Frustrated Ambition

C&C

CAMPAIGNS & COMMANDERS

GREGORY J. W. URWIN, SERIES EDITOR

CAMPAIGNS AND COMMANDERS

Frustrated Ambition

General Vicente Lim and the Philippine Military Experience 1910–1944

Richard B. Meixsel

University of Oklahoma Press | Norman

Library of Congress Cataloging-in-Publication Data

Names: Meixsel, Richard B., 1955– author.
Title: Frustrated ambition : General Vicente Lim and the Philippine military experience, 1910–1944 / Richard B. Meixsel.
Description: Norman : University of Oklahoma Press, [2018] | Series: Campaigns and commanders ; volume 61 | Includes bibliographical references and index.
Identifiers: LCCN 2017026957 | ISBN 978-0-8061-5905-8 (hardcover : alk. paper)
Subjects: LCSH: Lim, Vicente, 1888-1944. | Generals—Philippines—Biography. | Philippines. Army—Officers—Biography. | World War, 1939–1945—Campaigns—Philippines. | Philippines—History, Military—20th century. | Philippines—History—1898–1946.
Classification: LCC U55.L54 M45 2018 | DDC 355.0092 [B] —dc23
LC record available at https://lccn.loc.gov/2017026957

Frustrated Ambition: General Vicente Lim and the Philippine Military Experience, 1910–1944 is Volume 61 in the Campaigns and Commanders series.

The paper in this book meets the guidelines for permanence and durability of the Committee on Production Guidelines for Book Longevity of the Council on Library Resources, Inc. ∞

1 2 3 4 5 6 7 8 9 10

Interior layout and composition: Alcorn Publication Design

To CMSgt and Mrs. Perry C. Meixsel, USAF, Ret.

Contents

Illustrations

Figures

Maps

Acknowledgments

Many individuals have supported my prolonged effort to produce this book, and I am pleased finally to have the opportunity to acknowledge their assistance in print. James Madison University, where I have taught history for more than twenty years, has provided both leave and funds for research-related travel and writing. My thanks go to department chairs Professors Michael Galgano and Gabrielle Lanier for their indulgence throughout this process. A long-ago Fulbright student fellowship provided the opportunity to conduct archival research in the Philippines and to interview veterans of the Philippine Army. At Camp Aguinaldo's "The Last Watering Hole," social center for retired officers, I found many who were more than willing to bend a visiting American's ear. Most of those to whom I spoke have since passed away, but I am especially indebted to Lt. Gen. Leonico Tan (11th Division staff), Brig. Gen. Luis A. Villa-Real (21st Field Artillery), and Brig. Gen. Dionisio Ojeda (41st Division staff) for their many insights into the prewar army and candid comments about their wartime experiences. Mr. Mariano Infante (41st Engineers), the then-historian of the 41st Division Association, shared his extensive research and introduced me to many other veterans. They are too many to list here, but interviews with Clodualdo G. Bias (41st Infantry), Domingo G. Gabitan (43rd Infantry), Francisco Joves (22nd Infantry), Cesar B. Mendoza (22nd Infantry), Alfredo S. Morado (43rd Infantry), and Ernesto V. Santos (aide-de-camp to General Lim) were especially fruitful.

Brig. Gen. Fidel Segundo's daughter, Mrs. Lourdes Segundo de Leon, allowed me to read the general's diary and reminisced about her father. Conversations with Maj. Gen. Paulino Santos's daughter, Dr. Rosa Santos Munda, were equally revealing about the personalities of the prewar army staff. Dr. Helen Mendoza was untiringly helpful in finding people whose names I had read in prewar newspapers and wanted to meet, such as Rosario and Maria Escolar, sisters who drew the first numbered slips in the draft-lottery held in Manila's Araullo High School in May 1936, and Mr. Jose Malvar, one of the first to register for the military draft in Manila in April 1936.

I benefited from conversations and correspondence with Lt. Col. Clyde Childress (31st U.S. Infantry, 61st Philippine Army Regiment), Col. Arthur G. Christensen (II Philippine Corps staff), Col. Maximiano S. Janairo (Philippine Scouts, Philippine Army engineers), Col. Thomas Jones (26th Philippine Scouts Cavalry), Col. John Olson (57th Philippine Scouts Infantry), Lt. Col.

Leon F. Punsalan (West Point class of 1936; aide to Maj. Gen. Basilio Valdes), Col. James Ord and Lt. Col. James Ord (son and grandson, respectively, of Lt. Col. James Basevi Ord), Lt. Col. Santiago Guevara (Philippine Scouts, 1st Philippine Army Division), and Mrs. Carmen F. Guevara. I was also privileged to interview the late Col. Winston Jones, the last surviving American adviser to the wartime 41st Division.

Others who showed an interest in the project, read sample chapters, or passed along relevant information include Alex Duckworth-Ford, Richard Frank, Allen Manzano, Peter Parsons, Manuel L. Quezon III, Paul Ropp, Joseph Suarez, and the late Col. Karl Lowe (31st Infantry Association historian). The late Mrs. Dell Benzel provided access to Col. Malcolm Fortier's papers. My thanks also go to Dr. David Patrick for gathering documents on my behalf from Mrs. Benzel. The family of the late L. Scott Harrison made available his extensive collection of interviews and correspondence with veterans who had served in the Philippines. Prof. Michael Onorato, an authority on the Philippine governor-generalship of Leonard Wood, happened to mention to me that he had donated to the University of Michigan his copies of records from the British National Archives dealing with military and political issues in the Philippines in the 1930s, many of which have been first used, so far as I know, in this biography.

No one can work in this field without calling repeatedly on the assistance of Mr. James Zobel, longtime archivist at the MacArthur Memorial in Norfolk, Virginia, and Dr. Ricardo T. Jose of the University of the Philippines, the leading authority on Philippine military history and on the history of World War II in the Philippines. General Lim's great grandson Vicente P. Lim made readily available the family photographs used in this book; Mr. Michael G. Price provided photographs of places associated with General Lim's life and career.

My wife, Dr. Christine Sternberg Patrick, retired associate editor of the Papers of George Washington, reviewed the manuscript and offered useful suggestions for improvement. I am grateful for the genealogical research provided by my Aunts Dorothy Dawson Duett and Margaret Dawson Smith and the Spanish translation untaken by Mary Hackett, retired editor of the Papers of James Madison.

Finally, I was fortunate to have had the opportunity to meet the late Capt. Roberto H. Lim and Mr. Vicente Lim Jr. and am exceedingly grateful for the kindnesses they showed to me, both in the Philippines and in the United States. *Frustrated Ambition* is probably not quite what they had in mind, but I do believe that they would find something of their father here.

Frustrated Ambition

Introduction

He was a big man, for a Filipino, a soldier for thirty years before the war, known throughout the two armies in which he had served for an especially stern sense of duty and a lack of tolerance for those who did not share it. Dwight Eisenhower knew him in Manila in the 1930s and thought him difficult to work with but acknowledged his "high standards of personal honor and integrity." "It is either black or white with him," wrote the author of a character sketch that appeared in an English-language Philippine daily in 1937, soon after he had retired from the United States Army to accept a commission in the newly formed Philippine Army. "There are no half-tints and no half-way measures. You are either his friend or you are not." Nor did he accept "sloppiness in any man who wore the uniform," remembered a veteran of his wartime division. "The general was known to bawl out not only Filipino but American soldiers as well, both officers and enlisted men," which, this former sergeant admitted, "disqualified the general from my list of persons I would like to meet."[1]

Months of rigorous wartime imprisonment left Brig. Gen. Vicente Lim much diminished. Upon his release in July 1942 from the Capas prison camp that had held the surrendered soldiers of Bataan, Lim set to work trying to build an underground organization capable of challenging his country's Japanese occupiers. "Lim had," postwar U.S. Army investigators into claims of wartime service accepted, "a long-range plan of unifying all guerrillas on Luzon, and he had a tentative cadre of high ranking Philippine Army men who were to constitute the backbone for a planned division."[2] But by early 1944 Lim had to admit that his plans remained largely that, just plans. His continued activity in Manila would lead only to his arrest. He determined to join guerrilla forces in a remote part of the archipelago or possibly make his way to Australia.

Along with a few comrades, Lim escaped the city in early June 1944. They went south through Batangas and at the coast boarded a batel, a large sailboat, to continue their journey. A Japanese patrol boat they spotted the next morning appeared to be headed for another sailboat—a good sign, because the Japanese tended "to inspect only one boat among several seen plying these waters at [the same] time"—but an unlucky shift in the wind pushed Lim's batel across the patrol boat's course. It approached, signaled them to stop, and three soldiers jumped aboard. Their cursory inspection was near an end when "the last Jap[anese] soldier in the hull of the batel gave a shout": he had discovered a pistol. The Japanese looked more closely and now found a radio transmitter and generator. Lim and his men were transferred to the Japanese motor launch and taken to nearby Mindoro Island. Five days later a detachment of Japanese soldiers sent from Fort Santiago escorted the captives back to Manila.[3]

The Japanese military police had made the former Headquarters of the United States Army's Philippine Department the center of their operations. The Spanish-era fort rapidly gained a reputation as a place to be avoided. "Brutal and barbaric treatment" at the hands of the Japanese was so widespread that prosecutors at the Tokyo war crimes trials would deem it "impractical to detail the treatment received by each individual." Instead they offered a summary "in general [of] the forms of torture" that were commonplace in Fort Santiago "from the time of the Japanese occupation in January 1942 to February 1945."[4]

Lim must have known what to expect. A fellow captive, a nephew who survived, was in a different cell but on occasion was able to exchange a few whispered words. Lim confided that he was, like the others, being beaten and had been forced to go long hours without sleep. "He was pale and had lost weight, very much thinner than he used to be," his nephew observed. The beatings had aggravated an eye condition too, "his eyes sort of giving this fluid," and his speech was at times incoherent.[5] The men were eventually moved to larger cells, and other prisoners reported seeing or hearing of Lim. A journalist named Adalia Marquez had been picked up with other wives, mostly as a hostage to her husband's return, and was relatively free to move about the fort. She once looked past a Japanese guard and claimed to have seen Lim—his hair long, his features gaunt, seated on a cement floor in a cell "along with some two hundred other sets of skin and bones." She was surprised to see him. No one she knew had caught a glimpse of him since he had been brought to the fort, and all assumed he had already been killed.[6] Lim expressed to his nephew the belief that he might yet find a way out. But for now, in the waning months of 1944, he waged an inner struggle to survive the torments of Fort Santiago, as the outside war in which he had hoped to play a leading role finally returned to the Philippines.

Vicente Podico Lim was once his country's best-known soldier. In 1914 he had become the first Filipino to graduate from the United States Military Academy at West Point, New York. Lim was atypical in being both a Filipino and an academy-trained officer. Before World War I, most officers assigned to the "Philippine Scouts"—the locally recruited soldiers of America's army in the

Philippines to which Filipino officers' commissions were restricted—were American enlisted men holding temporary commissions renewable upon the needs of the army and the adequate performance of duty. Service with the Philippine Scouts represented the pinnacle of their careers. By contrast, Lim chafed at the professional constraints of Scout duty and constantly sought opportunities to expand his military education and experience.

Lim attempted without success to get sent to Europe as a military observer during the world war. He was then attached to the Philippine Constabulary, the country's militarized national police force that in coming years would vie with the Philippine Scouts to become the nucleus of a Philippine army. He was the only Filipino officer whose professional assignments gave him a foot in both camps. In 1918–19 Lim served in the Philippine National Guard, a short-lived organization but an instructive experiment in army building (now almost entirely forgotten) that held important lessons for successfully implementing a military system in the 1930s, when the Philippines would gain a measure of political autonomy. Lim's superiors evaluated him as the best Filipino graduate of West Point assigned to the national guard.

The status of Philippine Scout officers underwent significant change in the 1920s. When Lim joined the army, the Scouts served mostly in companies and battalions in remote parts of the archipelago as infantry auxiliaries to the regular U.S. Army garrison. By the 1920s, the Scouts had been reorganized into regiments of cavalry, infantry, and artillery, numerically and operationally the mainstay of the Philippine Islands' defense force. Regular army officers began to serve with the Philippine Scouts as part of their routine two-year tours of duty in the Philippines. Filipinos and those few Americans whose commissions remained restricted to the Scouts could nevertheless now be promoted as high as the rank of colonel and were allowed to attend postacademy army schools in the United States. No one was more successful at doing so than Vicente Lim. He completed the Infantry Officers' Advanced Course at Fort Benning, Georgia, and the Command and Staff College at Fort Leavenworth, Kansas. During his lifetime, Lim was the only Filipino graduate of the Army War College in Washington, D.C. His three-year sojourn in the United States (from 1926 to 1929) solidified his reputation as first among Filipino soldiers.

The United States Army's limited institutional interest in the Philippine Islands evaporated when Congress passed an independence act in 1934. The army's disengagement freed Lim to position himself to play a leading role in shaping a military system for the independent nation that would emerge at the end of the ten-year transitional period called for in the Tydings-McDuffie Act. His attempt to be put at the head of the Philippine Constabulary came to naught, but Lim was the behind-the-scenes author of significant military-related legislation passed by the Philippine Assembly before the inauguration of the Commonwealth government in November 1935.

The last American governor-general of the Philippines, Frank Murphy, vetoed the legislation, and the soon-to-be first president of the Philippine Commonwealth, Manuel Luis Quezon, returned from a visit to the United States in late 1934 to announce that he had, instead, asked Congress to authorize a military mission to oversee the creation of a Philippine defense force. Quezon later revealed that U.S. Army Chief of Staff Gen. Douglas MacArthur would head the mission. Placed next to those of the American general, the Filipino officer's achievements of course paled to insignificance. MacArthur's arrival in the Philippines in October 1935 effectively—and purposely—pushed Lim to the margins.

The shadow of Douglas MacArthur looms large over the subsequent course of Philippine history. If Vicente Lim was the best-known Filipino soldier during the American era of Philippine history, MacArthur remains, in the words of historian Samuel Eliot Morison, "the greatest single figure in the military history of the Philippines."[7] However, for all his much-remarked-upon association with the country, MacArthur had remarkably little to do with the Philippines compared to many other officers of his generation. At a time when officers might expect two or more assignments to the Philippines, each two or more years in length, MacArthur had spent less than a year there, from late October 1903 to early October 1904, initially working on engineering projects in the Visayas before landing a softer billet in Manila. His Fort Leavenworth–based battalion had received orders to the Philippines in 1912, but then-Captain MacArthur had been allowed to remain behind to teach at an engineering school.

Left to his own desires, would he ever have returned? His reintroduction to the Philippines in 1922 after an absence of nearly two decades was, so a much repeated story has it, an unsought wedding gift from Gen. John J. Pershing. The then army chief of staff had been linked romantically to MacArthur's bride, Louise Brooks, and supposedly displayed his displeasure at their marriage by exiling them to the Far East. Whether being punished or not, MacArthur enjoyed his time in the Philippines. After completing his tour of duty in early 1925, he arranged for a third assignment to the islands.

MacArthur commanded the Philippine Department from October 1928 to October 1930, during which time he became more intimately associated with Quezon. He had probably first met the Filipino leader during his 1922–25 tour of duty. Restored to bachelorhood, MacArthur enjoyed frequent "trips to the fights, polo games, and vaudeville shows," as one of his soberer biographers confirms. He eventually took up with a much younger mestiza mistress, whom he would bring to the United States when he became chief of staff in 1930. Or, as Vice Governor Joseph Hayden later put it to the British consul in Manila, at this time MacArthur acquired the "mud" that invariably clung to anyone too closely involved with the Philippines' leading politician.[8] Nevertheless, it was this very intimacy, combined with the sympathy MacArthur had shown toward Filipinos and the confidence he had placed in them in his official acts as commanding general of the American army in the Philippines, that would lead Quezon to seek MacArthur's assistance in building a new army for a new nation.

As usually presented, the subsequent "military history of the Philippines" is well known and fairly brief: The military system devised by the American military mission soon foundered on financial constraints and MacArthur's deteriorating relationship with Quezon. Retired from the army in 1937, but kept in Manila by hubris and pecuniary interest, MacArthur had grown old and almost forgotten by 1941. World War II resuscitated his career. The defense of Bataan and Corregidor made MacArthur a heroic figure. He escaped to Australia, there to build an avenging American army that would liberate the Philippines from Japanese oppression in 1944–45.

It is no secret, though too seldom emphasized, that soldiers of the Philippine Army constituted the bulk of MacArthur's United States Army Forces Far East (USAFFE) command. General MacArthur directed his troops from Corregidor Island; General Lim commanded a Philippine Army division at the front on Bataan. Whatever their limitations as a fighting force, Lim's 41st and other Philippine Army divisions were to make Bataan possible—the siege, the battle, the "symbol [in the words of journalist Hanson Baldwin] of moral victory, of glorious defeat."[9] Lim could do nothing to prevent USAFFE's ultimate surrender, but as the American high command turned its thoughts to getting out, Lim turned his to preparing for the underground struggle against the Japanese that was sure to follow and in which he expected to play a prominent part.

Scholarly and popular interest in the military history of the Philippines is mostly confined to two events that bookend the American period of Philippine colonial history, the Philippine-American War (1899–1902) and World War II (1941–45). Histories of the Philippine Scouts and Constabulary, the most substantial of which are decades-old unpublished doctoral dissertations, focus on those organizations' founding periods, a half-decade or so in the early twentieth century when Filipino officers were few in number and without authority or influence. As for the Commonwealth-era army of the 1930s, it remains mostly incidental to the careers of Douglas MacArthur and his chief of staff,

Dwight Eisenhower. Their many biographers have charted the rise and fall of the Philippine Army while seldom seeing any reason in the process to mention a single Filipino officer by name. The United States Army's official history of the 1941–42 Philippine Campaign, still the standard account more than a half century since its publication in 1953, merely identifies Lim as the commanding general of the 41st Philippine Army Division. There is no comprehensive history of the Philippine guerrillas in World War II, and no examination of the role played by Lim, the only surrendered Filipino general who accepted no position in the Philippine government during the period of Japanese occupation.

During the thirty years he spent in uniform, first as a company and field-grade officer of the U.S. Army's Philippine Scouts and then as a general officer in the Philippine Army, Vicente Lim's career intersected every significant military-related development that took place in the Philippines. My goal in *Frustrated Ambition* is to use Lim's experiences to shed light on forgotten episodes in Philippine history, to offer new perspectives on military affairs during the American period of occupation, and to return some agency to Filipino soldiers who attempted to affect the course of their own country's history, a history from which they have, for far too many years, remained largely absent.

Prologue

In 1934, for some no-longer-known reason, the United States Army decided to compile a historical record of its native-manned regiments serving in the Philippine Islands. At the time, no one knew who exactly broached the idea of recruiting Filipinos into American service during the Philippine-American War three and one-half decades earlier, but Warrant Officer Charles Franklin, compiler of a never-published but liberally distributed typescript, "History of the Philippine Scouts," identified a letter that Lt. Matthew Batson had sent to higher headquarters dated 16 July 1899—half a year into the war—as the "first official" record of a proposal to arm native collaborators.[1] A former enlisted man with ten years of service behind him at the outbreak of the war with Spain, Batson had joined the 4th U.S. Cavalry Regiment, operating north of Manila, in April 1899 and experienced firsthand the challenges posed by that region's difficult terrain. Brig. Gen. Arthur MacArthur's 2nd Division of the 8th Army Corps had seized the Philippine Republic's capital of Malolos, twenty miles north of Manila, on the last day of March 1899; continuation of the drive farther into Central Luzon opened the division's left flank to a "maze of small rivers, estuaries, and arroyos [that run] into Manila Bay," a watery wilderness from which insurgents could strike with near impunity against the division's outposts and supply lines.[2]

The area also happened to be home to the Macabebes, a community known to be fiercely opposed to General Emilio Aguinaldo's Philippine Army. James LeRoy, whose *Americans in the Philippines* remains one of the better works on the early period of American occupation, explained that "most of the land [around the town of Macabebe] was owned by a prominent Spanish family, the Blancos, to whom the people bore feudal relations." Formed into military units by the Blanco family, the Macabebes had "remained loyal to Spain when all the other native troops deserted." The Englishman John Foreman, one of the relatively few English speakers who had traveled widely in the country at the time and thus gained a reputation as an authority on the Filipinos and their history, characterized the Macabebes as being "the only Filipinos who have persistently and systematically opposed the revolutionary faction of their own free will, without bribe or extraneous influence. No one," he wrote after visiting the area, "seems to be able to explain exactly why they should have adopted this course." A quartermaster aboard one of the ships that brought the American army to the Philippines in mid-1898 chose an inopportune time to sightsee in an area controlled by Aguinaldo's forces and subsequently found himself confined with Macabebe prisoners of the Philippine Army. "I spoke to many of them" in poor but rapidly improving Spanish, Albert Sonnichsen recalled, "inquiring the cause of this racial feud" and could learn nothing more than that "it dated far back from the time of the rajahs, and would," he quoted one of the Macabebes as saying, "continue until doomsday."[3]

The Macabebes' antipathy toward the revolution was thus well known. Batson wanted to hire Macabebes to patrol their home region and prevent "small bodies of insurgents from operating against our lines of communications." In late July 1899, Batson went off with a detachment of the 4th Cavalry on an expedition south of Manila, during which he performed a feat for which he would receive the Medal of Honor, while his proposal worked its way up the chain of command. Maj. Gen. Henry Lawton, commanding general of the 8th Army Corps' 1st Division, strongly endorsed Batson's request. From the moment he landed in Manila, an aide later wrote, General Lawton had "placed great importance and faith in the necessity and usefulness of native troops as auxiliaries for the army in the Philippines." MacArthur had been leery of the Macabebes, but he now affected to believe that Batson's concept was worth trying so long as a "skillful officer" was put in charge. The unenthusiastic commanding general of the 8th Army Corps, Maj. Gen. Elwell Otis, told Batson that the Macabebes were likely to "put a bolo [knife] in [his] throat and then we will have more American rifles to fight," but reluctantly agreed that Batson could "draw up plans for the organization of a company of Macabebe scouts."[4]

By the middle of September 1899 Batson had a one-hundred-man-strong company of Macabebes "patrolling the rivers and nipa swamps of Pampanga." On his own initiative he enrolled another hundred men and with the two companies surprised and dispersed an enemy force. In early October he raised a third company. Two companies then marched east to join Lawton's new force being organized to push north through Nueva Ecija and close off General Aguinaldo's escape routes into the northern mountains. The third joined MacArthur's division affront the main part of the Philippine Army near Angeles. Within a few days, Lawton had instructed Batson to return to Macabebe and bring back two more companies of veterans. While Lawton's troops fought poor weather and challenging terrain, Batson and his "Macabebe Scouts" kept pace with Brig. Gen. S. B. M. Young's cavalry brigade that Lawton had permitted to "break loose" and live off the land in an attempt to get across Aguinaldo's line of retreat. A dilatory American subordinate allowed Aguinaldo to escape at Porzorrubio in mid-November, but what few men remained of what a month earlier had been a thousand-strong flying column—"eighty troopers from the 3rd Cavalry and the remnants of Batson's Macabebes"—continued close on Aguinaldo's heels. In a report summarizing his brigade's activities, Young highlighted the remarkable "bravery, coolness, skill and judgment shown by Lieutenant Batson throughout [the chase]." He seconded a recommendation that Batson receive the Medal of Honor. Lawton suggested that Batson be made a major of volunteers "especially as he is now commanding a battalion of Macabebe scouts."[5]

Batson did not last out the war. On 19 November 1899, still in pursuit of Aguinaldo, Batson was shot in the foot at Aringay, near the coast in northwestern Luzon a few miles south of San Fernando, La Union. (Aguinaldo escaped, but another force of Macabebes led by different American officers would entrap him at Palanan, along the remote northeastern coast of Luzon, in March 1901.) Batson went back to the United States to recuperate and spent his leave pressing the War Department to turn his Macabebes into a Philippine cavalry squadron.[6] He returned to the Philippines in mid-1900 to take command of the unmounted squadron, but his physical condition deteriorated and eventually the "hardships of service in the Philippine Islands" sent him home for good. A leg had been amputated, and he was forced to quit the army in 1902. Batson died fifteen years later after a colorful and controversial second career as a builder and booster of the newfangled flying machines, long before Charles Franklin began work on the Philippine Scout history. Why Batson, in particular, had been attuned to the potential of using natives as soldiers went unrecorded, though he seems to have seen the issue as much through a racial as a political lens. Many years later, Batson's daughter would tell the military historian Edward Coffman that her father had been "highly impressed by the . . . performance in combat" of the African American soldiers of the 9th U.S. Cavalry he had led in Cuba in 1898.[7] If black men would fight for a country that largely denied them political rights, why not brown?

Batson knew he was not the first to think of recruiting Filipinos. His private papers include a letter dated 1 June 1899, six weeks before Franklin's cited document, in which Batson mentions that his cavalry troop had provided an escort for Capt. William Wren of the 17th Infantry, who "a few days ago" had been assigned to recruit a company of Macabebes.[8] Other officers had the same idea. In looking to co-opt Filipinos into helping America secure its possession of the Philippines, the United States Army followed a path long blazed by earlier colonizing powers, including Spain. Until the outbreak of the Philippine Revolution in 1896, the "Spanish" army in the islands had for many years consisted mostly of Filipinos. Only in 1897 had Spain begun to send a significant number of *peninsulares* to soldier in the archipelago, but the Filipino contingent of the army remained substantial, some 14,000 men at the start of the American war. The Spanish governor-general had also raised militia forces in 1896–97 and did so again in 1898. Most of the latter joined the revolutionary cause, but Filipinos of the "old native regiments" remained loyal to Spain.[9] Occupation of Manila had brought the Americans into contact with one of these, the 72nd Regiment, made up of those Macabebes who later so impressed Lieutenant Batson. Within a few days of the start of the Philippine-American War in early February 1899, the Macabebes had approached General Otis offering "to join the Americans . . . armed and equipped, and needing only rations."[10]

The Americans had little difficulty finding Filipinos willing to cast their lot with a new colonial master. About the same time that Batson had been recruiting Macabebes, another former enlisted man turned officer, Capt. Percival Lowe, had raised a mixed company of white soldiers and Tagalogs. As the army moved farther north, hundreds of Ilocanos sought service under the American flag. By the end of 1901, the army had battalions of "native scouts" in both northern and southern Luzon. Given a lack of American soldiers in the Visayas to the south of Luzon, officers took the initiative to raise Filipino troops in these islands as well.[11]

The Macabebes would soon pass from the scene. They made up only a fraction of the Filipinos serving the Americans by the 1920s, by which time most Filipino soldiers would be Ilocanos and Visayans, but while the war lasted, they were instrumental both in hastening the Philippine Republic's collapse and undermining nationalist claims that the Philippine Islands were something more than the congeries of quarreling tribes that army officers would long maintain they were. The onset of guerrilla warfare only magnified the war's challenges and made the use of locally recruited soldiers more attractive. Of the 4,165 American soldiers who would die in the Philippine-American War, more than three-fourths (3,161) would succumb to disease, drowning, heat exhaustion, and other maladies largely reflective of the physical hardships of soldiering in the Philippines. The guerrilla phase of the war pointed more urgently to the need for soldiers who could speak the local languages and better withstand the rigors of a tropical climate. The utility of the Macabebes and other collaborators exceeded expectations, so much so that not long before his death in battle in December 1899 General Lawton would refer to them as the army's "main reliance and support" in the ever-harsher war against the *insurrectos.*[12]

Officers were a different matter. Within weeks of recruiting his first company of Macabebe volunteers, Batson had sought permission to appoint Filipinos as junior officers in his new command. Batson explained to his superiors that he had initially intended to use white soldiers as both officers and noncommissioned officers but had been impressed by the quality of his Macabebe recruits and unimpressed by some of the white enlisted men assigned to work with local troops. Many of his Macabebes had fought for Spain, and Batson had appointed these experienced soldiers to fill the NCO ranks. He thought that several would make good officers too. At this further proposal to draw on indigenous resources to prosecute the war in the Philippines, however, General Otis "drew the line." American officers supportive of the use of native troops held native officers in low regard, suspecting that they would be untrustworthy, lack initiative, and prove disloyal. By 1900 the integration of Filipinos into the army in the Philippines had found support at the highest levels of the administration of President William McKinley but invariably with the proviso that native soldiery serve "under American officers."[13]

Despite this, and for reasons not explicitly given in the available records, the Army Reorganization Act of February 1901, which allowed recruitment of a maximum of 12,000 Filipinos for service in the army as "scouts," included a brief statement authorizing the appointment of Filipinos qualified by "their services and character" as lieutenants in the Scout companies. Published debate on this aspect of the Reorganization Act focused on the appropriateness of enlisting some Filipinos into the army for the purpose of suppressing other Filipinos—"to copy the infamous policy of Great Britain in the present and in the past," as one critic summarized the matter—not on whether Filipinos should be officers. Over the next decade four Filipinos would receive commissions—three in 1902 and one, a long-serving enlisted man, in 1907.

The success of these few native officers reflects an anomaly in the army's institutionalized racism. While the army viewed Filipinos, as a group, as unworthy of commissioned status, individual American officers might extend patronage to individual Filipinos whose mettle excited their admiration. This phenomenon appeared in the commissioning of African American officers, the most noted example being the first black soldier to reach general officer grade, Benjamin O. Davis. A commissioned veteran of the 10th United States Volunteer Infantry Regiment and sergeant in the regular 9th Cavalry, Davis impressed several of the regiment's white officers with his education, bearing, and experience. They supported his effort to obtain a regular commission, and in 1901 Davis became one of two black soldiers to do so.[14]

The pattern for the first Filipino officers was similar. Commanding General William P. Duvall of the Philippines Division, for example, interceded to advance the careers of Lieutenants Ygnacio Abelino and Crispulo Patajo after they failed to qualify for promotion in 1908. Abelino joined one of the original companies of Macabebe scouts in 1899, enlisted into the formal Philippine Scouts organization when it was established in 1901, and rose to the rank of sergeant major before being rewarded with an appointment to second lieutenant in 1907. Patajo had served as then-Colonel Duvall's "chief of detectives" in La Union during the war and had been instrumental in destroying the guerrilla movement in that northern Luzon province. Gen. J. Franklin Bell was quoted as having said of Patajo that during the insurrection his "services to the U.S. Army [had been] equivalent to a regiment." Patajo—billed in stateside papers as "Uncle Sam's First Filipino Soldier"—acquired some formal military training at Fort Leavenworth, Kansas, in 1903–1904, but an American contemporary who served with the Scouts recalled that Patajo lacked the education and training to be a successful officer. Later, during World War I, Philippine Scout Mateo Capinpin, the only enlisted Scout not a veteran of the Philippine-American War to become an officer prior to World War II, was also, like Benjamin Davis, "assisted and urged by [his] superior officers" to obtain a commission.[15]

However sympathetic some army officers may have been to granting local commissions to a few Filipinos who had demonstrated their loyalty to the United States, it remained for civilian William Howard Taft to set in motion the process of creating a corps of professional Filipino military officers. Taft had arrived, reluctantly, in the Philippines as chairman of the Second Philippine (or Taft) Commission in June 1900. The First Philippine Commission in 1899 had been an information-gathering body; Taft and four fellow commissioners were meant to rule. Or so Taft thought. Coming from a country in which the army traditionally had little presence, the extent of the army's influence in the Philippines took Taft and his fellow commissioners by surprise. "There are more captains, majors, and colonels here than we had any idea existed," commission secretary Daniel Williams recorded in his diary. Williams was being facetious, but his observation that "military authority is supreme—omnipotent" was on target, and few soldiers would have quarreled with his conclusion that many in the army "think it will take years to crush the insurrection and restore public order. This would mean the indefinite continuance of military rule—a prospect much more alluring to many of our officers than the advent of civil government."'[16] To underscore the point, the islands' military governor, Major General MacArthur, had greeted the new commission and the consequent diminution of his own recently acquired power with poor grace. As Taft depicted the scene in a letter to his wife, "the frigidity" of MacArthur's welcome "had made his perspiration stop" on the hot afternoon at the Ayuntamiento in Manila's old walled city when the two proconsuls first met. To Taft's commiserating comment that MacArthur retained considerable authority despite the commission's presence, the army general is said to have replied, "That would be all right, if I had not been exercising so much more power before you came."[17]

The story may be apocryphal—historian Rowland Berthoff claimed it was "dramatic but imaginary"—but it was soon evident that the two held opposing views on the nature of the war in the Philippines.[18] General MacArthur had been in the country about two years when Taft arrived. He had reached Manila with the Third Expedition in July 1898 and had led a brigade in the assault on the Spanish-occupied city in August. In the summer of 1899 he had commanded the 2nd Division in its drive against Aguinaldo's forces north through Central Luzon. Although he was not the senior officer in the islands, he had more field experience than any other and in May 1900 had succeeded General Otis as military governor and commander of the army in the Philippines. All along, according to his biographer, Kenneth Young, MacArthur "read everything he could find on the Filipinos and the former Spanish administration." MacArthur accepted that the Filipinos' war for independence enjoyed significant popular support; consequently, the army needed to maintain a strong presence throughout the country, and it was far too early to consider a transition to civilian rule.[19]

In sharp contrast to the army commander's depiction of broad-based opposition to American authority, Taft purported to believe that resistance was confined to a few malcontents. He brought with him the conviction that Filipinos possessed neither the competence nor the ambition to rule themselves. Taft's arrival in the Philippines happened to coincide with a lull in combat activities. He visited safe areas and spoke to Filipinos favorably disposed toward American protection. Taft held the corresponding view that the army presence in the islands could be significantly reduced, and that the army's presence generated anti-Americanism among Filipinos otherwise inclined to accept the legitimacy of American rule. If military force were required, it could be provided by locally raised units of Filipinos whose officers would find themselves subordinate to civil authority. At the end of July 1900, Taft, who had been in the islands an entire month by that time, wrote that "it would be possible to raise militia among the Filipinos at an early date." One or two regiments might be formed "at once." Nor did he doubt that Filipinos could do "as good work as our own soldiers." The only real obstacle to raising a native force was General MacArthur, a dull-witted martinet who moved, Taft confided to his brother Charley, "with a slowness that is most exasperating in the matter of organizing militia and a constabulary."[20] In July 1901, within a few days of MacArthur's departure for the United States, the commission enacted legislation that created a national police force, to become known as the Philippine Constabulary, under the command of an army officer who took his marching orders from the civil government.

The larger issue, Taft told one correspondent, was "the military tendencies to hold onto power." Many soldiers regretted the army's loss of authority and would continue to look back with longing to the "Days of the Empire." Fairly or not, Taft concluded that the army had no positive role to play in the political maturation of the Filipino people, and he never changed his mind. Returning to the Philippines as Secretary of War to participate in the inauguration of the Philippine Assembly near the end of 1907, Taft publicly applauded the army's centrality in "bringing about order in the Islands" but privately told President Theodore Roosevelt that the "attitude of [the] military [was] just what it had always been—that of suspicion and expectation of the bursting of the volcano and all that sort of thing." Nothing had changed in the four years since Taft had given up the post of civil governor at the end of 1903. "I have," Taft wrote, "the same opinion of their judgment that I have always had."[21]

As civil governor, Taft had championed the recruitment of Filipino soldiers to replace American regulars in the islands; he now decided that Filipinos should have the opportunity to command those soldiers too. Taft had hardly returned from his final trip to the archipelago when he asked the House of Representatives Committee on Military Affairs to permit Filipinos to attend the United States Military Academy. Taft acknowledged that the Reorganization Act allowed Filipinos to be appointed as junior officers in the Philippine Scouts, but he assumed that most such appointees would be drawn from the enlisted ranks, just as American Scout officers were. He was of the opinion that "we have not any Filipinos that are [currently] fitted to be made officers." Congress had allowed citizens of other countries "to enjoy the benefits of education at West Point"—why not Filipinos?

Democratic Party opposition to measures that seemed to cement further U.S. ties to the Philippines ensured that Taft's proposal would, for the most part, move along the by then predictable contours of Philippine-related legislation. When the academy appropriation bill for fiscal year 1909 came before Congress in May 1908, a Texas Democrat named James Slayden took the lead in denouncing the proposal to allow Filipinos to attend West Point as "a cheap bribe" calculated "to break [their] loyalty to their own race and to the cause of Philippine independence." He decried the country's increasing association with the "Malay hybrids" of the Philippines. To Slayden, the "Filipino mad" Taft's request that Filipinos be allowed to attend the military academy "indicate[d] a policy" of growing involvement in Asia that was costly, militarily dangerous, and deleterious of the nation's racial exclusivity. It was a policy he did not hesitate to condemn.

Not every Democrat agreed. What better way to justify granting independence to the Philippines than by making the Filipinos capable of mounting their own military defense and thus undermine retentionist claims that the Philippines could not be free because Filipinos could not protect themselves? So argued Representative Richmond Hobson. The Alabaman reminded his colleagues that, if the United States "would hasten the day when the Filipinos could be safely intrusted [*sic*] with the responsibility of self-government, [it] must carry forward their education in the science and art of self-defense." Hobson pointed out that in "the absence of a large, mobile Army in America and of transports," only the Filipinos could provide the necessary troops to defend the islands. Hobson, a "big navy" advocate and former naval officer, was an outlier when it came to his party's attitudes toward the military and the Philippines (as well as in his openness toward allowing nonwhites to attend the military academy, an attitude that would later cost him a seat in the Senate), but he articulated themes relative to the building of an indigenous military force that would be raised again and again in the coming decades. With Republicans dominant in Congress and some friendly Democrats on board, passage of the legislation was assured, but while Taft had recommended that seven Filipinos be allowed to attend the academy, one for every 1 million inhabitants of the islands, the approved legislation provided for only four, one for each year of the four-year course of instruction.[22]

The army remained conspicuously silent throughout the debate. The few commissions granted so far had been based on proven loyalty through active service against their fellow countrymen. Filipinos with much different backgrounds and expectations might now gain commissions. Hints of the army's attitude could be seen in the *Army and Navy Journal*'s editorial support of Taft's proposition with the proviso that the Filipino cadets be chosen from the enlisted ranks of the Philippine Scouts or Constabulary, which was precisely what Taft was trying to avoid. Another hint came in 1912, when Judge Advocate General E. H. Crowder queried now-president Taft on the proper interpretation of the 1908 law allowing Filipinos to attend West Point. The academy would accept its fourth Filipino student the following year, and Crowder pointed out that the wording of the law was the same as when "individual foreigners are admitted [to the academy] and not the language . . . for establishing permanent representation." The law specifically mentioned four Filipino students, and, once the fourth had been admitted, perhaps no more were to be accepted? Taft replied that it had been his intent that Filipinos have "permanent representation" at the military academy.[23]

In selecting Filipino candidates for the military academy, the insular government evolved a selection process similar in detail to that used in the United States though somewhat more meritocratic. Army officers—or their biographers, anyway—are not agreed on the openness of the process that led to an academy appointment in the early twentieth century. Stephen Ambrose believed that when Dwight Eisenhower sought an appointment in 1910 most congressmen allowed any applicant to participate in an "open, competitive examination" and selected the one who scored highest. But when his subject,

Lucius Clay, went to West Point in 1914, "there were no competitive examinations and few merit appointments," Jean Edward Smith asserted, since "most legislators looked on their appointments as patronage rewards for the sons of deserving supporters."[24] Of course, in the Philippines as in the United States, the process discriminated against those who lacked the schooling necessary to attempt the qualifying exam and bear the expense of traveling to the academy. The army provided a bunk on a West Coast–bound transport, but the successful Filipino applicant had to pay his own way on to New York and had to make a deposit of at least 200 pesos—$100—to meet the cost of uniforms.[25] With the exception of Emilio Aguinaldo Jr., who was appointed second alternate in 1923 without taking a qualifying exam, there is no evidence that during the period of American control any favoritism was shown to a particular Filipino candidate for entry to West Point.[26] In the Philippines, the applicant who obtained the highest passing score on a test given by the Bureau of Civil Service was designated as candidate, while other successful applicants, if any, were designated as first or second alternate. These alternates could proceed with the army's physical and mental tests for admission to the academy.[27]

Not for several years would any Filipino pass the qualifying exam. Few even tried. It soon became evident that Secretary of War Taft had embraced the cause of Filipino entry into West Point more avidly than had Filipinos. By the mid-1920s, thirty or more applicants would sit for the Bureau-administered qualifying examination each year, but that was far from the case before World War I.[28] In a Philippine Bureau of Education circular dated 29 June 1911, Director of Education Frank R. White informed his division superintendents that no one had showed up for the test in May. It was rescheduled for August, and White urged superintendents and teachers "to assist in securing desirable candidates for this examination." Little had changed the following year when acting education director Frank Crone revealed that no one had passed the May 1912 test. He suggested that "properly qualified Filipinos" were apparently unaware of the "exceptional opportunity" for a free education "at one of the best American colleges," with an annual salary of 3,400 pesos ($1,700) afterward. He asked teachers to encourage suitable students to take the examination.[29] Again in 1913, however, student response to the examination announcement was depressingly familiar. The insular government was once more trying to "scare up" interest in attending West Point, a military weekly in the islands reported. When only two candidates showed up for the exam in May, the government rescheduled it for September 1913. Ten sat for that exam, the War Department having made it easier to obtain applicants by reducing the physical requirements for acceptance.[30] Despite the less-than-portentous start, by that time the first Filipino cadet was well along in his studies.

The Philippine Islands. Copyright © 2018 by The University of Oklahoma Press, Publishing Division of the University. All rights reserved.

CHAPTER 1

An Untiring Advocate of Independence

First Cadet, 1910–1917

Why Vicente Lim chose to be a soldier is lost to history. His family did not have a military background, though Vicente had reputedly "organized the children his age to serve as couriers" for revolutionary troops during the Philippine-American War. Years later, a journalist wrote of him that "even in his youth, young Lim showed a fondness for military life and had a profound and consuming love for the glitter of the uniform and well-disciplined life of men in the service."[1] When asked near the end of his life why he had joined the army a half-century earlier, a contemporary of Lim's, Mateo Capinpin, answered: for "the same [reasons] as any other young man, looking for adventure and attracted by the smart uniform." Eighteen years after Lim left for New York, Maximiano Janairo sought an academy education because it offered a "sure job after graduation" and a chance "to see what America was like." Similar goals may well have motivated Vicente Lim.[2] If Lim was attracted to military life, he nevertheless probably knew little of the Philippine Scouts, to which he would be assigned. A few months before he was scheduled to graduate, the third Filipino to enter West Point, Rafael Garcia (class of 1916), asked the Bureau of Insular Affairs to send information about the Scouts. "I think it would be of great benefit to me," Garcia wrote, "if I know a little of the organization I am to join soon." Garcia explained that the class of 1915's Filipino graduate, Anastacio Q. Ver, had tried to find something about the Scouts in the academy library without success.[3]

Perhaps no place was more emblematic of a nascent Philippine nationalism than Lim's birthplace of Calamba. The town lay thirty-five miles south of Manila in the heart of the Tagalog-speaking region of Luzon. A ten-hour ride by pony cart in the late-Spanish period when Lim was a boy there, Calamba was one of the larger settlements in Laguna, a province that extended around the southern half of the large lake known as Laguna de Bay. Compilers of the official government gazetteer of the Philippines wrote that Laguna had been labeled "the garden of the Philippines" because "every variety of tropical plant and tree known to the archipelago" grew in the province. Calamba is best known as the home of nationalist icon Jose Rizal. Rizal's family was involved in a celebrated dispute between tenants and Dominican landlords of the Calamba estate in the late 1880s and early 1890s and so too, reportedly, was the Lim family. The Lims had arrived in Calamba sometime late in the nineteenth century. Lim's father was a Chinese immigrant from Fukien (where Lim was a common surname); his mother was a Philippine-born Chinese mestiza. Most of the Philippines' many Chinese immigrants became involved in merchant activities, but the very arrival of large numbers of immigrants after midcentury pushed the Chinese mestizo community out of the traditional retail trades and increasingly into agriculture. Jose Ayala (a baptismal name) Lim-Yaoco and his wife, Antonia Podico, leased land to farm at Calamba and opened a small store in the town. Jose Ayala Lim died in 1897; Antonia outlived her husband by many years, during which time she gained a reputation as a shrewd and successful businesswoman.[4]

Vicente (the spelling was changed from Vi*n*cente while Lim was at West Point) was their third child. Like most mestizos, the Lim children "grew up identifying themselves with the Filipino rather than the Chinese community," but Vicente thought his Chinese heritage worth emphasizing. On the academy admission form he listed his father's "nationality" as "citizen of Phil. Is. but of Chinese blood." Not until the appointment of the Philippines' fourth cadet, Luis R. Salvosa of Lucena, Tayabas, did candidates begin unequivocally to state their parents' nationality to be Filipino. The late Eugene Ganley, an army officer who spent two decades gathering material for a never-completed history of the Philippine Scouts, corresponded with many former Scout officers, and one named Issac Nichol, who had attended the Army War College with Lim in the late 1920s, informed him that American contemporaries tended to think of Lim more as Chinese than Filipino.[5]

Given the tumultuous events in the Philippines at the turn of the century, Lim had acquired a better-than-average education before applying to West Point. Lim was eight years old when the revolution against Spain started and fourteen when the war against the Americans ended. Nevertheless, he got a solid grounding in the basics in public school and at the private Liceo de Manila. Founded in 1900 to provide young Filipinos with "*la educación de estos dias, la educación moderna*," the school's curriculum emphasized Spanish, Latin, arithmetic, geography, and English. At the Liceo, he proved to be a poor student. His family gave him too much spending money, and as a result he neglected his coursework. A year spent "deported" to a provincial school in Batangas Province (to Tanauan, a large town a few miles south of Calamba and a place where Lim spent several years of his childhood) taught him to take education more seriously, and Lim returned to Manila to receive what he called "a real schooling" at the Philippine Normal School.[6]

Begun by American educators in 1901, the Normal School was considered by its founders to be "the crown of the educational system of the islands" prior to the establishment of the University of the Philippines in 1908. But in those days, graduation from the Normal School was the equivalent of completing the second year of what by the 1930s would be a four-year high school course of instruction. Lim was one of a small number who actually studied to become a teacher; most students were interested in the school's professional and college preparatory classes. Lim completed a teacher education program in 1908, taught for six months at a public school in Santa Cruz, Laguna, and then returned to the Normal School for additional study. According to a report in a Manila daily several years later, Lim had been "well known as a baseball player at the Normal School" and had passed the school's final examination with "flying colors."[7]

Encouraged by one of his teachers there, in 1908 he took the first West Point qualifying examination administered by the Philippine Bureau of Civil Service.[8] None of the fourteen or so applicants passed the test, but Pablo del Villas of Nueva Caceres (now Naga) and Lim were considered "promising candidates" for admission, and Governor-General James F. Smith designated them candidate and first alternate, respectively.[9] Concerned about their chances of success, the War Department's Bureau of Insular Affairs lined up a second alternate in the United States, Sotero Baluyut, a student at Iowa University. But Lim passed the army's qualifying test and arrived at West Point to begin his military career in March 1910. Taft had expected the first Filipino cadet to enter in 1909, but Lim could not have received his acceptance letter until mid-January 1909, and, by then, it would have been too late to have found a berth on an army transport that would have allowed him to meet the academy's reporting date. However, the delay meant that by the time Lim arrived at West Point he was, by less than a week, too old to join the corps of cadets and thus indulged in the time-honored practice of adopting a birthdate more amenable to academy regulations. At the time, cadets officially reported to West Point on 1 March and could not have passed their twenty-second birthday by that date. Army records show Lim's birthday as 5 April 1888, but *To Inspire and to Lead*, published by the Lim family, gives 24 February 1888. Had Lim acknowledged the latter date, he would not have been eligible to attend the academy.[10]

Lim was not the first noncitizen to attend the United States Military Academy, but such cadets remained an uncommon sight. Most of the very few foreign cadets came from Latin American republics. The first Asians to make it through the academy, "two unusually bright Chinese boys," had left the year before Lim arrived. According to a newspaper report, they had been popular students, the American cadets being convinced that one was a nobleman and that the other—smarter, more popular, and, naturally, the better English speaker—was sent along as his companion.[11] Lim's arrival at the academy coincided with a campaign by West Point's new superintendent, Maj. Gen. Thomas Barry, to upgrade potential cadets' preparatory training. Barry was scornful of foreign cadets, whom he claimed were routinely "carried along" despite their failure to meet academy standards. He had hardly more favorable words for many American applicants.[12]

Lim entered West Point at a time of significant changes in the academy. The obligations of empire had led to the enlargement of the army and a concomitant need for more officers. The corps of cadets had nearly doubled in size over the previous decade and would double again by the time the country entered World War I. An average class in the 1890s graduated about sixty students. Lim joined more than twice that number of entering cadets at West Point in 1910 and was one of 107 to graduate in 1914. To provide the housing, training, and administrative facilities needed to accommodate the additional students, Congress since 1902 had authorized $6 million in construction costs.[13] Much of the academy that Lim saw was newly built.

For many cadets, the first year at the academy was the hardest. Rigorous academic work and homesickness took their toll, and the initial summer months could be especially punishing. Cadets found themselves subjected to a regime of relentless physical activity and "disciplining" by upperclassmen. The hazing of "plebes" had become so out of control by the early twentieth century that Congress conducted an investigation into the practice and in 1901 passed a law forbidding the abuse or harassment of cadets. It had little effect. One of Dwight Eisenhower's biographers claimed that when the future president arrived at West Point in 1911, "hazing was more widely practiced than at any other time in the academy's history." Congress held additional hearings into allegations of hazing at West Point in 1909, 1910, and 1914.[14]

Lim was helped through the ordeal by First Classman Clyde Selleck (class of 1910), an officer who would, like Lim but with less success, command a Philippine Army division on Bataan thirty-two years later. If Lim underwent the full rigors of "Beast Barracks" and experienced the other unpleasantries of plebe life, however, common sense suggests that President Taft's known interest in the Filipino cadets stayed the hand of even the most obtuse upperclassman. By contrast, the few black Americans who overcame the many hurdles to an academy appointment were spared the usual harshness of the cadets' first weeks only to show that they were not wanted and did not belong. As it happened, a senator from Wyoming appointed an African American as alternate to fill the state's West Point quota in 1910. Even the suggestion that "for the first time in more than a quarter of a century, West Point [would be] confronted with the possibility of having soon to admit a negro as a cadet" left the academy's officers and students apprehensive. Their opinion was unanimous that it would be better for all concerned that no African American come to the academy. "A negro cadet is never hazed," officers reportedly sympathetic to the plight of black Americans explained. "He is ostracized, and lives . . . a being absolutely apart."[15] There is no evidence to indicate that Lim or any future Filipino cadet confronted that even more unpleasant welcome to West Point. An explicit public statement addressing the treatment of Filipino cadets was left by Angel Miguel Jr., one of three Filipino cadets at the academy in 1924 (none of whom graduated), in which he asserted that they were treated just like the white cadets. Lim, however, bunked alone his first year at the academy and found a roommate only when the second Filipino to enter West Point, Anastacio Ver, arrived in 1911.[16]

Unfortunately, Lim left little record of his cadet days. Fellow cadets whose academy years corresponded to Lim's and who gained enough stature to generate biographies or memoirs seem to have found his presence unremarkable. At least, they or their biographers say nothing about him. The academy archives do include a large collection of letters written by Donovan Swanton, whose five years at West Point (1912–17) overlapped those of Lim and the other early Filipino cadets. Swanton occasionally mentioned the Filipino cadets in his letters. In one, Swanton wrote that he had met the other fifteen Catholics in his class and commented that "the Filipino [Rafael Garcia] is a comical chap and everybody laughs at his antics." In another letter he noted that he had gone to a "hop" and danced with several cadets, including "a Filipino cadet in the second class." Other passing references to Filipinos suggest that they were familiar to Swanton's correspondents and that their presence did not excite particular attention.[17] The cadets tagged Lim with the nickname "Cannibal," no doubt a reflection of their ignorance of the Philippines and possibly some residual memory of the much-hyped Filipino presence at the 1904 St. Louis Exposition, in which the headhunters of northern Luzon and other esoterica featured prominently. The Philippine exhibit left the impression, wrote a foreign resident of the Philippines, "that the inhabitants of these islands were a race of naked cannibals and savages."[18] The cadets demonstrated little imagination. When the second Filipino arrived in 1911, they gave him the nickname "Cannibal" too. Lim must not have objected to the moniker—he reportedly continued to use the name with his classmates for the rest of his life—but thereafter the trend was toward nicknames that Americanized the Filipinos rather than exoticized them: Rafael Garcia was "Ralph"; Luis Salvosa, the fourth Filipino entrant, was "Sal"; and so on.

Aside from a two-month furlough between their second and third years at the academy (during which many cadets returned home, although Lim obviously could not, given that Manila was more than a month's journey away by rail to the West Coast and army troopship across the Pacific), cadets enjoyed few extended opportunities to leave West Point. One Christmas, Lim visited New York City and Washington, D.C., where he honed card-playing skills that would stand him in good stead in the years to come. More importantly, Lim's academy years fell within Manuel Luis Quezon's tenure as Philippine resident commissioner. The former governor of Tayabas (now Quezon) Province and an assembly representative, Quezon was only thirty-one years old but already one of his country's most prominent politicians when he arrived in Washington, D.C., in December 1909. When he returned to Manila in January 1917, he took with him credit for having overseen passage of the Jones Act, a grant of autonomy and presumption of independence that ensured Quezon would find a position of greater political authority in the islands. He served as president of the newly created Philippine Senate from 1917 and would ultimately, in 1935, become president of the Philippine Commonwealth. Even as an army officer presumably isolated from the web of familial and social relationships that were the necessary precursors to preferment in the Philippines, Lim could benefit from Quezon's close ties to American officials who oversaw Philippine affairs. Later, with the establishment of the Commonwealth and the ten-year transition to a republic, Quezon's support for advancement in the new national army would be essential.

As part of the process of socializing cadets into army life, officers and their families assigned to the post were encouraged to invite the young men into their homes for dinner and other social events, while "cadet hops" provided the opportunity to meet suitable young ladies from the surrounding area. The latter posed obvious but not insurmountable obstacles to Filipino students. One cadet in the late 1920s, Eligio Tavanlar, dated a white woman from New York and introduced another Filipino cadet, Rufo Romero (class of 1931), to the woman's younger sister, Lorraine. Romero and Lorraine Becker later married.[19] Whether based on his own experiences or on observation of the Romeros and other unhappy marriages between Filipinos and Americans, when his sons later attended the military and naval academies, Lim counseled them to have nothing to do with American women. Referring vaguely to some episode of his own at the military academy, Lim would advise his son Roberto, then a student at Annapolis, to "get along as much as possible with the people who surround you and mind your own business."[20]

Despite his "fondness for military life," while at the academy Lim did not excel in purely military subjects such as drill regulations and practical military engineering. He was close to the bottom of the class in both subjects. He performed near or above average in philosophy and mathematics and stood near the head of the class in Spanish, a subject in which he proved "a never tiring helper of goats" (although one of his sons recalled that Lim did not speak the language fluently, at least not by the 1930s). He was found deficient in English but was not turned back to complete his studies with a later class.[21] In entering the academy, Lim had less educational preparation than Filipino cadets who followed, but in 1910 probably was equal to or not far behind most of his American classmates. (After World War I, some Filipino cadets had at least one year of university work, usually at the University of the Philippines, before arriving at the academy. Since Reserve Officers' Training Corps participation was mandatory at the university, they also had some knowledge of military basics.) A decade of tightening the academy's once-derisory admission standards had gone some way toward bringing West Point up to the level of schools with which it aspired to be compared, and many of Lim's American contemporaries were at least high school graduates. But that was an era when "high school" might consist of only two or three years of schooling, and standards varied considerably across the country.[22]

Lim graduated seventy-seventh in his class. He later claimed that he could have done better; he had not bothered because he knew doing so would have no impact on his standing in the army. He came to believe that he should have tried harder, if only to make a name for himself in a country that much prized the label of academic "top-notcher."[23] Lim and the other Filipinos who graduated before World War I had little incentive to excel academically. With their service restricted to the Philippine Scouts, then exclusively organized as infantry troops, the usual perquisite for those who finished near the top of the class—a choice of career path (engineers, artillery, cavalry, and infantry, in order of usual preference)—was not available. Until the reorganization of the Philippine garrison in the early 1920s, all Filipino graduates became infantry officers.

Lim received his commission as a second lieutenant on the morning of 12 June 1914. Secretary of War Lindley M. Garrison's commencement address was the briefest anyone could remember having heard in years. He then rose from his seat only twice to acknowledge individual cadets: once to shake the hand of William Holcombe, the class honor man, and once again to recognize Vicente Lim, foremost in a long line of Filipinos who would graduate from the U.S. Military Academy in the decades to come. Quezon was on hand to watch and claimed to have awaited the presentation of Lim's diploma with "his heart in his mouth" since there were so few Filipinos in the audience. At the calling of Lim's name there erupted "a clamorous round of applause, more prolonged than the tributes for any other cadet," Quezon would soon tell readers of his independence-minded journal, *The Filipino People.* A widely distributed illustrated news feature of the graduation ceremony concurred. Lim "had become so popular among his classmates" that "rousing cheers" greeted the presentation of his diploma.[24]

What did Lim take away from the academy? Preeminently, for most cadets the academy marked the beginning of friendships and acquaintances that would shape careers lasting—unless dismissal, resignation, or death came first—until they reached retirement age forty or so years in the future. Despite the enlargement of the previous decade, the army officer corps remained very small. The graduates' paths would cross again and again at the same few post and school assignments. The "personal relationships" established at the academy, one of Lim's contemporaries, Matthew Ridgway (class of April 1917), would write, were an important legacy of an officer's cadet years.[25] Lim could not say the same. Given Philippine Scout commissioning and assignment policies when Lim joined the organization in 1914, there was every likelihood that he would never serve with any of his American classmates.

Yet another graduate of the April 1917 class, J. Lawton Collins, recalled from his cadet days "the thrill that crept up [his] spine as the Star Spangled Banner was played at retreat and the flag fluttered down at Trophy Point." Dwight Eisenhower (class of 1915) remembered that the oath-taking ceremony that marked the start of his academy years brought "a feeling . . . that the expression 'The United States of America' would now and henceforth mean something different than it ever had before. . . . Suddenly the flag itself meant something."[26] For American cadets, the academy years reinforced an innate patriotism, but if a sense of patriotism drove Lim to an army career, it was love of his own country, not that of the United States. The authors of the academy annual referred to Lim's "never tiring advocacy of independence" for the Philippines. Graduation from West Point gave Lim the beginnings of a professional military education that could, he hoped, be put to his country's use and provide him with the credentials to claim preeminence in Philippine military affairs in the years to come.

World War I began less than two months after the class of 1914 graduated. Two of Lim's classmates would die in France (one killed in action; another struck down by influenza, both in October 1918), but for the present most of the newly commissioned officers turned their attention south, to the Mexican border. A fourth of the class would serve with the Punitive Expedition, and many others would receive orders to camps along the border. Before reporting for duty, however, the cadets enjoyed a lengthy leave, their first in two years. Lim was one of several who went to Europe, "in order to have an idea, however superficial [Quezon would write], of the military organizations of the various nations of the old continent." He intended to continue to the Philippines via the Siberian railroad. When World War I began in August, Lim was somewhere in Russia. He arrived in Manila in October after an absence of four and a half years and there received orders to join a Philippine Scout company on the island of Panay that garrisoned a small post known as Fort San Pedro near the city of Iloilo.[27]

Lim returned to find an American army undergoing significant reorganization and retrenchment. Maj. Gen. Leonard Wood, a onetime commander of the Philippine garrison (from 1906 to 1908), was completing four years as chief of staff in 1914 and had long been concerned that the regimental rotation system by which the army manned the Philippine garrison was both uneconomical and detrimental to war readiness. While Lim was at West Point, Wood had ordered the implementation of what was known as the Colonial Army System. No longer would entire regiments rotate in and out of the Philippines on tours of duty lasting about two years. Now, six regiments of the regular army were designated for permanent Philippine service. Officers and enlisted men would be individually assigned to these "colonial regiments." To cut costs and allow regiments to serve as entire units at locations on Luzon, rather than be distributed by company or battalion among several different posts as had typically been done in the past, Wood decided that no army regiment would any longer be assigned to a post in the Visayas. Under Wood's initial plan, one regiment of infantry and two squadrons of cavalry would remain on Mindanao, but in 1913 those troops transferred to Luzon as well.[28]

Iloilo was one of several posts at which Filipino soldiers replaced Americans. When Lim reported for duty in 1914, Maj. Houston V. Evans, a West Point graduate (class of 1896) who had served in both the Philippine-American War and the 1913 Moro expedition, commanded the 10th Battalion, Philippine Scouts, at Fort San Pedro. He was the only officer holding a regular commission in a racially mixed garrison that included ten other American officers (all enlisted men holding Scout commissions); four noncommissioned officers of the regular army drawn from the quartermaster, medical, and ordnance departments (at least one of them an African American); and about three hundred Filipino enlisted men assigned to the 38th, 39th, and 40th companies of Philippine Scouts.[29]

Fort San Pedro (later demolished after World War II) stood on a promontory to the south of Iloilo. The fort was built by the Spanish in the early seventeenth century to guard against the depredations of Muslim pirates from the southern Philippine Islands and the threat to Spanish rule posed by other European interlopers. An English report of the mid-eighteenth century described it as having walls "cracked in several places" but as difficult to approach by sea. Later, the Spanish used San Pedro as a prison, a function continued by the Americans after their arrival in 1899 and again by the Japanese during World War II. Until the withdrawal of regular army forces, the American infantry regiment assigned to Camp Jossman on nearby Guimaras Island provided two companies of soldiers to guard the prisoners.[30]

Beneath its romantic veneer, Fort San Pedro was physically unappealing. The annual inspection reports for the years of Lim's assignment portray a dreary, dilapidated, and neglected post. The old fort itself held one barracks building along with storerooms and the prison. Other barracks and a half dozen officers' quarters ran along a seawall to the north. A few hundred feet to the southwest stood the only modern concrete structure on the post, the headquarters building completed in 1913. The second story of the building served as officers' quarters as well. Here, presumably, is where bachelor officers like Lim lived. The remainder of the post was taken up by a large open area immediately to the west of the fort and buildings. The area is labeled "salt marsh" on a contemporary map of Fort San Pedro. There was no electricity on the post, nor was there a source of freshwater that could be piped to the post.[31] An officer who inspected the fort in 1915 wrote that most of the buildings were in such poor shape that even painting them would be a waste of money. Termites had so badly damaged the timbers under the barracks flooring that the buildings could not be repaired and were not safe to live in. Suitable furniture was available only for the commanding officer's home. There were four typewriters at the post; all were broken. The post commanding officer was fully aware of Fort San Pedro's shortcomings, but funds to improve the place were repeatedly denied him. To add to the difficulties of making the fort more habitable, War Department guidelines cautioned that nothing was to be done to destroy or diminish the "artistic beauties" of historic places like Fort San Pedro that had fallen into the government's hands as a result of the war with Spain.[32]

In this intimate military community Lim learned the routines of regimental soldiering. Lim's company, the 39th, had only recently arrived from Ludlow Barracks at Parang, on Mindanao. Its commander, Capt. Emil Speth, was one of the first officers in the Philippine Scouts. He had come to the Philippines in 1898 with the 18th U.S. Infantry and had been one of seven enlisted men in that regiment discharged in 1901 to accept Scout commissions. Speth's unit was invariably rated one of the best-trained Scout companies; his enlisted men reputedly spoke English with the German accent Munich-born Speth never lost.[33] Lim ultimately formed a low opinion of his fellow American Scout officers. In 1927, long after most of the Americans had left the Scouts, Lim reminded Maj. John Sullivan of the Bureau of Insular Affairs of the need to "eliminate the unfit" Americans still serving with the Philippine Scouts. "I have many friends in the

Scouts," Lim wrote, "but I can frankly state that as a whole they are the greatest handicap for the government. . . . The great majority of them are even disgusted with their ownselves." But he held his first company commander in high regard. Speth, Lim wrote years later, "taught me the value of work, industry, responsibility, initiative, and self-reliance." He considered Emil Speth to have been one of the most influential teachers he had had in the army.[34]

Like the other junior officers on the post, Lim was obliged to attend the various garrison officers' schools and to demonstrate his competence in military law, field engineering, hygiene, topography, and the Spanish language.[35] Periodically, Lim and the soldiers of his company would venture across the strait to Guimaras, where the post's firing ranges were to be found, or travel farther afield to Regan Barracks, near Mount Mayon in southern Luzon, where the Scouts also conducted target practice. Lim sat on investigative boards—one to determine the physical soundness of the 39th Company barracks, for example; another to investigate the theft of cigarettes from the post store—and courts-martial, served as officer of the day, and supervised athletic events. Lim's year and a half at Fort San Pedro would be among the longest uninterrupted periods spent "with troops" in his army career.

Lim also found opportunities to socialize in nearby Iloilo. Only a few minutes' walk from the fort, Iloilo vied with Cebu "for the dignity of ranking as the second city" of the archipelago. During the second half of the nineteenth century, Iloilo's growing importance as a port for the transshipment of sugar grown on nearby, but harborless, Negros Island to all parts of the world had made it "the premier port" of the Visayas. The introduction of mills and port facilities on Negros in the 1890s and early 1900s would ultimately contribute to Iloilo's economic decline, but initially the advent of new milling technology "augmented Iloilo's prosperity" and fueled "a boom in construction, conspicuous consumption and commerce," as one of the leading historians of the area has written.[36]

Foreign visitors came away with conflicting images of the Philippines' "second city." Margherita Hamm saw Iloilo near the end of the Spanish colonial period, before a large portion "of the best business and residence sections" of Iloilo burned when American forces first occupied the city in February 1899, and dismissed it as "extremely unprepossessing," with unpaved streets, one cheap hotel, no places of amusement, and no restaurant worthy of the name. Dean Worcester—later so prominent in Philippine affairs—had been equally unimpressed. The "second city of the archipelago [was] by no means attractive," he wrote in his influential *The Philippine Islands and Their People.* He and four companions had found themselves marooned in a "miserable" hotel in the city until a foreign businessman took pity on them and invited them to stay in his guesthouse on Guimaras. The American traveler Paul Gilbert agreed that "nothing especially of interest [was] to be found at Iloilo," although he was one of the few to mention San Pedro. The "usual stone fort," he wrote (without giving its name), "seems to belong to some scene of a comic opera." Other evaluations of the city were more positive. An Englishwoman who arrived in Iloilo in 1904 described it as "a big town, with long straggling streets, and the houses all two stories high . . . separated by little bits of garden with palms and flowering trees." The effect, she observed, made Iloilo look "quite pretty." An American writer who visited Iloilo in 1914 commented approvingly of the city's "first-class shops, . . . electric lights, telephones, [and] ice plants."[37]

Lim certainly found Iloilo agreeable. The attractions of the city were such that he was "led astray by young pleasures" until sobered by a sharp report written by Captain Speth. In Iloilo, Lim continued to develop the network of friendships and acquaintances that would allow him to pursue interests outside the army. In the United States, he had been befriended by Quezon and other members of the resident commissioner's staff, such as Maximo Kalaw. Now, Jorge ("George") Vargas, an up-and-coming lawyer who had recently been admitted to the bar and had opened a short-lived law office in Iloilo, became one of Lim's acquaintances. Vargas told Kalaw that he saw Lim often and that the two had "become quite intimate."[38]

Lim's ability to socialize in the Filipino community represented the flip side of the ever-present issue of race. The observation by Edward Coffman, the leading social historian of the "Old Army," that soldiers "brought to the Philippines the mores of turn-of-the-century Americans, including attitudes toward race," need hardly be belabored. Introduction to the Philippines only reinforced existing attitudes. "The American Army . . . does not as a rule," army officer Harry Bandoltz wrote matter-of-factly after ten years' residence in the islands, "admit Filipinos even of the highest class to social equality. . . . Orders on this subject could have no good effect that would outweigh the bad one of directing attention to this unfortunate fact."[39] From Fort San Pedro, Lim complained to Quezon of the many petty annoyances he confronted in the army, most of which, he implied, could be traced to race prejudice. Earlier, at the academy, Lim had argued with a professor who had made disparaging remarks about people from Asia. Later, in Manila, Lim reportedly physically assaulted an American policeman who had insulted him. Lim then refused to apologize, even after being told to do so by both the governor-general and Quezon.[40]

Racial tension had been heightened by the arrival in 1913 of a new governor-general committed to increasing Filipino visibility in government, which meant, of course, diminishing the American presence. To some unmeasurable extent, Lim served unwittingly as a symbol of a new policy of Filipinization to which the army had responded viscerally, even though the new governor, Francis Burton Harrison, had no authority over the army itself. There was, one officer would later write, "evident deterioration in every department [of the insular government] from the moment Burton Harrison took over and began to apply the Democratic reforms of the new Wilson administration." The army community became even more socially isolated than it was normally inclined to be and abstained "from all but strictly official life." Harrison got even—and ensured the army's lasting enmity—by writing a book drawing attention to the criminality of some American soldiers and the provocative acts of others intended to undermine Harrison's Filipinization policy.[41]

Certainly, Lim and other Filipino officers suffered nothing like the overt ostracism inflicted on the army's few other nonwhite officers. African American Benjamin O. Davis Jr., for example, entered West Point in 1932 and almost immediately found himself "silenced." This treatment, usually reserved for cadets who violated the honor code and then refused to resign, ensured that Davis dined alone, bunked alone, and spoke to no one other than in the line of duty until he left in 1936. As Davis knew from the start, the other cadets subjected him to silencing simply because most did not want black officers in the army. A black cadet who had been "found" for academic deficiency in 1929 had faced the same treatment as did a cadet dismissed in 1935. To Davis's surprise and disgust, this treatment continued after he graduated from the academy. Among other slights, he was denied membership in officers' clubs both in the South, at Fort Benning, Georgia, and in the West, at Fort Riley, Kansas. Like his army-officer father before him, Davis faced the dreary, demoralizing prospect of repeated assignments to Reserve Officers' Training Corps units at black colleges or with one of a small number of black National Guard organizations, "professionally disadvantageous" but "safe" assignments where he would not command white enlisted men nor outrank a white officer.[42]

By contrast, Filipino officers could join the local military clubs and participate in the garrison's social activities. An American officer who served in the islands in the 1930s observed, however, that the Army and Navy Club normally excluded Filipinos from membership "no matter how lofty their position in Filipino circles" and only begrudgingly tolerated those commissioned in the Scouts "since they were in effect Army officers."[43] References to Filipino officers were often flattering but seldom failed to include the phrase, "judged as a Filipino." In this way, then Col. George Marshall evaluated the otherwise "popular [and] hard-working" Maj. Rafael Garcia in 1935.[44] Maj. Edward M. Almond, who served with the Philippine Scouts' 45th Infantry Regiment in 1930–33, found the Filipinos to be "good officers" of high quality, again "within their capabilities." Capt. Charles Ivins, who also spent a tour of duty in the Philippines with the 45th Infantry in the 1930s, considered the Filipino Scout officers to be "the highest type of native," a generously meant but open-ended compliment.[45] Mariano Sulit was certain that racial prejudice once cost him a lieutenancy in the Scouts. Sulit had been a private in the regular army in the United States preparing to ship out to France when he was awarded a commission in the Philippine Scouts in 1918. He returned to the Philippines and was ordered immediately to retake the commissioning exam. Without time to prepare, he failed the examination and was not allowed to attempt it again, because, Sulit later told Quezon, the examining officers had not wanted to give a commission to a Filipino. (He regained the commission in 1920.) Another Filipino officer commissioned just after World War I, Narcisco Manzano, thought that racism had worked to his advantage. He felt that he had been given a commission over better-qualified applicants because his mixed Filipino-Spanish ancestry meant that he was much lighter skinned than most Filipinos.[46]

Whether race was the main issue or not, Lim's tour of duty at San Pedro was marked by a series of incidents that challenged his resolve to remain in military service. In a speech he gave before cadets of the Philippine Military Academy in July 1941, Lim revealed that during his time at San Pedro he became "disgusted" at the way in which his commanding officer treated him. He complained to higher authority, and the officer was relieved of duty. Lim gave no further details, but contemporary post returns suggest that Lim crossed swords with Maj. Charles Morton, a regular army captain who had assumed command of the 10th Battalion in February 1915 following Evans's death of apoplexy. The post returns report that a colonel from the inspector general's office was conducting an investigation of an unspecified nature at the fort in January 1916. That same month Morton was stripped of his temporary major's commission and ordered back to his regular army billet. Another army captain, Frederick V. S. Chamberlain, who had been at San Pedro awaiting assignment, took Morton's place.[47]

This was not the last unpleasant incident at San Pedro involving Lim. In May 1916, Lim preferred charges against an American soldier at the post, Private First Class Roy Lee, whom Lim accused of having behaved in a disrespectful manner toward him in Iloilo. The court officers found Lee guilty and fined him one month's pay, but at the same time appended an extraordinary addendum to the court-martial papers condemning Lim's behavior as well. Lim, the officers wrote, had treated Lee in an "unnecessarily harsh, overbearing and tyrannical" manner. Lim's conduct toward an enlisted man was "unbecoming an officer and a gentleman" and his conduct before the court itself was found to be extremely offensive. Chamberlain allowed the addendum to be attached to the trial papers and forwarded to Manila. Lim's tour of duty at Fort San Pedro came to an abrupt end. One month later, he received orders to leave Iloilo.[48]

If Fort San Pedro represented the least the army had to offer in the way of professional opportunities, in some ways Lim's new post represented the most. The 42nd Company of the Philippine Scouts, to which Lim was now assigned, was stationed at Fort Mills, on Corregidor Island. The army had occupied the small, tadpole-shaped island at the mouth of Manila Bay soon after arriving in the Philippines, using it initially as the site of a convalescent hospital. Soldiers in those days called the island "the graveyard" because, it was rumored, only the sickest men were sent there, but by the time Lim reported for duty, Corregidor was nearing completion of its conversion to the massively armed coast artillery fortress that guarded the entrance to the bay. Most of Mills's heavy guns had been emplaced prior to Lim's arrival, but the fortress infrastructure had yet to be completed and construction of gun batteries continued on adjacent islands.[49]

Although Fort Mills lacked the physical amenities and even the tropical ambiance (which came only in the 1920s and 1930s after numerous palms had been planted on the island) that later made an assignment to Corregidor a delight to army families, it nevertheless had a sizable and growing community of nearly five thousand officers and men, making it the largest army garrison in the Philippines. Coast artillery officer Frank Clark served on Corregidor during these early years of construction and remembered that "new ideas burgeoned and were encouraged [and] the whole atmosphere was electric with progress and achievement." Lieutenant Clark's enthusiasm for the assignment was not typical—this was a time when a Philippine tour of duty had yet to achieve the popularity of the post–World War I years—but Corregidor offered a wide array of professional and social opportunities. Among other things, in 1916 it was the site of the only military aviation unit in the Philippines. A young Lewis Brereton, whom Lim would meet a decade later at Fort Leavenworth and again in the Philippines in 1941, was stationed on Corregidor that year. Corregidor was also close to Manila. The city could easily be reached by army and civilian ferries that made the thirty-mile, three-hour'-long trip to and from the capital several times daily.[50]

Lim's own job was less rewarding. The Philippine Scout troops on the island guarded the civil and military prisoners who built the fortifications. The Scout garrison included thirty officers; Lim was the only Filipino. He may well have preferred Fort San Pedro, where at least a substantial civilian community existed only minutes away. At any rate, Lim remained barely four months on Corregidor. By the end of October 1916, he was in Baguio, instructing at the Philippine Constabulary school there. It was an assignment made at his request.[51]

The first two years of Lim's regular army life can hardly have been satisfying. To his fellow Scout officers, service with Filipino soldiers marked the pinnacle of their professional careers, but Lim felt constrained by the parochialism of Scout duty in remote provinces. "I feel ashamed that I am not doing what I should or could do [for] my people," Lim had written to Quezon from Fort San Pedro. "I will get out of the scouts at any cost if I could only widen my education on military subjects," he confided. Lim was keenly interested in European military events, and the young lieutenant sought Quezon's help in getting assigned to Europe as a military observer. The education he would receive, Lim believed, far outweighed any risk to his life.[52] Quezon could do nothing for him, but perhaps service with the Philippine Constabulary in Baguio would provide opportunities for advancement and achievement that would forever remain beyond Lim's reach as a company-grade officer in the Philippine Scouts.

The Philippine Constabulary with which Lim now found himself associated shared a history contemporaneous with and not too dissimilar from that of the Scouts. Like the army's Filipino-manned organization, the Constabulary had been founded in 1901 to mop up remnants of the revolutionary army and put an end to brigandage. It was organized, again like the Scouts, into company-sized units of Filipino enlisted men under the command of American and European officers, most of whom had been enlisted men or junior officers in volunteer regiments during the Philippine-American War. A few regular officers of the U.S. Army occupied the senior positions in the Constabulary. The Scouts and Constabulary were about the same size, roughly five thousand men each. A law passed by Congress in 1903 allowed the chief of the Constabulary (at that time an army captain who, thanks to the new law, held the local rank of army brigadier general) to command both Constabulary and Scout units on field operations. The men wore slightly different uniforms, and the Constabulary carried older rifles, but Governor Taft's insistence that the Philippine Constabulary was "not a military force" was less a description of real conditions than a calculated justification for eroding the army's authority in the islands. "The distinction drawn" between the Scouts and Constabulary, wrote an American familiar with the contemporary Philippine political scene, "is a distinction without a difference."[53]

Differences had begun to emerge by 1916, however. American army officers still held senior positions in the Constabulary, but their role had been declining since passage of the so-called Manchu law in August 1912, which made it more difficult for the army to retain officers on detached service, and would end entirely in 1917.[54] More importantly, the Constabulary officer corps had always included Filipinos, and the percentage of native-born officers in the organization was growing rapidly. The Philippine Commission Act of 18 July 1901 establishing the Constabulary had allowed the recruitment of Filipino officers, and 27 of the organization's 183 officers at the end of 1901 were Filipinos. Many of these "Filipinos," one critical American officer observed, were Spanish mestizos—"much more Spanish than Filipino"—who tended to perpetuate "Spanish traditions of the 'ruling race.'" Nevertheless, natives of the islands, whatever their ethnic origin, constituted a significant portion of the officer corps from the start. There was, of course, opposition to the trend. Looking ahead to a time when more Filipinos would apply for entry to the Constabulary's officer ranks, in 1908 the Constabulary's acting director, James Harbord, raised the examination standard for appointment to third lieutenant. "I think I can see that time coming," Harbord wrote fellow army officer Chief of Constabulary Harry Bandholtz, "and desire to have the examinations high enough to stop the rush."[55]

These and other steps suggested to halt the ingress of Filipino officers had limited effect. America's entry into the world war in April 1917 precipitated the departure of many white officers, who sought appointments in the rapidly expanding U.S. Army or rejoined the armies of their European homelands, but the war only accelerated an existing trend toward Filipinization. In 1916 the Filipino-dominated legislative body had set out to Filipinize the officer corps by purposely reducing entry-level pay for officers, thus ensuring, the governor-general acknowledged in his annual report, that "no more Americans [would] come from the United States to enter as third lieutenants." The passage of a retirement act (the Osmeña Act) for Philippine civil servants in February 1916 allowed officers and other American officials with six years of service to depart with gratuities, with the clear implication that that was the best to which an American could look forward. At the end of 1916, 190 American and 159 Filipino officers served with the Constabulary; by the close of 1918, the officer corps included only 39 Americans, while Filipino officers numbered 308.[56]

The Filipinization of the Constabulary officer corps presented opportunities for promotion to senior grades and positions of authority that neither Filipino nor American Scout officers could ever achieve, since they were, at that time, limited by law to the ranks of lieutenant and captain. At the same time, talk of amalgamating the two organizations continued. The Philippine Commission had routinely called for "the consolidation of the Philippine Scouts and Constabulary into a single homogeneous native force under the control of the insular government," and the Bureau of Insular Affairs schemed to unite the two organizations as late as 1917. It foresaw joint U.S.-Philippine government financing and administration of a combined force.[57] The army's reluctance to state firmly that the Scouts were a part of the "regular" army only fed such speculation. These trends—Filipinization and amalgamation, combined with recurrent talk that the Philippine Constabulary might one day become the Philippine Army—encouraged an ambitious officer like Lim to associate himself with the Constabulary. He was uniquely well placed to benefit from such an association. The fact that Filipino officers of the Constabulary had to begin as third lieutenants placed Lim higher on the promotion ladder than most of them (only eight Filipinos held a rank higher than that of first lieutenant in 1916), and no young Constabulary officer could match his educational and professional credentials.

The Constabulary school itself was in the process of a significant transformation from its origin at the Santa Lucia Barracks in Intramuros in 1904 as a sort of orientation course for newly appointed officers. The school had retained its brief three-month duration when it moved from Manila to Baguio in September 1908, but in 1917 instruction lengthened to two years. This expansion may have encouraged the positive response to Lim's request, since the school now needed more and better-qualified instructors. In fact, the act upgrading the academy's standards had been rewritten to include a provision allowing instructors to be non-Constabulary graduates of "military academies or colleges." Like the other changes taking place in the organization, the expansion of the school at the instigation of the national legislature looked deliberately to the time when the Philippine Constabulary might form the basis for a Philippine army. The enlarged school could provide officers not just for the government's national police force but also for a national guard. It would be "a sort of West Point for the training of officers for the armies of the independent republic of the Philippines when it shall materialize."[58]

In addition to the professional opportunities that promised to flow from his assignment to the Constabulary academy at Baguio, Lim's personal life took a new and rewarding direction. In August 1917, he married Pilar Hidalgo. The Hidalgos were a prominent merchant family, resident in Manila but from the town of Boac, on the island of Marinduque. Pilar was already well known in the islands. She had been one of the first women graduates of prestigious Manila High School, in 1910, and of the University of the Philippines College of Liberal Arts, in 1913. Fabian de la Rosa's "portrait of Miss Hidalgo" had drawn "the admiration of thousands" when displayed at the 1915 Panama-Pacific International Exposition in San Francisco. At the time of her marriage, Pilar was an instructor in mathematics at the University of the Philippines, an accomplishment that led a newspaper account of the engagement to call her "the first Filipino woman mathematician." The Lims were married in Quiapo, Manila, on 12 August 1917. Decades later, Pilar Hidalgo told Lim's biographer Juanito Rimando that the wedding ceremony had included military ushers who attempted to "cross sabers" under which the newlyweds would pass. Many guests were not familiar with the practice and, thinking they were about to be attacked, fled the church in alarm.[59] The Lims spent several days after the marriage in Calamba. By then, they knew they would not make Baguio their home, since Lim had received orders to return to duty with the army. America's entry into the European war presaged significant changes in the army garrison in the Philippines, and none would be more dramatically affected than the officers and men of the Philippine Scouts.

CHAPTER 2

"A Good Future before You"

At Home and Abroad, 1917–1929

The legislative act that permitted Filipinos to attend West Point obligated graduates to spend at least eight years on active duty, but Lieutenant Lim would have had little expectation of serving with the Philippine Scouts (PS) into the next decade. Only a few weeks after returning from Lim's commissioning ceremony, Quezon publicly asserted his belief that "sooner or later" the Philippine Constabulary would "be converted into the army of the Philippine Islands." It would want well-trained native officers, and Filipino students in Washington, Quezon wrote, were already "call[ing] Lim 'the future Chief of Staff of the Philippine Army.'" The young cadet's interaction with the resident commissioner and his staff would have encouraged a belief that he faced a promising career in a Filipino army. In 1914 independence seemed imminent. The Nacionalista party, with its repeatedly stated goal of "immediate independence," dominated the Philippine Assembly, which had been formed in 1907 with the partial transfer of legislative power from an appointed commission to a body of elected representatives. Heightened expectations of self-rule accompanied Woodrow Wilson's accession to the presidency, since the Democratic Party platform called for "an immediate declaration of the Nation's purpose to recognize the independence of the Philippine Islands as soon as a stable government can be established." Wilson was less the anti-imperialist than party pronouncements suggested, but his victory in November 1912 "produce[d] a general feeling of jubilation" in the islands. At a "monster demonstration" held on the Luneta to celebrate Wilson's triumph, a crowd estimated at thirty thousand applauded Quezon's assurance "that it was Mr. Wilson's intention to bring about the political independence of the islands" and Assembly leader Sergio Osmeña's promise that "the victory of Woodrow Wilson meant for the Filipinos their entry into the concert of nations." Wilson's choice of governor-general added to the anticipation. Francis Burton Harrison arrived in Manila in October 1913 to tell Filipinos that "every step we take will be taken with a view to the ultimate independence of the Islands."[1]

War was the other context for optimism. Like colonial elites elsewhere, during World War I Filipino leaders expected military contributions to lead to political concessions from the colonizing power. Even before April 1917, the deterioration of relations between Mexico and the United States and Washington's decision to send an expedition to Veracruz had had repercussions in Manila. Osmeña cabled Quezon with a plan for forming a "Filipino army" to serve alongside the American forces in the expected war with Mexico. Quezon passed along to Harrison his response that war was, in fact, unlikely, and the situation called instead for "quietness and self-control."[2] The War Department gave no consideration to the proposal either, but the determination to form a Filipino army persisted. The Bureau of Insular Affairs compiled a thick file concerning efforts by members of the Philippine Assembly to gain official sanction for a military force.

As an advocate of Philippine independence, Harrison took seriously the Philippines' need to develop a capacity for self-defense. In late 1916 he informed Washington that legislators were discussing a bill to make military service compulsory and to establish a committee of national defense. The committee would develop plans for a Philippine army, Harrison noted approvingly, and he emphasized the possibility of converting the Constabulary with which Lim had just become associated "into an insular army." On 17 March 1917, three weeks before the United States formally cast its lot with the Allies, the Philippine Legislature passed the Militia Act. The act did not stipulate when or how officers and men would be recruited for the "organized militia" (to be called, following American practice, the national guard) but authorized the governor-general to consider means of doing so. Volunteers might fill the ranks of nine projected regiments, but Harrison had authority to compel service if necessary.[3]

World War I and America's slide toward belligerence merely quickened and legitimized Filipino attempts to create an indigenous military force as an outward manifestation of political maturity. The American declaration of war on Germany in April encouraged the government to proceed with raising a division of Filipino soldiers. The legislature itself could do little to press forward against American opposition, but no one was keener on the national guard than Harrison himself. He had served in a volunteer regiment during the Spanish-American War, and he fully expected to be appointed major general in command of the guard and lead it to France.[4]

The subsequent history of the Philippine national guard was short but instructive. Many of the problems that would confront the military mission in 1935–40 made an appearance in 1917–18. Central to the success of the national guard, for example, was the support of the local U.S. Army garrison—the only force to possess the necessary expertise, supplies, and training areas that would allow the guard to achieve its objectives. The cooperation of the local army commander could also legitimize the project to a suspicious general staff in Washington. Maj. Gen. Hunter Liggett, commanding general in the Philippines in 1916–17, proved immediately helpful. Harrison learned that there were 25,000 Springfield rifles held in reserve in the Philippines, and he could count on their use by the guard. In other concrete ways, the army extended its support and guidance. Army officers had assisted in preparing the Militia Act. Now they assumed prominent positions in the guard's command structure and participated in training guard officers. When Liggett left in mid-April 1917, the new commanding general, Brig. Gen. Charles J. Bailey, was equally supportive.[5]

Bailey's replacement, however, was not. Brig. Gen. Robert K. Evans, a retired Philippine-American War veteran recalled to active duty to head the Philippine Department, was a popular commanding officer, the local press reported, but he had little intention of supporting the Philippine national guard. He took command in August 1917 and acted promptly to hinder the guard's development. The Springfield rifles were shipped back to the United States, and other war reserve supplies (such as tents and cooking utensils) the guard had hoped to borrow were suddenly unavailable. Even condemned "fencing muskets" that earlier had been offered for the guard's use were instead dumped into Manila Bay.[6]

Evans's refusal to cooperate with the Philippine government immensely complicated the task of organizing the Philippine National Guard (PNG). Especially devastating was the enlargement and reorganization of the Philippine Scouts from battalions into regiments. The Scouts' transformation reduced access to regular army officers, noncommissioned officers, and potential recruits. As Harrison noted in alarm, "The increase of the Scouts and the organization of our division cannot go on satisfactorily at the same time."[7] The decision undermined the guard's ability to obtain sorely needed professional leadership and training, and it appears to have been calculated to do exactly that. Evans first proposed the reorganization of the Scout battalions into regiments soon after assuming command of the garrison. When the War Department did not concur, he persisted in advising regimental status "in October and [again] in mid-December 1917."[8] Incensed by Evans's obstreperousness, Harrison demanded his removal. A new commander, Brig. Gen. Henry Greene, proved more obliging, but by the time he took office in August 1918, an irreplaceable year had been lost.

When asked four decades later about the situation in the Philippines during World War I, Noel Perley, the army officer first assigned to the PNG (before Evans's arrival), told Eugene Ganley that "everything was fantastic." No one knew what to expect. Officers arrived from the States on one transport only to receive orders to return on the next. Perley agreed that the Philippine Department—filled with "has beens" and others resentful at having to remain in the islands while everyone else went off to war—hated the guard and had been egged on by the War Department to quash it. Local opinion held that the real source of the guard's problems was not so much Evans as the department adjutant, Col. Edwin Landon. Quezon finally asked the resident commissioner to see what could be done "to secure the transfer of Col. Landon."[9] But an American Scout officer pointed out that Evans had to concern himself with the immediate defense needs of the islands, not with the development of an indigenous military force. With most of the "colonial regiments" ordered back to the United States or on the Siberia expedition (Colonel Landon along with them), the Philippine Scouts remained the only trained and presumably reliable source of American authority in the islands. The gist of Evans's correspondence with Harrison suggests that the general thought the guard would be a failure even with army support; thus resources turned over to the insular government would simply be wasted. If Evans was not actively encouraged to hinder the guard's development, his actions must have had the tacit approval of his superiors. In 1923 the War Department awarded Evans the Distinguished Service Medal for his service in the Philippines. He had, the medal citation read, handled "many difficult problems" with "rare judgment, tact, and great skill."[10]

Of course, accommodating a Philippine guard division could not be an army priority in April 1917, but when pushed to consider the matter, army officials in Washington rejected the use of Filipino troops either in France or along the Mexican border or anywhere else guard officers fantasized about being sent—Mesopotamia, some thought, or perhaps Indochina and India, where Filipino troops could maintain order while French and English troops fought in Europe.[11] Prodded by the Wilson administration, which had received the formal offer of a division of Philippine troops from Quezon (president of the recently established Philippine Senate) when he visited Washington in June 1917, in January 1918 Congress approved the organization of the Philippine guard in the same fashion as the national guard of the United States and authorized calling it into federal service. War Department assistance was still necessary to bring about the training and subsequent utilization of the guard, and in mid-April 1918 Brig. Gen. Thomas Hartigan of the PNG, a onetime West Point cadet who had served in the Philippine-American War and now made his home in the islands, traveled to Washington to outline the accomplishments of the guard and its potential use in the war effort. In presentations to war college and general staff committees in the capital, he stressed the leading role played by army officers in writing the Militia Act, which, he assured his listeners, conformed closely to the National Defense Act of 1916.

His audience remained unconvinced. Opposition to the guard, Hartigan cabled Harrison, was "incredible and violent." Hartigan did not reveal that Harrison himself was a focus of hostility. According to Jaime C. de Veyra, the Philippine resident commissioner, the initial impression of the offer of Filipino troops had been favorable, but when the War Department learned that Harrison expected to be the division's commander, support turned to opposition. The Spanish-language *La Vanguardia* newspaper's correspondent, Alfredo Roa, took a broader view. The army would not tolerate any civilian being given a prominent military role, Roa reported from Washington, not even the president of the United States. To that extent, the Philippine National Guard represented an amateur entrepreneurial military tradition that the army had effectively suppressed in the United States. The regular army was no more sympathetic to the martial ambitions of the governor-general and his staff of Manila merchants and lawyers (Hartigan was one) than it was to those of former president Theodore Roosevelt and his proposed volunteer division. That the much-despised Harrison happened to be the guard's commander was merely icing on the cake.[12]

Real as it was, the War Department's opposition extended beyond distaste for Burton Harrison. The army's disinterest in making use of Filipino soldiers, however unpalatable to ambitious politicians and soldiers in the Philippines, was entirely predictable. The army was willing to accept Filipino recruits in the United States (sixty-seven Filipinos would die while serving with the army in 1918), and the U.S. Navy carried out a successful recruiting campaign in the Philippines during the war. But only the direst need for men on the western front would have turned the army's attention toward the Philippines, with the inherent logistical, not to mention racial, difficulties to be overcome in making use of Filipino manpower. Even sympathetic observers in the Philippines conceded that guard enthusiasts had overlooked some salient features of modern warfare in their rush to seek combat. A division of men could be lost in a single day's fighting, the Philippine Revolution general Jose Alejandrino commented in a newspaper interview, yet no one in the Philippines seemed to be considering the thousands of additional Filipinos who would be needed as replacements, were the guard's supporters to get their wish.[13]

Ultimately, the War Department achieved its goal. It thwarted the guard's ambition to see active service outside the Philippines. Although the authorization to accept organized Filipino militia forces had come at the beginning of the year, the Philippine National Guard was not federalized until 20 November 1918.[14] When the guard finally disbanded in February 1919 after two additional months' training at the insular government's expense, many of the men parleyed their guard experience into positions with the Philippine Constabulary, the Philippine Scouts, or the navy. Those organizations had set up recruiting offices at Camp Tomas Claudio, the national guard training area (named for the first Filipino soldier to be killed while serving with the army in France) located not far from Fort McKinley.[15]

The obvious need for mutuality of effort and understanding between army authorities in Washington and Manila in order for the creation of Philippine armed forces to succeed could not have been lost on Manuel Quezon when fifteen years later he asked Douglas MacArthur to be the Philippine government's military adviser. MacArthur's effort to retain authority as chief of staff even as he served in Manila and his attempts to place supportive officers in positions of authority in both Manila and Washington suggests that he had been made well aware of problems the national guard confronted in 1917–18.

The Filipino soldiers' experience was also instructive. As was often the case, elite enthusiasm for the political and social potential of military service sometimes surpassed the willingness of the populace to perform it. The Philippine record in 1918 was mixed. D. R. Williams, the former commission secretary and an outspoken opponent of Philippine independence, claimed that even Filipinos well informed about the war and desirous of an American victory remained passive onlookers. Only with great difficulty had the government been able to induce men to join the guard, despite "the service [being] painted in most attractive colors."[16] In some parts of the country, the guard did face considerable difficulty recruiting. The province of Albay, for example, raised 21 men to fill an 800-man quota; farther south, a mere 74 patriots stepped forward to fill Cebu's 2,000-man quota. But support was striking elsewhere. The *Cablenews-American* editorially dismissed talk of the guard as an incipient national army as "sheer twaddle," but it nonetheless noted considerable enthusiasm for military service. In the northern Luzon province of La Union, San Fernando provided 450 men to fill a 200-man quota after a recruiting drive of only a few days, while in the southern part of the island, 600 volunteers oversubscribed the Camarineses' provincial quotas by 200 men. In the Camarineses, the paper admitted, "everyone of the required age is willing to join the guard." Serving as a recruiting officer briefly on Negros in 1918, Lim reportedly had little difficulty filling his quota of recruits.[17] A close reading of the PNG correspondence also suggests that recruitment success relied only partly on either patriotism or compulsion; for many enlistees, the attraction of military service was its promise of full-time work with decent pay.[18] As the authors of the 1930s-era military system would learn, the military offered economic security that many Filipinos could not achieve through other means. For many other Filipinos in 1917–19, interest in military service was directly tied to the possibility of active service, another lesson that would be relearned in 1935–40.

Whether or not the Filipino people had genuinely supported the PNG, its popular legacy was Filipino enthusiasm for military service, dedication to the cause of Philippine independence, and adherence to the concept of the citizen-soldier. If in truth most provinces had failed to fill their enlistment quotas in 1918 and contemporaries had lamented that so many "names of young men of worth" were missing from the list of student officers undergoing training with the guard, Filipinos later remembered things differently. Maximo Kalaw, Lim's friend who would sit on the national defense committee in the Commonwealth-era assembly, recalled that "hundreds of our choice young men—the flower of our youth—left their high governmental and professional positions to join America's colors" during the war, while so many men stepped forward to serve that the recruiting goal was quickly oversubscribed. The successful first mobilization test of the Philippine Army in May 1939, Iloilo mayor Dr. Ramon F. Campos would tell the Commonwealth's citizen-soldiers, reminded him of the many who had volunteered for the Philippine National Guard twenty years earlier. Years after the national guard's demise, Quezon claimed to believe that had only the United States supported the effort to create an organized militia, the Philippines would have been well on the way to being able to defend itself as independence approached.[19] In this sense, the national guard had continued symbolic importance into the 1930s as Filipinos confronted the security needs of a new nation.

Of course, as a junior officer Lim had no influence on policy and, until Evans left, little possibility of seizing whatever chance of active service the PNG might present. For much of the war period, he was on duty in Mindanao. The Philippine Scouts abandoned most posts in the Visayas and Mindanao in 1917–18 to replace departing American regiments on Luzon, but the army kept one Scout battalion at Zamboanga and Sulu. Lim was transferred there in August 1917 and remained for about a year. He served first with the 50th Company, Philippine Scouts, at Augur Barracks, on Jolo, and then with the 52nd Company at Pettit Barracks, Zamboanga.[20] In truth, Mindanao was as close to the possibility of fighting as a Philippine Scout was likely to get during the two decades Lim spent with the organization, and the last awards of the army's Philippine Campaign medal would be made to Philippine Scouts engaged against Moros in July 1917.[21] Throughout the American period of occupation, orders to Mindanao would appeal to the more adventurous army officers who found themselves on duty in the Philippines. Lim can only have chafed at the assignment. Two years earlier, while still at Iloilo, Lim had sought Quezon's help in getting assigned to Europe as a military observer. Now Lim was as far from the Great War as it was possible for a soldier in the U.S. Army to be.

With General Evans gone, the Filipino officers were at last able to seek assignments with the national guard, which even at that late date held out the only hope for active service. Within a month of Greene's arrival, the Philippine Department had issued a special order sending Lim and seven other Filipino Scout officers to the guard for instructor duty. When the insular government decided to fund extra training for the guard, the Philippine Department allowed the Scout officers to remain on duty with it. Lim was given the rank of major in the guard and placed in command of the 2nd Battalion, 9th Infantry Regiment. Lim remained with the unit only a short while, if indeed he ever actually reported for duty. Prior to the guard's demobilization, Lim was also on duty with the 2nd and 3rd Infantry Regiments. Given the short period of time the PNG was activated, Lim could hardly have seen much service with any of these regiments, but nonetheless he impressed the adjutant general and regimental commanders. Based on their observations, Lim was rated the best of the West Point–educated Filipino officers serving with the Philippine National Guard.[22]

The belief that the guard division might become the basis for a postwar Philippine Army was widespread and probably was shared by Lim and the other Filipino Scout officers. Potential army recruits "need have no fear about their future," General Ralph Jones had assured provincial governors charged with overseeing local recruitment efforts. Those who wanted to be would be kept on active duty after the war, because Harrison had agreed that the national guard would be "the nucleus of the future Filipino army."[23] However, the end of the war meant the demise of the PNG. The wartime economic boom ended, and a scandal involving criminal investments by Philippine National Bank officials came to light; both events reduced government resources that might have sustained the guard in peacetime. A new governor-general, army general and Republican presidential aspirant Leonard Wood, had been a leading proponent of "preparedness" in the United States and would push for military training in local colleges during his years at Malacañan (1921–27), but he was also determined to cut costs and roll back his predecessor's Filipinization policy.

Still, for Lim and others who returned to army service at war's end, the postwar era would witness a sea change in the organization of military forces in the archipelago, creating in the process opportunities for greater responsibilities for Filipino officers. Washington had virtually denuded the islands of American soldiers during the war, and the army had abandoned most posts located outside Manila and central Luzon. After 1917, American and Filipino troops never again garrisoned any post in the Visayas, nor, aside from Pettit Barracks, any post on Mindanao. The army fully expected to rebuild the garrison after the return of peace, but the changing economic and political environment of the postwar period placed severe restrictions on its ability to do so. The army therefore placed increasing reliance on Filipino manpower.

For officers and those who sought to be officers, the 1920s started on a high note. Ten Filipinos received commissions in the Philippine Scouts in 1921. Narcisco Manzano, author of the only memoir to have been written by a Filipino Scout officer, was one of those who joined at this time. Like other new officers, Manzano had served in the national guard and wanted to continue a military career. Thanks to the indulgence of sympathetic army officers, the intelligent but underweight and physically slight graduate of the engineering program at the University of Santo Tomas obtained a commission in August 1921. He and the nine others commissioned that year made up nearly one-third of all Filipinos who obtained Scout commissions throughout the period of American occupation.[24]

Two years later, the Philippine Scouts received their first officer from the naval academy. Because graduates were not offered navy commissions and there was no legal requirement that Filipino graduates be given commissions in the army, applicants to Annapolis never approached in number those who sought to attend West Point. The first year the qualifying test was offered, in 1916, fourteen applicants attempted the exam and six passed. That was an encouraging start, but that was also the highwater mark for Filipino applicants. By the mid-1920s, thirty or more would-be soldiers took the West Point test each year, while three or four usually showed up for the Annapolis exam. All too often, only one or two, if any, passed. The Bureau of Civil Service began doing for the navy what it had done for the army before World War I; asking schoolteachers and college professors to identify suitable young men and encourage them to try to get into the academy. Three Annapolis graduates ended up with commissions in the Philippine Scouts: Jose E. Olivares in 1923, Emilio M. Bataga in 1925, and Bienvenido M. Alba in 1927. Like the cadets destined for West Point, Annapolis-bound cadets would be informed in early 1931 that they would no longer be offered commissions in the Scouts.

The status of Scout officers changed significantly in the 1920s. Until 1920, Lim and the other Filipino academy graduates had been among the few Scout officers who had had to meet regular army commissioning standards, though their opportunities for service and promotion were limited to those available to the army enlisted men holding temporary Scout commissions. The army had also obtained Scout officers from civilian life through competitive examinations (three Filipinos won commissions on that basis while Lim was at West Point), but in 1916 the army decided that American enlisted men would receive preferment in test-based competitions for Scout commissions and offered commissions to several who failed the examination.[25]

Eventually, for Americans, a Philippine Scout commission became a consolation prize for failure to obtain a commission in the regular army. Applicants whose lack of educational attainment, or merely poor timing, prevented them from qualifying for a regular commission sought service with the Scouts or the Philippine Constabulary, also a stepping-stone to an army commission in the pre–World War I period. The second-class nature of such commissions was a constant source of aggravation to those who held them. During his tenure as governor-general, Harrison complained that Scout officers were "in a state of continual dissatisfaction" and were forever politicking to receive regular status. One Scout officer who had insisted that a regular army enlisted man be court-martialed for having spoken disrespectfully to him complained that everyone knew "the white troops" looked down on officers who served with native troops. Some American regulars agreed. One wrote that he "wouldn't want [American Scout officers] in my outfit." They had little formal education and were "jealous" of the regulars "since their service was limited to the islands." Maj. W. W. Taylor Jr. observed that "the bulk of [the American Scout officers] were not of the officer type in the first place, and very few of them have succeeded by study and effort in overcoming their early deficiencies in education and ethical standards." In addition, many had "forgotten that they were white men." Personally, Major Taylor had been incensed while serving in the Philippines that he had "had to quarter his family adjacent to the native family of a white Scout officer." He saw no reason to continue this "double standard" for commissioning. Scout officers should be required to meet regular army standards.[26]

The National Defense Act of 1920 provided that all Scout officers who were United States citizens could be recommissioned in one of the branches of the regular army, if qualified. Those who failed to take or pass a qualifying exam could continue serving with Scout units. In either case, they were now to receive the promotion and retirement benefits enjoyed by other commissioned officers. Americans would no longer be eligible for commissions exclusively in the Scouts.[27] Filipino officers would still be restricted to Scout service, but, like the Americans, they could be assigned to other branches of the army (not just the infantry), they could attend service schools in the United States, and they could be promoted to senior ranks. Not every American left the Philippine Scouts, but the trend was clear. The March 1923 edition of the *Army List and Directory* listed 105 Philippine Scout officers, of whom 83 were American, while the April 1935 edition showed 58 permanently attached Scout officers, of whom only 32 were American. By 1941 only 12 American Scout officers would remain on active duty.

The immediate postwar period brought important changes to enlisted Scouts as well. In the space of five years, Filipino soldiers underwent a complete conversion from "scout" to "soldier." In 1917 Scouts continued to serve in dispersed infantry companies or battalions; by 1922 the Philippine garrison had come to include Filipino-manned regiments of all arms and most supporting branches, numerically integrated into the line of the regular army. The wartime 1st Philippine Infantry (Provisional) became the 45th Infantry (PS), to which Lim would be nominally assigned for most of his remaining years in the Philippine Scouts; the 2nd Philippine Infantry (Provisional), with which Lim served briefly, became the 57th Infantry (PS); the 1st Philippine Artillery (Provisional) became the 24th Field Artillery (PS); and so on. When the 9th Cavalry ended its long sojourn at Camp Stotsenburg in 1922, some officers remained behind to take charge of Filipino recruits in a new cavalry regiment, designated the 26th. The Philippine Department created a Scout signal company and an engineer company. An existing medical regiment was stripped of its American enlisted men and filled with Filipino soldiers. In addition, economic retrenchment gave Filipino troops numerical dominance in the garrison. Before World War I, the Scouts had composed one-fourth to one-third of total army strength in the Philippines; from the early 1920s, Filipino soldiers would make up about 60 percent of the Philippine garrison.[28]

The use of enlisted Scouts in virtually all branches of the army partly explains the significant changes that came about in the Scout officer ranks after World War I. Leadership in the Scout regiments now required the services of professionally qualified officers, which excluded enlisted men given temporary officer status while serving with Filipino troops. After 1920, most officers who served with Scout units would be regular army officers fulfilling their two-year-long foreign service obligation in the Philippine Islands.

The greater use of Filipino manpower was not indicative of army confidence in the capacity of Filipino soldiers. Economic concerns drove the decision to rely on them, not the belief that Filipinos were really capable of performing the assignments. Lest any officer fail to discern the limitations of Filipino ability, Philippine Department Headquarters at Fort Santiago commissioned a psychological study of the Filipino soldier, the purpose of which was to remind officers of Scout inferiority. Authored by an "acknowledged authority on the subject" who remained anonymous, *The Psychology of the Filipino* painted a demeaning portrait of the local soldiery. The "Filipino character" had many "grave defects," the reader learned. It was emotional, illogical, ignorant, unformed, easily influenced, swayed by preference and prejudice, submissive yet vain, slothful, inert, careless, and lacking in forethought, competitiveness, pugnacity, creativity, and perseverance. Only superficially and with difficulty could the Filipinos develop the innate fighting ability of the white soldier. *Psychology of the Filipino* was an abridgment of a classified report authored by Col. Edward Munson.[29] In Munson's view—one obviously shared by senior officers of the Philippine

Department—it was "illusory" to place any faith in the ability of Filipino soldiers to defend the islands. Despite an appearance of soldierly skill, "the practical results of [military] training," Munson insisted, "will never produce more than a low grade fighting efficiency in the Filipino soldiers." Munson's report was required reading for all American officers. Department intelligence officer Maj. Walter Prosser told a correspondent in Washington that it was "the best thing [he had] seen on this subject." When Eugene Ganley began research for his history of the Philippine Scouts in 1959, he soon learned about *Psychology of the Filipino* from an American officer who had spent more than twenty years with the Scouts. Col. Frederick Ward fully agreed with Walter Prosser's view of the book: "It was," he informed Ganley, "[the] best estimate of Filipino character I have read."[30]

Munson's report was not completed until mid-1924, and the pamphlet version was not published until 1925. *Psychology of the Filipino* was meant to address a specific concern—the growing reliance being placed on Filipino reserves in contemporary defense projects (discussed in the following chapter)—and was not supposed to be made available to Filipinos. They were unlikely to have been surprised by its content. The passage of time had done little to change racial attitudes. Lim claimed that he was ordered transferred from Fort McKinley to Corregidor in 1922 to free up living quarters at the post for an arriving white officer. He angrily refused and the orders were canceled.[31] Later, as a student at the war college, Lim contrasted the attitude of army officers in the United States toward Filipinos with the attitude of army officers serving in the Philippines. "While travelling on army transport," Lim offered as an example, "it is the consensus of opinion of all the Filipino personnel that there is considerable difference between the American officers going to the Philippines and those returning to the United States." His service in the United States, he explained, "has been most pleasant and satisfactory, while during [his] twelve years service in the Philippines prior to 1926 [the year he came to the United States], there was always a question of how long [he] would stay in the army."[32] His was a widely held feeling among native officers of the Philippine Scouts. A few years earlier, a front-page article in one Manila daily, headlined "Filipinos in Army May Quit," had disclosed "a general discontent among the Filipino scout officers." They were both "discriminated against" and "not given positions of responsibility commensurate with their ranks." Their solution was to be detailed to the insular government to serve in a variety of technical capacities, just as several American officers were doing. They could draw their American salaries while working with Filipinos.[33]

Some perceived little reason to remain in the army if other opportunities beckoned. Strength reductions in the early 1920s led to many officers being reduced in rank and drove others from the service altogether. Lim and several other Philippine Scout officers were uncertain as to their commitment to continued service with the United States Army. The end of the war presaged the onset of a lengthy period of inactivity and parsimonious military budgets, and officers began to seek opportunities elsewhere. When legislation passed in 1922 offered early-retirement benefits, Lim and Rafael Garcia signaled to Quezon their willingness to get out of the army, if the Philippine Senate president could suggest a way in which their services might be more valuable to the country. A few officers did quit. Maj. Vincente Barros, the former Constabulary officer who had been commissioned in the Philippine Scouts by examination in 1912, retired in 1922 to become the superintendent of the San Ramon penal colony. Luis Salvosa, an April 1917 graduate of West Point, also left the army in 1922, as did Crispulo Patajo, the only Filipino officer remaining on active duty whose service dated back to the Philippine-American War two decades earlier.[34]

A further discouragement experienced by Filipino officers early in the decade was the threat to their promotion opportunities. The National Defense Act placed Scout officers on the regular army promotion list, or so it seemed at first. The longest-serving Filipino officers, Captains Patajo, Barros, Pedro Dulay, and Esteban Dalao, received their majorities on 1 July 1920. A closer reading of the new defense act suggested that it prohibited Filipino promotions beyond captain. The government ruled that the four who had already received gold oak leaves could keep them; all others would have to be content with remaining captains. The Scout officers were understandably upset. "The effect of the decision is to kill our military careers," Lim told Quezon. Lim was at the forefront of founding the Filipino Officers Society, with the purpose of lobbying to defend the officers' rights. Within months, passage of the army appropriations bill for 1923 made all Filipino officers eligible for promotion to colonel. Lim advanced to major in April 1923. In theory, at least, Filipino officers had the possibility of commanding regiments of Filipino soldiers.[35]

Lim unwittingly found himself playing a prominent part in the one event that brought the Philippine Scouts to unwelcome public attention in the 1920s: the Scout mutiny of July 1924. Unhappy over the disparity in pay and benefits between Filipino soldiers and their American counterparts, some junior enlisted men determined to "strike together" until their demand for equal pay was met. On the morning of 7 July, most men in two battalions of Fort McKinley's 57th Infantry (PS) refused to drill. The following day, over two hundred soldiers of the 12th Medical Regiment failed to report for duty. While Scout complaints focused specifically on the inequality in pay—a Scout private had originally received one-half the pay of a regular army private; by the early 1920s he received little more than one-third—the mutiny took place against a backdrop of wider discontent. In recent months, there had been strikes of Filipino workers in Hawaii, of civilian employees at the Cavite Naval Yard, and even of students at the University of the Philippines. Furthermore, in early 1924 the army had only narrowly thwarted "a daring and nearly successful attempt by Filipinos to cut off the water supply of Corregidor." "Other sabotage threats" had been made against air service facilities at Camp Nichols near Manila and Clark Field at Stotsenburg.[36] The army blamed outside agitators and the "seditious political knavery and discontent" of Filipino politicians for undermining the loyalty of the Philippine Scouts but could not prove the involvement of any "outside influence" in the affair.[37] No member of Lim's regiment, the 45th Infantry (PS), joined the "strike," but the regiment's officers had no reason for self-congratulation. That regiment's sergeant major had refused to tolerate any disobedience on the part of the 45th's soldiers. He had earlier been accused of misusing his immense influence over the men and had been told that any further trouble would result in his demotion. Military authorities were soon approached "by many individuals" from the 45th affirming their loyalty to their officers and to the United States.[38]

Ultimately the army charged 225 soldiers with inciting mutiny or refusing to obey orders. Tried collectively in two large groups, the accused men chose a popular American officer of the 26th Cavalry (PS), Maj. John Considine, to be their individual counsel; a reluctant Lim accepted appointment as the soldiers' defense counsel. They had a difficult task. For all but fifteen ringleaders, who were tried separately, the issue before the court was straightforward: had the accused soldiers refused to report for duty as ordered or had they not? The adequacy and fairness of army pay was irrelevant. Lim decided to concentrate on the language problem. He knew that most of the men could comprehend little beyond the simplest commands in English, and that, conversely, officers could not speak the men's languages. In what the local press labeled derisively the "Tower of Babel Defense," Lim argued that language difficulties prevented the soldiers from understanding the nature and seriousness of their actions. Not only were there many more and distinct dialects spoken by the soldiers than most officers seemed to be aware, but there were many words in army regulations that could not be easily translated. "There are few interpreters in the whole Philippines who can off-hand translate into the native dialects questions asked in English," he stressed to the court. The thought that poorly educated enlisted men were up to the task was too ludicrous to contemplate.[39] But while it was easy enough to establish that there were serious communication problems between American officers and enlisted men within the Scout units (one officer, for example, could not identify men in his company who were seated before him at the trial), too many soldiers had obeyed their officers for the rest to claim that they had not understood what was being said to them. The eight American officers of the court-martial board, headed by Douglas MacArthur, the commanding general of the 23rd Infantry Brigade at Fort McKinley, acquitted only six men. Four ringleaders received ten- to twenty-year sentences at Manila's Bilibid prison. The rest of the accused received dishonorable discharges and sentences of five years at hard labor with the penal battalion on Corregidor.

Little had been said by or about Filipino officers during the affair, but Walter Prosser, the Philippine Department intelligence officer, wrote that the department suspected "that native officers of the Philippine Scouts were not ignorant of the Soldiers' Union," and he claimed that one retired officer wrote an article under an assumed name in support of the strikers' actions. The army's investigation of retired officers could not establish their involvement in the strike. Nevertheless, for Filipino officers, the Scout mutiny starkly exposed the dilemma of colonial military service. If Filipino soldiers had, as Chief of Staff Malin Craig would later state, "taken our part against their own people," how could Filipino officers maintain their bona fides as professional soldiers while at the same time developing links with political elites whose patronage would be necessary to transform their identity as officers of an occupying power to nationalists worthy of commanding the army of an independent republic?[40] A few years after the mutiny, an American officer in Manila prepared a lengthy memorandum presenting some ideas to "improve" the Scout organization in the course of which he posed a question about the Scouts that must have been on everyone's lips back in 1924: If the army thought it reasonable to pay Filipino enlisted men only a fraction of what it paid American enlisted men, why did Filipino officers receive the same pay as American officers? If the mutiny was all about money, then the native officers of the Philippine Scouts had no reason to make common cause with their enlisted subordinates. They received the same pay and benefits as Americans. But if money was only the outward manifestation of the soldiers' wider discontent with their second-class status, then officers were as discontented as the enlisted men and as potentially disloyal.

Lim and the other Filipino officers found themselves caught up in the minutiae of garrison life. A fellow member of West Point's class of 1914 happened to be stationed in the Philippines in the mid-1920s, and he wrote that Lim was known as "king of the range at Fort McKinley." Lim also served as "barrio officer" and assumed the hat of "athletic officer" for the 45th Infantry in July 1924, when Mateo Capinpin, who had held the position, left for the infantry school at Fort Benning.[41] Lim was frequently involved in organizing athletic events in those years. In January 1923 Col. William C. Webb, a field artillery officer from Camp Stotsenburg, and Captain Lim managed the Philippine

Department's annual "military tournament" at Fort McKinley. That success led to Lim's involvement in the Sixth Far Eastern Games in Osaka, Japan, later that year. Lim took charge of the military and civilian Filipino athletes who competed in the games, shepherding them through training at Fort McKinley and organizing their camp at Osaka.[42]

There were opportunities for professional advancement in the 1920s that had not existed when Lim joined the army. The 1920 amendment to the National Defense Act made Filipino officers eligible for assignment to military schools in the United States, and officers took full advantage of that provision. For the most part, they attended lower-level technical schools. Where Filipino officers found themselves lagging behind was in access to the army's most prestigious schools. Those at the peak of the army "educational pyramid" included the Command and General Staff School, the Army Industrial College, and the Army War College. Attendance at the Naval War College and certain foreign military schools offered equal prestige.[43] Most of the Filipino academy graduates lacked the necessary time-in-service to attend upper-level schools prior to 1936–37, but those who had graduated earliest fell short of their American contemporaries' achievements. Of the 116 members of the West Point class of 1915 who remained in the army by the time their classmate Anastacio Ver retired in 1934, only 15 had not attended the Command and General Staff School, the Army War College, or the Army Industrial College. All but 17 of Rafael Garcia's 87 classmates of the class of 1916 remaining on active duty attended one or more of the three schools before 1937. Even a substantial portion, more than one-third, of the class of August 1917 had attended a senior service school by 1937. Their classmates Fidel Segundo and Salvador Reyes had not done so.[44]

Lim was the exception to this generalization. Although Lim was not the first to depart for the United States, no officer proved more adept at gaining admission to these schools. In 1926–27 he attended the advanced infantry officers' course at Fort Benning, and in 1928 he graduated from the Command and General Staff School at Fort Leavenworth.[45] Until several officers serving with the Philippine Army were sent there in 1937, Lim remained the only Filipino graduate of the staff school. A third and final year in the United States allowed Lim to attend the Army War College in Washington, D.C., a feat not achieved by any other Filipino before World War II. Lim had not intended originally to remain away from the Philippines for three years, but his success at each school in turn and the cost of transportation to and from the islands made the army amenable to his requests to continue his professional education.[46]

Lim took advantage of his three years in the United States not only to improve his professional knowledge but to increase his circle of military and political acquaintances. When the army chief of staff hosted a luncheon at the

Army and Navy Club in May 1929 for Manuel Roxas, Sergio Osmeña, and other Filipino dignitaries visiting the capital, for example, Lim was one of the few military guests below the rank of brigadier general. He even attended the annual "wallow" of the Military Order of the Carabao that year. The three hundred army and navy veterans of the Philippine-American War and their guests who gathered at Washington's Willard Hotel in February included congressmen and general officers as well as old friends and acquaintances like Frank Ahern and Col. Fred Chamberlain, Lim's commanding officer at Iloilo. The only Filipino guest at a raucous gathering all too well known for its racist overtones and ridiculing of Filipino aspirations, Lim made a brief speech commending the army for crossing "the Pacific to destroy the Spanish power in the Orient" (diplomatically avoiding mention of what the army did next) and reiterated a theme of his war college research, that "America's presence in the Philippines makes for stability in the Pacific region." Secretary of War and soon to be Philippine governor-general Dwight Davis was in attendance and pronounced Lim's "the best speech of the evening." On his own initiative, Lim approached the War Department about providing aviation training for Filipinos and suggested that Filipinos be sent to the United States to attend flying schools just as *pensionados* attended American universities. He also urged that the governor-general take steps to increase Filipino numbers at West Point. An article in the *Washington Post* announcing the graduation of the 1929 war college class was mostly about Lim, followed by an almost unreadable (because the print was so small) list of names of "the other graduates."[47]

Lim's success in the United States was personally rewarding and buttressed his standing as first among Filipino officers, but his presence and prominence may have brought unwelcome attention to Filipino officers as well. By the late 1920s, the steady progression of Filipinos through company grades (lieutenant and captain) and into field grades (major, lieutenant colonel, and colonel) posed a potential dilemma for the army. Typically, majors commanded battalions, and colonels commanded regiments. It was not that Filipino officers had never held command positions, but the changed organization of the 1920s army meant that Filipino officers would eventually gravitate to the command of the new Scout regiments or senior staff positions. They would also command the regular army officers who now filled most of the officer billets in the Philippine Scouts.

In 1928 Brig. Gen. George S. Simonds, assistant chief of staff for the War Plans Division, drew the General Staff's attention to what he called a "problem" that could become "seriously embarrassing" within a few years. Four Filipino officers had obtained their majorities in 1920, and three others followed in the course of the decade. "There will be difficulty," Simonds wrote, "in finding places for these officers appropriate to their grades." He suggested that no more Filipinos be commissioned. If the government still desired to allow Filipinos to attend the military academy, graduates might receive commissions in the Philippine Constabulary. At any rate, they should not continue to be placed on the regular army list.[48] No Filipinos received direct commissions from civil life or from the enlisted ranks after November 1921. Throughout the 1920s, Filipinos did continue to receive commissions in the Philippine Scouts after graduation from the academies, although the cadets who would have graduated with the West Point classes of 1927, 1928, and 1929 failed to complete the course of instruction.

Leon F. Punsalan won the 1931 competition in Manila for the military academy appointment. His knowledge of algebra proved unequal to the task of passing the further army examination, but he placed first again the following year and, this time, was soon on his way to New York. Both in 1931 and 1932, he received letters from the governor-general informing him that the government would honor its obligation to fund his studies at West Point, but that he would not receive a commission in the Philippine Scouts. Punsalan, who felt fortunate to obtain a third lieutenancy in the newly formed Philippine Army when he graduated in 1936, credited the decision to Depression-era fiscal constraints, but Simonds's plea of 1928 had found receptive listeners. By early 1930 the War Department had decided to end its "embarrassing" situation and no longer grant commissions to Filipino academy graduates. To prevent adverse reaction in the Philippines, the decision was not publicized. The last academy graduate to obtain a commission in the Scouts was Emmanuel S. Cepeda, who graduated with the class of 1933. He had entered West Point in 1929, only a year after Simonds had first raised the issue of commissions for Filipinos.[49]

If graduation from the army's premier schools usually set an officer on the path to positions of increased responsibility, Lim's accomplishments can only have added to his frustration. Just as the army continued to allow Filipinos to attend the military academy even though it had no intention of offering them commissions, so it acquiesced in providing advanced training to Filipino officers, even though it had equally little intention of assigning them to positions that made use of their training. Opportunities for advancement in the islands remained limited. Entering the 1930s, Filipinos served on neither the Philippine Department nor Philippine Division staffs, and Lim, with young children and a talented wife with career ambitions of her own, faced the dreary prospect of a return to troop duty with the 45th Infantry Regiment (PS) and consignment as a range, laundry, barrio, or post beautification officer doing the service-related tasks that had become the work-a-day lot of Filipino officers of the Philippine Scouts.[50] Fortuitously, Lim's return to Manila at the end of the

1920s coincided with the tenure of Philippine Department commanders determined to emphasize the contribution Filipinos could make to the archipelago's defense. The time was propitious for an expansion of university-based cadet programs that could provide junior officers to the Filipino-manned divisions called for in contemporary war plans, and in October 1929, immediately upon his return from the United States, Lim became commandant of cadets at the Colegio de San Juan de Letran.[51] He would remain there until retiring from the U.S. Army in 1936.

CHAPTER 3

"KEEPING DOWN FILIPINO LEADERSHIP"

War Plans Orange and the Filipino Soldier, 1929–1934

When Lim stepped off the troopship *Grant* early in October 1929, the United States Army had been in the Philippines for just over thirty years, but formal routinized planning for the defense of the Philippines was less than a decade old. In the early years of occupation, war planning had been something of an exercise in hesitancy and contradiction. In 1908, ten years after the army had first arrived in the Philippines, six years since the insurrection had been officially suppressed, and a year that opened with nearly 30 percent of the overall army on duty in the islands, Chief of Staff Maj. Gen. J. Franklin Bell had admitted that the War Department had yet to make a "thorough and systematic study" of the organizational or operational needs of the Philippine garrison, a fact he blamed on the government's failure to articulate a definitive policy toward the archipelago.[1] An ongoing controversy over whether a major naval base should be placed in Subic Bay (the navy's preference) or Manila Bay (the army's) complicated planning further, but over the next decade the army's strategic posture in the Philippines—the navy having decided to have little more to do with the matter—came to center on the fortifying of Corregidor and three smaller islands that spanned the mouth of Manila Bay and the occupation of nearby Bataan Peninsula. To summarize the matter briefly, as general staff officer Maj. Munroe McFarland did before a war college class in 1915, "practical unanimity" had come to exist that "Corregidor must be held to the last and in order to do this [Japan] must be prevented from placing his heavy guns in folds of the Mariveles Mountains [on Bataan] within range of the batteries on Corregidor."[2]

Still, only in November 1919 had the general staff's recently established War Plans Division instructed the army's three overseas departments in the Philippines, Hawaii, and the Panama Canal Zone to prepare, following a common pattern, what it termed defense "projects" and defense "plans" that could be reexamined annually by planning boards in Washington and in department headquarters. According to the WPD memorandum, projects were to indicate "policy and usually form the basis of estimates and legislation"; plans would stipulate schemes "for attaining some definite end and consist of a detailed and methodical arrangement of the means or successive steps believed to be necessary or conducive to attainment of the object in view." The War Department would review and then approve, modify, or reject locally authored projects, while "responsible territorial and tactical commanders" would prepare plans. Asked to clarify the distinction between plans and projects by an army reserve officer in the Philippines, WPD's Col. LeRoy Eltinge confirmed that "[t]he plan of defense which is concerned with the actual defense on the ground, tactical and strategical, is a function of the Commanding General of the Philippine Islands and is not ordered or in any way directed from Washington."[3]

Presumably, what had been an ad hoc process that left one generation of officers unaware of an earlier generation's labors would become routinized and bring to an end a tendency to reinvent the wheel. Maj. Gen. Johnson Hagood, to give one example of that tendency, once sent Maj. Gen. Ewing Booth a long letter reminding him of their work on a so-called "Corregidor Project" in 1913, which had involved ensuring that the island fortress-in-the-making possessed appropriate facilities and adequate resources to withstand a lengthy siege. Hagood's most recent tour of duty in the islands, in 1926–28, he told Booth, had revealed that "all this work had been forgotten." The reports they had compiled "had been lost and no one, either in the Department general staff or at Corregidor, had ever heard of any of [it]." In early 1921, to cite another example, the army adjutant general had responded to a Philippine Department report on the deliberations of a local army and navy defense board that had identified a suitable "combined mission" for local forces by applauding the "highly gratifying . . . spirit of cooperation" shown by the army and navy commands in the Philippines before drawing the department commander's attention to the fact that the Joint Board in Washington (created in 1903 to coordinate activities that involved both the army and the navy) had already stipulated what the mission would be and had so informed the department commander. That had been in 1916. The adjutant general went on to observe that the planners did not even appear to be aware of instructions concerning the "approved garrison of the Philippine Department" sent to the department commander only a few months previously.[4]

Now, commonality of purpose and knowledge between local planners and those in Washington would emerge, and, through regular reviews and revisions of projects and plans, create an institutional memory of the problems and solutions identified by earlier planners. The 1919 War Plans Division memorandum set the stage for a two-decades-long series of Philippine Defense Projects and Philippine Defense Plans (all directed against Japan, or "Orange," in the army's color-coded war plans of the day) that would culminate with the well-known HPD "War Plan Orange 3" of 1940–41.

Filipino officers, even those like Lim who had achieved the highest level of formal staff training, did not participate in any substantial way in preparing the department's war plans or projects. At no time did the army consider seriously that it might benefit from the continuity and expert local knowledge that would follow from bringing Filipino officers into the planning process. Nevertheless, in the changed context of the post–World War I era, the War Department's insistence that HPD think systematically about the islands' defense pushed Fort Santiago's planners to consider an enlarged role for Filipinos in local military forces.

The idea that Filipinos should and could be relied on to fill the ranks of the "American" army in the Philippines had a long if somewhat idiosyncratic pedigree. Matthew Batson, a founder of what became the Philippine Scouts in 1901, had thought that the United States would have to recruit a Filipino army if for no other reason than that Congress would never appropriate the money necessary to support an American-manned force large enough to hold the islands. Maj. William Johnston, who commanded the model Scout battalion that had been a sensation at the St. Louis Exposition in 1904, came up with a more detailed project. He argued that Philippine Scout strength should be raised to 25,000 men or more. The Filipino soldiers could then both defend their homeland and be used in overseas expeditions. There was much talk of an expedition to China at the time, and, as Johnston explained, "[when] battle losses are announced the American public will view the enterprise with much less discontent than if each death vacated a place at an American fireside." Cameron Forbes, governor-general from 1909 to 1913, had suggested raising "a mountain militia" of some 30,000 "worthy savages" who after a period of military training would assist the regular garrison in preventing insurrection or invasion.[5] Forbes's successor pushed Washington to support a national guard during World War I. Nothing much came of any of this and the army adamantly opposed the re-creation of a national guard, but the defense projects that emerged from Fort Santiago by 1923–24 nevertheless legitimized and institutionalized at least the idea that the army give Filipinos a greater role in the defense of their homeland.

Bearing in mind the Joint Board–dictated mission of maintaining control of Manila Bay, a task explicitly defensive in nature, the authors of the Philippine Department Basic "Orange" Project for 1924 (the first that remains in its entirety) accepted that "the mission of the command implie[d] the strategic defensive" but further asserted that it would "be executed by energetic offensive tactics." Philippine geography alone made "purely defensive measures" futile and a defensive posture sacrificed "the advantage of operation on interior lines and [was] contrary to too many of the Principles of War and to the Doctrine of War." The 1924 project did not abandon the focus on fortifying the islands of Manila Bay and occupying the nearby mountain slopes of Bataan Peninsula overlooking Corregidor, but it did enlarge the concept of defense.[6]

Energetic offensive tactics required more than the modest troop strength authorized for the peacetime garrison, nor under wartime conditions would it be possible to await reinforcements from the United States. In short, the Americans needed Filipino help. Both the 1923 project (the first, of which only fragments remain) and 1924 project linked the accomplishment of the army's mission in the islands to the progressive development of the Philippines' manpower potential. American forces would serve as only the nucleus for the "necessary native reserve forces."[7]

Local interest in military training played a part in drawing attention to the potential for developing reserve programs in the Philippines. Support for a college-based officers' training program like the Reserve Officers' Training Corps (ROTC or PROTC, as it was sometimes called in the Philippines) was particularly strong. In 1921 University of the Philippines president Guy Potter Benton had approached newly appointed governor-general Leonard Wood about the possibility of upgrading the university's modest drill program. Weekly drill had been "an unwritten requirement for graduation" since 1912, and in 1917 the university had formalized the requirement that all physically qualified male students participate in drill, but the program had never amounted to much more than "elementary close order movements with wooden rifles." Benton wanted to establish an army-supported Department of Military Science and Tactics similar to those found at American universities.

Leonard Wood had been a leading advocate of military preparedness in the United States and brought the same attitude to the Philippines. "Military science should be taught intensively in all schools," a university newspaper quoted Wood as telling school officials and students, "because a strong system of national defense for this country is essential." The hardest part, Wood explained, would be creating "a force of well-trained officers." With Wood's backing, Benton persuaded the army to send an officer to the Philippines specifically to serve as the university's professor of military science and tactics (PMS&T). Aided by a grant from the board of regents, surplus property of the army and the national guard, and the assignment of several other officers and NCOs, Capt. Chester A. Davis, a decorated AEF veteran, directed a program of one thousand cadets when the school year opened in June 1922. "We are going to cut out this parade stuff," Davis declared, and make ROTC fit to become "the nucleus of the army that will defend the Filipino soil." By 1923 some 2,150 cadets trained on campuses of the University of the Philippines, the Ateneo de Manila, and National University.[8]

War Department assurances "that a loyal and dependable force of native troops" could be established with relative ease in the Philippines did not persuade Congress to act. Committing funds to insular forces would only reduce the sums needed to put the reserve system in the United States on a firmer basis, and the unsettled political status of the islands made Congress wary of providing support for PROTC. The War Department continued to press for passage of favorable legislation but by early 1925 had to admit failure. Attempts to legalize the reserve provisions of the National Defense Act for use in the Philippines would have to await "a more propitious time."[9]

Relying on Filipinos to bolster the islands' defensibility did not sit well with many American officers. Opposition started at the top. Maj. Gen. Francis Kernan, department commander from November 1919 to March 1922, was against both the Filipinization of the islands' forces and the reorganization of the garrison's mobile army into the Philippine Division (a tactical organization subordinate to the Philippine Department). Kernan thought a division neither feasible nor desirable. The designated troops were "scattered in many parts of the Islands and China," making their physical concentration into a division unlikely, while the department's paucity of officers made the creation of a divisional staff an unnecessary burden. More importantly, forming a combat division would only "divert attention from the main military problem in the Philippines, which was the defense of Manila Bay by means of Corregidor, and would shift that attention over to the land defense of the Island of Luzon and the city of Manila which was an impossible proposition" and which would also—short of Congress's unlikely funding of the regular army's return to the Philippines—of necessity turn attention toward the greater use of local manpower. The army tended to "forget history," Kernan complained, and viewed the garrison's requirements only in light of the potential for repelling invasion rather than of still possible insurrection.[10]

It was partly to refute Kernan's arguments that army chief of staff Gen. John J. Pershing, himself a veteran of nine years' service in the islands, offered his own view of the role of Filipino soldiers in America's largest overseas possession. In May 1922 Pershing informed a new Philippine Department commander, his former West Point classmate William Wright, that "any American force" would be inadequate for the islands' defense. The general staff was therefore considering "training, organizing and employing native troops in the defense of the country." "It seems to me," Pershing wrote, "that we have a distinct obligation to prepare the Filipinos for the exercise of an increasing measure of self-government and to prepare and to employ them for the defense of their country to the greatest extent possible and consistent with safety and our political aims." Pershing admitted that he had "not any too high an opinion of the ability of the Filipinos to govern themselves" but felt that nonetheless they had "made material advancement" and deserved more opportunities for growth. Wright agreeably responded that it was "quite practicable gradually to perfect, under Federal control and supervision, a system of insular reserves, officered in part by Americans and largely by Filipinos, with a scheme of military training imposed and regulated by our government." These reserves could, in time of emergency, be used to bring regular army units up to war strength and to form native divisions.[11]

Still, throughout the period of American occupation, fear of losing authority over those Filipino military forces that might be raised set limits to what even sympathetic Americans were willing to tolerate. Leonard Wood can serve as the template for this conundrum. As we have seen, Wood was a vocal supporter of military training for Filipinos, both as a character-building exercise and to meet the islands' defense needs. He happened to become governor-general at the same time a navy-voiced reappraisal of American planning for an Orange war seemed to suggest that the Philippine garrison would be abandoned to its fate. Wood protested vehemently and argued in favor of "the progressive development of organized reserves." Once the "General Staffs of the Army and Navy" came to understand "the possibilities of organizing and developing the military strengths of the Philippine forces in the Regular Army," Wood surmised, they would have confidence in the garrison's ability to withstand an enemy attack.[12]

But even as Wood championed reliance on Filipino troops to sustain America's presence in the Far East, he lacked confidence that imparting military training to Filipinos would end up serving American interests. In his diary, Wood told the story of a Filipino Scout officer (Pedro Dulay, one of the three Filipinos commissioned by examination while Lim had been a student at West Point) assigned as a university instructor in military science who was suspected of telling his cadets things that were "not conducive to a real sense of loyalty to the United States." Wood was "having the matter looked into." Wood's attitude created a dilemma he could not resolve. He touted military training as a means of reshaping Filipino character along more modern and progressive paths, yet he distrusted Filipino leadership and loyalty and did not want to rely on Filipinos for military security. Wood's contradictory missives—the Filipinos are loyal, yet we need more American troops—first perplexed and then irritated officers in Washington. The War Department concluded that his increasingly hysterical letters mostly reflected his difficulties with local political leaders. The head of the War Plans Division finally recommended that the chief of staff simply stop answering Wood.[13] Nonetheless, the officially sponsored appearance of

Colonel Munson's racially charged *Psychology of the Filipino* makes clear that Wood was not alone. Although the pamphlet happened to have been published after the Scout mutiny, it had been written earlier for the express purpose of questioning defense projects and plans predicated on the building up of native manpower reserves.

The remainder of the 1920s witnessed a hiatus in defense planning. The Philippine Department commanding general as the end of the decade approached, Maj. Gen. Frederick Sladen, revealed his distance from more-ambitious predecessors when his views were sought in preparation for the Joint Board's reappraisal of the army and navy missions in the Philippines in late 1927. Agreeing with the findings of a local planning committee, Sladen responded that holding "that portion of Manila Bay covered by the Harbor Defenses" was sufficient. Nothing should be done by "our present small forces," he continued, "to attempt any operations prejudicial to the best defense of these areas."[14]

Sladen was adding his voice to the side of caution in an ongoing debate among army and navy planners in Washington over the desirability of adopting a "formula that would produce victory in a war with Japan" by means of a "strategic offensive in the Western Pacific," rather than continue an existing plan of remaining on the "strategic defensive" that envisioned wearing down Orange through "economic pressure and raids on Japanese commerce." "Faced with this choice of strategies," army historian Louis Morton wrote, "the Joint Board . . . directed the planners to prepare a plan based on the concept of a strategic offensive." They reworded the mission statement for forces in the Philippines. "The primary mission of the Army forces," according to the then-current Joint Board directive, was "to defend Manila and Manila Bay in conjunction with the Asiatic Detachment by operating on the offensive-defensive against enemy forces in the Luzon Area." In mid-1928 the Joint Board revised the statement to read that the army's "primary mission [was] to hold the entrance to Manila Bay." It now had a "secondary mission" of holding the "Manila Bay Area as long as possible consistent with successful accomplishment of the primary mission."[15]

Meant to emphasize the importance of preserving a base for the arrival of the sailing-to-the-rescue United States Fleet as opposed to using locally available forces actually to defeat an enemy, the Joint Board's new mission statement provided a more-than-adequate excuse for keeping Filipinos out of department war plans. Lim's prominence in army circles in the United States at this time may have been entirely coincidental, but the then chief of staff's memoirs reveal that his interest in developing Filipino military potential was nonexistent. Charles Summerall, army chief from November 1926 to November 1930, expected that in a war with Japan "the troops stationed in the Philippines would retire to Corregidor, without resistance or losses, and hold the fortifications until relieved. . . . These did not include Filipino troops, whom no one could have considered as effective." When Summerall learned that President Calvin Coolidge was concerned about the large percentage of "Filipino troops" on Corregidor (Coolidge meant the Philippine Scouts), Summerall promised to "correct the situation" and subsequently ordered an American antiaircraft regiment transferred from Fort McKinley to the island fortress.[16]

It is thus something of a mystery why department commanders at the end of the decade determined to disinter and enlarge upon the 1924 Orange Project, in the process once again pushing to the fore the issue of Filipino manpower. Knowing that Douglas MacArthur commanded the Philippine garrison at the end of the decade, historians have tended to read history backward and interpret his 1928–30 command as a precursor to his ill-fated military advisership to the Commonwealth later in the 1930s, one explained by a romantic and even irrational embrace of the islands along with an inflated sense of self-importance. However, the process of once again enlarging the scope for Filipino participation in the Philippines' defense began not with MacArthur but rather with his short-tenured predecessor in Manila, Maj. Gen. William Lassiter. An instructor at the academy when MacArthur arrived as a cadet in 1899 and the last member of his West Point class of 1889 to remain on active duty, Lassiter was an officer of an older generation whom no one could accuse of having adopted either a romantic or irrational attachment to the Philippine Islands.

Manila newspapers were reporting as early as October 1927 that MacArthur would replace General Sladen, but while en route to Manila to take up his new post as governor-general, former secretary of war Henry Stimson visited Lassiter in Chicago and discovered that his old friend was willing to join him in the islands. He "had always assumed," Stimson soon enthused in a handwritten letter to General Summerall, that Lassiter, "like most officers," preferred to be stationed in the United States and had been delighted to learn instead that Lassiter "really cherished the Philippines as his first choice."[17] Lassiter followed Stimson to the Philippines neither expecting to serve a full tour of duty nor having received instructions from the War Department to do any more, or less, than his predecessor had done. However, aboard the troopship taking him to the Far East in April 1928, Lassiter met Brig. Gen. George Simonds of the chief of staff's office. Simonds, who was traveling to Manila for a brief visit to examine the "housing situation" there, told Lassiter "that there was no [recent] project in the War Department for the Philippines and that one was desired at as early a date as practicable."[18]

Lassiter quickly decided that centering the islands' defenses on Bataan and Corregidor was ill founded, no matter how the Joint Board worded the mission of the Philippine garrison. He noted the obvious: "The practical point is that the forces here are expected to have a base ready for our fleet when it arrives." Holding the "entrance to Manila Bay" was of no purpose if meanwhile the enemy took "all the rest of Luzon, including the shores of Manila Bay." Aside from purely tactical considerations, Lassiter believed that the deliberate isolation of American forces in Bataan would forfeit "the psychological advantage of having the natives on our side." It was crucial that the United States pursue a policy of "getting the natives on our side" and harness that support in defense of the islands.[19] With some success, Lassiter took steps to strengthen the existing university-based military training programs and pushed army bureaucrats to interpret regulations in ways favorable to supporting a local reserve system.

Why he bothered to do so remains a puzzle. MacArthur had been informed that "the exigencies of the service [had] necessitated the ordering of General Lassiter to the Philippines," but Summerall had merely accommodated Stimson. Lassiter knew that the assignment was to last only about six months.[20] Once in Manila, however, Stimson saw no reason why his friend should be replaced and requested instead the revocation of MacArthur's orders. The chief of staff took the position that the cancellation of MacArthur's orders would at this late date be unjust and embarrassing.[21]

MacArthur reached Manila on 1 October 1928 to begin his third tour of duty in the islands. Had MacArthur returned with the intent of pushing forward the development of Filipino reserve forces? Summerall had told Lassiter that there "was nothing special about the situation in the Philippine Department or in the Orient" that he could not learn from Sladen after he reached Manila.[22] There would have been no reason to tell MacArthur something else. According to his friend General Hagood, however, MacArthur was "very much embarrassed" by the "same old stand and run plans"—whatever that phrase meant—of his "immediate predecessor" that he found in place when he returned as commanding general and took up the task of revising the Philippine Department's defense projects and plans. The criticism was unwarranted and not shared by the War Department. "General Lassiter," General Simonds pointed out, "asked not for the ground troops which he desired but for the ground troops which he thought there was some possibility of getting." Simonds believed that MacArthur's own plans were "along the same general lines" as Lassiter's.[23]

Of course, MacArthur had to do more. Lassiter's one division of locally recruited soldiers was not enough; MacArthur wanted at least three divisions. The United States would bear the cost of this expansion at first, but the insular government would progressively take over support of the Filipino troops. In this, MacArthur insisted, he had the cooperation both of the governor-general and of the leading legislative and business leaders. "All," he informed the War Department, "pledge heartiest support." In addition, MacArthur believed that control of these troops could remain in the hands of the army, even as the Philippine government assumed a large share of the costs. It was at this time, in 1929–30, that members of the Philippine Assembly began to introduce defense-related legislation: a bill to encourage "field training" for the UP's cadet corps, for example; another to establish a tax to collect the money needed "for the construction and maintenance of military training camps."[24]

The army tried to do its part. It now decided that Filipinos could participate in Citizens' Military Training Camps and pushed for the program's extension to the Philippines as the primary builder of reserve forces. Lassiter had investigated means by which CMTC might be implemented in the archipelago, and no one had been a more ardent booster of such camps in the United States than MacArthur himself, when he had commanded the army's 3rd and 4th Corps areas from 1925 to 1928.[25] The volunteer program (participants received food, clothing, and transportation) attracted far more applicants in the United States than the army could accommodate; surely it would prove equally appealing to Filipinos. After the War Department informed HPD that "CMTC should start in fiscal year 1931 with three thousand candidates from Luzon only," MacArthur pressed forward with a well-publicized plan to conduct training at Fort McKinley.[26]

MacArthur's preparation of war plans predicated on the availability of Filipino officers and enlisted men once again focused attention on the role of ROTC. His 1929 "Basic Project" included an ambitious Philippine reserve program to be developed over a ten-year period. Like Lassiter, MacArthur urged that PROTC be put on an equal footing with ROTC in the United States. Despite its inability to gain formal support for ROTC earlier in the decade, the army had continued to provide officer and enlisted instructors and weapons and allowed the cadets to train on army posts. It also provided most of the costs of the final two years of the four years of instruction (ninety-four centavos of each peso spent).[27] Given the failure to do so only a few years earlier, the War Department was reluctant to attempt to get congressional support for PROTC, but it continued to believe that officers could be acquired through the existing military training programs in the islands' colleges and universities "without formally associating these schools with the ROTC." The army had to remain circumspect, since the suspicion remained—and no one wanted a legal challenge to find out for certain—that the army was not supposed to be providing such support. When MacArthur decided to upgrade the status of cadet training at the Colegio de San Juan de Letran and requested arms and equipment for it, for example, the BIA pointed out that there was no legal authority to support educational institutions in the islands; rather, local custom had apparently legitimized such support.[28] Thus Vicente Lim could return from his three-year-long educational sojourn in the United States to enter the growing ranks of professors of military science and tactics. Assignment as a PMS&T was little more than a detail in an American officer's career; in the Philippines, by the 1930s, to be a Filipino Scout officer meant, for most, to be a PMS&T.

Lim's stature might have suggested that he was the officer to direct the important University of the Philippines program, but that position was already marked for Capt. Fidel Segundo, an equally prominent Scout officer who would become one of Lim's competitors to head the Philippine Army later in the 1930s. An Ilocano from Laoag in Ilocos Norte Province, Segundo had attended UP before reporting in 1914 to West Point, where he had graduated with the abbreviated class of August 1917, in which he had placed a respectable 64th in a class of 151. A story current among university cadets before World War II (although some of the details have gotten garbled along the way) was that when the United States declared war on Germany, "Smoke" Segundo had been so anxious for active service that he "jumped out of the window to be number one to enlist."[29] Segundo had had no better luck than Lim in getting to Europe during the war and, like Lim, had had to be content with attachment to the national guard in 1918–19.

During the 1920s, Lim attended the highest-rated army schools; Segundo attended the wider variety. He had been one of six officers chosen from among dozens of applicants to participate in an aerial observer's school offered by the 3rd Aero Squadron at Camp Stotsenburg in 1920. In the United States, he graduated from the field artillery battery officers' course in 1925 and from a cavalry officers' course in 1926. At the time of the Scout mutiny, there had been talk of having Segundo assigned to the Bureau of Insular Affairs as a Philippine Scout liaison officer. He was, senior officers agreed, "an able and capable officer and absolutely loyal to the United States." American officers consistently rated him "outstanding" and considered his military record to be "far superior" to Lim's. High praise had not led to significant assignments. In 1929 Segundo joined five other Scout officers at the University of the Philippines as executive officer of the military department and in 1931 became commandant of cadets, a position he would hold until 1936.[30]

The commandancy of cadets at Letran was a significantly less-important assignment. Located in Manila's old walled city, or Intramuros, the Dominican-run Colegio de San Juan de Letran marked its three hundredth anniversary the year following Lim's appointment as professor of military science and tactics. It was one of the oldest and most prestigious schools in the islands, but it was very small. Letran had conducted since the early 1920s "an elementary disciplinary military course" for boys aged fifteen to eighteen. Lim found spirited students eager to participate in a rejuvenated cadet course, but the students had only wooden guns with which to drill and "no organization at all." He obtained obsolete weapons from the Philippine Constabulary and succeeded within a few months in replacing them with modern Springfield rifles, courtesy of MacArthur's determination to boost ROTC. Major Lim also designed a new uniform that, he reported, "every *Letranista* could look at with a feeling of pride and satisfaction." The Philippine Department's intelligence office recognized Lim's improvements with a backhanded compliment: Plan Brown, the plan of action in the event of insurrection, now included the Letran cadets on a list of potential security threats.[31]

One of Lim's sons would recall that his father found the Letran years in some ways the most rewarding of his career. He established contacts in the business community that would provide him with welcome opportunities to supplement his military income. Although Lim could not openly participate in political activities (one Scout officer was reprimanded for doing so in 1931), he enjoyed more freedom to strengthen ties to local political leaders. From Letran, Lim could advance his own interests while also facilitating communication between the civilian and military communities. In one of the last efficiency reports Lim received before retiring, the Philippine Department commander, Maj. Gen. Frank Parker, acknowledged the Filipino officer's "great value in contact with the civil authorities."[32] Nevertheless, command of the Letran cadet corps can hardly have satiated an ambitious officer's desire for recognition and advancement, and within a year or so of his assignment to Letran, Lim had begun to seek other opportunities.

Lim attempted to reassociate himself with the Philippine Constabulary. It remained the only alternative to the Philippine Scouts open to Filipinos of a martial disposition. Although its duties had become almost entirely oriented toward law enforcement, the Constabulary embraced the military legacy of its early years. Both officers and men, a serving officer acknowledged, "resented [being] called or referred to as 'policemen.'"[33] The American editor of the Constabulary monthly magazine, *Khaki and Red*, lamented that although "times have changed [and] the Constabulary operates as a military organization only in the District of Mindanao," still "the military aspect predominates in all [the Constabulary's] training." In the editor's opinion, military-oriented training "must serve a diminishing purpose" in the Philippine Constabulary.

That was in 1926, the very year Constabulary officers began graduating from the U.S. Army's infantry school at Fort Benning, Georgia. Since the Constabulary was destined to be "the nucleus of the Philippine military forces of the future," said the first graduate, Lt. Elias Dioquino, more officers should attend the school. By 1934 five others had done so. These officers subsequently authored numerous articles on professional military development and were among the most articulate defenders of the Constabulary's right to become the army of an independent Philippines.[34] Even as the Constabulary assumed an ever larger burden of police and other nonmilitary duties, making the range of its responsibilities "practically unlimited" according to one official study, the military aspects of Constabulary service continued to beguile officers and aspirants into service. Like Philippine Scout officers, Constabulary officers served as college instructors in military science and tactics. They made plans to participate in the army's annual division maneuvers. Constabulary cadets staged their own "war games" involving the invasion of one province by another.[35] If its military competence was more imagined than real, nevertheless the Constabulary—unlike the Scouts—belonged to the nation and as an object of the Philippine Legislature would find political support to give weight to its demands.

Nor would its officers willingly give way to Lim's ambitions. Lim had worked with the Constabulary as an instructor at the officers' school in Baguio, but familiarity had not bred respect. Over the years, Lim had formed an unfavorable opinion of the Constabulary officer corps and had not been shy about saying so. In a radio address on the topic of Philippine national defense broadcast in February 1930, Lim had dismissed the Constabulary's pretensions to be "the nucleus of the future Philippine army." Its police duties were broad, essential to the nation's well-being, and could not be sloughed off onto municipal police forces, which were but "the dumping-place of political favorites." The Philippine Constabulary could not be both a law enforcement agency and an army.[36] The frustrating reality remained, however, that Constabulary service offered more opportunity for advancement than was possible in the Philippine Scouts.

Lim's awareness that both Filipinos and Americans were unhappy with the senior leadership of the Constabulary in the late 1920s and early 1930s suggested that he might reattach himself to the organization—this time as something more than an academy lecturer. In 1917 the departure of Herman Hall, the last Chief of Constabulary contributed by the U.S. Army, had opened the way for the Constabulary to acquire its first Filipino commanding officer, Rafael Crame. A bemedaled longtime veteran of Spanish military service in the Philippines who had found his way into the insular police in 1902, Crame had benefited from Governor-General Harrison's Filipinization policy and remained Constabulary chief until his death on 1 January 1927, after nine years in office.[37]

The governor-general at the time was Leonard Wood, one of whose "pet projects" was that American army officers should resume the senior billets of the Philippine Constabulary. If Wood had his way, Crame would be both the first and last Filipino Chief of Constabulary. When General Crame had recommended Maj. Guillermo B. Francisco for promotion to lieutenant colonel in 1924, for example, Wood frankly told him that he "was not in favor of promoting Filipinos to very responsible positions because of the *tayo-tayo* system. They cannot succeed."[38] The War Department fended off attempts to reassign its officers to the Constabulary, however, and the best Wood could do was to prevail upon the Philippine Department commanding general to recommend army NCOs for Constabulary commissions. In addition, he sought BIA support to canvas the ranks of American ex-officers and recommend some who might be willing to return to Constabulary service. Several accepted reappointment with immediate promotion to the rank of major. He did not plan "to extensively re-Americanize the Constabulary," Wood declared in his annual reports, but the Constabulary needed more American officers who would not face the pressure to form "local affiliations."[39] The eleven ex-soldiers who joined the Constabulary in 1926, followed by eight more in 1927, together more than doubled the number of Americans in the force, but Wood's hope that Americans would come to fill 30 percent of the officer corps proved wildly optimistic, and few of the Americans who first entered the Constabulary in the 1920s remained with the corps for more than three or four years.[40]

Though Wood was notoriously distrustful of the competence and reliability of Filipino officers, attempts to re-Americanize the Constabulary did not end with his death in August 1927. Governor-General Stimson supported Wood's goal of finding more American officers, at least to serve in the non-Christian districts of Mindanao, and urged his successor, Dwight Davis, to do the same. Stimson also reportedly "started the business of getting the law amended to permit army officers to be so detailed [as senior officers of the Constabulary]," and Davis went so far as to invite Col. George Marshall to accompany him to the Philippines "as prospective Chief of Constabulary." The future U.S. Army chief of staff, who had not enjoyed two previous tours of duty in the islands and did not wish to return for a third, declined the invitation.[41]

Unsuccessful at placing an army officer at the head of the Constabulary, Wood had appointed as Crame's replacement Swedish-born Charles E. Nathorst, a former enlisted man and veteran of the Spanish- and Philippine-American Wars who had joined the Constabulary in 1901. That appointment, combined with the recommissioning and rapid promotion of a few American officers earlier in the decade, promised continued American dominance of the organization's senior leadership positions for years to come. Naturally, Filipinos objected. When Nathorst retired in April 1932, Quezon sounded out retired officer Lt. Col. Paulino Santos about becoming the new head. Colonel Francisco, then district commander of the Visayas, was also mentioned as the possible next Chief of Constabulary, as was recently retired Col. Jose de los Reyes. None found favor with the governor-general. The senior leadership of the organization remained in disarray throughout this period, with Nathorst briefly replaced by the sickly Lucien Sweet, who died in the United States in December 1932 without having taken up his post. Despite Quezon's disapproval, another superannuated former army private and Philippine-American War veteran, Clarence Howard Bowers, was appointed acting chief during Sweet's tenure.[42]

American command of the Constabulary satisfied neither Filipino nor American political leaders in the islands. Filipinos wanted a Filipino to command the force; Americans wanted an outsider, preferably an army officer. That Americans continued to occupy most of the higher posts in the Constabulary—at the end of 1933 that meant the sole brigadier generalship, three of the five colonelcies, and two of the four lieutenant colonelcies—did little to reassure the government. Their ages, questionable habits, and the general impression that the only Americans who stuck with the Constabulary were those lacking in ambition and ability were bad enough; in addition, intermarriage and long residence in the islands made them susceptible to the same pressures that lessened American confidence in Filipino officers. In early 1934 Governor-General Frank Murphy (appointed to the post by President Franklin Roosevelt in 1933) informed the Bureau of Insular Affairs that it was "essential" to reorganize the Constabulary "to separate that body from political influence, place it on a merit basis and generally improve its morale." Murphy thought that neither Bowers nor any other of the ranking American officers was up to the task.[43]

Lim was confident that he would assume the PC's commanding generalship. By the end of 1933, seventeen Filipino officers whose original commissions predated Lim's served in the Philippine Constabulary, but only three were senior in grade to Lim and none possessed his professional military credentials. The Philippine Department intelligence officer was told that Lim had been assured by Quezon that he would, eventually, be the Constabulary head. There was public speculation throughout 1932 and into 1933 that an "outsider" would be appointed to command the Constabulary. The outsider, of course, was Lim. According to the *Philippines Herald*, Lim was to serve as colonel and assistant chief before moving up to the organization's senior post after Bowers left. The paper expressed confidence in Lim's ability to lay "the foundation for our national defense" in harmony with "the best military techniques" and Filipino needs.[44]

The long-suffering Bowers finally received promotion to the Constabulary's single brigadier generalship; the *Herald*'s congratulations to Lim proved premature. Governor-General Theodore Roosevelt Jr. announced that the War Department had turned down his request for Lim's assignment to the

Constabulary. Senator Sergio Osmeña was in Washington at the time that Lim was scheming to transfer to the Constabulary and also spoke to the BIA on Lim's behalf, to no avail. Lim's hopes were not entirely dashed. Murphy became governor-general the next year and reopened the issue. Murphy sought the War Department's advice on appointing a Filipino officer to command the Constabulary, an American army officer with two or three additional army officers as assistants (an option he admitted would not gain local support), or a Filipino graduate of West Point.[45]

Lim was the "Filipino graduate" to whom the governor-general referred, but, as it had only the previous year, the army again declined to allow its officers to serve with the Constabulary.[46] Murphy then turned to the Constabulary's head surgeon, Col. Basilio Valdes, for a new Chief of Constabulary. The editor of *Khaki and Red* expressed "pleasant surprise" at the appointment. Presumably Valdes, who had joined the Constabulary in 1921 and had been serving since January 1933 as the acting commissioner of health and public welfare, would prove immune to the blandishments of political interference.[47] It would not be the last time that Lim's ambitions took a back seat to Basilio Valdes's more intimate ties to Manuel Quezon.

By that time, it was more than apparent to Lim and the other Filipino officers overseeing the development of the reserve officer corps that they were marching in place. The Filipino manpower-dependent war plans of Lassiter and MacArthur had come to nothing, brought down by a combination of Depression-era fiscal constraints and the hostility or indifference of new commanding generals. MacArthur's successor in Manila, Maj. Gen. John L. Hines, was a veteran of three previous assignments to the Philippines and a former chief of staff (1924–26) who had spent the preceding four years overseeing ROTC and CMTC programs in the United States. He had pledged "enthusiastic support" for MacArthur's proposals and felt that MacArthur would be able to do much to further those goals from Washington.[48] But even by the time MacArthur departed Manila in October 1930, it was clear that he would leave behind more expectation than accomplishment. Little came of the training programs stipulated in his defense project. In August 1930 the War Department had informed MacArthur that Congress had eliminated CMTC funds for fiscal year 1931. They were restored but no monies existed for a program in the Philippines. The War Department could only console the Philippine commander and insist that "plans for such training be retained."[49]

Hines's successors showed no interest anyway. Brig. Gen. Stanley Embick reported for duty as the commanding general of the Harbor Defenses of Manila and Subic Bays in June 1932. Embick was a friend and influential subordinate of Hines's replacement, Maj. Gen. Ewing E. Booth. In an April 1933 memorandum to Booth, Embick offered his much cited analysis of America's military position in Asia in which he decried the "madness" inherent in the army and navy's joint war plan. "The Philippine Islands have become a military liability of a constantly increasing gravity," Embick intoned, and he could see only two "broadly opposite" options: the constructing of huge naval facilities and the placement of a fleet in the Philippines, or the neutralization of the islands and the withdrawal of American military and naval forces. He recommended the latter course. While Embick felt that his country had legitimate interests in the Far East, "the American economy, he was sure, could easily survive if foreign commerce stopped." Consequently, Embick supported a severely restricted "defensive perimeter."[50]

Hines had followed Lassiter's and MacArthur's lead, authoring plans that called for confronting the enemy on the beach and projects that converted Philippine Scout infantry companies, field artillery batteries, and cavalry troops into cadres for training thousands of Filipino reservists, but it is instructive that the Orange projects prepared under his immediate successors were the only ones to include the words "first phase" in their titles. Their authors had little patience with the mobilization of additional Filipino divisions included in earlier schemes. Subsequent defense projects continued to outline the garrison's enlargement through four mobilization phases, from phase one during which the garrison expanded from peace to war strength, to phase four, by which time presumably a 3rd Philippine Division would exist. Booth included data on these subsequent phases in his defense projects, but in prioritizing the garrison's needs, support for manpower reserve programs (upon which third and fourth phase mobilizations were predicated and which ostensibly justified the assignment of Lim and other officers to local ROTC units) appeared last, and would be funded only after every other objective, including construction funds for the peacetime garrison's quarters and barracks, was met.[51]

The companion war plans mirrored the complete lack of confidence in constructing a reserve system in the Philippines. In the 1934 First Phase, Plan Orange (completed in late 1933), Philippine Department planners conceded that the enemy was most vulnerable at landing places but feared that an enemy amphibious assault on Bataan might quickly cut off a mobile force dedicated to maneuvering across the Luzon plain. The mobile troops were thus to concentrate along "a defensive position in southern Bataan." Only "if time permit[ted]" would a negligible portion of the Philippine Division contest the Japanese advance elsewhere and only if doing so did not jeopardize retirement to the Bataan defensive area. The American 31st Infantry Regiment would proceed immediately to Corregidor for beach defense. The department commander was to be guided in all his actions by the primary goal of defending the harbor defenses "to the last extremity."[52] Filipino reserves, and Filipino officers, had no place in these plans.

The insipid, implicitly defeatist Philippine Department war plans of the early and mid-1930s did not go uncriticized. In 1933 Brig. Gen. Charles Kilbourne, Embick's predecessor as commander of harbor defenses and now head of the War Plans Division, queried the focus on the defense of Bataan, a provision deemphasized in Lassiter's and MacArthur's Orange plans. He pointed out that the new Philippine Defense Plan gave "missions for existing units only." What had become of the Filipino-manned divisions envisioned by previous commanders? When Booth's successor, Frank Parker, continued in the same vein, Kilbourne prepared a sharp response for the chief of staff's signature reminding Parker that he, like Booth, had not "studied and weighed the solutions" to the Philippine Department's perennial problem of few men and overwhelming Japanese strength. "By organizing and equipping Filipinos, under natural leaders," Kilbourne wrote, "there were possibilities of harassing and delaying operations not only embarrassing to the invaders but tending to encourage the population in an attitude of loyalty that would be lacking if it were made immediately evident that we meant to abandon everything except the fortifications and southern Bataan."[53]

General Embick assumed Kilbourne's position as WPD chief in 1935 and lost little time acting on his conviction that army forces could serve little purpose in the Philippines. Embick thought General MacArthur was neither "objective [n]or realistic" when considering Philippine defense planning and was instead "guided by his vanity and his emotions." Convinced that the growth of airpower and Japanese possession of the mandated islands had irrevocably undermined the once sound (pre–World War I) Philippine defense plans, General Embick worked with navy planners to devise a more cautious plan to defeat the Japanese navy and return American authority to the Western Pacific. The army and navy war plans divisions settled on a scheme to "advance in progressive stages" across the Pacific, a plan that would inevitably delay relief of the distant garrison. Embick ostensibly sold MacArthur on the revised plan for war against Japan, "disingenuously" maintaining that the plan in substance remained unchanged.[54] Unknown to Embick, by the end of 1934 MacArthur had secretly agreed to return to the Philippines as military adviser and fully expected to use Filipino manpower potential to overturn the premises on which the army's War Plans Orange—those authored in both Washington and Manila—were based.

Army war planning for the Philippines in the early 1930s also took place against the backdrop of growing expectation of independence. The Philippine Legislature's ninth independence mission had reached Washington in January 1932 to find a political environment made hospitable by the onset of the Depression. Many in Congress were determined that Filipinos should have their independence, whether Filipinos wanted it or not. Resistance on the part of the administration of President Herbert Hoover and dissension within the ranks of the leading Filipino politicians added drama and a measure of uncertainty to the scene, but Congress finally agreed to an independence bill, the Hare-Hawes-Cutting Act, and passed it over Hoover's veto in January 1933. It was not accepted by the Philippine Legislature mostly because it had been negotiated by Quezon's political competitors, Sergio Osmeña and Manuel Roxas, and its acceptance would have worked to their benefit and not his, so he organized its defeat. Quezon then went to Washington himself and returned with a similar bill, the Tydings-McDuffie Act, which Congress passed on 23 March 1934 and President Roosevelt signed the following day. Like Hare-Hawes-Cutting, it granted the Philippines independence following a ten-year transitional Commonwealth period. The Philippine Legislature approved the measure on 1 May 1934.

With freedom for the country in sight, Lim might have returned to duty with the Philippine Scouts. There was a general assumption that the Scouts would play a prominent role in the military forces of an independent Philippines, and presumably the departure of white officers would lead to accelerated promotions for native officers.[55] That might not happen for several years, but the army could, if it wanted, position the Scouts during the Commonwealth period to serve as the basis for a Philippine army. Lim himself had publicly argued that it was the Scouts, not the Constabulary, that should be the starting point of a future Philippine army. The department's intelligence officer observed that "the presence of a highly trained body of professional soldiers, as exemplified by the Philippine Scouts, is not being overlooked by prominent Filipinos in the event of independence."

In truth, the organization had an ambiguous status, among both Americans and Filipinos. In the course of testifying before Congress on the inefficiencies of army organization in 1933, General Hagood recommended that the Philippine Scouts be abolished. Hagood was of the opinion that in the event of hostilities between Americans and Filipinos, the Scouts would prove disloyal. Contemporary war planners in the Philippines had no higher opinion of the Scouts. The HPD Plan Brown of 1932 accepted that almost all native troops "are either disloyal or cannot be trusted," while a "large percentage" of the Filipino soldiers were aged and physically unfit for the rigors of field service. Nor could they match the Japanese soldier in loyalty to the cause for which they would be called on to fight, should Japan attack the Philippines while it remained under American occupation. General Parker said it hardly mattered, since "by the time [the United States] withdrew, practically all those [Scouts] in the service now will have been retired on Federal pension." There was no guarantee an independent Philippine government could or would sustain the Scouts. As a cost-saving measure in 1932, Congress had considered transferring the maintenance of the Scout organization to the insular government. If passed, Resident Commissioner Camilo Osias noted, the measure would impose a ruinous financial burden on the Philippine government. Even a retentionist like Lim's brother-in-law Vicente Villamin (from whose opinions Lim kept a safe distance, at least publicly), a lawyer and economist who was among the most-quoted commentators on Philippine affairs in American newspapers in the prewar years, admitted that the transfer of the Scouts to Philippine authority would mean the organization's disbandment. The Manila government simply could not afford the Philippine Scouts.[56]

After twenty years on active duty, Lim had come full circle. In 1934 the army had no more interest in allowing Filipinos to pursue careers as military professionals than it had had when Secretary of War Taft had suggested allowing Filipinos to attend West Point back in 1908 or when Lim had graduated from the academy in 1914. It no longer offered commissions in the Philippine Scouts. The army's limited resources in the Philippines would have been better devoted to developing an indigenous defense capacity, since no one thought the navy could reach the Philippines in time to prevent the small garrison's surrender, but, as always, the attitude of most American officers remained suspicious and short-sighted. Assignment of Filipino officers as PMS&Ts to university cadet corps had become merely another avenue for marginalization.

For all that, not since 1914—when many Filipinos had expected their country soon to be free of American occupation—did Filipinos interested in military affairs have such scope for action. The Tydings-McDuffie Act stipulated the formation of a ten-year "Commonwealth" to precede Philippine independence, during which time the United States would remain responsible for the defense of the archipelago. The act did not require the Commonwealth government to create its own military to take the place of the American army, but it did not forbid it from doing so either. In fact, the act's wording—that the United States could command "all military forces organized by the Philippine government"—led some to believe that the United States was at least tacitly encouraging the Philippines government to develop its own military forces.[57]

Lim did not wait to see how things developed. The one significant piece of military-related legislation passed in the run-up to the inauguration of the Commonwealth showed Lim's determination to play a central role in the new nation's military affairs. This was an "act creating the Bureau of National Defense in the government of the Philippine Islands" approved by the legislature near the end of 1934. Once selected by the "chief executive of the Philippine Islands with the consent of the Senate," the "chief of the Bureau of National Defense" had wide-ranging authority "to establish the different branches of military service and organizations which may be necessary for effectively defending the National Territory," but the bureau's immediate focus would be on the acquisition of officers and the oversight of military and citizenship training in public and private schools. All schools would be obliged to provide office space, storerooms, and training facilities for military instruction, and private schools would have to bear the cost of military instructors. Any school that refused would be denied government recognition. In introducing the bill in the House of Representatives, Claudio Sandoval of Palawan Province had stressed "the importance of a strong officers' corps." "Armies today," his statement read, "are as effective as their officers are." The act presumed that the United States and other unnamed countries would allow Filipinos to train in their "different military and naval academies, and schools of aviation." The government was to fund 185 military scholarships in the four years following passage of the legislation.

Despite Lim's expression of confidence that he would do so, there was little chance that the governor-general had ever intended to support the Bureau of National Defense Act. It was just one of many bills passed by the legislature that Murphy vetoed, though Murphy's biographer seized upon the bureau act as a particularly "badly thought-out measure" and summarized approvingly Murphy's veto message, which was about as long as the bill itself. Murphy conceded that the act addressed an important policy issue, but he argued that it had not undergone the necessary degree of public scrutiny and that it obligated the government—a government that was not yet in existence—to assume onerous financial burdens. Nor was national defense an urgent matter given that the United States remained responsible for the Philippines' security during the Commonwealth period. Murphy's veto of the bureau act was only half the blow to Lim's ambition. At the same time, the governor-general approved a significant increase in the size of the Philippine Constabulary.

Major General Parker, the garrison commander, provided another justification for opposing the bill by publicly expressing the opinion that the proposed bureau might conflict with the army's authority, and Col. Frederick Manley, the governor-general's "military adviser," had told Sandoval that Murphy's office was working on its own national defense plan. Lim thus credited the bill's defeat to the governor's staff, which, he informed Quezon, was determined to perpetuate "the old political strategy of keeping down Filipino leadership."[58]

For Lim the significance of the bureau act was not just what was in it but what was not: the Philippine Constabulary and its academy would not be important sources of officers for a future Philippine army. Although the word "constabulary" was nowhere mentioned in the legislation, Sandoval had mimicked Lim's earlier comments about the Constabulary's unsuitability as a military force. "The Philippine Constabulary was created for police work and its very existence has been predicated upon that understanding. When an organization has served so long and so faithfully and has acted in such a manner efficiently, that organization is indoctrinated into such a system, departure from which is a hard process." A police force could not perform the functions of an army. In other words, the bureau act represented an attempt by the Filipino officers of the Philippine Scouts to take charge of the Philippines' military future. Lim and several other Scout officers had testified in favor of the bill, and Claudio Sandoval had introduced it and shepherded it to passage. Sandoval had no military experience, nor had he evidenced any special interest in military matters in the past. What he did have was a brother-in-law in the United States Army's Philippine Scouts named Vicente P. Lim, and knowledgeable observers drew the obvious conclusion: Sandoval had been mouthing Lim's thoughts on the republic's military needs, and Major Lim intended himself to be the chief of the Bureau of National Defense.[59]

CHAPTER 4

"We May Even Be There Indefinitely"

Origins of the Philippine Military System, 1934–1935

Passage of the Bureau of National Defense Act represented the fleeting high point of Vicente Lim's attempt to shape the future course of Philippine military affairs prior to the establishment of the Commonwealth. Neither Lim nor any other Filipino officer would be involved in determining an appropriate military system for what was, presumably, a soon-to-be-independent nation. That decision would have its origin not in Manila but in a continent—and a culture—an ocean away, in Washington, D.C., where Philippine Senate president Quezon negotiated for the services of the United States' senior-ranking soldier as military adviser to the islands' government. The Philippine military system dates to November 1934, when Douglas MacArthur accepted Quezon's offer of renewed service in Manila and put several officers quietly to work devising a program of military training and organization suitable for a Philippine republic. The ten-year transitional Commonwealth government called for by the Philippine Independence Act would not be inaugurated for another year, and Quezon would not make public his hiring of MacArthur until well into 1935, but Quezon had long been the islands' dominant politician, had put his imprimatur on the Tydings-McDuffie Act, recently approved by the Philippine legislature, and could look forward to becoming the Commonwealth's first president.

Precisely why and in what manner Quezon acquired Douglas MacArthur's services remains cloudy. The way Quezon put the matter in his posthumously published autobiography, *The Good Fight*, was that he had "sought a conference" with MacArthur as soon as the independence act had been "introduced" and after he "became certain that the new bill would become a law." "Do you think that the Philippines can be defended after they shall have become independent?" he asked MacArthur. "I don't *think* so," MacArthur emphatically replied; "I *know* that the Islands can be protected." Quezon then inquired if MacArthur would be willing to come to the Philippines as military adviser. MacArthur answered that there was "nothing [he] would like more" than to help the Filipinos "organize their own defense." MacArthur's encouraging responses to his queries led Quezon to proceed "at once" to gain President Roosevelt's and Secretary of War George Dern's approval of MacArthur's assignment as Commonwealth military adviser.[1]

Quezon did not write portions of his autobiography and probably had not read it in its entirety before he died, but this account of how Quezon acquired MacArthur's services, or some slight variant of it, has been repeated in almost every MacArthur and Quezon biography and history of Philippine-American relations. It is not a story Quezon told consistently. When they first met on the afternoon of 18 November 1935 at Malacañan Palace, Quezon told the members of the National Defense Council, established ostensibly to advise on military affairs (though it rarely met thereafter), that he had approached MacArthur *after* Congress had approved Tydings-McDuffie, and MacArthur, expressing his belief in the Philippines' ability to defend itself, had said that he would be "delighted" to assist "as far as constructive policies or works are necessary during his term of office as chief of staff." He did not agree at that time to become the Commonwealth's military adviser.[2]

MacArthur's military subordinates are no more enlightening. Maj. Dwight Eisenhower, who had worked closely with the general since 1932, wrote that before visiting the chief of staff in Washington, Quezon had "through correspondence . . . already expressed to General MacArthur a hope that the General would come to the Philippine Islands as 'Military Adviser.'" He accepts that when MacArthur asserted his belief that the Philippines could be defended, Quezon immediately asked if MacArthur would accept the military adviser post and that MacArthur answered "in the enthusiastic affirmative," but Eisenhower dates that exchange to a visit Quezon made to Washington in spring 1935, not fall 1934. (Quezon was in the United States from March to May 1935.) Yet Capt. Thomas J. Davis, the general's personal aide from 1928, recalled that Quezon "first approached" the chief of staff seeking his services as military adviser during a trip to Washington in "the late fall of 1934" and that the two agreed to the terms of MacArthur's services at that time. These are contemporary statements, written respectively in November 1935 and February 1936, by two men who should have known the truth of the matter.[3]

What seems to have taken place is that when Quezon was in Washington to negotiate changes to the Hare-Hawes-Cutting Act in late 1933 and early 1934, he approached MacArthur to discuss the military needs of the proposed Philippine republic. MacArthur agreed to use his authority as chief of staff to devise "constructive policies or works" that would help the Philippines prepare militarily for independence.[4] In fulfillment of that promise, in July 1934 the head of the War Plans Division, General Kilbourne, cabled the Philippine garrison's commanding general asking his views on the "organization, strength, equipment, distribution, duties and financial support of the Commonwealth forces, release of reservations to the Commonwealth for the use of such forces, [and] relations [of] federal forces and Commonwealth forces." Other senior officers were also asked to provide WPD with their thinking on the same topic.

The other officers had little to say—that the army be sure not to leave any valuable property behind was the thrust of their contributions—but in mid-August 1934, Maj. Gen. Frank Parker responded with a modest proposal to combine the Philippine Scouts with the Philippine Constabulary to produce a ten-thousand-man force "organized for both military and police purposes." He saw "no possibility of adequate defense against aggression by a powerful nation." The Philippine government need only concern itself with ensuring domestic tranquility. Parker, however, shared the view of those who saw the Philippines as America's commercial entrepôt in the Far East. The Tydings-McDuffie Act allowed for the possibility of a continuing American naval presence in an independent Philippines, and Parker wanted "Corregidor and its system" transferred to the navy for retention by the United States. "Under no circumstances or conditions," he wrote, "should this installation be relinquished."

The War Plans Division chief was unimpressed. Kilbourne was himself a soldier of unusually broad and sympathetic Philippine experience. He had won the Medal of Honor in the Philippines in 1899, commanded the first coast artillery unit assigned to Corregidor, served with the Philippine Constabulary, and even authored a boys' adventure story based on his Philippine experiences. The year before, he had chided Parker for his failure to rely more heavily on Filipino manpower in preparing local defense plans, and he now dismissed Parker's conservative suggestions. Ultimately he recommended to MacArthur that the army use the ten-year transition period leading to independence "to exert an influence on the nature of forces to be raised by the Commonwealth and to be maintained by the subsequent Republican government." During this "period of tutelage," Kilbourne believed, the army could guide the Filipinos through "every phase of the question of their national defense." Kilbourne suggested something similar to the national guard as a basis for a Commonwealth army. With "generous details of Regular Army personnel as commanders [and] inspector-instructors," a creditable military force would exist by 1946. The army could further build up a Philippine army by releasing for military service to the Philippine government all men of the Scouts who could be spared and by leasing "for a nominal sum" the necessary military reservations for training and housing the Philippine Army.

MacArthur's response showed that he had by then agreed to become Commonwealth military adviser. He was no longer interested in others' opinions about the Philippines' military needs and acted to suppress any further official involvement in the matter. Although he had approved the original query in July, he now handed back Kilbourne's memorandum and dictated a much different response than the one his subordinate had suggested. "No action will be taken," Kilbourne subsequently informed General Parker, "which could effect [*sic*], in any way, the initiative of the Filipinos in determining the character of the defense forces to be developed." MacArthur approved this cable for transmission only after deleting the sentence that had ended Kilbourne's draft message: "Should [the Filipinos] ask advice or assistance, you will inform them they should submit [a] request to the War Department for the detail of the necessary officers." When Kilbourne raised the issue again soon after, in early December, MacArthur responded with a handwritten note that read, "Take it easy and do not force developments in this matter. We may be there [the Philippines] ten years—we may even be there indefinitely." At this time, too, MacArthur added his voice to those opposed to the Bureau of National Defense Bill.[5]

In November 1934 Quezon had made an official request to the secretary of war for the assignment of "professionally trained military leaders of wide experience" (mentioning no officer by name) to the Philippine government to assist in the preparation of a "defense system." He asked that an act of May 1926 allowing the detail of military and naval personnel to American republics to assist "in military and naval matters" be amended to include "similar assistance" for the Philippines. The Philippines' inclusion in the 1926 act gave MacArthur a basis of authority independent of the local garrison commander, but he did not stop there. In other ways, MacArthur acted to ensure himself a free hand in the Philippines. As noted, he advised against approval of Lim's handiwork, the Bureau of National Defense Bill. When General Parker refused to have the army vacate the Santa Lucia military quarters in Intramuros that MacArthur wanted as his headquarters, MacArthur strutted his knowledge of "Things Filipino" and put Parker in his place, informing the Philippine Department commander that Santa Lucia had originally been "the Constabulary Club and [its] title still rests with the Insular government." The quarters, then occupied by the 31st Infantry Regiment's commanding officer and his family, were to be "cleared and ready" by mid-October. More important was MacArthur's letter of instruction to Parker. Over the army adjutant general's signature, General Parker received an extraordinary letter ordering him to furnish any personnel, reserve matériel, and "every possible help [in] accomplishment of the mission of establishing an adequate native national defense for the Commonwealth." The head of the military mission was "empowered to use his own judgment" in demanding "whatever assistance he may require." In short, MacArthur gave himself carte blanche to raid the resources of the local army garrison. Parker told Governor-General Frank Murphy that he had "never seen such orders in his entire career."[6]

As the request for adding the Philippines to the list of countries eligible for military advisers made its way through Congress, MacArthur set his subordinates to work devising a Philippine military system. In a handwritten draft describing the establishment of the military mission, Eisenhower wrote that in November 1934 the commandant of the Army War College was asked to set up a "special committee" to prepare "all necessary studies, plans, laws, proposed speeches and other essential documents" for a Philippine military system. Maj. James Basevi Ord, a West Point classmate of Eisenhower's serving as an instructor at the college, was placed in charge of the committee, on which sat "several of the ablest officers of the army." Such committees were not uncommon, but this one was short-lived. There is no record of it in war college files, and in the final version of what would become the introduction to the mission diary, Eisenhower wrote that "the details of the original plan were worked out" by Ord alone, with "intermittent assistance" from unnamed others at the war college.[7]

Eisenhower's subsequent prominence and Ord's death in an airplane crash in Baguio in January 1938 has left Ord overshadowed in accounts of the mission's activities, but contemporary evidence makes Ord the primary author of those "studies, plans, [and] essential documents." Ord was credited with doing "much of the work connected with organization of the Philippine defense force" by a *Washington Post* appreciation published at the time of his death as well as by Eisenhower and by Maj. William Hoge, an officer of the 14th Engineers (PS) at Fort McKinley who worked with the military mission in 1936–37. Hoge recalled that Ord "had more sense and knew more about" the Philippine military system than either MacArthur or Eisenhower. Also, unlike his colleagues, Ord was an accomplished linguist who counted Spanish as just one of several languages he spoke fluently. Once in the islands, he would have the task of explaining the military system to members of the Philippine legislature, where Spanish remained an official language. Army Air Corps officer William ("Jerry") Lee, already in the Philippines working to help the PC establish an air patrol capability when the mission arrived in 1935, remembered Ord as "the politician" of the group, whose job consisted largely of "trying to sell the Filipinos on various things that the military adviser wanted."[8]

Ord's career had followed an unusual trajectory. After graduating from the Military Academy in 1915, Ord had served with the Punitive Expedition in Mexico in 1916. In combat for the only time in his career, at Parral on 12 April 1916, wounded and under heavy fire, Ord dismounted to assist an injured soldier. Ord received the Distinguished Service Medal for his bravery that day. Ord spent time directing refugee camps in New Mexico and Texas and briefly serving with a reserve officers' training camp in Georgia before he arrived at West Point to join the Department of Modern Languages. Like Eisenhower and Lim,

Ord missed out on service with the American Expeditionary Forces during World War I but soon after the Armistice arrived in The Hague as an assistant military attaché. He remained there until October 1922. Ord spent much of the next decade in France. He attended the prestigious Ecole Supérieure de Guerre from 1922 to 1924 and returned to Paris as an assistant military attaché in 1928. He held that position until late 1932 when he was assigned to the Army War College, first as a student and then as an instructor. In France, Ord met with Eisenhower and Richard Sutherland, the man who would take Ord's place on the military mission. The three attended Marshal Ferdinand Foch's funeral in 1929. While in France, Ord also met MacArthur, during an official visit by the chief of staff to Europe in 1931.[9]

Ord did not lack familiarity with the Philippines. Eisenhower had performed his foreign service in Panama in the 1920s and never saw the islands until 1935, but Ord had served a two-year tour of duty as a battalion commander with the 31st U.S. Infantry in Manila from 1926 to 1928. His birth in Mexico and native fluency in Spanish may have given Ord more of an interest and ability to socialize with upper-class Filipinos than would have been typical of army officers, but, despite the Philippines' growing reputation as a sought-after duty assignment, Ord had had no interest in being sent there at the time. When he learned that the army did not count his years in France and Holland as foreign service and that he would have to serve in one of the army's overseas garrisons, Ord had asked to be sent to China, where an army regiment guarded the American legation at Tientsin. By all accounts, as a member of the military mission, Ord worked and socialized easily with Filipinos, so much so that Eisenhower would write that MacArthur grew jealous of Ord's rapport with Filipino officials.[10]

Ord left nothing behind describing the sources he used to devise the military system, but a memorandum (now in the MacArthur archives) dated 2 November 1934 directed the chief clerk of the army library to give Eisenhower five manuscripts dealing with French military organization. These were reports issued by the French Ministry of Defense and translated and annotated by the army attachés in Paris. Ord had been involved in preparing these or similar reports, and Ord drew on his considerable knowledge of French military practice to design a military system for the Philippine Commonwealth. France's military affairs were the most widely studied by U.S. Army officers in the interwar period, and France was one of the few world powers that persisted in a peacetime conscription scheme after World War I.

Ord's last assignment to Paris had coincided with far-reaching changes in French conscription practice. War weariness and the perception that Germany's war potential had, momentarily at least, been blunted, had led the government to reduce military training time to eighteen months in the mid-1920s and to twelve months in 1928. Previously, conscripts had remained with their regiments for one or two years following this initial period of military training. Now, most would return home upon completion of training. Conscripts would no longer train in line regiments but in special training centers. Far from the *offensive à outrance* philosophy that had permeated French military thinking before the war and had necessitated longer service times and ready-to-march combat units, the law of March 1928 committed France to a demonstrably defensive military posture. The French recognized that the 1928 law ultimately would mean that "the defense of the nation would rest squarely upon the shoulders of young, untested, short-service soldiers and reservists who had never been under fire." Thus, most deputies in the French legislature thought it "prudent to reinforce an army of reservists with bastions of concrete"—that is, to build the Maginot Line.[11]

The short training period was a concession to French leftists who feared the conservative socializing effects of longer periods of military service. For their part, tradition-bound officers feared that the resultant military forces would be ineffective. Ord no doubt understood that French conscription practice reflected as much the give and take of divergent political forces as any objective military factors, but if he had any appreciation that that might not transfer to the Philippines, he left nothing behind saying so. He ignored the context and concentrated on the details. The year at which all French males had to register (age twenty), their division into "classes" based on month of birth, the year their training began (age twenty-one), the establishment of regional mobilization centers—these and other elements of the French military system would find their way into Philippine practice. Even the nominal wage of five centavos a day that would be paid to conscripts while undergoing basic military training seems to have been borrowed from the French model. French conscripts during World War I had received the nominal sum of five centimes per day.

Some of these were commonplace components of all conscription systems, of course, and in other ways Ord clearly did not copy French practice. French conscripts trained for a full year, for example, not the five and a half months Filipino draftees would initially be required to train. The short training period for Philippine "trainees," however, does point to one way in which French practice may have had a direct, and disastrous, impact on the Philippine military system: Ord borrowed the concept of premilitary training (also referred to as "preparatory military training," or PMT) from the French. For decades, French republicans had championed school-based premilitary training, and that such training would be implemented underlay French Socialists' belief that as little as six months of formal military training would suffice for conscripts. In accepting a reduced military service requirement in 1928, French military planners had understood that military-oriented training given before recruits reported for one year of active service was essential to the successful working of their military system.[12]

PMT became an important but mostly unrealized component of the Philippine military system. It was to continue from ages ten to eighteen, during which time students would gradually acquire basic military skills. The purpose of cadre training was to enhance these skills and offer company-level infantry training. MacArthur justified providing a mere five and one-half months of basic training to Filipino conscripts "*only*" on the understanding that trainees would already have completed PMT, Eisenhower wrote.[13] Yet by 1938, less than half of the Philippines' student-age population was attending school, and hardly 7 percent of high school–age Filipinos could be found in high school. The government's emphasis on primary education (grades one to four) meant that a large percentage of Filipino children entered first grade, but barely half of those children were still attending school four years later.[14] No one thing indicated more clearly the chasm between the military mission's conceptualizing in Washington and the reality of conditions in the Philippines than the expectation that most Filipino males would receive several years of "premilitary training" in school prior to reporting to an army training camp.

In outline, like most conscription-based military systems, the Philippine military system began with the concept that all physically qualified males were obliged to make themselves available for military service. Each April, beginning in 1936, every Filipino celebrating his twentieth birthday during the calendar year was to register for military service. The next month, on 15 May, a portion of those registered would be chosen by lottery to report the following year for basic military training lasting five and one-half months. A select few would be given the opportunity to receive additional training. The original intent was that, starting in 1937, 6,000 conscripts would be called to service. That number would grow until ultimately about 40,000 conscripts were to be trained each year, beginning in 1942. Upon completion of basic training, the conscripts then passed into the first reserve. At age thirty-one, they entered the second reserve; at age forty-one through age fifty, the third and final reserve. Eventually, the reserve would include several hundred thousand trained men. Conscripts who successfully completed training would be assigned to reserve "divisions" that would correspond geographically to the Philippines' ten military districts, from the 11th Division (i.e., the first district's first division) in northern Luzon to the 101st Division on Mindanao. Each division would total about 7,500 officers and men, small by contemporary standards but about the size of Union army divisions during the American Civil War.[15] As more reservists completed training, more divisions would be formed in each district. The 1st Military District would have the 11th Division, then the 12th Division; the 2nd District would have the 21st Division, then the 22nd Division; and so on. The military mission also planned to develop a "professional force" of 930 officers and 7,000–10,000 enlisted men, which would devote much of its time to training the reserve portion of the force.[16]

For MacArthur, the conceptualization of Philippine defense needs always returned to the question of numbers. The historical problem of defending the Philippines, he would lecture a group of officers at his Intramuros headquarters, was lack of numbers. "The professional soldier and sailor," MacArthur declared, thoroughly understood that the Philippines could not be defended "*with its present garrisons*." MacArthur's thinking on the problem of Philippine defense was grounded in his experience with the Philippine Department's Orange war plans. The creation of the Commonwealth government resolved the intractable dilemmas of war planning in the 1920s: the failure to support large officer and enlisted reserve programs; the lack of commitment on the part of too many American officials to associating Filipinos with the defense of their own country. The establishment of a semiautonomous government with the authority to support military forces pointed the way toward resolving the Philippine dilemma. Through his letter of instruction to Parker and by retaining his status as chief of staff, MacArthur would be able to draw on the resources of the existing regular force in the islands—essentially, American officers and Philippine Scouts—to develop a Philippine army, just as projects of the late 1920s and early 1930s had recommended. Still, given the Commonwealth's "limiting budget," MacArthur further reasoned that only a peacetime draft could produce economically the large numbers of soldiers needed to defend the Philippines from foreign aggression. Aside from reminding them of the financial strictures that had to be confronted, MacArthur's only guidance to the officers who would devise the military system was to insist that "the defense system should be based primarily on universal conscription."[17]

Little evidence suggests that the military mission shaped the Philippine military system in ways that reflected an awareness of how Filipinos might respond to the imposition of conscription; at least the mission eschewed the racial and cultural prejudices underlying army planning for the use of indigenous manpower in the past. The U.S. Army had in fact considered the possibility of implementing conscription as part of the 1924 defense project. The planners had concluded that "considering the social and political system and practices characteristic of the Filipinos, it is probable that any system of compulsory service administered by them would be characterized by corruption, ignorance of requirements, and careless administration."[18]

That is not to say that the idea of compulsory military service had neither history nor constituency in the Philippines. There had been some sort of conscription (the details of which are now obscure) in the Spanish Philippines, and the World War I–era authorization for a manpower draft, though never implemented, remained in force. More recently, the constitutional convention's national defense committee, nine of whose twenty-one members had some kind of military experience, ranging from two former generals of the revolutionary army to a retired United States Navy petty officer with three campaign medals to his credit, had recommended a provision borrowed from the 1931 constitution of the Spanish republic that read: "the defense of the state is a prime duty of government, and in the fulfillment of this duty all citizens may be required by law to render personal military and civil service." It dismissed out of hand the "volunteer system" of military recruitment. Not only was it too expensive for the Philippines to support, but it was also "undemocratic" (the poor would end up in the army while the "sons of the wealthy" would evade military service) and involved "the objectionable feature of entrusting the sacred mission of defending the country to men lacking in capacity who have proved failures in other fields of activity." The committee saw little need to justify further compulsory military service "for the reason," chairman Jose Alejandrino wrote, "that the consensus of public opinion is in favor of the measure proposed." The committee did not, however, recommend military conscription in a form similar to that subsequently adopted by the Commonwealth government.[19]

An authority on the history of the military draft in the United States has observed that "if America has no tradition of a draft absent an ongoing war, hot or cold, [America does have] a tradition of the intellectual elite longing for some form of national service. The issue is not so much the need of the country for the labor of these conscripted citizens, but the benefits that would be wrought on a young person having served the country for some period of time. . . . What was needed, they argued, was compulsory service to transform the unredeemed and to make them better citizens." The observation is not really applicable to the interwar period, a time when Army Chief of Staff MacArthur would find himself embroiled in a "feud with pacifists," but similar thinking did motivate many Filipinos in the 1930s, starting at the top: "We are not only interested in having citizens who will be competent soldiers," but "in having soldiers that are competent citizens," Quezon said in defense of the Philippines' conscription program in a speech given at the annual Military Order of the Carabao banquet in Washington in 1937. No one would prove to be a more fervent supporter of army training as a means "to produce useful citizens" than Paulino Santos, the Philippine Army's first chief of staff. In fact, Santos thought the purely military functions of the army something of a distraction. A staff officer quoted Santos as saying that he did not expect the Philippines to be at war during his lifetime nor "even during our children's generation nor our grandchildren's." Army funds thus would be better expended on vocational training that would make reservists "useful in their respective communities."

Every senior officer attempted to draw public attention to the "nonmilitary" aspects of military training. The PMT portion of the defense program, Constabulary colonel G. B. Francisco said, would develop a national spirit, make young men both physically strong and morally confident, and instill loyalty and respect for constituted authority. General Valdes told members of the Manila Rotary Club that military training would teach Filipinos to subordinate local and personal interests to national interests. The citizen army would be "an instrument of national development." Army training was a "great leveller," West Point graduate Rafael Garcia asserted. It would bring rich and poor together, encourage a democratic spirit, end social division, and, not least, stop an "increasing physical tendency toward effeminacy" among Filipino boys.

Such sentiment extended beyond the army. The director of the Office of Adult Education, for example, Segundo Infantado, saw army training camps as having great potential to promote adult literacy and be "agencies for the dissemination of culture." The president of the Philippine Women's University wanted a military cadet–like program for young women. "Our whole national defense program is justified as a character-forming movement," she pointed out. Would not women benefit as much as men from such training? Similar expressions filled contemporary Philippine newspapers and journals.[20]

What did Lim think of all this? His studies in the United States in 1926–29 provide few clues. As a student at the army's advanced schools, Lim had passed up the opportunity to focus on topics of the sort that would have served as a basis for devising a military system, such as manpower mobilization or army organization. Dwight Eisenhower, for example, had been through the war college the year before Lim and had prepared a paper on the necessity of forming an enlisted reserve for the regular army and how to go about doing so. Lim preferred the broader canvases of military history and what a later generation would label geopolitics. At Fort Benning he had written a paper on Aguinaldo and the Philippine Revolution and, at Fort Leavenworth, a paper on Philippine defense in case of a Japanese invasion. (Neither paper survives.) His war college thesis argued the importance of the Philippines to America's security and economic interests in the Far East.[21]

Lim had, however, begun thinking about the military needs of the Philippines long before the establishment of the Commonwealth. His first known opinion on a proper military system for his country dates to 1919. Then, Lim, like Paulino Santos later, had argued in favor of a "useful" army in which vocational or industrial work played a part equal to that of military training. "Our people do not need as much discipline as the Europeans or Americans [since] we are naturally disciplined," Lim had written at that time.[22] When Lim returned from the United States in 1929, he was invited to deliver several lectures on the topic of military training and national defense to be broadcast over the radio. Lim argued that Filipinos needed to become military minded, cognizant of the Philippines' vulnerable position in a predatory world system, and willing to commit themselves to "intensive training to prepare them for any emergency." Ten more years of army life, nearly a third of which had been spent in the United States, had matured his views and changed his mind about the natural discipline of his countrymen. Cultural attitudes were a major obstacle to military mindedness. An "*Ang Dios na ang bahala*" (God will provide) mentality, combined with the human tendency to follow the easier path through life—"hence the big numbers that seek the white-collar positions," Lim observed—formed the biggest challenges to be overcome. He recommended beginning in the public and private school systems, where the scope of existing "military training or some form of mass physical education" could be greatly expanded. The government "could establish yearly military training camps" and send young men abroad for advanced training.[23] (These ideas reappeared four years later in the failed Bureau of National Defense Bill.) In an address before the Philippine Reserve Officers' Association in February 1934, Lim reiterated the theme of military mindedness:

> If our country were rich enough to be able to afford a large professional army, it would be an easy task to develop a plan of defense that will be adequate to the needs of our scattered islands. But every one of us is aware that our economic condition will not bear the burden of expenses incident to a complex military organization, and therefore we shall have to resort to universal military training—a system that can succeed only if supported by public opinion and undertaken willingly by all Filipinos.[24]

The need for "national discipline" was a recurring theme of Lim's public statements. Filipinos talked a lot about nationalism, Lim lamented, but "have miserably failed to ascertain the moral and spiritual foundation upon which national unity should be predicated." He had some harsh words for his countrymen. Too many "evils of the old order" survived the introduction of new governmental forms. He decried the persistence "of the *compadre* and *tayo-tayo* system, of red tape, of downright dishonesty in the conduct not only of the masses of our people but more appallingly so in those upon whom great and solemn public responsibilities are reposed." Military training would reshape cultural norms. It would "teach our boys the value of discipline," lead them to embrace "greater national ideals," and put an end to the "many evils of the old order." Citizenship training is what Lim really meant, and for this reason he was an early and persistent booster of the Boy Scout movement. When the Boy Scouts of America in the Philippines gave way to the Boy Scouts of the Philippines, Lim was a charter member of the new organization and helped oversee its growth from 17,000 men and boys in 1936 to more than 30,000 by 1939.

Whatever else it represented, then, to this extent the military mission's scheme was a happy marriage of Filipino elites' embrace of compulsory military service as "an instrument of national development" (to quote again General Valdes) and the U.S. Army's Uptonianism unimpeded, as it was in the United States, by congressional oversight.[25]

Although no copy of the military mission's original plan appears to have survived, few substantive changes were made to it once the military mission arrived in the islands in October 1935 and began the work of getting the plan accepted as the Commonwealth's national defense act. Ord met almost at once with members of the national assembly to explain the details of the plan. A critical Frank Murphy, unhappy with both the provisions of the proposed bill and the military mission's freedom from the High Commissioner's oversight, also had his staff dissect the plan. It quickly concluded that the plan was financially unsound and that the High Commissioner had the authority to challenge it, but Murphy was unwilling to clash publicly with Quezon and MacArthur. In short, while the mission's national defense plan had "to be rewritten insofar as arrangement and much of its language was concerned," Eisenhower acknowledged, "its basic provisions were . . . retained intact." MacArthur assured Murphy that "with minor modifications," the proposed bill was the same as prepared by the American army's general staff and war college. In sum, for the most part, the military system was just as the High Commissioner would later describe it: a plan "prepared in a staff school as a solution of an academic military problem."[26]

The versions of the proposed national defense bill published in the Manila newspapers toward the end of November 1935 differed little from the final version approved in late December; changes were mostly cosmetic. Where early versions of the legislative bill derived from the plan contained the word "Commonwealth," for example, the final version used the word "Philippines." The initial bill stipulated that annual registration for conscription would take place in March followed by a lottery drawing in April. In the approved bill, these months were changed to April and May, respectively. The Assembly's national defense committee chairman, Lim's brother-in-law Claudio Sandoval, opposed any amendment that challenged the structure of the proposed military system, and his opposition was invariably upheld by the Assembly. Other provisions, however, were open to revision, even if they made the system more financially burdensome. For example, the first draft of the bill authorized payment to conscripts for travel to training camps if they had to journey more than forty kilometers. One legislator wanted to reduce the figure to ten kilometers; the disputants settled on twenty.[27] The Assembly approved the national defense act—Commonwealth Act no. 1—on 19 December 1935, and Quezon signed it two days later.

The defense act was thus largely the work of the military mission, accepted with little debate by a compliant national assembly. A representative from La Union Province, Camilo Osias, mounted the only extensive attack on the act. Osias, a resident commissioner in the United States from 1929 to 1935 (and Lim's companion to Osaka in 1923), once pledged undying devotion to Quezon but had since soured on his onetime patron. Osias now questioned both the provisions of the proposed defense act and an Assembly resolution that President Quezon's defense scheme be accepted without further ado. Public statements that the Assembly's defense committee had prepared the bill, Representative Osias stated, were nonsense. "What I know," he said, "is that there was a bill handed to us, and some little changes were made." The whole matter was very "irregular and somewhat misleading," he claimed.[28] Quezon admitted as much in a speech made on the occasion of the Commonwealth's sixth anniversary (15 November 1941). The Assembly's support for the defense program, Quezon asserted, "was done more in the nature of a vote of confidence in my leadership than because there was a general conviction that the plan of national defense recommended by me upon the advice of General MacArthur was of real and practical value." That the Assembly had played little role in the affair had really never been a secret. A widely used civics textbook of the day baldly stated that the military mission "was actually responsible for all the plans and organization of the Philippine Army."[29]

Quezon's dominance of the Philippine political scene ensured the passage of any defense-related legislation he cared to sponsor. Why did Douglas MacArthur need to stand at his side while he did so? The general's biographers have tended to emphasize that MacArthur's acceptance of the military advisership may have resolved personal dilemmas that would accompany the conclusion of his term of office as army chief of staff. Still nearly a decade short of the army's mandatory retirement age in 1935, MacArthur was a highly decorated combat veteran and battlefield commander. He had commanded corps areas and an overseas department, as well as having enjoyed a longer than usual term as the army's top-ranking officer. What fields were left to conquer?

These facts may partly explain MacArthur's interest in returning to Manila; they say nothing about why Quezon wanted MacArthur in Manila. Of course, as Quezon knew, the involvement of an officer of MacArthur's stature and seniority in creating a Philippine army might obviate some of the problems experienced by the national guard during World War I. The former chief of staff would presumably have the influence to draw on the resources of the local army garrison and overcome opposition to Philippine ambitions that might arise in Washington as well as at Fort Santiago. Looking back on the episode decades later, Eisenhower was of the opinion that "in Quezon's judgment, no other man could generate in the Philippine people the esprit as well as the willingness for work and sacrifice needed in the development of defense forces that had to be created from scratch." Such was the resonance of the name MacArthur among the Filipinos.[30]

Of course that recollection came with later knowledge of Bataan and Corregidor and all that had followed to make MacArthur "the single greatest figure" in Philippine military history. What Eisenhower wrote at the time, in December 1935, was something different: MacArthur "consented to act as Military Adviser" because he believed "that the development of adequate defense forces in the Philippines would constitute a distinct service to the United States." As for why MacArthur and Quezon alone insisted on the implementation of a military system that so many well-informed others thought unnecessary and unworkable, Eisenhower had an answer for that too: "Manifestly, such a system [as MacArthur contemplated for defending the Philippines] cannot protect any Island Nation against the consequences of a blockade by sea [but it gives hope] that through preservation of territorial integrity . . . powerful allies" might come to the besieged nation's rescue.[31]

He no doubt meant the United States, which is precisely what contemporaries feared. Quezon and MacArthur were up to something. Vice Governor Joseph Hayden thought their actions amounted to "a deliberate plan"—"perhaps 'plot' would be a better word"—to turn the Philippine Commonwealth into "a semi-independent state or protectorate." Hayden made those remarks in a letter (perhaps unsent) to a friend in the United States in late 1935 but returned to the issue in his monumental *The Philippines: A Study in National Development.* Hayden completed this work only days before the attack on Pearl Harbor, and by then, of course, events made speculation irrelevant. But after surveying "the MacArthur-Quezon defense plan" with which "many military experts disagree," Hayden asked "why two such able men as President Quezon and General MacArthur should have sponsored a defense plan which on the face of it cannot defend the nation"? One answer to the question, Hayden noted, emerged in contemporary legislative debates: "America will more likely stay here when we have trained men to help her."[32]

It was Lim's friend Maximo Kalaw who spoke those words; it is unlikely the two had not discussed the issue. The belief that the Philippines could be of value to the United States should Americans place faith in Filipino ability would have resonated with the Scout officer. That, after all, had been the theme of Lim's Army War College thesis in 1929: "The Philippine Islands—A Military Asset." In his paper, which the commandant of the college had labeled a "study of exceptional merit" and passed along for reading to the War Plans Division, Lim had identified the Philippines as a "strategic position" of such value that its occupation had given the United States "a commanding influence and importance in the Pacific Region." He denied "the theory that the Philippines has no place in the economic structure of the United States." The islands could provide "the majority of the raw materials" to meet America's growing need for tropical goods, and if the United States did not take advantage of the Philippines' economic potential, Japan certainly would. Militarily, "as far as the defense of the Philippine Islands at present is concerned, it is purely a liability to the United States." But that was only because the government had failed to train and equip Filipinos "in whom there is a strong desire to learn the art of war."[33] Lim publicized these views in a radio address in the Philippines made in early 1930 and in an article published in the *Infantry Journal* in 1931. He was effusive in his praise of the United States. Nearly three decades of "American tutelage" had wrought "an almost incredible transformation" in the lives of Filipinos and had made their country an inspiration for "every part of Asia, where the people dream of free institutions and representative government." The "work of America in the Philippines has meant to the Filipinos peace and security, progress and prosperity, liberty and opportunity." Furthermore, "the economic value of the islands [to] the United States" was immense. The Philippines could provide "tropical products" to the United States "in sufficient quantities to free them from dependence upon foreign countries." The two countries' mutual strengths could lead to a strong and profitable partnership—and thereby resolve the "Philippine problem," as Lim put it—were it not for the attitude of "not a few Americans" who, Lim lamented

> have not been always thoughtful about the self respect and susceptibilities of so sensitive and high spirited a people as the Filipinos. Thus, instead of touching their better nature and enlisting their self interest, they succeed only in hurting their pride and arousing their passions. . . . Americans are made to appear in the light of foes rather than as friends, of condescending masters rather than willing helpers. With so baneful an atmosphere, it is not astonishing that in spite of the Filipinos' deep feeling of appreciation for the blessings America has given them, they have raised a cry against the continued relationship with their benefactors.[34]

Nonetheless, whatever Lim might have thought of the future of Philippine-American relations, Quezon's hiring of MacArthur was deeply disappointing.

Lim's status as the Philippines' foremost soldier, the one who must inevitably play a leading role in the development of a Philippine-authored military system, paled next to the luster of a MacArthur. Quezon may have intended just that. Choosing an outsider allowed Quezon to avoid choosing between Scout officers and Constabulary officers, who continued to fight for preeminence in creating and leading a Philippine army. No officer in either group dared challenge the authority of one of America's most valiant and accomplished soldiers. A few weeks after he had arrived to take up the advisory position in October 1935, MacArthur wrote to old friend John O'Laughlin, editor of the *Army and Navy Journal*, that "the mantle of Lafayette has fallen on my shoulders insofar as the Filipino people are concerned and my activities and position are treated on a higher plane of almost veneration and reverence."[35] MacArthur presumably had in mind the Marquis de Lafayette who had made a triumphal tour of the United States in 1824. Lim knew American history too, and may well have wished that, like the elderly Lafayette, MacArthur would content himself with the plaudits and gifts of a grateful nation—and return home.

CHAPTER 5

"El Entusiasmo de Nuestros Jovenes"

Implementing the Military System, 1935–1939

Like that of most Filipino officers, Lim's participation in the early years of the army-building enterprise is poorly documented. His insider letters to his children in the United States do not begin until August 1938, after his son Roberto had entered the United States Naval Academy (from which he would graduate in 1942). The published semiofficial mission diary kept from 1935 to 1939 by Dwight Eisenhower includes Lim's name, once, in a list of officers with whom the military adviser's chief of staff played cards. Little more than passing journalistic reports and a small number of archival documents allow Lim's activities during this time to be sketched. The *Manila Daily Bulletin* reported at the end of 1936 that Lim was involved in an effort to settle a dispute between local and army officials over the use of public facilities at Albay, buildings of the old Regan Barracks near Daraga in the far south of Luzon in which Lim had trained as a young officer two decades earlier. A January 1937 memorandum in the Quezon Papers identifies Lim as serving on the National Transportation Board. In the first letter he wrote to his son, Lim took pride in the success of his most recent major responsibility—organizing the Occupation Day parade. Lim declared it to be "the most wonderful parade that had ever been exhibited in the Philippine Islands." It was indeed a magnificent parade, led by President Quezon, followed by an estimated 100,000 participants, so lengthy a procession that it took some four hours to pass the reviewing stand. Occupation Day, commemorating the day the American army took possession of Manila on 13 August 1898, had long been a public holiday; this was its first observance in which Filipinos had shown any substantial interest.[1] Like Lim's other assignments, however, it was mostly busywork. By August 1938 he was already grumbling about retiring. The contours of the military system had been set by others, and, perversely enough, only the system's failure was likely to offer an opportunity for Lim to play a significant part in his own country's army.

MacArthur had hoped that the Philippine Scout regiments could form the new army's building blocks. In a November 1934 speech, Quezon—his words clearly reflecting recent conversations with his military adviser—had stated that the Philippines would adopt a military system based on conscription but that the Scouts would likely form the army's "backbone."[2] Quezon did not specifically mention the Scouts' few Filipino officers, but they were an obvious source of expertise, however limited, for a Philippine army that would possess few technically trained officers. Thanks to a propitiously timed army retirement act, approved by Congress on 31 July 1935, most of these officers would be able to leave the American army with pensions, although they were far from having completed the thirty or more years of service normally required to receive retirement benefits. Under the terms of the 1935 act, any officer with at least fourteen years, six months, and one day of service could apply for retirement and receive a prorated pension. By early 1936 two-thirds of the Filipino officers were, or soon would be, eligible to retire under this act.

Service with the Philippine Army allowed Filipino Scout officers to obtain positions of authority and responsibility they would never achieve in the United States Army and provided a means of continuing their careers beyond 1946, since the War Department did not intend to allow Filipinos to remain on active duty with the regular army, or even on the retired list, after the Philippines attained independence. The army expected that Filipino soldiers on active duty would be "wholly retired" and paid a lump sum compensation based on the length of time they had spent in the army. Those Philippine Scouts already on the retired list by 1946 "would be wholly retired with a lump sum compensation based on the rate of their retired pay and their life expectancy."[3] Scout officers who hoped to continue military careers after 1946 had to embrace service with the Philippine Army; that they would necessarily do so proved to be just one of many demonstrations of the mission's ignorance of local realities. By the end of 1935, Eisenhower and Ord had met frequently with individual Scouts in an attempt to determine the terms on which each would be willing to join the Philippine Army but had found no common ground.[4]

Several factors explain the Scouts' hesitance. One was their undisguised dislike of the Constabulary, and it was the PC—not the Philippine Scouts—that in January 1936 became the nucleus of the Philippine Army. MacArthur was asked about this—would the Constabulary become the army?—as soon as he arrived in Manila, but remarkably the military mission does not appear to have expected the PC to play a significant role. The organizations' officers could hardly stand one another—hostility that dated back at least to the national guard era when the Scouts' contempt for PC officers had been the subject of frequent complaint as both groups sought to find a future in the PNG. For many years, one Constabulary officer publicly acknowledged, "an intangible but ever present unsympathetic feeling" had existed between army and Constabulary officers. The more recent struggle to define a future Philippine army, which had led the Scout officers to get behind legislation abolishing the Constabulary academy and creating an alternative source of officers through the Bureau of National Defense, had only increased ill-will between the two groups. With the later integration of Scout and Constabulary officers in the Philippine Army, "an extra good effort" was made "to see that nothing [was] said about" this traditional hostility, without much success. In the words of a Manila journalist: "cut throat rivalry between Scout officers and Constabulary men" persisted. Scout officers resented being subordinate to Constabulary officers, whom they considered less professionally qualified, and were dismayed at the preponderance of Constabulary officers in the senior ranks of the army. Promotions were likely to be blocked for years.[5]

Another obstacle was financial. Most of the Scout officers were reluctant to sacrifice the security offered by the U.S. Army for an uncertain future in the Philippine Army. The *Philippines Herald* reported in early January 1936 that Quezon had discussed with Lim, Segundo, and Rafael Garcia the question of Scout transfers to "the future Philippine Army," but some officers were unwilling to transfer "since the status of the high command . . . has not been determined," and they objected to a pay cut. The Scout officers' salaries were generous by local standards. A first lieutenant in the American army (the rank held by most Filipino officers) received almost as much as a lieutenant colonel in the Philippine Army.[6]

Initial talks between the officers and the mission were based on the assumption that the Scouts would have to quit the U.S. Army to join the Philippine Army. None cared to take advantage of the 1935 retirement act. Only when the War Department agreed that Scout officers could be assigned to the Philippine Army without losing their status and benefits as U.S. Army officers did Scouts begin to transfer to Commonwealth service. By mid-1938, all but three of the Filipino Scout officers still on active duty were serving with the Philippine Army.

Still, many remained unwilling to commit themselves to permanent service with their nation's military force. Their discontent flared into the open in late 1938, when several staged a walkout from the Philippine Army, with serious repercussions for the reputation of the Scout officers. Lim was not a disinterested observer, but his is the most extensive available account of the episode. As he explained in a letter to one of his sons, Eisenhower and Ord (presumably with MacArthur's approval) made promises about promotions that were not fulfilled. Some officers, the more junior of the Scouts who had agreed to be seconded to the Philippine Army, did not receive the promotions they expected and angrily returned to duty with the Philippine Scouts. The officers were "not discontented or disloyal," the *Herald* informed its readers, but they had been unable "to readjust themselves to certain requirements and policies of the Philippine Army." A member of the Manila municipal board was less politic. He denounced the officers as "unpatriotic," and Quezon was equally scathing. "We cannot have and we do not want in the Philippine Army," he told the chief of staff, officers who put their personal ambitions above "the service they can render to the state and to their country." According to Lim, Quezon had been led to believe that he had engineered the "entire walkout of Scout officers." Lim maintained that he had watched the fiasco play itself out from the sidelines. The officers involved who had cared to ask his advice, he informed Quezon, had invariably decided to remain with the Philippine Army. Lim pointed out that he had earlier suggested that officers quit the American army "by retirement or resignation" before accepting a place in the Philippine Army. By not doing so the Scout officers on loan from the American army would always be free to resign their Philippine Army commissions whenever they received orders they did not like.[7]

Eisenhower had been out of the country at the time, but he commented on the episode after returning to the Philippines in early 1939. As Eisenhower told the story, the Scouts had become discouraged by MacArthur's "unsatisfactory" attitude toward them. Several had stormed out, and MacArthur in turn had "worked up the President to the point" that Quezon believed the Scouts were going to seize "the government a la Cuba!" The Scouts eventually convinced Quezon that he had been misinformed about their intentions, and Quezon apologized for the intemperate words he had used at the time.[8] For Eisenhower, the Filipino officers were peripheral to the affair, which was but another example of Quezon's declining faith in MacArthur. By accepting the Scouts' version of what happened, Quezon was explicitly repudiating his military adviser. For Lim, the episode served to boost his standing with the Philippine president, disassociate from the seemingly mercenary Scout officers, and position himself as an alternative to MacArthur and the military mission as a source of military expertise.

Lim himself had tentatively decided to accept an appointment in the not yet formally existent Philippine Army by the end of 1935, though the little evidence available suggests that he may not have jumped at the chance to do so. Burton Harrison, who had returned to the islands in 1935 as a sort of unofficial adviser to the Commonwealth president, learned that Lim was "ready to give up his rank in the United States Army to serve in the Philippine Army *if really needed*—otherwise not." Lim wanted to be in charge of something and hoped to become chief of the Manila police department when the last American to hold that position retired in early 1936. Tellingly, that job, like that of Constabulary chief two years earlier, went to someone with closer ties to Quezon.

Lim soon made the expected decision. The Letran Cadet Corps honored him with the presentation of a golden saber at its commencement exercises on the afternoon of 4 March 1936 (put on display in Brias Roxas's show window on the Escolta, then Manila's main shopping thoroughfare, the sword disappeared during the war); he retired from the U.S. Army under the provisions of a service-connected disability regulation on 30 June. The next day, he became a brigadier general in the Philippine Army. Ultimately, only he and Maj. Mateo Capinpin had been willing to cut their links with the United States Army in order to assume positions in the Philippine Army. Capinpin, the former enlisted man who had been commissioned during World War I when the army faced a pressing need for additional officers, was the solitary Scout officer who had completed thirty years on active duty (as of September 1936) and was thus eligible to retire with full benefits.[9]

Lim took charge of the Philippine Army's War Plans Division, a billet commensurate with his training and interests and one for which he alone was considered to have the technical qualifications. Despite his ambition to do so, he probably had little expectation of commanding the army in 1936. In fact, denoting a senior officer for the new army turned out to be yet another example of an obstacle unanticipated by the military mission. The wholesale conversion of the Philippine Constabulary into the army should have allowed its commanding general to assume the comparable position in the Philippine Army, which would be known, following American practice, as chief of staff. The Chief of Constabulary in 1935—the only Filipino officer wearing a general's stars—was Brig. Gen. Basilio Valdes. A protégé of Quezon and of the late Leonard Wood, Valdes was (like Wood) a medical doctor by training who, until chosen as Constabulary chief in 1934, had spent his entire career in the Constabulary's medical division. Quezon's biographer Carlos Quirino claimed that it was not Valdes's lack of military experience that kept him from becoming chief of staff; rather, Quezon refused to appoint the handsome and affable Valdes, whom many people wrongly thought was from Spain, for fear of being thought "too partial to white people." "I need a darker man," Valdes recalled Quezon as saying. "I need a man who can mix with the politicians, who can play poker with them, and get immediate passage of this law creating the army."[10]

According to a memorandum describing the process by which senior officers were selected that had been published in full after the choice of army chief had become a matter of public controversy, President Quezon had stated his determination that "favoritism, friendship and political preference"—that is, the usual criteria—would play no part in the appointment and promotion of officers in the Philippine Army. He directed MacArthur, as a "quasi-government official completely outside the currents of local and personal interest, to make a complete study of the qualifications of all individuals available for appointment to higher positions in the army, and to submit the resulting slate to the President for approval." In early January 1936 the military mission presented Quezon with a list of "definite recommendations." It settled upon Paulino Santos, a retired PC lieutenant colonel, to be chief of staff, with Valdes as his deputy, both to be advanced to major generals. Eisenhower wrote that "soon after" the mission's arrival in the islands, MacArthur had "announced his intention to secure the appointment of Colonel Paulino Santos as the chief of staff." Santos was, Eisenhower agreed, "the only logical person to serve as chief of staff of the Philippine Army. He understands organization and the necessity for systematic procedure in handling an army."[11]

Now largely forgotten outside of Mindanao's Coronadal Valley, where he founded an agricultural settlement prior to World War II and where a city bears his name, Paulino Santos deserves a less obscure fate. His life story could hardly have been improved upon by rags-to-riches author Horatio Alger Jr., a comparison journalists seldom failed to make when writing about the Philippine Army's first chief of staff. As with Alger's fictional heroes, luck, pluck, and hard work carried Santos to the senior ranks of his chosen profession in a remarkably short time. By most accounts, he fully deserved his good fortune. British Consul General L. H. Foulds would describe Santos as, next to Quezon, the most impressive Filipino he had met. He carried, Foulds wrote, "the proverbial baton in his knapsack."

Paulino Santos had enlisted in the Philippine Constabulary in 1909. Eighteen at the time, he had already spent two years as a schoolteacher in his native Camiling, Tarlac, and had tried but failed to enlist in the navy. Santos had wanted a free trip to the United States, where he hoped to study law, but a cholera outbreak near Cavite at the time closed the navy to Filipinos. As a *soldado*, Santos rose to the rank of sergeant. He spent his entire enlistment with the general service company in Manila, and when he was discharged in 1912, he accepted a clerk's position that provided the opportunity to remain in the city and attend school at night. Over the heads of dozens of other competitors, some of them graduates of military colleges in the United States, Santos won a commission to third lieutenant, and in April 1914 finished at the top of a Constabulary officers' course conducted for newly commissioned American and Filipino officers.[12]

His career did not start well. During his first assignment, to Malolos, Bulacan, Santos made an enemy of the provincial governor and was transferred to Mindanao. He spent the next decade assigned to Moro Province. There he won acclaim for "pushing forward school work, and in develop[ing] agriculture and lines of communication." For these achievements, the Constabulary awarded him the Distinguished Service Star. Nor was Santos lacking in martial ardor. In 1917, in the action for which he eventually (in 1935) received the Medal for Valor (the Constabulary equivalent of the Medal of Honor), Santos led an attack on a *cotta* in Lanao. The high walls of the small fort proved difficult to scale, and every soldier in the attack was wounded.[13] Santos suffered wounds twice in action during his service in Mindanao, and in 1917 he was promoted to captain over the heads of thirty-six ranking first lieutenants.

Hard work combined with good luck to advance Santos's career the following year, when two American officers sang patriotic German songs at a social gathering in Jolo, and both were cashiered. One had been the provincial commander, a position now filled by Santos. Santos was appointed governor of Lanao in 1921, but his rigorous application of the law created a tense situation there, and by early 1924, Governor-General Wood decided that Santos had to go. Wood arranged with General Crame to make it appear as if Santos's services were needed on Luzon and offered Santos the post of adjutant general. Six years later, Santos was appointed assistant district commander for southern Luzon. Barely forty years old at the time, he was clearly destined for the Constabulary's single generalship.[14]

Surprisingly, Santos soon retired. Officially, his retirement was a result of physical disability, but Santos immediately became director of the Bureau of Prisons. He quickly gained plaudits for cleaning up the mess left behind by the bureau's former officials. After only a few months in office, lauded the secretary of justice, Santos "succeeded in creating a general spirit of contentment among the prisoners[,] . . . provided better rations, meted out more humane treatment, outlawed favoritism and undue discrimination, and gave evidence of greater interest in the welfare of the prisoners." As head of the prison bureau, Santos directed a substantial establishment of nearly 4,000 employees overseeing the needs and security of 8,000 to 9,000 prisoners. The system included several large facilities located throughout the islands to which Santos added the penal colony at Davao. It was expected to become "the greatest productive unit of the Bureau of Prisons." A few years later, the British consul reported that he had read a "description of the Penal Colony so lyrical that it must have tempted some of its readers to commit a crime in order to be sent there!"[15] His directorship of the Bureau of Prisons brought out a self-help, self-sufficiency, self-improvement philosophy that Santos would attempt to inculcate in the Philippine Army.

Despite the high regard in which Santos was held by disinterested outsiders, Quezon did not want him. Harrison shared a cabin with Santos during a sea voyage to Mindanao in 1936 and saw that Quezon was "very cold . . . at first" toward the newly designated chief of staff.[16] And Santos had other critics, some of whom thought he was too close to Quezon. Fellow Constabulary officers resented his rapid promotion; Scout officers belittled his lack of formal education and professional military training. "His personality and social grace," read an article in the *Philippines Free Press* defending his appointment, "were considered a handicap, scornfully pointed out as the reasons for his promotion." Even MacArthur's declaration that he, and not Quezon, had put forward Santos's name as army chief did not quell public acrimony and accusations that Santos's appointment represented the reintroduction of "politics in the army."[17]

When presented with the military adviser's recommendations for senior appointments in the army, Quezon temporized. Instead of being installed as chief of staff when the army was officially established on 11 January 1936, Santos was left in his position as director of prisons and given a minor post as secretary to the inconsequential Council of National Defense. Quezon announced that another retired officer, Jose de los Reyes, would be acting chief of staff. The mission had planned to recall Reyes as provost marshal but had never considered him a potential chief of staff. According to the *Philippines Herald*, Reyes was "the man least expected to be appointed." The editor of *Khaki and Red* agreed that the promotion "came as a surprise" and was presumably "but a reward" for long years of loyal service in the Constabulary.[18] Quezon had expected Reyes to "supervise only in a most general way the processes of organizing the Philippine Army," but instead Reyes began issuing "specific orders" that "badly handicapped current work." Reyes almost immediately announced a full slate of staff appointees, all of whom were serving Constabulary officers, even as the military mission negotiated assignments to the same positions with Scout and other Constabulary officers. Harrison met Reyes about the time the army was formed and found him "tired and old, . . . hardly able to cope with new problems," but William Dosser, a long-serving American Constabulary officer who remained in the Philippines after retiring in 1939, thought that Reyes took his role as head of the army seriously and grew "disappointed and disillusioned" when pushed aside after only four months as acting chief of staff.[19]

Finally, MacArthur insisted that Santos assume the army's top position. On 4 May 1936 Santos became head of the army with the rank of major general and a less than ringing endorsement from his commander in chief. Quezon frankly acknowledged that General Santos was not "endowed with the knowledge that a chief of staff should have in building up" the Philippines' national defense, but Santos would, after all, have General MacArthur's guidance. Santos, too, felt compelled to defend his appointment. He asserted that he was "not a professional soldier" but rather a "citizen-soldier," a distinction he thought to be an advantage given the Philippine Army's recruitment basis. And he acknowledged that his appointment had led to discontent in the officer corps. His fellow officers would, Santos commented (with greater optimism than future events would warrant), put patriotism above personal feeling.[20]

There is some evidence, albeit contradictory, that Lim's prominence put him in the running to be chief of staff. While Lim was not the most senior of the twenty-six Filipino officers on active duty in the American army in 1935, he was the one most frequently quoted on military matters in local papers and invariably identified as the Philippines' leading professional soldier. The authors of a lengthy *Army and Navy Journal* article describing the military mission, published as soon as the news of MacArthur's appointment was made public, expressed the opinion that Lim was "a likely selection" as "leader for the Philippine Army," and, in his memoirs, Victor Buencamino recalled that Quezon had sounded him out about who would make the best first chief of staff: Basilio Valdes, Fidel Segundo, or Vicente Lim? Each officer had his strengths, but Quezon was most concerned that the army commander be able to establish "personal and social" contacts with MacArthur and other American officers, whom he had "just asked . . . to come over and help build a citizen army." Buencamino agreed that, in that case, the "socially polished General Valdes" was the best choice.[21] Although Buencamino is clearly in error on one point—leaving aside "acting" chief of staff Reyes, Valdes was the army's second chief of staff, not its first—his recollection reinforces the belief that Paulino Santos was not Quezon's choice as chief of staff.

If social grace trumped the need for professional knowledge, then Lim was not the man for the top job, at least not for now. Smooth interpersonal relationships were not his forte. Issac Nichol, the former Scout officer who had attended the war college with Lim in 1928–29, called Lim an "outstanding" officer and thought he had the respect of all who knew him well. But, Nichol admitted, Lim "lacked tact and could be truculent" and did not have as many friends as the other Filipino officers. He had a temper. In the not-too-distant past, Lim had made the front pages of the Manila press for having knocked down the student colonel of the University of the Philippines cadet corps. Thousands of "carnival-mad guests" had crowded an auditorium to witness the coronation of Miss Philippines at the 1930 Manila Carnival, and Lim told a group of rowdy cadets to "show their education." They responded in a disrespectful manner, and Lim floored cadet colonel Antonio Quirino, a younger brother of Quezon protégé, member of the Philippine Senate, and future Philippine president (from 1948 to 1953) Elpidio Quirino. In response, the students prepared a resolution that denounced Lim's "haughty and insulting manner" and "use of his rank to gain advantage over the students using unnecessary and brutal force and violence." None of this was unknown to the military mission when it set out to pick a chief of staff. Lim's mid-1935 evaluation (extracted from no-longer-extant efficiency reports) read: "Bright—egotistical—arbitrary. Has been frequently in trouble."[22]

Controversy over the selection of the senior army officer was yet another untimely distraction from the mission's major responsibility: beginning the process of registration, conscription, and training. Less than four months separated the passage of the National Defense Act in December 1935 from the initial registration period scheduled for April 1936. Eisenhower recorded in mid-January that little had been done "to organize the administrative machinery to accomplish registration," and he was pessimistic about the government's ability to do so.[23]

On the surface, at least, registration was one thing that went well. Politicians returned home to drum up support, landowners urged their workers to participate, and military officers attended community assemblies to "broadcast the provisions of the [National Defense Act] in the dialect best-known to the majority of the inhabitants." Informed by newspapers, posters, and word of mouth, and urged by army and other government officials, Filipinos came forward in large numbers to register for military service during the first week of April 1936. "Brisk scenes" characterized Manila's five registration sites, and the city surpassed its expected number of registrants by 4 April, halfway through the registration period. Newspapers reported equally heartening news from well beyond the capital city. Nueva Ecija Province witnessed "a record enlistment," despite the fact that it was "supposed to be another hotbed of communists and agitators" opposed to the government's military scheme. Adjacent Pangasinan Province also saw enthusiastic crowds of registrants. Far to the south, in Bacolod, capital of Negros Occidental, the large number of young men who packed the municipal building soon exhausted the supply of registration cards. In Cebu City, the registration period was marked, one newspaper headline read, by "el entusiasmo de nuestros jovenes." The army had expected perhaps 135,000 registrants; by the end of the week, over 148,000 men had registered for military service.[24] A jubilant President Quezon wrote to an American friend: "I am beginning to think that, perhaps, there is more strength and more will power, more determination on the part of the Filipino people than the world has suspected."[25]

This initial enthusiasm would require much effort to sustain. Filipinos themselves had a phrase for the phenomenon: *ningas kugon*, or flaming grass—enthusiasm that blazed brightly at the start of some enterprise but quickly died down to ashes. It was common to all sorts of programs. Once the hoopla surrounding the Commonwealth's inauguration had subsided, the Philippine government would inevitably face the difficult task of maintaining public interest in military service. And despite the outward appearance of success, a close reading of the April 1936 registration figures provided troubling indicators of future problems. While it was true that many more men than expected had registered, in twenty-one of the country's forty-nine provinces totals had failed to meet army expectations. There were important regional differences in registration as well. The city of Manila and two Visayan provinces, Iloilo and Negros Occidental, accounted for 72 percent (11,442 out of 15,915 registrants) of the numbers in excess of projected registration figures.[26]

The "enthusiasm of our young people" was less evident in later registration periods. From 1937 to 1941, nothing demonstrated more clearly the failure of the military system to find support among the population than the declining registration figures and, more important, the declining number of registrants as a percentage of those legally obligated to register. Over 148,000 men registered in April 1936, but only 104,722 did so the following April, though the army had expected close to 140,000 registrants in 1937. The army suggested that 34,000 males born in 1937 must have died prior to reaching age twenty, perhaps in the 1918 influenza epidemic, but subsequent registration periods were even more worrisome (army estimates, in parentheses, follow the actual numbers of registrants for each year except 1938, for which no estimate is available): in April 1938, there were 85,471 registrants; in 1939, 87,604 (97,200); in 1940, 90,733 (119,100); and in 1941, 93,655 (120,200).[27]

If these figures were not discouraging enough, the 1939 census (the first taken in more than two decades) revealed that the army had tended to underestimate significantly the number of Filipino males turning twenty years old each year. The army had supposed that there would be at most about 135,000 registrants in 1936. As we have seen, more than 148,000 men registered. When the 1939 census appeared, however, it showed 166,536 male Filipinos born in 1916 as still living. There had not been too many registrants in 1936; there had been far too few. Of males born in 1917, the census showed that over 138,000 remained alive. The census counted 154,866 twenty-year-olds born in 1918, and there would be 122,058 twenty-year-olds born in 1919 available (barring deaths) to register in 1939. The census listed 183,353 males born in 1920 and alive in January 1939; less than half that number would register in 1940.[28]

Officials conceded that registration figures and the initial appearance of popular acceptance of the military system had been misleading. The British consul passed along the view of his invariably pessimistic American army informants that "many young men above or below the age of 20 registered [in 1936] because of unemployment, with the idea that once in the army they would be housed, fed and clothed." Philippine Army officials surmised that "many over and under aged men not knowing their exact age" had registered "for fear of being prosecuted."[29] The perception that "fear" propelled young men to registration sites in April 1936 belies press depictions of buoyant youths anxious to demonstrate their patriotic ardor, but it is in keeping with registrants' memories, albeit long after the event. One of the first to register in Manila was Jose Malvar. As a grandson of the well-known Batangueño Revolution–era Gen. Miguel Malvar, twenty-year-old Jose's name figured prominently in newspaper accounts of the first military registration. Interviewed nearly sixty years later, however, Malvar defined his overriding attitude toward registration as, in fact, "fear" (his word). Malvar had earlier been expelled from one university for not attending obligatory ROTC drills, and he expected further disruption of his studies at a different school were he not to register for the draft.[30]

Nor was the government prepared to rely on voluntary compliance with the National Defense Act. Many trainees registered because they were told to do so by those in authority. Alfredo S. Morada, who lived near Manila, in Pasig, and turned twenty in 1937, recalled that the town mayor had a list of twenty-year-olds and visited their homes to ensure that each registered. Morada's name was not on the list because he had been born elsewhere, and although his father held a prominent civil position, Morada did not correct the mayor's oversight. He had no interest in the military and suspected that he would be required to leave college to attend a training camp. (Morada completed his university's ROTC course and served with the 43rd Infantry Regiment on Bataan.)[31] A spirit of volunteerism was no more evident in some rural areas. In Pililla, Rizal, Clodualdo Bias registered in 1936 because local officials checked birth records to confirm that all who were supposed to register, did so. Bias's father and uncle had fought the Spanish and Americans at the turn of the century, but their war stories, he recalled, had only convinced him never to be a soldier. He did not want to register, and neither did any other young man he knew in Pililla. Pedro H. Millante, born in 1918 in the southern Luzon province then known as Ambos Camarines (now Camarines Sur), also remembered a local official's arrival with a list of names. Thus news of the requirement to register for military service came to Millante's barrio on remote Lagonoy Peninsula.[32]

The recollections of these former trainees reinforce another of the army's observations: community attitudes were as important as those of individual registrants in the successful working of the military system. Public commitment to the system could help ensure continued high turnouts in registration months. In addition, the providing of training sites and building materials was partly contingent on local government and private means. In Negros Occidental, for example, wealthy citizens made cash contributions in support of the local training program, and landowners provided the space for a training camp at Magallon, one of four in the province. During a visit to Negros in April 1937, Santos expressed his appreciation to the owners of the Binalbagan Sugar

Central for having improved the nearby cadre's barracks and drill grounds. The provincial board agreed to string power lines to the training camp at Murcia and provide the camp with free electricity. It also set an example to other employers by paying the salaries of conscripted government workers while they underwent military training.[33]

But such largesse, while not unique, was neither widespread nor sustained. Just as the individual registrant's interest and commitment waned, so too did the community's. This at least was the army's conclusion. Declining registration numbers, the army came to believe, reflected what "look[ed] to be an indifference on the part of local officials in many provinces" to ensuring a good turnout.[34] Pushed by authorities in Manila and district commanders, provincial administrators carried out periodic drives to punish nonregistrants and draftees who failed to report for training, but these had little lasting effect. Judicial records for the years 1936–1939 for the province of Negros Occidental are available, and the pattern of prosecutions for violating the National Defense Act is telling: 2 prosecutions in 1936; 119 in 1937; 10 in 1938; and 291 in 1939. The records may be incomplete but are nonetheless suggestive. Without constant vigilance and the application of force by authorities, a large number of young men simply did not bother to register.[35]

Despite the publicity that accompanied the introduction of registration and conscription, the military system was poorly understood. This was something else Eisenhower blamed on MacArthur, who had "pooh-poohed the idea" that "an intensive, intelligent, educational program" had been needed in 1936 to gain public support and understanding for the defense plan.[36] Many people did not realize that registration did not mean military service would follow. Here was a major and important difference between the Philippine military system and its European model. In France, for example, with the exception of a few who received deferments and the physically unqualified, most young men registered and most then served in the military. In the Philippines, the fact that many—indeed, most—of those who registered were not called for service only furthered confusion about the system. By design, the majority of registrants would never be called for training, and service lay months ahead even for those who would be. In Manila, of the 7,000 April 1936 registrants, only half would have their names drawn in the May lottery. Only half of those would undergo military training, and for half of those, the training would not begin until July 1937, more than a year in the future. The percentages were similar in every province.[37]

Registrants had expectations of service, yet nothing happened. In the meantime, their interest flagged. They got married, moved away, obtained jobs they were loath to abandon, or wondered why they had to perform military service while others did not. The editor of the Bacolod *Commoner* spoke for many when he observed that the problem with the military system was that many "idle and unemployed young men" who wanted to be soldiers were not called to service while those with livelihoods were.[38] Or, to broaden the lament of the University of the Philippines administrator who decried the army's demand that military science requirements for students be increased: what made the government think that *all* young men made good soldiers?[39] There is evidence that local acceptance boards had already begun to assign to military duty youths who seemed best fitted to perform it. One officer and provincial acceptance board member stated publicly that while the registration process was appropriate, the subsequent "luck of the draw" was not a suitable means of determining who would be required to perform military service. His attitude was shared by others. Francisco Joves, who attended a training camp in 1938 and later obtained an officer's commission, remembered that in his home of Malasiqui, Pangasinan, the local cadre commander and town mayor went over the registration list and selected appropriate candidates for military service—not for them the unpredictability of a lottery.[40]

Like some of those who had joined the national guard in 1918, many registrants thought they were entering an occupation offering long-term employment and financial security. For some, such as Alfredo Morada, who had good prospects elsewhere and little interest in a military career, this was reason to avoid registering for the draft. But for others, being dismissed to their homes after only five and a half months of training was a perplexing and discouraging experience. In the course of refuting charges that the regular army was having difficulty attracting recruits, General Santos revealed that in truth "thousands of men," especially trainees, were "anxious" to join the regular force. The Philippine Army, he explained, offered relatively high pay and good benefits. Later, Santos expressed his fear that many trainees would return to their homes thinking that they were owed jobs as policemen or government agents. As early as April 1937, a Cebu newspaper interpreted the drop in registration figures that year as reflecting the fact that many young men had been disappointed to learn that they were not joining the regular army but only the reserves. Other trainees understood that conscription did not guarantee employment but hoped that it would prove a first step to service in the regular (i.e., permanent) force.[41] This explains the ease and rapidity with which the Philippine Department was able to double the size of the U.S. Army's Philippine Scouts (from approximately 6,000 to 12,000 men) in a period of a few weeks in early 1941. Most of the new enlistees had earlier completed Philippine Army training and were keen to return to military service. Indeed, some of the new Scout enlistees assumed they were returning to duty with the Philippine Army.[42]

Even with the most obliging of populations, the government had to overcome immense hurdles to implement its military program. Army-directed funds comprised a big part of the government budget but remained inadequate for the task being attempted, as did training facilities and weapons. Experienced officers and noncommissioned officers essential for training the conscripts were in short supply. With only a few months to prepare the training program, many of the cadres remained unready to accept conscripts. Reportedly, not even one of the seven sites housing fifteen cadres on Panay Island in the 6th Military District was close to completion at the start of the first training session. Many in the first contingent of trainees had to devote considerable time to clearing land, constructing barracks and other facilities, and engaging in other unsoldierly activities hardly calculated to encourage either them or their friends and relatives to look forward to military service. Nor were existing camps all they should be. Eisenhower visited a number of cadres in central Luzon during the first training session and found them "in a filthy, dirty condition." So unsanitary were cadres that the army ordered cadre officers to have barracks and beds thoroughly cleaned even at the cost of curtailing normal training. Low sanitary standards probably did not bother the trainees as much as they did cadre inspectors, but the old soldier's complaint of "bad food and not enough of it" combined with the inability to return home for the Easter holiday made for many unhappy trainees in 1937.[43]

None of this is to say that the system could not have worked. There was hardly time to find out before the Japanese invasion swept it away. By the 1930s, almost every independent nation in Asia had implemented a conscription-based military system, none with much success, at least initially. But an abrupt decision in May 1936 to accelerate the building of the citizen-soldier army complicated immensely whatever chance the Philippine military system had of succeeding.

Originally, only 6,000 registrants were to be called to service in 1937, the first full year of training. New officers would practice their profession on this small contingent of trainees, 3,000 of whom would train from January to June followed by a second group of 3,000 from July to December. Not until 1942 was the army expected to accommodate the full 40,000 trainees per year called for in the mission's plan. Even this scheme may have been overly ambitious, yet rather than conscript just 6,000 registrants in 1937, it was soon decided that 40,000 registrants be trained that year, and every year thereafter. As Eisenhower would write in a 1942 memorandum destined for President Quezon, this decision had momentous and entirely negative consequences. It caused "considerable changes in construction, in training and organization programs, and eventually resulted in a growing shortage of qualified instructors when trainees [conscripts] reported to training camps." Moreover, he continued, "this change of planning . . . eliminated the financial reserve that was expected to pile up during the first few years and so created difficulties in the purchase of equipment that was desired."[44]

Who made this decision, and why? Eisenhower first credited the military adviser. In a May 1936 diary entry, Eisenhower explained that MacArthur "quite suddenly" determined "to take in the full quota of forty thousand conscripts during the year [1937] instead of the total of six thousand contemplated under the original plan." "After several months' local experience," a staff memorandum quoted MacArthur as saying at this time, he "became convinced that these studies had ignored certain vital psychological factors," primarily that the military system had to be seen to be working throughout the archipelago. Three years later, in April 1939, Eisenhower recorded in the mission diary the details of a lengthy conversation he had with Quezon that told a different story. In regard to a Philippine Army study he had been given that questioned the continued training of large numbers of conscripts when the army faced more pressing needs, Quezon asked Eisenhower why the decision had been made to increase trainee numbers. Eisenhower now remembered that he and Ord had been told in 1936 (presumably by MacArthur, although the general's name was not mentioned) that *Quezon* "believed the psychological reaction of the people would be bad if only a small number of trainees was inducted promptly after the first registration of military manpower." According to Eisenhower, in response Quezon "just said, 'I never heard of such a thing.'"[45]

In his April 1939 conversation with Eisenhower, Quezon "speculated" that MacArthur had increased the number of trainees to produce an army large enough to justify the general's "desire to be Field Marshal." Of course, by that time, attitudes toward MacArthur had changed significantly from what they had been in 1936. Quezon did not mind blaming MacArthur for the problems besetting the army; Eisenhower did not mind recording Quezon's jibes in the mission diary. Quezon had been enthusiastic about the successful draft registration in 1936 and may well have wondered, along with his countrymen, why so few registrants (less than 5 percent, if the original plan had been followed) would subsequently be called to service. Other explanations thus present themselves: One is that MacArthur had discussed the issue with Quezon in 1936, and the two had agreed to increase trainee intakes to gain public support for the endeavor; another is that MacArthur—pushing along his "plot" with Quezon—was determined to demonstrate the usefulness of a Filipino army in meeting America's strategic needs in the Far East and to do so as quickly as possible. In 1936 a sizable Philippine Army was important as a symbol of what the Philippines could offer the United States; having an armed force that was well trained and competently run—something that would take many years to achieve—was secondary.[46]

On these activities central to the success of the military system as devised by General MacArthur and the military mission, Lim appears to have left no fingerprints. He was not involved in registration or camp construction or training of conscripts. Lim had no say in the decision to increase trainee numbers in 1937. Although one of five general officers in the Philippine Army in 1936 and one of only three by 1939, he had no real authority. An article in the *Philippine Forum*, a short-lived monthly from the early Commonwealth, illustrates the point. It revealed that one of Lim's WPD projects was to devise a ten-year schedule for the "gradual transfer" of American army reservations in the islands to the Philippine Army. Fort McKinley would pass into Filipino hands in 1938, Fort Stotsenburg in 1939, Nichols Field in 1940, and so on. Nothing came of the plan, since the posts remained the property of the American army until 1946, and it had neither need nor interest in cooperating with the Philippine Army's chief of war plans.[47]

There remain a very few official HPA WPD documents, one of which describes activity by Lim that may have been consequential. In March and April 1937 Lim made a tour of portions of Mindanao to study the possibility of establishing "a system of army camps and roads focused on the southern coast." He returned concerned about the large Japanese presence on the island. "Superficially," Lim observed, the Japanese appear to be engaged in "peaceful activities," but a careful observer could see that a "slowly creeping but absolutely certain territorial invasion" was taking place. Could there be a connection between Lim's report and the higher-than-average draft quota (as a percentage of total registrants) assigned to parts of Mindanao?[48]

Of greater consequence to the military mission's success was that Lim and other Philippine Army officers began almost immediately pushing back against its assertion of control over all things military related. In October 1936 Bureau of Insular Affairs chief Brig. Gen. Creed Cox heard from the director of foreign sales at Remington Arms that a company representative recently back from Manila had found the army's general staff and the military mission working at cross purposes. Frank Jonas, a well-known arms dealer, had been told upon arrival in the country in August that Lim (who had already initiated correspondence with Remington in the United States) wanted to talk to him. On Eisenhower's advice that he "deal direct with the office of the Military Advisers," Jonas intended to brush off Lim but after "checking up on his importance" decided it would be unwise to do so. Lim introduced him to Rafael Garcia, the army's supply chief, and Jonas learned that the general staff wanted to stockpile millions of rounds of ammunition and build an ammunition-making factory.

When asked how all this could be paid for within the limits of the army's annual appropriation of 16 million pesos, Lim, Jonas reported, "scoffed at the idea" that military spending would be limited to that amount. Jonas found himself in an "embarrassing position": Eisenhower and Ord said one thing; senior Filipino officers said another. When Ord suggested that Jonas discourage Lim from thinking that a factory might be built, Jonas learned that General Santos also wanted a factory and so, too, according to Santos, did Quezon. On the surface, Jonas wrote, the Filipino officers "appeared to be working hand in hand with the Military Advisers [but] they are not going to sit by quietly and be dictated to by the American[s]." The correspondence made its way from the BIA to an alarmed general staff and State Department. Misinformed by Manila press articles that suggested Ord had spoken in favor of building munitions factories in the Philippines (he had not), authorities in Washington instructed MacArthur to put a stop to the whole business.[49]

Lim did not, presumably, act purposely to undermine MacArthur's position with the War Department; his actions nevertheless played a part in creating the unreceptive environment that greeted MacArthur and Quezon when they journeyed to Washington in early 1937 to confront growing official hostility toward the Philippine military system. The Roosevelt administration's subsequent effort to recall MacArthur to the United States and put an end to the military mission would lead, instead, to MacArthur's decision to retire from the United States Army at the end of 1937. He would remain in Manila as the well-paid but increasingly marginalized military adviser to the Commonwealth government.[50]

For Lim, the hard-to-accept reality was that Eisenhower and Ord were doing the things he wanted to do. As Lim had foreseen, the mission's presence marginalized Filipino officers and proved to be a source of endless frustration to those ambitious to shape the development of the nation's military forces. Members of the military mission inspected cadre sites, served on review boards, dealt with the national assembly, and handled weapons acquisition and budget matters. "The closeness of the official relationship" between MacArthur and Quezon, Eisenhower confirmed, further enhanced the mission's status. The field marshal was not formally in the chain of command, but Filipino soldiers looked to him for validation of their ideas and actions, so much so that Philippine Army headquarters eventually informed officers that the practice of corresponding directly with the military adviser without first contacting HPA would have to stop. The adjutant general was not to forward mail to nor "seek advice from" the military adviser "unless the proper general staff section" had first studied the matter and made recommendations.[51]

On paper at least, Lim was as well qualified as Eisenhower and Ord to devise a military system and oversee its implementation. Seniority still counted for a great deal in the U.S. Army, and Lim had graduated from West Point before they had. He, too, had attended the premier army schools, and, having been promoted to lieutenant colonel in November 1935, he outranked them at the time he retired from the army. Furthermore, Eisenhower's refusal to accept advanced rank while seconded to the Philippine Army diminished the standing of those Scout officers who, like Lim, accepted higher grades in the national military forces. American army officers assigned to work in military capacities with the Philippine government traditionally, though not invariably, had carried higher local ranks, but Eisenhower rejected the promotion he had been offered, and because he did so, so too did subordinate Americans on the military mission; as a result, more-senior Philippine Army officers found themselves in the position of seeking "advice" from lesser-ranked Americans.

Of course, it was equally true that whatever the recitation of professional qualifications found in the annually published *Army Register* might suggest, Lim had nothing like the background in wrestling with the problems of army organization and manpower mobilization that Eisenhower had acquired in the six years he had labored in the offices of the undersecretary of war and chief of staff; nor did he share Ord's familiarity with the minutiae of foreign military systems imbibed over many years as an attaché. Lim conceded that they were probably "the best minds that can be selected from the American army," but in sharp contrast to them, he was, as he reminded Quezon in an unused resignation letter from early 1939, intimately familiar with local conditions. Philippine Army officers needed to learn "to use our initiative," Lim argued, and doing that required lessening the authority and influence of the military mission.[52]

Aside from MacArthur, in his letters Lim rarely mentioned members of the military mission. Eisenhower almost never referred to Lim by name, but several negative references to unnamed Filipino officers point to Lim. When Ord, back in Washington in mid-1937 to cajole the War Department into providing more assistance, informed Eisenhower that an arms dealer recently returned from the Philippines (presumably referring to the exchange of correspondence between the BIA and Remington Arms the year before) had claimed that "many officers of the Phil[ippine] Army resent the presence of the American Military Mission and feel it could be dispensed with," Eisenhower responded that Ord should "not give another thought" to a report "alleging our unpopularity with certain elements of the Philippine Army." Eisenhower mentioned no name, but Ord had. "The remark," Ord had written, "seems to be attributed to Lim." Lim did not escape censure in Eisenhower's 1939 "Personal Estimates" either. Eisenhower criticized Lim's conviction that "no Filipino except a Scout can possibly be a good soldier" and his difficulty in working with others in contexts "that require cooperation rather than dictatorial control." In a long report on the army submitted to Quezon at the end of the year, Eisenhower enlarged the criticism: Scout officers, he wrote, "act on the theory that unless a Filipino has been a Scout, he cannot be a good soldier and officer." They "belittle the abilities of others" and promoted disunity in the officer corps. "Most of them," he added, "have an unusual degree of personal ambition." Elsewhere in the report, Eisenhower urged that "training of officers in American Military Schools should be continued as long and as comprehensively as possible." Most graduates benefited from the experience, he wrote, though "occasionally the individual gains nothing but an exaggerated ego." One officer to whom Eisenhower was alluding would have been apparent to President Quezon.[53]

The money rankled too. The disparity in remuneration between Scout officers and Americans working with the Philippine Army was a festering grievance, as was that between Scout and Constabulary officers. Financially, Lim made out better than most other Filipino officers because he drew his U.S. Army retired pay as well as his salary as an officer in the Philippine Army. Most Scout officers refused to retire and thus got only the greater of their American or Philippine Army salaries, with the difference, if any, paid by the Commonwealth government. The Americans enjoyed far larger incomes. Quezon's munificence to MacArthur is well known. When Roosevelt determined to recall MacArthur to the United States in 1937, the army chief of staff responded that for financial reasons, if for no other, MacArthur would instead simply retire and remain in Manila. He had been "reliably informed," Gen. Malin Craig told Roosevelt's military aide Edwin Watson, that in the Philippines MacArthur was receiving "more than three times his salary as an Army officer." Eisenhower, who felt the need to mention the sum several times in the mission diary, pegged MacArthur's income at $33,000 a year plus the free use of an air-conditioned penthouse in the Manila Hotel—the "finest suite of rooms in town," wrote former governor-general Harrison, who had visited all the finest homes in town—"*and* all expenses" (Eisenhower's emphasis). MacArthur even charged the food he and his family ate at the Manila Hotel to the Commonwealth government.[54] By 1938 rumblings about the field marshal's "enormous" income had begun to appear in print. Out of respect for MacArthur's privacy, government spokesmen refused to reveal how much he was being paid but claimed that it was less than British field marshals or military advisers to other countries such as China were paid. MacArthur did not, they emphasized, receive the "absurd" sum of $3.75 per minute that critics claimed.[55]

Had the issue stopped there, Filipino officers might have found the disparity in compensation tolerable. Who could claim achievements or experience approaching that of MacArthur? But it did not. The field marshal was not the only beneficiary of Quezon's largesse. The other mission members enjoyed substantial incomes as well. Eisenhower's annual base pay was $3,500; by 1938 the Commonwealth government was paying him an additional $6,000 each year and at his own insistence had moved him into air-conditioned rooms at the Manila Hotel at no added cost. His salary was greater than that of the commanding general of the Philippine Department. That income, his wife acknowledged, was the one thing that made life in the Philippines bearable. It put them "on easy street for the first time in their lives." Eisenhower's was "a hell of good salary," Jerry Lee had penned in his diary when told by General Santos what the mission's chief of staff was being paid. By then Lee himself was receiving a per diem of fifteen pesos, or $7.50, a pittance by field marshal standards but still a sum that more than doubled his annual income as an army first lieutenant. He was, he admitted, "going to hate to leave it when [he returned] to the United States."[56]

Had Quezon been in the habit of reviewing old correspondence, he might have come across a letter that Rafael Garcia had sent him years before, back during World War I when Filipino Scout officers still hoped through assignment to the national guard to have a say in the development of a Philippine army. Scout officers should be trained for higher positions now, Garcia had insisted, as it would be foolish to rely on the guidance of American officers "who would not stay a day in the Islands when our independence is granted us unless a very lucrative position is offered them."[57] Money was never out of the equation. When in early 1939 Eisenhower sounded out a friend at the war college about joining the mission, he noted that "in addition to your full pay and allowances from the U.S. Army," the Philippine government would contribute "a per diem of $10.00 (gold)." Maj. Thomas J. Davis and Lt. Col. Howard J. Hutter even insisted on collecting per diems from the Commonwealth government for several weeks after leaving the Philippines for good in February 1940. They knew that Eisenhower had been awarded "a bonus of two months per diems" amounting to an additional $1,000 when he had left a few months' earlier. The last letter Eisenhower wrote to George Vargas before leaving the Philippines in December 1939 included a plea that Vargas find money for the U.S. Army enlisted men serving as clerks in the office of the military adviser. They were, Eisenhower explained, the only Americans associated with the military mission not receiving additional pay.[58]

The money issue came up after the war too, when a retired Philippine Scout officer named Amado Martelino sought Eisenhower's aid in getting back pay for service with the prewar Commonwealth army. Martelino, one of those who had been commissioned by examination in 1921, insisted that the Filipino Scout officers assisting the military mission enjoyed the same status as the officers who had accompanied MacArthur to Manila in 1935 and thus deserved similar remuneration. Eisenhower claimed that in fact the mission had arrived surprised to learn that "[its] numbers were not sufficient to carry out the multitudinous tasks developing upon [it]." Only then had it sought the assistance of the Filipino officers. Furthermore, unlike the Americans, who were "detailed to duty in a foreign area," the Philippine Scouts were working on behalf of "their own nationalistic existence." This carefully worded letter was meant to ensure that the U.S. government incurred no financial responsibility toward the former Scout officers and, as the "native" officers evaluation of mid-1935 found in the MacArthur archives makes clear, was not entirely true. It does, however, underline the reality that confronted Lim: the Americans did not expect the Filipinos to do anything other than what they were told to do. Lim found the situation intolerable and placed himself at the forefront of the mission's in-house critics. In June 1939 a memorandum to the British Foreign Office from its consul in Manila noted the "friction between the Philippine Army and the United States military advisers" and identified Lim, by name, as the "leader of the opposition" to the continued presence in the Philippines of General MacArthur and the military mission.[59]

Wedding of Vicente and Pilar Lim, Quiapo district, Manila, 12 August 1917. *Courtesy of Vicente Paolo Lim.*

Pilar Lim, Rafael Garcia, Vicente Lim, and Fidel Segundo at the Lims' house on Vito Cruz Street, Manila, ca. 1938. *Courtesy of Vicente Paolo Lim.*

Vicente and Pilar Lim at home. *Courtesy of Vicente Paolo Lim.*

Calamba from Laguna de Bay. *Courtesy of Michael G. Price.*

Fort San Pedro, Iloilo. *Courtesy of Michael G. Price.*

Regan Barracks, Daraga, Albay. *Courtesy of Michael G. Price.*

Colegio de San Juan de Letran in the 1930s. *Courtesy of Michael G. Price.*

Philippine Scout Company on Corregidor, ca. 1915. *Courtesy of Michael G. Price.*

Lim surrenders on Bataan, 10 April 1942. From a wartime pictorial published by the 16th Division, Japanese Army, in Manila. The Japanese caption reads: "Meeting with Corps chief of staff Limto." *Courtesy of Ricardo T. Jose.*

CHAPTER 6

"We Will Handle the Army to Suit Ourselves"

Changing Direction, 1939–1940

Looked at from the usual perspective—that of Douglas MacArthur's or Dwight Eisenhower's army career—the Philippine military system was in dire condition by late 1939. Eisenhower was anxious to get back to the United States before the war in Europe he knew was coming passed him by once again. He left at the end of the year, finding it preferable to tell confidants that he could no longer afford "to go on teaching schoolboys" rather than to acknowledge that he had also lost his place in MacArthur's confidence. That place now belonged to Richard Sutherland, "an excellent officer" in Eisenhower's words, whom, ironically, Eisenhower himself had recommended as the late James Ord's replacement. With the now-obligatory Philippine Army Distinguished Service Stars pinned to their chests, the two remaining members of MacArthur's original party, Lieutenant Colonel Hutter and Major Davis, sailed from Manila in February 1940.[1] By then, MacArthur was increasingly isolated in what a disdainful High Commissioner Francis B. Sayre called an "ivory tower atop the Manila Hotel," his relationship with Quezon as frayed as that with Eisenhower. According to Sayre, who had replaced Paul McNutt as America's representative in the Commonwealth in May 1939, MacArthur's answers to some hard questions about Philippine defense posed by Quezon early in 1940 had been unsatisfactory. The field marshal's pronouncements had once inspired heady confidence; Quezon now privately referred to MacArthur's statements on the defensibility of the Philippines as "idiotic" and "fantastic." The military adviser was "crazy," Quezon said. Finally, he asked High Commissioner Sayre "to have [MacArthur] relieved." Since MacArthur was a private citizen employed by the Philippine government, it was, in fact, up to Quezon to dismiss his military adviser, and Sayre wisely declined to get involved. Lim may not have been privy to this exchange, but he certainly knew where MacArthur stood with Quezon. The president, he informed his son Roberto in a February 1940 letter, was "disgusted with MacArthur [and] wants to get rid of him."[2]

As 1939 wore on, the confluence of unpropitious trends—the upcoming departure of the much respected Eisenhower, absence of widespread public acceptance of the obligation to register for military service, Quezon's awareness that he had saddled himself with a high-priced and largely ineffective military adviser whom he could not publicly afford to repudiate—had opened the way for Lim to position himself as the voice of Filipino opposition to the military mission's continued presence. Things had appeared very different at the start of the year. Then Lim had seemed determined to resign. When he finally managed an interview with the president at the end of March, he expected a confrontation and was surprised, so he told his son, to find Quezon conciliatory and receptive to Lim's complaints. The president, it turned out, shared Lim's anger at the misconduct of too many officers and wanted to hear more about Lim's ideas for pushing the army in a different direction. Eisenhower noted in the mission diary that MacArthur "has apparently been quite disturbed lately concerning the President's attitude toward the defense program." The general "says that the President does not really believe in the plan, and is ready to sabotage it at the [first] opportunity." Although another nine months would pass before he left the Philippines, "more and more," Eisenhower wrote at this time, "it becomes obvious that constructive action on this job has almost ceased." Eisenhower cannot have been as unaware of what was going on as this diary entry suggests, because Lim wrote that he had told Eisenhower the same thing he had told Quezon: too many resources were being used to create "an army of enlisted reserves without adequate trained officers." This was not news to Eisenhower, who had himself railed in the mission diary about the "hordes" of trainees, but he lacked Lim's freedom to criticize MacArthur's ideas to Quezon, though the Commonwealth president had given him the opportunity to do so, often enough. In other words, Eisenhower's cessation of "constructive action on this job" was but the flip side of Lim's "from now on the Philippine Army will be run by the Chief of Staff with the help of the Central General Staff"—on which Lim, of course, would be the senior staff officer. This explains why Eisenhower decided that, after three years of doing so, he could no longer suffer the "frequently irritating and patience[-]trying" practice of dictating to Filipino stenographers and why there is virtually nothing about the activities of the military mission in his diary after March 1939, even though Eisenhower remained in the islands until the end of the year.[3]

The Central General Staff proceeded to kick props out from underneath "MacArthur's plan." In June 1939 a conference between President Quezon and senior officers of the army and military mission provided the opportunity to air conceptual differences over the army's direction. The conference had ostensibly been called to discuss the question of whether "training would be improved by a greater concentration of stations for the instruction of trainees and if so, [would] mobilization efficiency be adversely effected?" But in a cover letter to a twenty-page report on the issue ultimately submitted to Quezon six months later, General MacArthur acknowledged that "during the consideration [of the issue] a suggestion for discussion was made as to the possible effect that would result were added emphasis to be placed at this time on the professional component, with a consequent diminution of the reserve element." MacArthur was adamantly opposed to such a reorientation of the national defense plan, which he equated with replacing the citizen army with a professional force. The sixteen members of the board who prepared this report were supposedly unanimous in concluding that "there shall be no diminution in the number [of men] trained annually." In fact, the report had been reworded to disguise the growing divide between MacArthur and the Central General Staff, which had nearly led to the issuance of a minority report by the Filipino members of the board.[4]

Eventually signed by both MacArthur and Philippine Army chief of staff Maj. Gen. Basilio Valdes, the report nonetheless stipulated that "experiments in the cadre training of high school cadets be undertaken" not later than January 1941. Thus began the turn away from the concept of "universal service, with equal liability for all" that stood at the center of the military system. Financial pressure played a part (or at least provided an excuse) in the decision to reduce the annual number of trainees; nevertheless, the decision played into the hands of in-house critics of the military system. Emboldened to strike out on their own and even suspicious of MacArthur's competence, in the short time remaining before the war general staff officers would increasingly focus on the Philippine Army's need for officers. Lim and other army officers had convinced Quezon that too much money and effort had been wasted on training large numbers of conscripted enlisted men while many officers remained, as Lim put it, "not even half-baked." President Quezon would state publicly that the defense-building process was being slowed because the army had "been training men so rapidly that there [was] a lack of trained officers."[5]

Already the army had decided to reduce the annual intake of trainees by 25 percent. It would order fewer than 30,000 conscripts to the training camps for 1939, and the number of trainees was reduced even more, to 25,000, in 1940. Lim wrote that the army wanted to call up even fewer conscripts but was concerned that doing so would alarm the public. But a mere 5,802 men would attend the January–June 1941 training period.[6] In addition, to focus on presumably more-trainable recruits, the army implemented high school cadre service. Fourth-year high schoolers who were at least seventeen years old and physically fit were required to attend military training in April and May. The army began conducting training at high schools from January to March of each year to prepare graduating seniors for summer cadre service.[7] The reduction in trainee numbers also allowed the army to concentrate training in a few well-established camps. By early 1941 more trainees would be reporting for duty to Camp Murphy near Manila and Camp Del Pilar (Camp Dau) on the Stotsenburg reservation than to all of the other training cadres of the country's ten military districts combined.[8]

It is tempting to speculate—and the available evidence allows for little more than speculation—that growing social discord during the Commonwealth period also contributed to the decision to restrict military service to the "better off" and more politically reliable segments of society. Confrontation between haves and have-nots was nothing new, but prior to 1935 the *independencia* rhetoric of nationalist politicians like Quezon had masked much of the country's internal discord. With independence promised for 1946, peasants no longer felt a need to subordinate demands for change to the imperative of presenting a common anticolonial front.[9] President Quezon responded by articulating a policy of "social justice," but whether that policy meant the poor were to be aided in any significant way, or instead the policy was intended to provide rhetorical cover to subvert peasant aspirations, remains a topic of dispute. Nonetheless, by 1940, Quezon had "moved systematically to destroy the independent peasant organizations" and eventually placed seven central Luzon provinces under Constabulary control.[10]

In such an environment, the government grew wary of giving military training to and placing weapons within reach of disaffected elements of society. This had been one of the reasons High Commissioner Murphy had opposed the activities of the military mission in 1935–36, and agitation in the provinces did draw the army's concern. There had been public speculation at the time of fighting in Lanao in 1937 that rebellious Muslims included army trainees who had stolen weapons from local cadres. Three years later, in response to labor unrest at the Calamba Sugar Estate in Canlubang, to cite one case for which a rare general staff document exists, the army reported that while the cadres were not affected, it had taken steps to ensure that weapons stored there would not fall into the strikers' hands.[11] Although there are few documented examples of government concern that continuance of the military system might embolden potential dissidents, well-known activist and Hukbalahap leader Luis Taruc may have had a good sense of what was being said privately among the governing elites. "There had been much talk before the war of a citizen army," he wrote in his autobiography, "but nothing had come of it. The thought of an armed peasantry did not sit well with the well fed of the country."[12]

As Taruc's words underscore, there had always been a strong class element in the working of the conscription law, or at least the suspicion that the "well fed" might avoid military service themselves. The members of the constitutional convention's national defense committee, who presumably knew the nature of their countrymen, had taken it for granted that adopting anything other than compulsory military service would lead to "the sons of the wealthy evad[ing] the sacred duty of defending their country." Universal registration had found favor among Filipino elites as a means of preventing any perception of a "rich man's war; poor man's fight," but while all males in theory registered for military service at the age of twenty, the sons of well-to-do families did not always appear on lists of trainees. There was nothing surprising about this. Manipulation of the registration process is common to most such systems. When the draft was implemented in 1936–37, General Reyes had commented to Burton Harrison that there had been a conscription lottery in Spanish times as well, but Reyes's name had not been drawn for service "because his family [had been] influential." The army admonished local acceptance boards to follow procedures and regulations strictly; otherwise, their actions "may give rise to suspicion and may substantiate rumors being circulated by some elements that only the sons of the poor are being sent to the training camps while the sons of rich and influential persons are being exempted or granted deferments."[13]

One way to target the better off—the "moneyed and upper classes" who, Lim complained, seemed indifferent to the army and national defense—and address the army's concern that potential leaders be developed was to renew the focus on ROTC. In the 1920s Philippine ROTC had been only fitfully embraced and produced few graduates. The promise of independence seems to have done little to make ROTC more popular. Articles poking fun at cadet pretensions or complaining of the onerousness of the ROTC obligation had been a staple of the student newspaper of the University of the Philippines before 1936 and continued to be so after the university affiliated its cadet program with the new Philippine Army. Law student Corban Alabado expressed what seems to have been a common attitude just before the outbreak of war: "Many students regarded ROTC as a course to be taken only as a requirement for graduation and all they wanted was to get it over with as quickly as possible." By 1941 enough students were evading ROTC by purposely taking fewer than the ten academic units that defined full-time status and thus mandated ROTC participation that the army was allowed to insist that students taking fewer credits still had to participate in cadet training.[14]

Enrollment statistics tell a similar story. The number of students attending the University of the Philippines rose throughout the Commonwealth period, but participation in the mandatory ROTC program declined. How did more students equal fewer cadets? One explanation is that exemptions were being abused. Documentation is sparse, but when student-cadets were called to active duty in August and September 1941, the university's board of regents was compelled to ask why some colleges had obtained so many exemptions. In the worst case, twenty-nine of the forty-nine students ordered to service from the College of Medicine had received deferments based on physical disability.[15]

Student disinterest in military training was not limited to the publicly funded University of the Philippines. The private University of Santo Tomas had begun a mandatory ROTC program in September 1936, but student support proved of short duration. By the start of the 1940–41 school year, there were so many "slackers" on campus that the *Rector Magnificus* issued "a strong ultimatum": get enrolled in ROTC or face suspension or dismissal from the university. "This year," the rector warned, "this rule will be strictly enforced."[16] The rule may not have been enforced (though the names of students recommended for dismissal were printed in the school paper), but if further evidence of the unpopularity of military training on college campuses were needed, it came with the government's approval of a mandatory three-year cadet program to begin in June 1940. The cadet reporter for the University of the Philippines student newspaper admitted that news of the added year had come as a "severe blow" to the students. Believing that they had "once and for all gone through the perhaps most hatedly wearisome phase of college life," he wrote, the students "were staggered by the enforcement of the new law."[17]

Mirroring the wider public response to annual registration, the Philippine Army–sponsored cadet corps started out strong but soon fizzled. Nine schools implemented ROTC programs in 1936, five in 1937, two in 1938, and only one in 1939. To the extent it was popular, ROTC found favor largely as a means of avoiding the draft, since completion of the two-year basic course exempted students from having to report to a training cadre. For that reason, ROTC was a major selling point for both public and private schools. For example, a few enthusiastic students and teachers had commenced an informal cadet program at Central Philippine College in Iloilo in September 1936, but college trustees had rejected making participation mandatory. They only relented after students complained that failure to offer ROTC would make them eligible for conscription. Confronted with the potentially adverse impact on enrollment, an officially sponsored cadet program began functioning in September 1937.[18] ROTC was thus sold less on patriotic grounds than on the relief it provided from the peasant's even more onerous citizen-soldier duty. When an eight-weeks-long summer camp was added to the ROTC program in 1939 in order to improve the quality of training and to bring college cadets into contact with enlisted trainees, school administrators insisted that ROTC be made mandatory for all colleges. They reasoned that with two months of training tacked on to the existing cadet course, potential students would just as soon take their chances at having to attend a training cadre. If ROTC was not mandatory, students would go to those schools that did not require it. Thus in 1940 the number of new ROTC programs jumped to ten. Another six were added in 1941. Eisenhower—whose thoughts on this matter were precisely the same as Lim's—urged the government to press on. He told Quezon that "no graduating certificate should be obtainable by an able bodied male student, unless he is also a graduate of R.O.T.C." Furthermore, any reserve officer who then failed to perform required military service should be punished by law and denied employment in "any government or quasi-government organization."[19]

Lim's interest in ROTC with its potential to provide the army with a pool of junior leaders reflected a recurring theme of his letters—the poor quality of officers in the army. "We have an army of crooks," an exasperated Lim exploded in more than one letter. Whether it fell within his purview as war plans' chief or not, Lim determined to take up the thankless but essential task of weeding out incompetent and even criminal officers. The initial mistake, at least in Lim's view, was converting the Constabulary into the army rather than create an officer corps mostly from the ground up, as he had recommended in the Bureau of National Defense Bill. Consequently, the new army suffered from low standards of professional knowledge and conduct on the part of too many officers, especially those of long service in the Philippine Constabulary, in which favoritism in assignment and corruption of law enforcement by politics were two long-standing traditions. This was not just Lim talking. Chief of Staff Santos once began a speech to academy graduates by warning them against the practice of seeking a "preferred assignment in a certain district." This had been one of his "greatest disappointments" in the old PC, which, he lamented, continued to be a problem in the Philippine Army.[20]

Outright criminal behavior was another matter. Eisenhower learned from Quezon that the "results of several courts-martial" had led the president to "distrust our present corps of officers." "He considers, properly," Eisenhower wrote, "that these courts have condoned offenses for which dismissal, and even prison sentences, would have been appropriate. He cited several instances."[21] The larger problem was the cascading effect of unqualified officers overseeing the training of other would-be officers who were then sent out as cadre officers with inadequate skills and experience to train the conscripts under their command. The end result was summarized for army intelligence by an American manager of a sugar central who visited one training camp and observed that the officer in charge was "still so patently a civilian that I felt sorry for him." MacArthur, this American quipped, "must have his tongue in his cheek when he sounds off about [the Philippine Army] or else he doesn't visit the training camps."

A 1939 memorandum destined for General MacArthur enlarged on the problem thusly: "The whole program [has been] slowed down by the disappointing discovery that all instruction, even for older officers, had to begin with fundamentals." "Most officers" demonstrated a lack of "professional knowledge and training" and, worse still, showed a "distinct reluctance . . . to accept responsibility." Furthermore, the memorandum continued, the high command had "been slow to adopt a firm attitude toward subordinate commanders and staff officers designed to compel a proper discharge of responsibility. Regulations for elimination of unfit officers have been administered clumsily and inefficiently." Of course, as Lim repeatedly pointed out, it was General MacArthur's insistence on training large numbers of enlisted reservists that led to the commissioning of large numbers of unqualified officers.[22]

This did not mean Filipinos could not be good officers, but, as Lim put it, "the officer corps has to build up its tradition, which everybody knows will take years to develop, not to speak of the number of years that it will take to train them in the different phases of the science of war." Even a sympathetic American observer like Col. Frederick Blesse, who worked with the Philippine Army in 1937–39, admitted that "leadership [was] still something of a problem in the Philippine Army." However, he thought that the commissioning programs based in the military academies and universities could produce "conscientious and capable" officers. Like Blesse, Lim agreed that the Philippine Military Academy would eventually solve the problem, but that would take years to achieve. (Its first class graduated in 1940.)

One way of addressing the problem was simply to re-create the Constabulary and reassign problematic former PC officers to it. Eisenhower noted in the mission diary that Quezon had said he wanted to "separate the Constab[ulary] from the rest of the Army" as early as April 1938. Eisenhower "wrote the bill [and] message [to the assembly] to accomplish this" and commented that "this would be a fine thing for the Army!" Some historians have interpreted this as yet another way that Quezon was showing his disapproval of MacArthur by stripping the field marshal of resources, but Lim told his sons that it was all about the necessity of improving the officer corps: "We have a plan of completely separating the two institutions," he wrote, "so that officers in the Philippine Constabulary will not have anything to do whatsoever with the officers of the Philippine Army," and he took credit for pushing the idea on Quezon. "Believe me," he told his son Roberto in his last letter of 1939, "by the time you join the service, we will have this Army pretty well cleaned up of crooks, liars, and inefficients."[23]

The diminishment of the military mission's stature and redirection of the army did not fulfill Lim's personal ambition. The army's senior post remained beyond reach. Passed over for the appointment when the army had been founded in 1936, Lim saw a second opportunity to become chief of staff arise in late 1938, when Quezon decided to replace Paulino Santos. Quezon claimed that Santos's relief was based on the American policy of changing chiefs of staff regularly, but Santos did not last the three years in office Quezon now proposed, let alone the four years most American chiefs of staff remained in Washington. Santos had not been Quezon's first choice for army chief in 1936, nor had Santos overcome internal army opposition to his appointment. Nevertheless, he had made a distinct mark on the army. He was convinced, Santos told the first group of officers to attend the Reserve Officers' Service School in Baguio, "that no people could make its defense effective that fail to grasp the importance of the agricultural, industrial, and financial forces of the nation." It was a theme he returned to time and time again in the many public speeches he made as the army's chief booster and public spokesman. He determined to use the cadres to introduce trainees to modern agricultural methods and sold both MacArthur and Quezon on the idea despite, as General Santos recalled, the "opposition . . . of my own colleagues." Army funds thus would be better expended on vocational training that would make reservists "useful in their respective communities."[24] But when Santos went, so too went any pretense that the army was seriously committed to vocational training. In 1939 army headquarters decreed that the term "vocational training" was no longer to be used. A trainee would engage in "industrial work" only enough "to break the monotony of his military existence and incidentally to provide him better food at less cost." Such labor was neither to be instructional nor to interfere with military training.[25]

Eisenhower thought that an additional nail had been hammered into Santos's coffin toward the end of 1937, when Santos was repeatedly in the news as a result of operations against Moros in Lanao and then because of the crash of Santos's aircraft while returning from Mindanao. In this dramatic episode Santos, Fidel Segundo, and American army pilot Jerry Lee were marooned on an isolated island off the east coast of Luzon for several days. The resultant publicity "irritated the President no end," Eisenhower wrote. The president's unhappiness with Santos was no secret. A reporter for the *Philippines Free Press* wrote that Quezon had responded to news of the recovery of General Santos and his colleagues with vigorous praise for the U.S. Army, whose pilots had found and recovered the officers, but with "ominous silence" regarding the Philippine Army. Santos had said that he and Segundo had talked about "who would be the next chief of staff if they were not found," but "now," the reporter observed, "it looked as if there were going to be a new chief, anyway." Quezon and others were determined "to relieve Santos [and] are working up an artificial sentiment of resentment against him," Eisenhower concluded. He credited

Santos's problems ultimately to racial politics: Santos was not a Spanish mestizo, and those who were hated having a "Malay" in such a high-profile position. When Santos was formally replaced, Eisenhower hosted a luncheon for him at the Manila Hotel to help disguise the fact that Quezon was firing the army's first chief of staff.[26]

An equally intriguing story holds that Santos was removed from office because he had acquired the reputation of being anti-American. Santos certainly had warm ties to individual Americans. Lieutenant Lee was a favorite. Santos was so overcome with emotion at a ceremony held to award Lee the PA's Distinguished Service Star that he could not speak and had to ask another officer to continue the presentation. Eisenhower characterized Santos as one of the "most able executives" he had met when the mission arrived in the Philippines in 1935 and, three years and many disappointments later, still thought him to be "a much abler man than his successor." However, Santos disliked the army's continuing reliance on American advisers. He was willing to concede that incompetence and irresponsibility in the officer corps had led the military adviser to rely more heavily on Americans than should have been necessary. Addressing fellow officers about the poor state of sanitation at the training cadres and MacArthur's decision to have U.S. Army officers inspect the camps, Santos lamented that "again the picture of the American appears, . . . and again I wonder how long we must be dependent upon them for these rudimentary inspections!" The comment was meant as chastisement for Filipino officers who could not be relied on to carry out even simple tasks, but "gratitude for this people who have done so much for us" eventually turned to resentment. The Philippine Department's intelligence office began to take note of disquieting tales about Santos's proclivity to denounce the American presence in the islands. The journalist and publisher A. V. H. Hartendorp told a story of having attended a cocktail party at MacArthur's Manila Hotel suite in late 1938 at which Santos "had a cocktail too many" and said to those around him that it was "tragic that the Philippines might be drawn into a war with Japan in which we would not be concerned." MacArthur claimed to think nothing of the comment, but within a few weeks Santos had been awarded a clasp to his Distinguished Service Star for all he had done "toward the attainment of essential standards of efficiency in the defense forces," put in charge of the Coronadal Valley settlement project, and shipped off to Mindanao. He would still be there when war came to the Philippines, wondering why he had not been recalled to active duty.[27]

When Santos went to Mindanao in late November 1938, Lim was certain that the army had seen the last of him, although Santos's official successor would not be in place until January 1939. For once, Lim viewed Santos's plight sympathetically. Probably no one had a better knowledge of the army, Lim conceded, but Santos's abrasive and egotistical personality—such was Lim's characterization—made him difficult to work with and turned people against him. (It was equally true, however, that no one was better qualified by inclination and experience than Santos to lead the Mindanao settlement project.) But if Lim hoped to be Santos's replacement, he was to be disappointed. An alternative reading of Victor Buencamino's memoirs suggests that at this time Quezon had considered making Lim the next chief of staff but had decided that Basilio Valdes could get along better with the military mission. "Valdes was," an American observer wrote, "a pleasant, mild-mannered man who made an excellent appearance in public. He was always ready to carry out instructions, but Quezon never depended upon his judgment either in military or other matters." Valdes wrote that Quezon had "forced him to accept the [chief of staff] position."[28]

The mission's prominence aside, a major obstacle to Lim's advancement was Quezon himself. Despite his disenchantment with the military adviser, Quezon remained reluctant to place full confidence in Filipino officers. To that extent, MacArthur remained useful as a foil to Filipino leadership of both the Scout and Constabulary varieties.

In some ways, Quezon had more military experience than any of his generals. As a young student in Manila at the turn of the century, he had watched the American assault on the city while serving as a corporal in a Spanish volunteer unit. He had played a more substantial role in the Philippine Revolution, in which he saw field service against the American army as a junior officer. His military record is not well documented, and knowledge of it is largely based on Quezon's own account. Years later, Quezon's Swiss doctor, Anton Trepp, reflected on Quezon's less than always courageous behavior on Corregidor and asked Manuel Nieto if Quezon had really done all the brave things he claimed to have done during the revolution. "Yes!" snorted Quezon's longtime aide, "[from] behind a tree." But in speeches made during the early Commonwealth years, Quezon drew on his military experience again and again to make this observation: Filipino soldiers, he said, were hardy and brave, but their lack of training and equipment left them horribly unprepared to meet a modern army on the battlefield. "We had no weapons to speak of and did not know how to use the few that we had," he was quoted as saying. The time came "when our best defense was our legs." The Filipino army "had no discipline; no organization. The war against America was no war; that was slaughter, pure and simple."[29]

Moreover, he had noted with approval the deference paid to foreigners with military experience who had aided in the war against the United States. Quezon had served under Gen. Tomas Mascardo in Pampanga, but the general had known "nothing about military strategy and tactics." Thus, he had appointed a Spanish colonel named Leysan—an officer "of ability and distinction," in Quezon's words—to be his chief of staff. Quezon also remembered that when Mascardo and Leysan had prepared a plan to attack the town of Angeles, Pampanga, they had made certain to consult the veteran Japanese officer, a Capt. Tei Hara, who was visiting the camp.[30] Still later, in 1914, Quezon had urged the retention of U.S. Army officers for service with the Philippine Constabulary after an army appropriations bill had included a provision restricting the army's ability to assign officers to the PC.[31] In all other ways he was a fervent supporter of Governor-General Harrison's contemporaneous Filipinization policy, but as Lim would discover, military matters were an exception to Quezon's insistence on a Philippines run by Filipinos—or at least by Vicente Lim.

Lim got a taste of Quezon's attitude when he reported to the presidential palace on 17 May 1939 to accept his advancement to deputy chief of staff. Hardly a week before, Lim had confidently confided to his son Roberto that Quezon "was rather rabid or displeased" with something MacArthur had done and implied that, soon, the establishment of a defense department would "do the real thing about the army," presumably by weakening MacArthur's influence. Lim was in for a rude surprise. Quezon used the opportunity to remind both the former Constabulary and former Scout officers that neither group had the background to direct the Philippine Army. "For some time," the president announced, "we will need the help, the leadership, and the advice of General MacArthur." Officers were required to remain behind after guests had departed to hear Quezon blast the many "untrue statements made by army officers and falsifications of documents and returns, all of which had been condoned by the Philippine army courts." He "was going to see that this ceased." Many officers "seemed to think," he continued, "that they were indispensable, but he, the President, was prepared to show them that they were not." Constabulary officers—"many [of them] liars and crooks," Segundo recorded Quezon as saying—were the specific target of Quezon's rebuke, but Scout officers heard some hard truths too. Whether they could be loyal "to their own country" had been an unanswered question when the army was created, Quezon admitted; furthermore, their expectation of the same high ranks given to Americans "temporarily assigned" to the Constabulary in years past was unrealistic if they expected to hold "permanent position[s]" in the Philippine Army. A chastened General Lim said nothing about his promotion in his next letter but did comment on the more comprehensive separation of the Constabulary from the army, a goal long sought by Lim. "At least," he wrote, "President Quezon listened to me in this respect."[32]

Toward the end of 1939, there remained for Lim the possibility of gaining ascendancy over the army through the new National Defense Department. The formation of the department is usually interpreted as Quezon's method of distancing himself from MacArthur and putting limitations on MacArthur's supervision of army-related activities. By 1939 Lim certainly hoped and expected it to have that effect, but since the idea of creating a defense department went back at least to the first half of 1936, presumably Quezon had not meant to send a message to MacArthur that his services were no longer needed. Eisenhower wrote in the mission diary in November 1939 that Quezon had begun talking about creating such a department "a couple of years ago." He did not say why Quezon wanted to do so, but at the time MacArthur had objected and Quezon had dropped the idea. Lim learned from Quezon in May 1939 that he intended to create the department, soon the news appeared in the local press, and the Assembly—obedient as ever to Quezon's dictates—promptly passed a bill authorizing the president to establish the department. MacArthur reacted with alarm. After a "satisfactory talk" with Quezon, however, the idea was seemingly dropped. Then, in a speech given at Lingayen in mid-October, Quezon announced that he had chosen court of appeals judge and former Pangasinan provincial governor Teofilo Sison to be secretary of national defense. The new secretary promptly told Quezon that since MacArthur carried no weight with the American government and did little to earn his "exorbitant" pay and allowances, he should be dismissed. Jose Yulo, the Speaker of the Assembly, added that a majority of legislators were willing to see MacArthur go and would like to see him replaced by either Valdes or Lim.[33]

Publicly, Quezon stated that the National Defense Department served notice of the new nation's determination to defend its inheritance, and some observers speculated that with the formation of the department the defense program would be "substantially accelerated."[34] Quezon may simply have been creating additional career opportunities for senior officers, which might explain why one assemblyman proposed an amendment to the defense department bill stipulating that no "military man" could head it. (Lim's brother-in-law Claudio Sandoval ensured that amendment's defeat.) General Valdes had been mentioned as the potential first secretary of national defense, and Lim was reportedly Sison's choice to be the new department's undersecretary. Lim turned the offer down because he did not like Sison and was holding out for the top spot.[35] Valdes still had over two years to serve as chief of staff; in the interim, Lim could console himself with the knowledge that he was, to quote a writer for the *Philippines Herald*, "the country's first professional soldier, and its outstanding military scholar" and would undoubtedly become the army chief of staff with the expiration of General Valdes's term of office.[36]

Although disappointed by his failure to be advanced to the head of the army, as deputy chief of staff Lim was now in charge of the day-to-day management of the army. (It is probably not coincidental that Eisenhower chose this very time to stop maintaining the mission diary.) Fewer men were being trained at better facilities. Officer development had moved to the forefront. The Philippine Military Academy would graduate its first class in a few months' time. The army was headed in a new and sounder direction.

The war in Europe changed everything. In Manila, as elsewhere, the events of late 1939 presented contradictory lessons. Poland's military forces had been easily defeated by the Wehrmacht in September, yet the plucky Finns had bloodied the nose of the Red Army in December. Furthermore, the Russo-German accord in August 1939 had led some to believe that with Russia's freedom to turn its attention east, Japan might seek accommodation with the United States in Asia, lessening the Philippines' security concerns. If, as is often claimed, Quezon was losing confidence in the military system and despaired of successfully defending the archipelago, his lieutenants had not yet gotten the message. Both the secretary and undersecretary of the newly established National Defense Department used the occasion of the army's December 1939 graduation ceremonies to reaffirm support for the Philippine military system. Addressing graduates of an officers' training course at Camp Ord, Tarlac, Secretary Sison drew attention to Finland's (so far) successful defense of its territory. With the Philippines' favorable geographical position, larger population, and the continued building of a "strong and trained army," he held "great faith in [Filipino] ability to resist foreign invasion." The next day, attending the graduation of forty probationary third lieutenants of the field artillery training school at Camp Dau, Pampanga, Sison expressed the belief that the defense program had produced satisfactory results and would continue "according to plan." A few days earlier, before the graduates of the army's first cavalry officers' course at Camp Claudio, Undersecretary Leon Guinto had frankly acknowledged that "recent events in Europe" had led many to question the ability of Filipinos to defend themselves. The task of the officers seated before him was not just to have confidence in the defense system, he said, but to inspire confidence in others. Filipinos must "shake off [their] inferiority complex" and strengthen their belief in the defensibility of the archipelago. Just as in 1916 Verdun-bound French soldiers had proclaimed, "They shall not pass," Guinto asserted that Filipino soldiers must take as their motto "They shall not land." Quezon's comments to the opening session of the national assembly in January 1940 struck a positive note as well. He observed that the army reserve forces were now more than 100,000 strong, a clear sign "that the youth of the land have responded patriotically to the call of duty" and an equally clear indication that "much has been accomplished in the execution of the National Defense Program."[37] Could their commander in chief be any less patriotic?

Public bravado masked private doubt for a while, but as the Commonwealth entered its fifth year the doubts began to emerge. Quezon, now persistently ill with the tuberculosis that would end his life in August 1944, was having second thoughts about just how much had been achieved in the way of national defense. Germany's success against Czechoslovakia and Poland, he admitted, led him to fear that perhaps monies spent on national defense were being wasted.[38] In an impromptu speech given at Rizal Memorial Stadium before the graduates of the Philippine Normal School on 26 March 1940 (and broadcast over Manila Radio KZRM), Quezon reportedly "startled his audience by asserting that he was no longer of the opinion that the Philippines [could] be defended against the aggression of a first class power." "I am saying this," he told his listeners, "because I want you to know the truth." A few days later, on 1 April, at the Manila Hotel Winter Garden—in MacArthur's backyard, so to speak—Quezon told an audience of alumni of the 1915 class of the University of the Philippines law school that "for a time, for a long time, I have believed confidently in the opinions of some people—some of whom are experts in this line—who have said that the Filipino people can defend themselves successfully against foreign invasion," but, in truth, he himself had grown pessimistic. As was often the case, listeners were not sure what to make of the Commonwealth president's utterances. The High Commissioner reported that no verbatim account of the Winter Garden speech had been published, and confusion persisted as to what exactly Quezon had said and what he had meant. The High Commissioner himself was of the view that Quezon was trying to make things look as bleak as possible in order to bring Filipinos around to the idea of remaining under American protection.[39]

Were Quezon's words a trial balloon intended to spark a reopening of the independence issue? Some senior Philippine Army officers thought so. Lim told his sons in a May 1940 letter that "the independence question is again in the limelight," and the issue might be "re-examined for the best interest of the Filipino and American peoples." But, he conceded, "whoever goes against independence is classed as not a patriot. That has been the biggest instrument of the politicians to gain the favors of the ignorant 'tao' [peasant]." Or were Quezon's comments, as legislator Benito Soliven explained in a lecture he gave on national defense at Taal, Batangas, meant to "galvanize [Filipinos] into effective determination to do their best" to prepare the Philippines for independence and to defend it?

Lim admitted that the senior officers of the army often had little better insight than the general public as to what Quezon really thought and whether his statements would have an impact on the working of the military system. Like everyone else, they read the newspapers and wondered. At the start of 1940, Quezon's mouthpiece, the *Philippines Herald*, reported that the "national defense plan swings uninterruptedly into its seventh semiannual conscription stage today," but soon other papers were hinting that the defense program was being curtailed. The *Manila Bulletin* quoted "authoritative military circles" as saying that the second training session of 1940 would be suspended (it was not) and the number of trainees reduced (it was). The government invariably responded to such articles with statements that the defense program would be "carried out faithfully," without revealing just what the "program" now consisted of. Meanwhile, army headquarters insisted that Filipinos still had to register for military service.[40]

The war gave Quezon cover to do what he been inclined to do for some time—"re-enforce and improve the Constabulary, even at the expense of the army," as Eisenhower had recorded MacArthur complaining as early as March 1939—and the courage to admit that critics of MacArthur's military scheme had been right all long. Lim called the general staff together in mid-July 1940 to talk about a published claim that the army would even be abolished. Quezon, he told them, thought that France's ready defeat showed the improbability of defending the country from an external foe and preferred an army to "keep peace and order." When Lim asked what the others thought of all this, Segundo responded by saying that if Lim understood Quezon correctly, what need was there for an army?

Lim preferred to believe that Quezon's talk was meant to undermine MacArthur, not the army. And the usual examples marshaled to illustrate that Quezon was turning against the army in 1940 can be misleading or are simply wrong. Quezon's cancellation of the 1940 mobilization exercise is frequently cited as an indicator of his determination to cut military spending and to some extent it was, but the military mission itself had since late 1938 contemplated reducing mobilizations to every other year. When Quezon canceled the 1940 exercise, he promised the army that it could carry out a more extensive training exercise for reservists in 1941, which it did. And far from "deemphasiz[ing] ROTC" (another commonly cited indicator of the president's declining faith in the military system), Quezon acquiesced in an army plan to extend mandatory cadet training from two to three years in 1940 and to four years in 1941. More universities would implement ROTC programs in 1940 than in any other year of the Commonwealth. Furthermore, despite widespread speculation (even by Lim) that military expenditures would be reduced substantially, in June 1940 the Assembly approved an army budget for fiscal year 1941 only slightly less than it had authorized for fiscal year 1940.[41]

All of this went by with hardly more public discussion than had accompanied the passage of the National Defense Act in December 1935. On the floor of the national assembly, Cebu representative Miguel Cuenco denounced the supposed reduction in defense expenditures and numbers of men to be trained and asked how such radical change could go unheralded. According to him, only one paper "had commented on it briefly."[42] Another assemblyman was equally suspicious and expressed "vehement opposition" to any reduction in defense spending. "War conscious" legislators introduced a bill to provide 50 million pesos for Philippine defense and another calling for universal military training, just two of nine military-related bills introduced in a special session of the Assembly in July. Segundo, the army's assistant chief of staff for training and operations, pointed to this "healthy feeling among the members of the assembly that the [army] budget should be increased" to suggest to General Valdes that the army prepare its own budget estimates and not limit itself to working within the administration's inadequate "dictated budget." Lim showed a copy of Segundo's memorandum to MacArthur, who rejected it out of hand. He reminded Lim that Quezon could raise and lower the budget "at will." Segundo should spend his time putting army training "on a proper basis," MacArthur said, and Lim should distance himself from Segundo's activities if he hoped to prosper in the army. That proved to be sound advice, since about this time the general staff was reorganized and Segundo—in certain respects "the most able officer of the army," in Eisenhower's evaluation—found himself sent off to Mindanao at the end of 1940.[43]

Lim's struggle in 1939–40 to reorient the Philippine military system paralleled a new Philippine Department commander's attempt to reinvigorate the moribund American defense posture in the islands. Perhaps more diplomatically than truthfully, Quezon had praised Maj. Gen. Lucius R. Holbrook's "incalculable assistance in the development of our national defense," but Holbrook's departure in early 1938 had, for the most part, put an end to active collaboration between the American and Philippine armies. Holbrook's successor, Maj. Gen. John M. Hughes, allowed a small number of Philippine Scouts to continue working with Philippine Army cadres and had had a few American officers observe the army's mobilization training in May 1939. He did nothing to further whatever plans Holbrook had had to incorporate the Philippine Army into department war plans. Maj. Gen. Walter Grant did virtually nothing noteworthy when he commanded the department from July 1939 to May 1940. There continued to be little interaction between the military adviser's office and the local army headquarters.[44]

Things changed in mid-1940 when the Philippine Department received a new commanding general, the department's sixth since MacArthur had come to the islands in 1935. Maj. Gen. George Grunert had arrived in Manila aboard the *U. S. Grant* on a previous tour of Philippine duty in October 1936. It was his first in the islands since having served more than thirty years earlier with the 11th Cavalry Regiment around Vigan in northern Luzon toward the end of the Philippine-American War. On this second tour of Philippine duty, Colonel Grunert briefly commanded the 26th Cavalry Regiment (PS) at Fort Stotsenburg. He was soon promoted to brigadier general and command of MacArthur's old outfit, the 23rd Infantry Brigade at Fort McKinley. He completed his tour of duty on 3 November 1938 and left the Philippines determined to return as soon as possible. In a letter written in June 1939, outgoing chief of staff Malin Craig informed Grunert that while he did not know what policy his replacement, George Marshall, would follow with respect to the assignment of general officers, he saw "no reason why you should not be seriously considered for the Philippines if you wish it." Barely seven months later, on 14 February 1940, Grunert was back in Manila and in command of the Philippine Division. A major general since December 1939, Grunert became commanding general of the Philippine Department on 31 May 1940, when General Grant returned to the United States.[45]

Grunert's years in the archipelago corresponded to a period of increasing tension between the United States and Japan, but America's condemnation of Japanese behavior did not, at first, translate into military action. As commander of America's exposed military garrison in the Far East, there was little reason for Grunert to think that the War Department would be sympathetic to his entreaties for men and matériel. Nevertheless, according to one officer who met Grunert aboard the *Grant* en route to Manila, Grunert was convinced that the United States would soon be at war with Japan and was "anxious to command our forces in the Philippines."[46] Like George Dewey in 1898, Grunert may simply have reasoned that as an older officer, approaching mandatory retirement, he had to be where the action was likely to be when the shooting started to stand a chance of participating in the war he felt was coming. The one new development observed by Grunert from 1936 to 1938 had been the creation of the Philippine Army. With the commencement of conscription in January 1937, there was now the promise that a large, militarily trained body of men would be raised by the Commonwealth government, and until 1946, when the islands would become independent under the provisions of the 1934 Tydings-McDuffie Act, this army remained legally available for use by the United States government.

At least a few individual officers in the Philippine Department began to think that the Philippine Army could help meet the needs of the U.S. Army, if only the War Department would take a sympathetic interest in it. Frederick Blesse, a medical officer who arrived in the Philippines in 1936, became familiar with the Philippine Army after he began working part-time with the military adviser's office in late 1937. In a lengthy letter to the army surgeon general describing his efforts to help the new army devise a medical service, he pointed out that the most important aspect of the "organization and training of these people" was that "this abundance of manpower" could be "the principal part in a logical plan of defense of these islands" in place of the army's current "defeatist plans."[47] There were other like-minded officers. Grunert himself had foreknowledge of Philippine government plans to raise a large citizen reserve army, because he had taught at the Army War College from 1932 to 1936 when the military system was being devised there. Grunert's papers include an intriguing letter to a friend, Col. William C. Koenig, who had been stationed in the Philippines from October 1937 until November 1940, during that time serving as the commanding officer of the 91st and 60th Coast Artillery Regiments. "I have been hammering for many months towards implementing the plan [of] which you have knowledge," Grunert would later write. "I took your proposals, whittled down the personnel and equipment [to what he thought he might obtain], and sent radio after radio."[48] What exactly Grunert meant by "your proposals" is unknown, but the statement suggests that there were officers in the garrison talking about what might be accomplished if only HPD could get its hands on the Philippine Army. Now that he was in charge, Grunert set out immediately to take control of Philippine Army troops and provide them with the training necessary to make them a reliable component of America's Philippine garrison—and to rewrite Philippine Department war plans to reflect the Filipino soldiers' availability.

Within days of assuming command of the Philippine Department, Grunert informed MacArthur that he planned to hold a conference to begin the process of revising the department's current war plan (WPO-2) and invited the military adviser to send representatives. MacArthur designated Lt. Col. Richard Marshall (his deputy chief of staff) and Maj. William Dunckel to attend the conference in Fort Santiago. It soon became apparent that Grunert's plans included Philippine Army troops. A complaint by an officer of the Philippine Army that officers from the Philippine Department had been visiting army headquarters to obtain information about the status of trainees, reservists, and weapons had already been noted in the mission's official journal. Department officers were ordered to deal with the Philippine Army only through MacArthur's office. An entry in the journal on 26 June 1940 registered Lim's complaint that the Philippine Department was making plans for using soldiers of the Philippine Army, and that the Philippine Army was not being invited to participate in the planning. The mission responded weakly that the department was not making plans for the Philippine Army "as an organization," which of course was exactly Lim's fear.

On 1 July 1940 Grunert met with MacArthur to discuss the new plan. The following day MacArthur told Lim that "so far we have no indication of what the [Philippine Department] war plan will be," but by 1 August HPD had revised the basic Orange plan, and on 19 August Grunert visited MacArthur to apprise him of its contents. Grunert had found the existing plan "inadequate," largely as a result of the failure to make use of Philippine Army troops. Grunert summarized the new basic plan for General MacArthur: The regular army would conduct beach defense operations while the Philippine Army mobilized; Philippine Army soldiers would then relieve United States Army troops as well as contribute to a reserve force, which would be "employed in expelling landed enemy forces . . . [or] in open land warfare." Only the "limited forces necessary" would withdraw to Bataan "when and if" forced to do so. In sum, Grunert was outlining for the military adviser what soon would be finalized as HPD WPO-3.[49]

The inclusion of the Philippine Army in the department war plan was only one aspect of Grunert's attempts to build up the garrison's strength. From mid-1940, the Philippine Department commander began "hammering" (his word) the War Department with cables, memoranda, and personal letters to the chief of staff requesting ammunition, antiaircraft equipment with operating personnel, harbor defense equipment, airplanes, and more troops. According to an official army history of this period, General Grunert sent eight "warning reports and recommendations" in July and August 1940 alone. Distracted by growing responsibilities elsewhere and uncertain of the Philippines' future in American defense efforts (and perhaps reading American newspapers reprinting Manila press articles predicting the demise of the Philippine Army), the War Department responded with sympathy, but little else.[50]

In early November 1940, General Grunert sought the War Department's authority to call Philippine Army troops to active duty for training. Grunert believed that as individuals the Filipino soldiers were valuable additions to the garrison but that the Commonwealth's army was deficient in any kind of advanced training and weak in officer leadership. With such training, Grunert hoped "to utilize elements of the Philippine Army on the island of Luzon . . . in units not larger than a battalion" if an emergency arose. He would supply "one experienced American officer" to each infantry and artillery battalion. The department commander recommended that "organized and equipped units of the Philippine Army be mobilized now" and given "a year of training, under competent supervision." A limited stock of ammunition led Grunert to ask for only those units located on Luzon for the present. Eventually, however, he wanted to include all army units, both for operational purposes and to bolster civilian morale. He asked for five hundred United States Army officers to oversee the training. In mid-December, the War Department responded that the plan was "inadvisable under present conditions." There was no money to support Philippine Army training, the American army was hard pressed to find qualified officers for its own use, and mobilizing Philippine forces might provoke a response from Japan. It did offer to send seventy-five reserve officers to the islands "to assist in training activities and for such other purposes as [Grunert] may desire."[51]

That was in mid-December 1940. Within only a few days, the War Department abruptly adopted a more positive stance toward Philippine defense needs. Near the end of the month, acting chief of staff for the War Plans Division, Leonard Gerow, reminded the chief of staff that Grunert's many requests had been disapproved because the War Department's policy had been not to spend money on the Philippines. "In light of the changed world situation," however, Gerow recommended a reappraisal of that policy. Acceding to Grunert's requests would raise morale, strengthen local defenses, "and exercise a deterring influence on Japan."[52] It was at this point that Grunert received word of the War Department's partial about-face in responding to his requests. The army notified Grunert that he could look forward to an increase in the manning levels of the Philippine Scouts, the 31st U.S. Infantry, and coast artillery regiments, and in construction funds. Grunert had asked for funds to build roads, docks, and storage facilities on Bataan, to expand Clark Field, and to construct a flying field near Camp O'Donnell, some $2 million in expenditures to which the War Department agreed. When sufficiency of supplies allowed, Washington would also ship antiaircraft and other guns.[53]

None of this was really secret, at least in the sense that the public knew that the United States was starting to build up Philippine defenses. Newspapers routinely noted the arrival of personnel and equipment, airplane crashes, and training exercises. When a new Philippine Department air officer (Henry Clagett, the first general-grade officer to fill that position) made an inspection tour of East Asia, for example, one paper published his photo alongside a map showing when, where, and in what order he had been visiting allied bases in China and Southeast Asia "with a view of [their] coordination with American defenses in the Far East." Of course, the press often exaggerated the extent of American interest. Just as the entirely forgettable General Grant had been heralded as a "great military strategist" whose assignment was demonstrative of a "new policy of appointing 'new blood' to strategic positions in America's far-flung insular defense posts" when he had arrived in the islands, so when aviators of the 20th Pursuit Squadron—the first additional air corps unit to be assigned to the islands since 1922—reached Manila in November 1940, the local press reported that the United States had not sent merely pilots; it had sent "only experienced flyers." In fact, the young pilot-officers were recent graduates of flight school and proceeded to wreck a respectable number of aircraft as they continued their flying instruction. The P-35 airplanes that followed were an improvement on the Philippine Department air force's P-26s (most of which would be given to the Philippine Army Air Corps), but the P-35s were already obsolete and no match for Japanese fighter aircraft. The enlisted men of the squadron were mostly recruits who received their technical training—be it as cooks, clerks, or mechanics—after arriving at Nichols Field.[54] Still, after years of neglect, the Philippines was beginning to receive attention. To Lim, it was clear that American interest in the Philippines as a potential counter to Japanese expansionism was growing. Now, in his view, the Philippines' task was to demonstrate that American resources would not be wasted and that Filipinos could be reliable allies.

It was in this context that Lim evaluated the untimely court-martial of Capt. Rufo Romero in late 1940, the first significant incident since the mutiny to bring the army's Philippine Scouts to, again unwelcome, public notice. Romero was a 1931 West Point graduate and an officer in the Philippine Scouts. He had been a brilliant student in the provincial schools of Tarlac and Pampanga and had finished four years at the military academy with the highest standing ever achieved by a Filipino cadet, sixteenth in a class of nearly three hundred graduates.[55] After two years with his regiment in the Philippines, he had returned to the United States to obtain a degree in civil engineering from the University of California and then had graduated from the army's engineer school with a superior rating. In 1935 he had gone back to duty with the 14th Engineer Regiment (PS) at Fort McKinley. Like the two other Filipino officers assigned to that regiment (Narcisco Manzano and Maximiano Janairo, the former commissioned by examination in 1921 and the latter a 1930 graduate of West Point), Romero was considered by his American superiors to be an officer of exceptional ability and great potential.

Captain Romero did not live up to his early promise. He went to the Philippine Military Academy in Baguio as an instructor in 1936 but soon had "differences of opinion with his supervisors" and returned to the Philippine Scouts. Lim wrote that Romero "began to deteriorate" after leaving the academy.[56] In the self-serving memoirs he narrated to a journalist in 1959, Romero blamed his problems on American racism and a grasping American wife, a young woman from New York City whom Romero had met during his first or second year at West Point and had married after she had misled him into thinking she was pregnant.[57] By 1940 Romero's womanizing and gambling were well known in the army and had drawn the concern of fellow officers. Some were suspicious of what their fellow Scout officer might be capable of doing.

When Romero returned to duty with the 14th Engineers after a period of leave spent with a civilian construction firm in late 1940, fellow engineer Manzano recommended that Romero not be reassigned to his previous billet as custodian of classified maps. Expressing indignation at Manzano's implication that an officer might commit treason, the regimental commander did not act on the suggestion.

Suspicious of his behavior and concerned that he would pass classified material to whoever would pay him for it, the army set up Romero: a police informant approached Romero and offered on behalf of the "Sultan of Mindanao" to pay substantial sums for military maps. But, as a *Philippines Free Press* article phrased it, "there is only one country which would pay money for Philippine defense plans." With his wife's help, Romero took secret maps, map overlays, and photographs from his office at Fort McKinley and made copies of them at home. Kept fully informed of Romero's activities, the army arrested him on 15 October 1940 and charged him with illegally removing classified material from his office, unlawfully reproducing secret maps of military installations, and passing those maps to persons not authorized to have them. Romero was not charged with having given anything to Japanese agents, although the army was certain he had already done so, some eight months earlier. One officer stated the army had not believed it had enough evidence to arrest Romero at that time. Romero did not testify. His defense counsel unsuccessfully tried to establish that Romero had been suffering from mental illness at the time the offenses had been committed. Romero did proclaim his innocence and "offered to undergo a brain operation for the purpose of removing the memory function from [his] head." He was found guilty on all counts and spent the next ten years in prison.[58]

There are conflicting accounts of how the army learned of Romero's attempts to sell classified maps, but Lim told his sons that he had brought Romero's activities to the army's attention.[59] Some Scout officers had considered supporting Romero as a fellow Filipino, but not Lim, who thought Romero had been given more than enough rope to hang himself. He was convinced that demonstration of Filipino ability would encourage further American support and had no sympathy for acts that sent the wrong message to the United States. "It's about time," he told his sons, that "Filipinos were punished for their crimes and made responsible for their actions." Even Quezon no longer escaped Lim's censure. Lim was sure that the Commonwealth president's transparent attempts to stay in power "until he was dead," aided and abetted by a supine Philippine legislature, alienated the Philippines' supporters in the United States at this critical time. Had these actions not led Americans to doubt Filipino loyalty, Lim told his sons, the Philippine Army might already have been federalized.[60]

CHAPTER 7

"Nothing Better to a Soldier"

Preparing for War, 1941

By late 1940, the increasingly grim international situation had the paradoxical effect of heartening Filipino attitudes toward their country's defense. The United States had begun to rearm, and the possibility had also grown that the Philippines would be the recipient of funds and armaments for its own defense. Quezon began to temper his earlier pessimism. Asked if he, too, would be willing to trade the United States naval bases for destroyers, as Britain had recently done, the Commonwealth president joked that if America gave some overage destroyers to the Philippines, it could have "half a dozen bases" in return. The United States had not turned down a recent request for military aid, and the War Department was, albeit still cautiously, responding favorably to the Philippine Department commander's requests for added resources.[1]

Lim confronted a further and less encouraging paradox. Though wary of the department commander and fearful that Grunert had imbibed the anti-Filipino attitudes common to U.S. Army officers, Quezon nevertheless had begun to develop a close relationship with the American official best placed to funnel resources to the islands. In 1935 that person had seemed to be Douglas MacArthur. Five years later, he seemed to be George Grunert, so much so that in early 1941 an article in the *New York Times* referred to Grunert's "quiet" takeover of the Philippine Army.[2] But while Grunert had Quezon's confidence, the department commander's interest was the short-term defense of an American colony, not the long-term development of an indigenous army. His policy left no place for an ambitious senior Philippine Army officer like General Lim.

Ever since his arrival in the Philippines, Grunert had determined to gain control of the Commonwealth's military manpower. Grunert's actions had had an immediate impact on the Philippine Army when early in 1941 he moved forward with augmenting the Philippine Scout troops in the garrison. The tactical needs of the Philippine Department had no bearing on the number of additional men to be recruited. The Army Reorganization Act of February 1901 had decreed that a maximum of 12,000 Filipino soldiers could serve in the Philippine Scouts, and, since the Scout organization already numbered about

6,000 men, four decades later this arbitrary and outdated figure restricted Grunert's options. He could enlist another 6,000 men. The increase was not just a means of building up the local U.S. Army garrison; it was a surreptitious way of funneling resources to Commonwealth military forces. The reserve ranks of the Philippine Army were to provide most of the recruits. Philippine Army soldiers who had already completed basic training would, after one year of service in the Scouts (rather than the normal three-year enlistment), return to their reserve areas, well trained and ready to assume leadership positions in the reserve divisions. The arrangement had been agreed upon following discussions between Grunert, High Commissioner Sayre, and Commonwealth government and Philippine Army officials. To minimize the impact on any one reserve area, the Philippine Department would send recruiting parties to northern Luzon and to the major Visayan cities in the south. Provincial recruiting also had the effect of restricting Tagalog access to the Scouts.[3]

The army met its recruitment goal by the first week of April 1941. Of more than 5,000 prospective enlistees who reported to Philippine Division headquarters at Fort McKinley, the army selected 3,803 and assigned most of them to the 45th and 57th Infantry Regiments. Another 1,100 recruits reported to the field artillery at Fort Stotsenburg, which expanded from one understrength regiment to a provisional brigade. "With the mobilization of these recruits," wrote an officer serving with the field artillery at that post, "half[day]-holidays disappeared from the old tropical schedule and reveille was pushed up to 4:30 AM." Within weeks, the twelve-hour days of "very intensive" drill and training that followed had erased the differences "between the new and the old Scout batteries."[4]

Merely increasing the number of Philippine Scouts could not in itself meet the Philippine Department's manpower needs. The limitation on Scout enlistments could be overturned only by congressional action, but Commonwealth forces were bound by no such restriction. It had not been the War Department's intent that Philippine forces be developed as a reserve for the U.S. Army—though the military mission had striven mightily to get Washington to see them as just that—but by early 1941 it was at least prepared to listen. Even as Scout recruitment and training proceeded, Grunert used local U.S. Army resources to improve the competency of the Philippine Army. Rather than continue to train at their own smaller and isolated facility in Subic Bay, for example, Philippine Army coast artillery reservists reported to Corregidor to undergo training with the U.S. Army's coast artillery regiments. Grunert assigned thirty officers to assist at Philippine Army camps at the end of March 1941, when reservists were mobilized for ten days of training. Many other officers visited the camps as observers as well.[5]

The March 1941 mobilization, the first for the Philippine Army since 1939, was a carefully scripted exercise that was as much about sending a message to the United States as it was about imparting serious military training to the 25,000 reservists called to active duty. Much like it had done at the implementation of draft registration in 1936, the Philippine government ensured that provincial governors and local officials understood that a successful mobilization required, as the secretary of national defense reminded them, their "readiness to comply" with the army's directives. Valdes, Lim, and other officials made radio broadcasts to rally support for the exercise and to explain how mobilization would be carried out. In one address, Lim took on a perennial complaint about the army's peacetime training cadres: "The problem of food has been given intensive thought," Lim assured listeners. He had personally gone over the menus, and no soldier would have reason to complain.[6] Ten days provided too little time to give anything more than refresher training to the reservists, but the mobilization was a convincing demonstration of the islands' manpower potential. More men reported for duty than had been ordered to do so, and according to Lim, who had toured camps on Luzon during the exercise, the reservists were "enthusiastic [about] licking Japan." If nothing else, the March practice mobilization helped to ensure that the real mobilization that began in August 1941 would go more smoothly, since, thanks to the earlier exercise, most officers knew what procedures to follow.[7]

Grunert continued to associate his activities with those of the Philippine Army, in ways both substantial and symbolic. An example of the latter was a gathering of senior American and Filipino military and civilian officials to attend the premiere of a military-themed movie—*I Wanted Wings*, with Ray Milland and William Holden—at Manila's Capitol Theater. The Constabulary band played before a soldier-filled audience with High Commissioner Sayre, Vice President Sergio Osmeña, Admiral Thomas Hart (the Asiatic fleet commander), General Grunert, and most of the Philippine and American general officers in the islands in attendance.[8] On a more serious note, Quezon said out loud what Grunert was urging the War Department privately: "The United States [should] send us more planes and more guns and ammunition to increase our power of resistance against invasion. We only need more equipment and more supplies, for we have abundant man power, have strong, intelligent young men who are eager to join the ranks for our defense."[9] In mid-June Quezon announced that the July to December 1941 trainee session was being postponed in the expectation that Congress would authorize defense appropriations for the Philippines. The training camps would be needed to hold the many thousands of reservists expected to be called to the colors for advanced training under the guidance of Grunert's Philippine Department.[10] Well before the White House–ordered mobilization of Commonwealth forces near the end of July, close cooperation marked the activities of the two armies. Philippine Army headquarters made "no important decision," wrote one contemporary observer, "without the approval of the Commander of the Philippine Department of the United States Army."[11]

That commander repeatedly emphasized the importance of the Philippine Army in his own war plans. The March mobilization had been held under the authority of the military adviser, but it had underlined Grunert's conviction that he needed to take charge of the Philippine Army. General Grunert radioed the War Department in April and again in May 1941 urging the mobilization of the "organized forces of the Philippine Army on the island of Luzon" for two to four months of advanced training under "his complete command, supervision, and control." In a lengthy memorandum sent in mid-June, he presented in detail his thinking on the use of the Philippine Army, leaving no doubt that the Philippine Department's War Plan Orange 3 reflected his ambitions for integrating the Philippine Army with the United States Army in the islands. As Grunert wrote:

> A frank and realistic appraisal of the combat capacity of our U.S. War Garrison, indicates the need for numerical increases and enlarged fire-power. The tactical possibilities, in our situation on Luzon, are those inherent in a position in readiness, with forces in observation in several sectors, and a central reserve, for operations on interior lines; this inescapable dispersion has the effect of weakening each element; the only remedy lay in early reinforcement; the most direct, and economical means, at hand, is the Philippine Army and its manpower. Our current W.P.O. is based on that conception.[12]

Lim viewed the trends of early 1941 with mixed emotions. He was understandably heartened by the promise of military aid from the United States, and he shared the perception that a strong Filipino army could benefit both countries. He told an audience of ROTC graduates at the University of the Philippines in March 1941 that the development of Filipino "fighting man-power" was a "fair exchange" for the American "economic protection" the Philippines would need in order to maintain its political independence after 1946.[13] Notably missing in Grunert's ambitions for the Philippine Army, however, was any mention of that army's senior officers. Grunert felt that the Philippine Army would not be useful in larger than battalion strength, and he expected to put American officers in command of those battalions. Where did a Filipino general fit in? Lim complained to MacArthur that "we need a lot of protection because Grunert and his staff do not care what happens to the Philippine Army as long as they can use the force to fight against Japan." MacArthur agreed and claimed that he had "had some heated arguments with Grunert about this."[14] Lim confronted a situation similar to that of 1917–18. Like General Evans before him, Grunert focused on the immediate security needs of an American colony; like the frustrated World War I–era Philippine Scout officers and national guardsmen, Lim thought in terms of what would confer long-term benefits to Philippine military capacity, as well as on his own opportunity to play an important part in the crisis.

Lim was pessimistic about his chances of making further contributions to shaping the army. The chief of staff position seemed further away than ever. When Paulino Santos had been replaced at the end of 1938, Quezon had claimed he was instituting a firm policy of naming a new army head every three years; that meant a new chief of staff should be announced by late 1941 when Valdes would have completed three years in office. Lim knew better than to assume Quezon would not change his mind and disclaimed any desire of wanting the position, but he insisted to MacArthur early in 1940 that the army needed "a Chief of Staff who will have the confidence of the public as to his professional ability and who can defend the army in its technical aspect." MacArthur responded by saying that he "would like to recommend [Lim] as the Chief of Staff."[15]

Lim claimed that Valdes had only accepted the appointment on the understanding that Lim would be his deputy and left to Lim the everyday running of the army. That did not sway Quezon, however. MacArthur told Lim that Quezon had long planned to make Constabulary head Brig. Gen. Guillermo B. Francisco the next chief of staff. Capinpin claimed to have heard the same thing. Lim could not bring himself to believe them. It was true that Francisco had been commissioned in the Constabulary in 1908, six years before Lim had been commissioned in the army, and that Francisco's was one name above Lim's on the officers' roster, but when it came to choosing the chief of staff, seniority had never counted in the past. Paulino Santos had not been commissioned until 1914 and Valdes only in 1921. Quezon could appoint anyone of the rank of colonel or higher to the post. Francisco—"an honest and impartial officer," according to a wartime Office of Strategic Services evaluation of his prewar career, though "not too bright" had been Eisenhower's characterization of him in the mission diary—had spent his entire career in the national police. If not personally, then at least institutionally, Francisco represented everything Lim thought was wrong with the army. If Quezon appointed Francisco, Lim saw no future in the army. By law, Lim could not be promoted beyond brigadier general either, unless he filled the chief of staff position. He spoke of leaving the army and even of going to the United States, probably by the end of 1941.[16]

General Grunert faced a more rewarding future. As events in the Far East grew more ominous, Grunert provided a resolute and comforting presence in

Manila. On the occasion of his sixty-first birthday on 21 July 1941, the *Philippines Herald* included a sixteen-page "General Grunert Birthday Supplement." High Commissioner Sayre, President Quezon, General Valdes, General Francisco, and other civic and military leaders offered felicitations. Grunert contributed a reassuring message for the Filipino people. "Hardened by vigorous training, the troops, both American and Filipino, have been forged into an efficient combat team, ready now to guard these islands against an aggressor," he reported. Two days later, in a letter to General Marshall, Grunert apologized for appearing to "push himself forward." He had been unaware that Quezon's mouthpiece planned such a generous tribute, but after all, he reasoned, personal prestige and reputation counted for much in the Orient.[17]

The once all-important military adviser seemed destined to follow Lim into obscurity. Sayre wrote in his memoirs that around this time he attended an "exceedingly important conference" in Baguio that dealt with defense planning. He invited Grunert to attend; he had assumed Quezon would invite the military adviser. "To my surprise," Sayre wrote, Quezon "did not do so and in our discussion the General was not referred to." MacArthur was reduced to getting one of the mission members, Lt. Col. Milton Hill, who ran the Philippine Army's General Service School in Baguio, to see if Emil Speth, Lim's company commander of long ago who now lived in retirement in the mountain resort, could learn from Quezon what was transpiring between Grunert and the Commonwealth president.[18] In earlier years, the Manila papers had routinely mentioned MacArthur's presence at Philippine Army ceremonies and exercises; by late 1940, the papers made note of meetings of Quezon with the High Commissioner, the Philippine Department commanding general, and the local navy commander, but not with General MacArthur. *His* sixty-first birthday, on 26 January 1941, had passed without "the usual official calls by Philippine Army and Constabulary officials." They had been "dispensed with upon the Field Marshal's expressed wishes."[19]

Finally, at MacArthur's own insistence, on 15 May 1941 he met with Quezon and demanded to know if rumors concerning the content of Quezon's conferences with Sayre and Grunert were true. Grunert, it was said, was to be named military governor in the event of war. MacArthur also promised to get out the military vote if Quezon decided to seek reelection later that year. In response, Quezon dismissed the rumor concerning Grunert and expressed outrage at the army's involvement in any political activity. Responding to what he believed was MacArthur's real concern, Quezon told his military adviser that no one under contract with the Commonwealth government could be guaranteed employment beyond 1941. MacArthur was free to return to the United States to seek other work, and the government would still pay his salary until the end of the year. Despite Quezon's added assurance of continuing "personal affection" for the Philippine Army's field marshal, MacArthur could not have drawn encouragement from the meeting. A few days later, on 28 May, MacArthur admitted to Lim that "he was licked." The combination of Sayre and Grunert had poisoned Quezon against him, MacArthur said, and he was therefore going to leave the Philippines, probably in September 1941. The next day, MacArthur wrote to General Marshall and stated his intention of closing down the military mission since "the Philippine Army [was] to be absorbed by the United States Army in the near future."[20]

If his intent was to force the issue of his future in the islands, he succeeded. By then, in Washington caution had given way to cautious optimism about America's ability to defend the Philippines. Financial constraints, the needs of its own expanding army, and concern that Japan would take action "to prevent or forestall" the arrival of whatever meager reinforcements might be sent to the Philippines had stayed the War Department's hand when Grunert had begun pressing for more resources in 1940. Now the commanding general had been allowed to double the number of Philippine Scouts. The number of American soldiers grew too. There had been about 4,800 in early 1941; by July 1941 they numbered 10,560. The one American infantry regiment in the islands saw its manpower increase by half. New fighter aircraft and antiaircraft guns and other war matériel became available. And though they would not arrive until much later in the year, already there was talk in Washington that "the newly developed B-17 heavy bomber" could turn around completely the situation in the Far East. The Philippines could not merely be defended; a bomber force placed in the islands could "deter Japan from further [southward] aggression."[21]

Who was to command the growing strength in the newly important outpost? In Manila MacArthur presented an image of solitude—publicly ignored by President Quezon, privately scorned by senior Philippine Army officers, and marginalized by Grunert's vigorous efforts to gain control of the Commonwealth's army. Until MacArthur's friend Joseph Stevenot, a well-connected American businessman with an interest in Philippine military affairs and a longtime associate of Lim's in the Boy Scout movement, showed up in the secretary of war's office on 21 May 1941 to complain that "Grunert and the President [Quezon] have been trying to ignore MacArthur," authorities in Washington apparently had little awareness of how inconsequential MacArthur had become in Manila. Stevenot later bragged about having gotten MacArthur recalled to active duty, but Stimson wrote that when he arranged for Stevenot to meet Marshall later that same day, the chief of staff "incidentally told [him] that in case of trouble out there, they intended to recall General MacArthur into service again and place him in command." MacArthur was "the logical selection for the Army Commander in the Far East should the situation approach a crisis." Marshall informed MacArthur of this decision in June and asked that the news be kept confidential.[22]

Ironically, Grunert's repeated insistence that if given more resources and training the Philippine Army was the key to a defensible Philippines would only have encouraged the view in Washington that MacArthur was the logical person to put in charge; the army was, after all, his creation. When Roosevelt froze Japanese assets and announced an oil embargo on 26 July 1941, he also ordered Commonwealth military forces into the service of the United States. MacArthur returned to active duty and took command of United States Army Forces in the Far East (USAFFE). That news, High Commissioner Sayre recalled in an unfortunate but popular metaphor, "fell like a bombshell on Manila." And if "Señor Quezon"—Roosevelt's flippant referent for the Philippine leader—needed a lesson in how little he mattered in Washington, he had it with the government's decision to mobilize Philippine military forces, recall Douglas MacArthur to active duty, and leave the general in the Philippines, without bothering to inform, let alone ask, the Commonwealth president.[23]

Lim, it turned out, had more confidence in the field marshal than MacArthur had had in himself. The story about his recall to active duty that MacArthur liked to have told by sympathetic journalists and sycophantic subordinates makes clear that MacArthur thought he was through in the Philippines. It goes like this: MacArthur was at breakfast on 27 July, a Sunday in Manila, when "he noted in a small box in the lower left-hand corner" of the front page of *The Sunday Tribune* a brief statement that the President of the United States had "ordered the incorporation of the Philippine army and navy forces into the armed forces of the United States" under the command of "an American army officer with rank of general." His response to this revelation was to do nothing. Only when a message from the War Department followed several hours later confirming that *he* was the general officer referred to in the earlier report did he telephone his chief of staff. Sutherland was golfing, so MacArthur called his deputy chief of staff, Richard Marshall, who found Sutherland, and the two men reported to MacArthur's suite at the Manila Hotel.[24]

Lim's letters reveal that MacArthur already knew of the president's order. That news had arrived in Manila very late on the night of 26 July. According to the statement MacArthur ostensibly read in the newspaper the next morning, "the Chief of Staff of the Philippine Army was advised of this dispatch on its receipt." Did General Valdes not bother to tell MacArthur? Lim informed his sons that he was called about midnight by a friend who read to him the text of Roosevelt's order. Lim claimed to have understood at once that Roosevelt meant MacArthur, and he called several other people to share the news, including Sutherland.[25] Is it conceivable that Sutherland went golfing the next morning having said nothing to MacArthur? It is, assuming that they thought the general officer was Grunert and that MacArthur no longer had reason to remain in the Philippines. Roosevelt's order calling into federal service portions of the Philippine military forces had placed those units under the command of an unnamed general officer, and several stateside papers identified Grunert by name as the proposed commander. Many Americans in the Philippines would have made the same assumption.[26]

Whereas MacArthur's arrival in the Philippines as Commonwealth military adviser in 1935 had pushed Lim to the margins, MacArthur's recall to active duty in 1941 brought Lim back into the mainstream. Lim managed to get in to see the now-busy field marshal on the afternoon of 27 July. "You could see the change in his face," Lim wrote to his wife the next day. MacArthur was like "a man who had gained victory in a field of battle." Lim thought he deserved some of the credit. Why had MacArthur remained in the Philippines into 1941, even as everyone in Manila whose opinion seemed to matter had come to hold him in disdain? Earlier, it had been Lim's opposition to MacArthur's insistence on continuing the mission-authored military system that had helped undermine Quezon's confidence in MacArthur. But when the possibility emerged that the United States would make available the resources and funding to support an enlarged army, Lim accepted that MacArthur was likely to be called on to lead Philippine military forces. "I would not say that I rescued MacArthur," Lim later recounted to his wife, "but sincerely I have helped him, not because he is a friend or an enemy, but I sincerely believe that he was valuable in our governmental set-up." Lim revealed that in a meeting of the central general staff presided over by the "former Secretary of National Defense" (he meant Teofilo Sison), he argued, much against the trend and at the cost of Quezon's goodwill, in favor of "the value and necessity of retaining MacArthur." Lim went so far as to suggest that had he supported "the contention of the President to eliminate MacArthur," MacArthur would have returned to the United States "long ago."[27]

MacArthur's assumption of command presented Lim with personal challenges as well as professional opportunities. Lim had come to see war with Japan as inevitable and even necessary, if the Philippines was to avoid being "gobbled up" either physically or economically by Japan. When the navy began sending dependents home at the end of 1940 and the army followed in early 1941, Lim began to think that his wife and younger children should go to the States too, and by March he was looking for space aboard an army transport. By that time, his two oldest sons had been students in the United States for several years (one at the Massachusetts Institute of Technology and the other at the Naval Academy) and his third son, Vicente Jr., had been appointed to fill the Philippines' slot at West Point, where he would graduate with the abbreviated class of 1944. Vicente left for America aboard the *President Taft* on 10 May 1941. Lim found berths for Pilar, their three younger children, and a niece on the passenger liner SS *Ivaran*, which sailed from Manila on 14 May and arrived in Los Angeles on 8 June.[28]

While MacArthur savored his victory, Lim pursued more disagreeable chores. At the end of July, he journeyed to Baguio to oversee the relief of the military academy's misbehaving superintendent Col. Rafael Garcia. That Garcia was a fellow West Point graduate and Philippine Scout officer made the task all the more unpleasant. To make things worse, on the trip north Lim's driver ran over and killed a young girl who had dashed into the road too suddenly for the driver to brake.[29]

Lim was soon able to devote his energies to the army's mobilization. The incremental incorporation of the Philippine Army began in mid-August 1941, with a brief ceremony at Zablan Field (a no-longer-existing airfield then located on the backside of Camp Murphy) that brought the Philippine Army Air Corps into USAFFE. Men assigned to reserve division infantry regiments began reporting for duty on 1 September with the last scheduled to mobilize in late November or early December 1941. By then, ten divisions—numbered the 11th, 21st, 31st, 41st, 51st (on Luzon), 61st, 71st, 81st, 91st (raised in the Visayas), and 101st (on Mindanao); and corresponding to the islands' ten military districts—would be fully formed.

Of course, the same predictable problems that had bedeviled the scheme of registration and conscription from 1936 to 1940 reemerged: some men called to serve did not wish to do so; others desirous of serving were not called. On paper, the reserve units had been overmanned by 20 percent to allow for wastage. By mid-September, Manila dailies were reporting that 5,000 reservists had not responded to mobilization orders, and for one reason or another, many who had were not accepted for service. An unusually large percentage of students at the University of the Philippines' medical college received exemptions, while Lt. Col. Amado B. Magtoto complained that army doctors held the reporting reservists to too high a physical standard and refused to accept many who could have served. Others simply did not heed the call to report for active duty. Since the army was being mobilized by unit and all trained reservists were already assigned to specific reserve formations, allowing individual reservists to volunteer to make up the shortfall could disrupt the mobilization schedule and create manning problems for their assigned units; nonetheless, MacArthur and Valdes decided to call for volunteers. President Quezon agreed, believing that allowing men to volunteer for service would relieve unemployment. There were reportedly "many jobless reservists" anxious to serve.[30]

The challenge of preparing the Philippine Army for war did not, for the moment, concern Lim. That fell to General Grunert. The sudden turn of events had left him stunned. Fort Stotsenburg's commanding general, Edward King, attended a conference at Grunert's office the morning after MacArthur's recall to active duty and wrote his wife that it "was like a funeral. It is very hard on [Grunert] to have General MacArthur put in command."[31] But Grunert still wanted to be in the Philippines. He continued as department commander and as such was responsible for training the mobilizing troops. To facilitate the training program, Grunert divided the Philippines into three corps areas. General King, an experienced field artillery officer who had arrived in the Philippines in November 1940, was put in charge of the first corps area, comprising the 1st, 2nd, and 3rd Military Districts. Brig. Gen. George Parker Jr., in the Philippines since May 1941 and serving as the "infantry adviser" to Jonathan Wainwright, the commanding general of the Philippine Division, took command of the 4th and 5th districts that made up the second corps area. The remaining five military districts, in the Visayas and Mindanao, became the third corps area. (Upon Grunert's departure, these corps would receive the better-known labels of North Luzon Force, South Luzon Force, and Visayan-Mindanao Force.) Grunert then held a series of conferences with "commanders of major tactical units then envisioned." Their goal, he told the American officers destined to work with the Philippine Army, was to get their units into shape for combat as soon as possible so that the Commonwealth forces could fulfill their mission of beach defense "under our War Plans." The peacetime army's emphasis on close-order drill, parades, and spit-and-polish was to "go by the board." All training was to be "combat training." Grunert commenced an active round of inspections that would take him throughout much of the archipelago. Early September found him visiting army camps in Batangas; the end of the month saw him north of Manila, at Camp Ord, Tarlac. He was far to the south in Iloilo by mid-October and told a correspondent that he expected to remain several more days in the southern islands.

Grunert failed to discern the extent to which MacArthur held him in disdain. On 27 October 1941, the *Philippines Herald* reported that Grunert had received orders to return to the United States. What the *Herald* did not reveal was that MacArthur had requested Grunert's recall. "It would be advantageous to relieve him," the USAFFE chief informed the War Department, "as I am loath, as long as he is here, to contract the functions of the Department commander." Publicly the War Department offered the excuse that the Philippine Department commanding general had completed his normal overseas tour of duty and was therefore being reassigned. The War Department's dissembling fooled no one, since all knew that Grunert's two-year Philippine assignment was not scheduled to end for several months. Many officer transfers had been put on hold; Grunert's was accelerated. He left the islands on 31 October 1941.[32]

Lim merely commented in passing in a letter to his wife in November that "Grunert is gone," but MacArthur's supplanting of Grunert gave Lim an opportunity he otherwise would not have had. MacArthur was not only, or even mostly, preparing military forces in the Philippines for an attack by Japan; rather, he planned to take advantage of the U.S. government's willingness to spend money to use the emergency period to compensate for all he had failed to do over the past six years as the Commonwealth's military adviser. Fully manned at authorized levels, ten Philippine Army reserve divisions would number about 75,000 soldiers, but MacArthur expected to form additional tiers of reserve divisions as well. Lim understood that MacArthur ultimately expected to put a quarter of a million men under arms. Furthermore, MacArthur was determined to mobilize all trainees and to resume the semiannual training program—with a full complement of 20,000 conscripts—in January 1942.[33]

In short, MacArthur intended to use the emergency period to create a Philippine Army that could stand on its own feet, and that meant a need for Filipino officers capable of commanding large units of Filipino soldiers. MacArthur's goal, a local paper reported, was to train Filipino officers "with a view to enabling them to succeed in the command of Philippine Army units recently integrated into the U.S. Army and placed under American officers."[34]

Lim still aspired to be the army's next chief of staff, but he realized that Philippine Army headquarters would play only an administrative role during the period of emergency. Even after MacArthur took over, there was no immediate intention of including the Philippine Army staff in USAFFE (that would not happen until after the war began). Selection as the commander of one of the mobilized divisions held out the best hope of public notice and future promotion. For the moment, Lim checked his ambition to be the Philippine Army's senior officer.

The identification of Filipino officers to serve in the senior ranks of the mobilizing units was a daunting task, one fraught with political and personal difficulties. Although "regiments" had existed in the tables of organization of the pre-Commonwealth Constabulary as well as in the Philippine Scouts, few Filipino officers of any grade or background had ever commanded large numbers of troops in either field or garrison. Each mobilizing division included a field artillery regiment, for example; no Filipino officer who had served with the field artillery had ever commanded more than a battery, and there were only six such officers on active duty in 1941. Lim himself had not commanded troops since serving as a battalion commander in the 45th Infantry in the mid-1920s and probably had not participated in anything that could be referred to as a "field exercise" since his schooling in the United States in the late 1920s. A central general staff committee racked its collective brain trying to devise a means of matching officers to units, without success. Lim said there was no answer to the problem. The Philippine Army did not have enough officers to command the many new units being called to service, and most senior officers did not have the experience to hold field commands commensurate with their ranks. Even so, they would naturally resent being passed over should more capable subordinates be given the superior commands.

Lim proposed, and MacArthur's chief of staff accepted, a sink-or-swim solution. Colonels were to be appointed to regimental commands, lieutenant colonels to regimental or battalion commands, and majors to battalion commands. U.S. Army officers would be assigned "to tutor them." If the American "instructor" came to believe that the Filipino officer could not handle the command, the officer was to be referred to a review board for elimination. His place would be taken by the next officer on the promotion list, who would be given a chance to show his worth. Eventually, capable Filipino officers would command all units, and the army would be rid of its "old fossils." The policy was typical of Lim's stern-faced approach to problem solving, but one that would be difficult to carry out in practice.[35]

Lim knew in early August that he would command a division. His seniority and connections got him the pick of the lot, the 41st Division, which drew its men from the provinces of the 4th Military District to the east and south of Manila: Rizal, Cavite, Laguna, and Batangas, as well as the three provinces that made up the islands of Mindoro and Palawan. Not only did that include Lim's home province, but the division had the most desirable of all cantonment areas, along breezy Tagaytay Ridge overlooking scenic Lake Taal. Thus Lim's joke to his wife that some Philippine Army officers rued their hasty decisions to decline assignment to his staff and Richard Mallonée's lament that he was stuck with lesser-qualified American instructors because the better-qualified (or the just better-informed) had rushed to volunteer for duty with Lim's division.[36]

Mateo ("Matty") Capinpin also received a division command, though his leadership record had been less than stellar in years past. Capinpin's superiors in the national guard had rated him among the least competent of the officers serving with that organization, and his performance at the infantry school at Fort Benning was reportedly so poor (or so one of Eugene Ganley's correspondents claimed) that he was ordered home without completing the course of instruction. (The *Army Register* credits Capinpin with having finished the company officers' course, his only schooling in the United States, in 1925.) Lim, for reasons he did not explain, had come to regard Capinpin as a "dangerous man" from whom it was best to keep one's distance. Eisenhower had admired Capinpin's personal traits—"a simple, straight-forward soldier . . . hard working and honest"—but was dubious about his capacity for high command. "If ever called for to serve in a high position," Eisenhower had written, he "should have some brilliant individual . . . as his principal assistant." Capinpin did have command experience. After joining the Philippine Army, he had commanded the 1st Infantry Regiment and later the 1st Regular Division at Camp Murphy. As a Scout officer, Capinpin had commanded the 45th Infantry's model drill company for many years, and by the time he joined the Philippine Army he had long since acquired the reputation of "a very strict disciplinarian." "He prided himself on knowing the drill regulations from cover to cover," wrote one officer who served under him just before the emergency period, and he would scan the camp through binoculars to spot litter and other shortcomings to bring to subordinates' attention. Capinpin himself told Ganley that it was his detailed knowledge of army regulations that had gotten him a commission in the Philippine Scouts in the first place, back during World War I. Capinpin would command the 21st Division during the Philippine Campaign.[37]

Division commands also fell to two American officers who had long years of service in the Philippine Constabulary behind them, spent mostly on Mindanao. One was Guy Fort, who by the time of his death in 1942 would have served longer in the Constabulary than any other American. In his secret evaluation of senior army officers, Eisenhower had recommended that Fort be retired immediately, and Fort was one of those whom Quezon had tried to dismiss without success in 1939. (Whatever his professional limitations might have been, Fort's dignity, bearing, and concern for his men left a favorable impression on many who knew him.) Fort's military service went all the way back to the Philippine-American War, and he had spent more than forty years in uniform as an army enlisted man, reserve officer, and Constabulary officer by the time World War II began. Fort would lead the 81st Division, which spent the war on Mindanao. Luther Stevens took command of the 91st, a Visayan division brought to Luzon before the start of the war. Nine years younger than Fort—Stevens was born the same year as Lim—but senior on the Constabulary officers' roster, Stevens had graduated from Mississippi A&M College to a commission in the Constabulary in 1910. He had never been an army regular. Like Fort, Stevens was among those who had left the Constabulary during World War I and had been reappointed in the early 1920s and advanced very rapidly when Leonard Wood was trying to re-Americanize the organization. He had benefited immeasurably from Wood's poor memory. (Wood thought he was promoting another officer named Leslie Stevens.) Quezon also had tried to get rid of Stevens, in the late 1930s, though Eisenhower had suggested he be allowed to continue to hold administrative posts on Mindanao. Stevens had completed the infantry school course at Fort Benning in 1939 and the command school at Fort Leavenworth in 1940.[38]

Other Philippine Army officers were either considered unsuitable for high command or were busy elsewhere. Colonel Garcia, the 1916 West Point graduate and a senior Scout officer serving with the Philippine Army, had hoped for a division, but the recent contretemps at the military academy that had led to his relief as superintendent had caused Quezon and MacArthur to lose confidence in him. Magtoto wrote that at the start of the war Garcia was considered for command of a provisional brigade, but "General MacArthur simply sa[id] 'No.'" Garcia was consigned to administer the 4th Military District, from which Lim would draw his division's replacements. Fidel Segundo requested a division command and was as well qualified as any Filipino officer to hold one, but Segundo had just replaced Garcia at the Philippine Military Academy, and Lim told him that directing the academy continued to be the more important task. Mobilizing the army was important but temporary; graduating superior junior officers from the academy remained the army's primary need, and HPA had run through the senior officers qualified to lead the academy. It is also possible that Segundo had burned too many bridges: Quezon had exiled him to Mindanao; MacArthur found him too outspoken; and Lim, Segundo seemed to have felt, had betrayed him by pretending that he had wanted Segundo to be chief of staff.[39]

Col. Pastor Martelino stood in line for a division too. Martelino was a 1921 graduate of West Point who as a Scout officer had served with the coast artillery. In the Philippine Army, Martelino had been superintendent of the military academy and training and operations officer on the central general staff. Eisenhower had referred to Martelino as "probably the best-rounded officer, from the standpoint of professional ability and general characteristics, in the army." (Martelino was the "brilliant individual" Eisenhower had in mind to assist the more senior but less able Capinpin.) Apparently, Martelino did not do as well as expected at the staff school in Baguio and instead became Clifford Bluemel's chief of staff in the 31st Division. Lim appreciated his potential and tried to get him in the 41st, but Martelino preferred assignment to a less desirable division in the belief that the chance of promotion would be better.[40]

Though more than thirty years had passed since he had arrived at West Point to begin his military career, had Lim remained on active duty in the U.S. Army, he would not have had the rank or time in service to justify a division command. All of the American officers designated as division commanders had been commissioned several years earlier than Lim. Filipinos who filled command positions thus found Americans serving alongside them.

Lim appears to have had no say in picking his own adviser. Lt. Col. Malcolm "Bob" Vaughn Fortier (pronounced "for-tear") was a battalion commander with the 31st U.S. Infantry when he was reassigned to the 41st Division in August 1941, initially as senior instructor to the 42nd Regiment. The approach of hostilities had found Fortier nearing the end of a two-year tour of duty in the Philippines. His military service dated to 1913, when he had completed a Plattsburg camp while a student at Washington State College. Commissioned in 1917 after several years as an enlisted man in the national guard, Fortier had not been in Europe during World War I but had served with the army of occupation. Returning from Germany in 1923, he was directing Civilian Conservation Corps activities in Washington and Idaho when he received orders to the Philippines in late 1939. With his wife and adult niece accompanying him, Fortier arrived in Manila aboard the same transport as General Grunert in February 1940.

Fortier had not volunteered for Philippine duty, but he and his family enjoyed the assignment. Many officers stationed with "Manila's Own" rented homes away from the regiment's barracks and offices in Intramuros, and so too did the Fortiers, in Pasay. They socialized with other army families at nearby Fort McKinley and at the Army and Navy Club, motored up to Baguio, and took shopping trips to Hong Kong and Shanghai. Their social horizons might have been broader than most since Fortier's niece, a graduate of Washington State College, taught at a private school in Manila that attracted European and Filipino students as well as civilian and military Americans.[41]

No other adviser's qualifications matched Fortier's. He had graduated from the advanced course at Fort Benning in 1929 and from the Command and General Staff School at Fort Leavenworth in 1931. An officer familiar with Fortier from the 31st Infantry told Lt. Col. Magtoto that Fortier was a severe taskmaster who had never been known to express satisfaction with his subordinates' work. Magtoto saw Fortier when the American was still the adviser to the 42nd Regiment and found him to be "one of the most efficient and exacting officers we have ever met."[42] Fortier's experience undoubtedly contributed to the division's success on Bataan, but in his subsequent letters Lim never mentioned Fortier's name.

Many Americans assigned to the Philippine Army (PA) came from Philippine-based units. And many, like Fortier, came from the 31st U.S. Infantry Regiment. Providing officers to PA divisions was that regiment's greatest, if least-appreciated, contribution to the subsequent campaign. Other Americans assigned to the Philippine Army came directly from the United States. Field artillery officer Richard Mallonée was one of those, and he was impressed by the officers being sent to the islands. "Workhorses all," he called them, with not "a polished desk topper among us." Another officer who had received "rush orders" to the Philippines in mid-October 1941 claimed that the chief of infantry had assured him that he and others sent to the islands at that time had been chosen for the duty because of their "splendid record[s]." Not everyone agreed. Arthur Whitehead, a Scout officer with the 26th Cavalry, ended up with the 61st Division after making his way from northern Luzon to Panay in early 1942. The American lieutenant colonel commanding the division's 63rd Regiment had been "recently called to active duty and in his words," Whitehead wrote, "'shanghaied' to the Philippines. His demeanor was that of a man resigned to his fate, but not happily so."[43] Col. Michael Quinn also had his doubts about some of these officers. "What in the name of God could the War Department [have been] thinking," he jotted in his prisoner-of-war diary, when it recalled to active duty an officer who had retired years earlier on medical disability and sent him to the Philippines? Quinn, a onetime Philippine Scout who had been the senior motor transportation officer on Bataan, wrote that some officers thought that "all regular officers who were ordered to the Philippine Islands, just prior to the war, had two strikes on them one way or another." A reserve officer friend of Quinn's wondered if the same could be "true of reserve officers."[44]

Not every officer sent to serve with the Philippine Army was chosen on the basis of merit. Medical officers at Fort McKinley used assignments to the Philippine Army as punishment. The large number of medical personnel who began to report to Fort McKinley and the 12th Medical Regiment (PS) by late July 1941 allowed the hospital staff to keep the new officers it liked, send the others to the Philippine Army, and threaten anyone who performed poorly with the same fate.[45] Bradford Chynoweth, who would command the 61st Division, was an experienced and even sought-after regimental commander, but his abrasive personality had led to an effort to dismiss him from the army in 1941. The attempt failed, but Chynoweth soon had unwanted orders to the Philippines. His friends concluded that he was being thrown "to the wolves."[46] At least a few officers, like Col. Maxon Lough (pronounced "luff"), actively sought assignment to the Philippines. A former Philippine Constabulary officer (served 1908–11) who would become a sector commander on Bataan, Lough added his own name to the list of those to be sent to the islands. At age fifty-five, he was too old to expect a combat command in the regular army. Service in the Philippines held out the only hope for a general's star.[47]

Along with the other proposed or contemplated division commanders and their staffs, Lim spent from late September to mid-November attending a staff officers' course at the Philippine Constabulary's Camp Henry T. Allen in Baguio. Instructed by American Colonels Clifford Bluemel, William Brougher, and Albert Jones (all designated to be division commanders), Philippine Army officers solved map problems, studied the proper organization and armament of infantry and artillery regiments, and learned how to prepare and convey an order. The school mostly provided the opportunity to evaluate each other's capabilities and to impress superiors. MacArthur and Sutherland visited Baguio on 21–22 October to watch Lim, Stevens, and other senior officers offer solutions to map problems. MacArthur spoke briefly and encouraged the officers "to question solutions to military problems." Later, at the U.S. Army's nearby Camp John Hay, MacArthur spent two hours in conference with the school's American instructors, presumably considering their evaluations of the Filipino officers.[48]

Lim thought the experience a personal triumph. The school at Baguio, he told his wife, gave him the opportunity to show "what I really am" by demonstrating his command abilities and loyalty to his staff. His "rather stern personality" (to quote one of his sons) had led officers who had avoided him in the past to now ask to serve with him. But the school also called into question the competence of some of the student-officers and encouraged the belief on the part of American officers that Filipinos lacked ability. Lim thought that several of the Scouts performed poorly. Bluemel made matters worse with a "slip of the tongue," a derogatory comment about the Philippine Army that embarrassed and angered Filipino officers. What Bluemel said might be true, Lim admitted, but it was not appropriate for an American who was scheduled to command Filipino soldiers to say so. Lim said nothing at the time but later urged Bluemel to apologize to the Filipino officers (which he did), if for no other reason than to keep MacArthur from punishing him.[49]

Lim was less optimistic about his future in the army once the emergency period had ended. He now knew that MacArthur and Capinpin had told him the truth: Quezon did not intend to appoint him army chief. The author of a study of the "main Filipino actors" during the Japanese occupation revealed that Quezon had long since "announced [to] his intimates" that Francisco would be the next chief of staff. This was, the author continued, a gross injustice to Lim, who was the much better soldier but who lacked the necessary "taste for partisan politics." In a letter written toward the end of his stay at Baguio, Lim admitted to his wife that he had to accept that he would not be the army's senior officer. Quezon wanted Francisco; or at the least, Quezon did not want Lim. The realization made him bitter. He had a long talk with Carlos Romulo about his failure to advance to the army's top post, and the two agreed, he told Pilar, that Lim could never be chief of staff mainly because he would not "suck up" to Manuel Quezon. He understandably could not resign during the emergency period, but he intended to get out of the army once it had ended.[50]

The training course concluded on 14 November 1941, and Lim hurried to Tagaytay to assume command of the 41st Division. He had told his staff officers

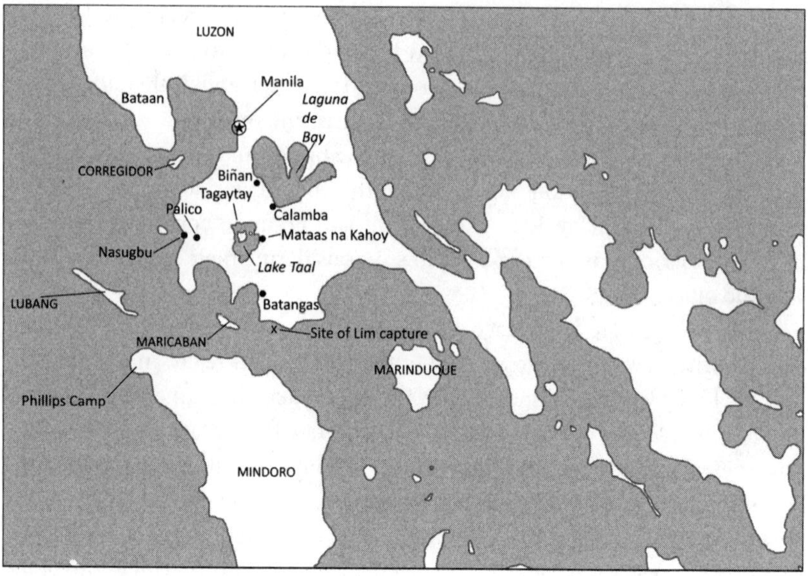

Southern Luzon.

at Baguio that the country was likely to be at war with Japan by the end of November. He wrote to Pilar that he had heard that the threat now confronting the Philippines had led people "who [previously were] not even interested in [him]" to approach President Quezon to insist that "one real military man" finally be put at the head of the army. According to newspaper accounts, he would probably be advanced to major general "for the duration of the emergency." He repeated the rumor but did not encourage his wife to believe it. Nevertheless, his mood had grown euphoric. He had told his wife when first selected for division command in early August that "there is nothing better to a soldier than to be in command of a fighting unit in the field." Now, even if Quezon did change his mind and offer Lim the army's top position, he could not accept it. General MacArthur, he confided to Pilar, considered him "the only Filipino who can really command a Division."[51]

CHAPTER 8

"The Only General with *Cojones*"

Lim on Bataan, I

News of the Japanese attack on Pearl Harbor first reached the Philippines at about 2:30 in the morning on Monday, 8 December, sent unencrypted in Morse code by a radio operator at a navy communications facility in Hawaii. The radio operator on duty at Asiatic Fleet headquarters in Manila thought it authentic and so informed the marine officer on duty. Thereafter, word that war had begun made its way to the scattered elements of the 41st Division, as it did elsewhere, by fits and starts. Maj. Gen. George M. Parker, commanding general of South Luzon Force, was in his quarters at Fort McKinley when he received a telephone call at about 4:00 A.M. telling him of the attack. He sent staff officers to his two division commanders, Lim and the 51st Division's Brig. Gen. Albert M. Jones, "with orders to alert their divisions." At the 41st Division's cantonment area along Tagaytay Ridge, the commanding officer of the 41st Engineers, Capt. Rigoberto J. Atienza, learned about the Japanese bombing of Pearl Harbor from his battalion's American instructor, Lt. Henry Harris, who had just heard of it on the six o'clock radio newscast. Captain Magtoto's battalion of the 42nd Infantry was in the process of being relieved from beach defense duties by another unit of the regiment when, near the town of Looc, the manager of a local hacienda rushed toward the soldiers shouting, "Señores, la Guerra está declarada!" Someone had telephoned him with news of the attack on Pearl Harbor.[1]

December 8 found the 41st Division better prepared than other reserve divisions. Lim had largely gotten his pick of staff officers and regimental commanders (to the ire of HPA G-3 officials, who were trying to assign officers on a rational basis); proximity to Manila and connections at army headquarters provided readier access to equipment. Still, Lim's division was on the same mobilization timetable as the others, and only one regiment, the 42nd Infantry, had completed the initial training cycle. Men of the final infantry regiment to be mobilized, the 43rd, had hardly begun reporting for duty. After arriving from Baguio in mid-November, Lim had busied himself with administrative duties, evaluated his officers for appropriate assignments, and inspected training areas. Lim was overly busy, wrote one American who saw him at this time. He thought Lim spent too much time doing things that should and could have been left to subordinates. On 29 November, Lim and other senior officers had been called to Fort McKinley to be informed of a War Department alert that war with Japan was imminent and told to send troops to the coast immediately. The 42nd Infantry assumed the initial responsibility of covering likely landing areas along the Batangas coastline; other units joined it once war had begun. The 43rd Infantry remained in reserve at Tagaytay, and as a result of "many false reports of [enemy] landings," several of its companies kept "dashing about," reported the regiment's American adviser. Lim moved his division headquarters closer to the coast, to Palico (Paliko). His staff had an animal shelter cleaned and turned into a command post, though they were careful to keep the building's exterior in its natural state and even left a few animals to graze in the surrounding pasture. If the animals failed to fool the Japanese, the men joked, they could always be eaten.[2]

The 41st Division area of responsibility included the Cavite shoreline and then continued from Nasugbu Bay south around Cape Santiago and along lengthy Balayan Bay as far as the Pansipit River at Lemery. Although the shoreline was extensive, potential invasion sites were few. Japanese landings would have been impossible in Cavite without prior neutralization of the fortified islands. The only deepwater port in Batangas was near the town of Nasugbu, where a single concrete pier capable of landing heavy equipment could be found. Shallow-draft landing craft could approach beaches at Balayan Bay, but the army assumed the craft could not accommodate heavy artillery or tanks. Palico stood at the intersection of the main roads leading inland from the coast, and there—should the Japanese get ashore—a steel bridge spanning the Palico River was readied for destruction.[3]

Batangas had long been considered a likely site for an enemy landing. From early in the century, U.S. Army troops had held periodic maneuvers in the province, debarking along the coast and advancing on Manila from the south. It was during one such exercise, in 1914, that a young George Marshall had made a name for himself by directing the operations of a 5,000-man invading army while only a first lieutenant.[4] Some of the earliest training exercises conducted by the Philippine Division in the mid-1920s involved marching to the south of Laguna de Bay to contest imaginary enemy troops advancing from Batangas and Lemery, and MacArthur himself had overseen a major divisional exercise directed toward preventing "the landing of an assumed enemy in the Batangas beach area" in January 1930.[5] Lingayen would become the focus of greater concern by the 1930s, but Manila remained vulnerable to attack from the south, an observation Field Marshal MacArthur seems to have been in the habit of making to anyone who cared to listen. Manila lawyer Marcial Lichauco recalled being told by MacArthur that "the enemy would probably attempt a landing in Batangas," as did the American author John Gunther, who passed through Manila in 1938 collecting information for an Asia-oriented companion to his best-selling *Inside Europe.*[6] Nor had the Philippine Department overlooked the area. Grunert's WPO-3 had assigned immediate responsibility for the defense of the region to the 31st U.S. Infantry Regiment. Once several of the 41st Division's units had mobilized in the area (WPO-3 did not call for activating the entire division), two battalions of the 31st would join the Department Mobile Reserve while the regiment's commanding officer remained with a third battalion to oversee the area's defense. Until the end of November 1941, however, nothing had been done to prepare beach defenses, nor had Philippine Army officers or their American advisers had an opportunity to reconnoiter the area.

Preparations now began in earnest. Lim's men dug fighting holes, cut down extensive cane fields to clear fields of fire, positioned machine guns and what few artillery pieces the division possessed, and strung barbed wire along the coast. Should the Japanese get ashore, reserve defense positions had been established and the bridges leading inland were prepared for demolition. Captain Atienza, who held a degree in civil engineering from the University of the Philippines and had been the engineer in charge of construction at several Philippine Army camps following his commissioning in the regular force in 1938 (as well as the top graduate of the Philippine Army infantry school in 1941), was convinced the division would give a good account of itself if the Japanese attempted to land. A visiting USAFFE engineer offered a less-flattering assessment of the division's preparations for war. Maj. William A. Gay, one of Brig. Gen. Hugh Casey's assistants sent to Tagaytay to oversee the emplacement of road obstacles, thought Atienza out of his depth as a battalion commander and General Lim entirely too optimistic about his division's capabilities. Even Colonel Fortier did not escape Gay's censure. The senior American instructor, in Gay's opinion, seemed hesitant to make "any kind of decision." Gay left the 41st Division "feeling that any enemy attempt to land in this area would be successful."[7]

The Japanese army had made substantial theoretical and practical progress in amphibious warfare training in the post–World War I period, and its war plans at least since 1918 had "stressed preparations for an opposed landing on Luzon." In 1926 army planners had gone so far as to dedicate three amphibiously trained divisions to operations against the Philippines. But the subsequent needs of the war in China had reduced the army's interest in amphibious warfare and led to omplacency.[8] The success of Japanese landings at Lingayen Gulf and Lamon Bay would reflect as much the inadequacy of USAFFE preparations at those places as Japanese competence in sea-to-shore operations. In northern Luzon, the bulk of defending USAFFE divisions could be found at the southern end of Lingayen Gulf, where the broad beaches between Dagupan and Lingayen City were thought to be the more logical landing areas. American forces would come ashore there in January 1945, but in 1941 the Japanese landed farther north, along the gulf's eastern shore.[9]

The main enemy landings in southern Luzon would take place at Lamon Bay, which USAFFE had considered unsuitable for an amphibious assault. Should the Japanese be so unwise as to debark at Lamon, the "rugged terrain" fronting the bay made the roads leading inland "easily defended," at least—the caveat in all American-authored analyses of the Philippine Campaign—with experienced troops.[10] The 41st Division's preparations may have been less sufficient than Atienza believed, but had the 41st been assigned farther east, at Lamon, rather than the more poorly prepared 51st Division and the hastily recruited 1st Division, the Japanese would have met a hotter reception.

As it was, the 41st Division's labored preparations did nothing to hinder the Japanese advance toward Manila. Gen. Masaharu Homma's 14th Army landed at Lingayen Gulf on 22 December and began pushing USAFFE forces before it down the central Luzon plain. That same day, a unit of the 51st Division (PA) clashed with a small Japanese force that had been making its way through Bicol since landing at Legazpi on 12 December. Those few Japanese troops posed no serious threat to USAFFE troops in southern Luzon, but early on the morning of 24 December the Japanese came ashore in greater force at Lamon Bay. The Japanese had in fact considered landing at Batangas but ultimately decided that the approach to Lamon, on Luzon's southeastern coast about seventy miles from Manila, posed fewer problems and was less exposed to American interdiction.[11]

MacArthur had already ordered a withdrawal into Bataan. No Filipino played any part in the decision. Quezon claimed to have been astounded when he learned, perhaps as early as the night of 10 December, of the possibility that MacArthur might order the army to Bataan. (The two ranking Filipino military officers, General Valdes and Constabulary chief Francisco, also went unconsulted. Their headquarters were not yet inducted into USAFFE.) General Sutherland later stated that MacArthur made the decision to abandon the beaches early on the morning of 8 December, as soon as he had learned of the attack on Pearl Harbor. MacArthur realized, Sutherland said, that with the incomplete mobilization and training of the Philippine Army, there was little likelihood of preventing enemy landings. If Sutherland was telling the truth and MacArthur doubted the capacity of the Philippine Army successfully to contest Japanese landings, that conclusion was never shared with his ground-force commanders, and the motive for his repeated (and amply documented) refusal to allow supplies to be moved to Bataan until well into December must remain, to quote biographer D. Clayton James, "a mystery."[12]

Wainwright received orders on the night of 23 December to withdraw to Bataan; Parker was informed at ten o'clock on the morning of the twenty-fourth at his headquarters at Biñan, about halfway between Manila and Tagaytay, and dispatched staff officer Maj. John H. Bennett to tell Lim that the 41st Division was to move at once to Abucay, Bataan. Through some never-explained mischance, Lim did not receive word of the order until late that afternoon. Leaving the 42nd Infantry behind as a covering force, the division boarded vehicles commandeered from the Pasay Transportation Company and drove through Manila and continued to Bataan, with General Lim buying up all the cigars he could find along the way. Most of the division was around Abucay by noon on Christmas Day; the remainder of the division straggled in over the next three days.[13] WPO-3's provision for withdrawing into Bataan would have been known to Lim and his responsibilities as head of WPD may have taken him to the province, but no documentary evidence remains to say so, and his letters are silent on the issue. Certainly few enlisted soldiers in the 41st Division were likely to have envisioned Bataan in their future. According to Captain Atienza, when the men boarded buses to make the move north—the soldiers did not know to where they were bound—they repeatedly asked why they were moving away from "the relative comfort of the beaches where they had worked so hard," away from the homes and the families they had expected to protect.[14]

"Bataan," author and veteran León María Guerrero wrote in a once-controversial but now long-forgotten essay, "was a Filipino fight. . . . This does not," he continued, "depreciate American participation in the campaign. The strategy and supreme command were American; the logistics and supplies were American; the [USAFFE] and two Corps headquarters, as well as many of the most efficient and gallant front-line commanders, were Americans. . . . But the men on the line were Filipinos."[15] No precise figure is available, but by December 1941, United States Army Forces in the Far East numbered about 150,000 troops. Just under 12,000 of these were Filipinos serving in the Philippine Scouts; American army units totaled 19,000 officers and enlisted men. That is, Americans made up about 13 percent of USAFFE, "the great majority" of whom, as Col. E. B. Miller of the 194th Tank Battalion underlined in one of the earliest and least-varnished accounts of the Philippine Campaign, were "not equipped or trained as combat elements." The rest of USAFFE was the Philippine Army.[16]

Not all of these men were on Luzon. Several Philippine Army divisions (the 61st, 81st, and 101st), and portions of some reserve divisions that moved to Luzon from the southern islands (the 71st Division's 73rd Infantry Regiment and the 91st Division's 93rd Infantry) remained in the south. Nor did all of those under arms on Luzon at the start of the war withdraw to Bataan. Some were killed, wounded, or captured during the early days of the campaign, while others found themselves cut off from retreating USAFFE units. But most of an estimated 13,000 Philippine Army soldiers who were serving with the North and South Luzon Forces on 8 December and who were not in or approaching Bataan by the end of the month simply "returned to their homes" during the retreat. This was not necessarily a bad thing. "The attrition of Philippine Army units due to desertion during the early fighting on Luzon," as one historian has observed, "actually constituted a process of selection contributing to the greater effectiveness of those units."[17]

Filipinos continued to make up the overwhelming number of soldiers on Bataan. With the exception of a few troops isolated in northern Luzon, the battalion at Pettit Barracks at Zamboanga, and 1,300 or so serving with the 91st and 92nd Coast Artillery Regiments on Corregidor, the Philippine Scouts were on Bataan. As for the 19,000 American soldiers in the Philippine garrison? Harbor defense command put the strength of the American army component of the Manila Bay forts—on Corregidor, El Fraile, Caballo, and Carabao Islands—at just over 5,000 in mid-April 1942. (This number included several hundred American soldiers who had escaped from Bataan.) Over 3,000 served in the 59th and 60th Coast Artillery Regiments and nearly 2,000 more filled support and administrative positions.[18] With 5,609 officers and men, the air corps approached almost a third of the American component of USAFFE. An unknown number, but at least several hundred (mostly officers), were able to escape the Philippines, and somewhere between 900 and 1,200 air corps personnel were assigned to Mindanao, as were about 250 U.S. Army officers and enlisted men who were on duty with headquarters and Philippine Army units off Luzon. Most of the remainder of the air corps, some 3,600 officers and men, were on Bataan.[19] In sum, over 80,000 Filipino and American soldiers crowded into the peninsula by early January 1942; roughly 85 percent were Filipinos, and nearly three-quarters of the total were in the Philippine Army.[20]

Bataan (unlike Americans, Filipinos pronounce distinctly each of the word's three two-letter syllables) was a pestilent, heavily forested peninsula some twenty miles in breadth and thirty miles from north to south dominated throughout its length by "supposed extinct volcano[es]." Mount Natib occupied the northern half of Bataan; the multipeaked Mariveles Mountains defined the southern half. Despite its importance in army war planning as a redoubt for American forces even before the 1920s, years passed with little done to prepare Bataan to withstand a siege. The department intelligence office's 1923 multivolume "Military Handbook of the Philippines" described the main route across the peninsula, from the province's capital at Balanga on the east coast to the small town of Bagac on the west—intended to link the major line of defense—as suitable for "men on foot and horses only" and probably impossible of passage during the rainy season.[21] A Philippine almanac published in 1926 confirmed that a daily "auto-buss" service connected San Fernando, Pampanga, with Balanga, but beyond that "other coastal and interior towns [had to] be reached on horse-back or by foot paths." Maps of Bataan in the early 1930s showed a "first-class" road running down the east coast only as far as Limay about sixteen kilometers south of Balanga, but being labeled first-class on a map of the Philippines, an author of the G-4 annex to the 1931 revision of the Philippine Defense Project explained, did not mean the road was suitable for military traffic. A sailor assigned to the navy's radio intercept station in 1935 when it was briefly located near Mariveles noted that even at that late date, trips to Manila from Mariveles were made by sea because only "brave souls" dared the overland route.[22]

J. Lawton Collins, a staff officer who participated in Philippine Division maneuvers in the Mariveles area in 1934, wrote that the exercise made clear "the necessity of improving road communications on Bataan," and in December 1934 Philippine Scout engineers and field artillerymen were put to work constructing an all-weather road from Limay to Mariveles and northwest to the Aglaloma River, which empties into the China Sea side of Bataan between Luzon and Quinauan Points. "For many years," another officer involved in the work recalled, "it had been customary of the 14th Engineers to work part time for the Department Engineer. Most work was done on Bataan during the dry season and consisted mainly of surveying, developing trails, and constructing bridges and roads." By 1940 maps of the peninsula indicated a paved east coast road to Mariveles with an unimproved road continuing up the west coast beyond Bagac. Only that year did it become possible to travel by road from Bagac north all the way to Moron. Until then, inhabitants of Moron who wanted to go to Manila would travel north by boat to Olongapo, in Subic Bay, and continue overland. By then, too, an improved road linked Bagac with the east coast town of Pilar.[23] When General Grunert took command of the department in May 1940, he sent Philippine Scouts of the 45th and 57th Infantry Regiments to the military reservation on Bataan to put a stop to illegal logging that was stripping the army-built roads and trails of their cover from aerial observation. The men also practiced jungle warfare techniques, fortuitously training near the same areas where they would confront the Japanese a year and a half later.[24]

The 41st Division moved into Bataan in late December unmolested by the advancing Japanese. To some extent, Japanese thinking mirrored that of the Americans: their plans were based on what they wanted to have happen,

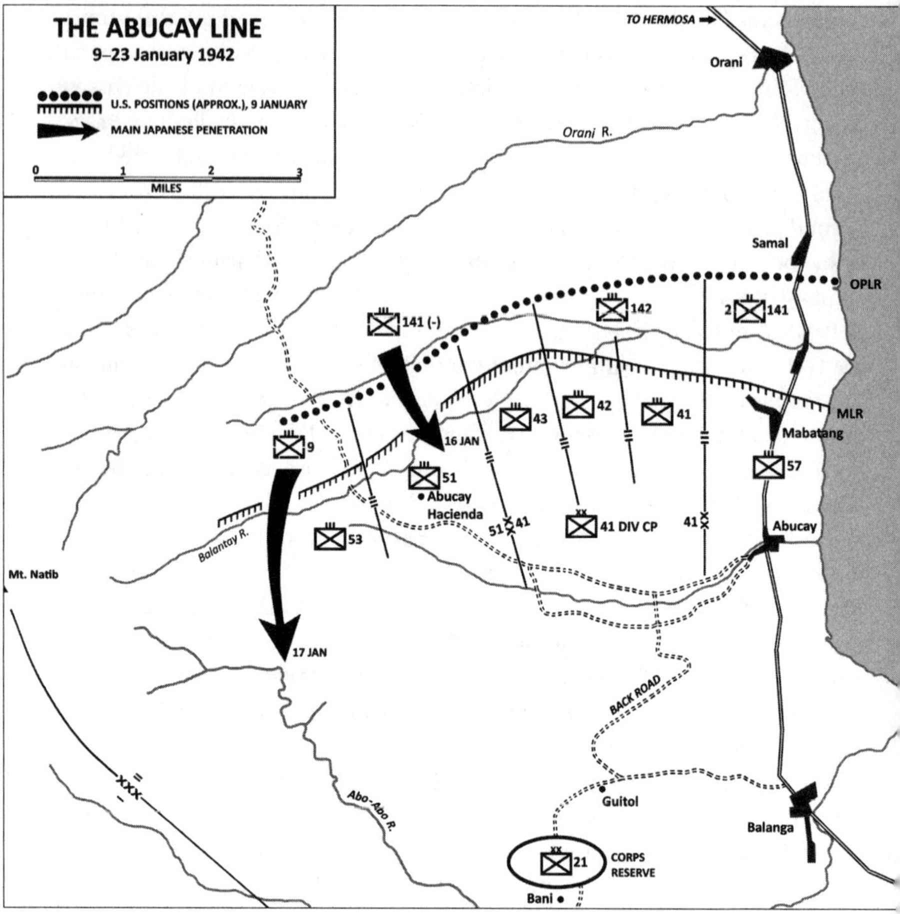

Bataan, January 1942.

not necessarily on what was likely to take place. MacArthur had projected a Japanese invasion in March or April 1942 because that is when Philippine Army training and the schedule of reinforcements from the United States would be well along, even though both USAFFE and War Department planners knew that every plan for the defense of the Philippines that had been written over the past two decades had foreseen a Japanese attack in either December or January. The latter months allowed the maximum amount of time for field operations before the rainy season set in, in late June or early July.[25] Similarly, the Japanese commander was handed a fifty-day schedule of operations because that is what the army counted on to meet its goals elsewhere, not because of a realistic assessment of both Japanese and Philippine-American capabilities. General Homma was to make the capture of Manila his objective. During a conference in October 1941, the idea that Filipino and American troops might withdraw into Bataan was raised but had been "brushed aside without discussion." When Homma began detailed planning for the Philippine invasion in mid-November 1941, his chief of staff, Lt. Gen. Masami Maeda, again pointed out that the enemy might retreat into Bataan and await relief from the United States. Homma queried the general staff: was Manila or the enemy army his target? Homma was instructed to make the capture of the Philippine capital his goal. Homma could not even get officers with recent knowledge of the Philippines assigned to his 14th Army staff because, the imperial general staff told him, "they had been posted elsewhere and were not available."[26] Nor had decades of intelligence-gathering activity in the Philippines prepared the Japanese for MacArthur's withdrawal into Bataan. The "my gardener turned out to be a colonel in the Japanese army" anecdote is a hoary staple of World War II in the Philippines lore, and Japanese agents had been apprehended for espionage from early in the American period of occupation, yet the Japanese high command apparently knew nothing of HPD's War Plans Orange.[27]

Fortunately for Lim, his untested division would not face the best the Japanese army had to offer. Based on evaluation of captured documents and interrogation of prisoners, a USAFFE intelligence officer would later conclude that the Philippine invasion force was one of "'pick-up' troops" that represented "a subordinate effort" in Japan's scheme of operations. Homma's "best division," the 48th, had swept USAFFE down the Luzon plain, but it was earmarked for further operations in Java. In its place, Homma received the 65th Brigade, a unit of minimally trained "mostly older men" suitable for occupation duties but unprepared for the rigors of Bataan. Its commander was Lt. Gen. Akira Nara, reportedly chosen to command because he had spent several years in the United States. In fact, then-captain Nara, a decorated veteran of the Japanese army's seizure of German possessions in China in 1914, had been something of a celebrity guest-student in the advanced course at Fort Benning when Lim had been there in 1926–27. Now, the fifty-two-year-old officer found himself hurried from Taiwan and supplied with intelligence from Homma's headquarters that significantly underestimated the size and composition of the enemy forces he was expected to overcome within a few days.[28]

Lead elements of the 41st Division arrived in Bataan midmorning on Christmas Day 1941 and, once corralled and pointed in the right direction, began taking up positions along what would be known as the Abucay line. Lim established division headquarters in the old cadre training camp at Balanga, four miles south of Abucay. After a few days, Lim saw that he was too far from the front and Balanga was being bombed too frequently by enemy airplanes, so he moved his forward headquarters into what had been a regimental command post along the Abucay Hacienda Road, about two and one-half miles behind the main line of resistance.

The Abucay line began at Mabatang, a coastal settlement a couple of miles north of the town of Abucay. From the beach inland about 1,500 yards, through the village and across the east coast road, the American 31st Infantry had begun organizing the ground for defense. Everything to the west—15,000 yards along the steep-banked but shallow Balantay River and up to the peaks of Mount Natib that marked the dividing line between I ("first") and II ("second") Philippine Corps—belonged to the 41st Division. No work had been done. Fortier complained that "not a blade of grass [had been cut] nor a shovelful of earth had been turned." The line to be occupied seemed to have been determined by officers who had only looked at a map and knew nothing of the terrain. Fortier commenced "a careful survey to determine the actual line to be held." While other units (including the 31st U.S. Infantry, replaced by the 57th Infantry (PS) at Mabatang at the end of December) held off the Japanese a few miles to the north, the division would be given nearly two weeks to make ready. "Too much praise," Fortier subsequently wrote, "cannot be given the men for the way they pitched in."[29]

The division's front was too wide for the number of soldiers available. The arrival of two regiments of the 51st Division (PA) at the start of the new year allowed Lim's men to shift eastward and strengthen their shortened portion of the line. The 51st Division had been bruised at Mauban, Tayabas, and moved to the Abucay line without its best-trained component, the 52nd Regiment, which had been consigned to beach defense. After the war, both the USAFFE chief of staff and the corps commander would tell army historians that the dearth of forces along the eastern slope of Mount Natib had been of grave concern to them. Nonetheless, at the time they were content to leave responsibility for the far left of the Abucay line to the 53rd Infantry (PA)—"the worst trained [regiment] in the entire II Corps," as characterized by the American author of the most detailed combat history of the Bataan Campaign. This area had initially been held by a battalion of the 42nd Infantry, whose men were "jubilant," according to Magtoto, when the 43rd Regiment had relieved them (the 51st Division then took the 43rd's place). The soldiers were certain that the difficult terrain meant they would see no action since the Japanese could not possibly attack over such ground. They were not alone in thinking so. Several officers from division headquarters had been ordered to the top of Mount Natib, and after a difficult daylong ascent they returned late the next morning convinced of the foolishness of trying "to defend these parts."[30]

Lim's division suffered its first death—self-inflicted—late on the night of 5 January. A lieutenant ordered his men to shoot at a suspicious sound in a bamboo clump, and soon uncontrolled fire was to be heard all along the line. The result was several wounded and one man killed, "shot squarely from the back." Until that night, many men had not fired their rifles. They now began to test their mettle against the Japanese. A soldier of one patrol sent out on the left of the division front, where the jungle made observation especially difficult, returned without his rifle but clutching a sword he had wrested from an enemy officer he had killed in hand-to-hand combat. Meanwhile, civilians passing through the line brought stories of homes looted and burned, men conscripted for labor, women attacked and raped.[31] Perhaps, too, at this time a few soldiers deserted.[32]

The war began in earnest with an enemy artillery barrage on the afternoon of 8 January.[33] To the division's right, the Japanese 141st Infantry Regiment had made the 57th Infantry (PS) its primary target. A strong attack against the Philippine Scout regiment's left flank on the night of 11–12 January forced one company to give way and brought the 41st Infantry into action. A counterattack by the regiment's C Company and Scout stragglers recovered much of the 57th's lost ground on the morning of 12 January.[34] While keeping pressure all along the division front, the Japanese pushed their assault steadily westward, testing in turn the 41st Infantry on the division right, the 42nd Infantry in the middle, and the 43rd Infantry on the division's left.

That regiment, like the third infantry regiment of every reserve division, had been the last mobilized and had had almost no training. Many of the men assigned to the regiment came from the islands of Mindoro and Palawan, and some had not been able to make it to Luzon to join the division. Lim had relieved its commander, a long-serving Constabulary officer who had undergone infantry schooling at Fort Benning, even before the fighting began at Abucay. According to the division history, the regiment had been forced off the main line of resistance as a result of an artillery barrage on the afternoon of 8 January. It regained the line, but on 13–14 January, the Japanese applied such "painful pressure" on the 43rd Regiment that reinforcements from the 23rd Infantry Regiment (PA) were called for.

The enemy finally found success on the far left. On 14–15 January, the 51st Division (PA) began to give way. Ironically, an unexpectedly successful counterattack by the 51st Infantry on the morning of 16 January—ordered by the corps commander against the wishes of the division commander—hastened the division's collapse. The Japanese moved quickly against the regiment's exposed flanks, forcing adjacent units to fall back or refuse their flanks, opening a path for the enemy. By the end of the day, the 51st Division was in retreat. The 53rd

Infantry Regiment headed west to try to link up with I Corps; the 51st Infantry reformed two miles to the south. Had the enemy continued pushing through the 51st Division area it might have gotten behind the 41st Division; instead it "flung itself against the left flank of the 41st Division." This gave USAFFE time to bring up two regiments of the Philippine Division, the 31st Infantry (U.S.) and the 45th Infantry (PS). They advanced against the Japanese on 17–18 January to recover the ground lost by the 51st Division.[35]

Lim left the division front once during the fighting. A renewed Japanese push against the Philippine Division on the left of the Abucay line in the early afternoon of 22 January threatened the 41st Division's forward command post and a nearby message center that could be reached down a ravine that cut southeast through the 43rd Infantry's regimental reserve line. By the end of the day, the enemy had pushed the Philippine Division back to about where it had started its offensive five days earlier. No reserves were available. The 31st U.S. Infantry Regiment was fully committed on the division's left; a provisional battalion of the 41st Engineers—the division's "ready reserve"—was already in action. If the enemy broke through, only a scratch group of forty-odd headquarters personnel would stand between it and the command post. Toward midnight the division chief of staff, Lt. Col. Tomas Domaoal, suggested that Lim go to Balanga. Lim demurred, but other staff officers and Fortier added their voices, and Lim allowed himself to be escorted to the rear command post (CP). He was back at the forward CP by daybreak.

During his absence, the division had its "first case of a man going crazy." One of the telephone operators began muttering, "My guardian angel is MacArthur." No one paid attention to him, but suddenly he jumped up, waved a pistol around, and cursed Americans as cowards for failing to lead the Filipinos to victory. The soldier was either knocked to the ground or "talked . . . into submission" and taken to a rear area hospital.[36]

At Abucay, the division had bent on both ends but had not broken. The 42nd Regiment at the division's center never moved off the main line of resistance. But while the 41st Division was holding locally, USAFFE elsewhere was losing the battle. On the far right, the 57th Infantry (PS) stood fast and in fact had seen no action since 15 January, but on II Corps' far left, the Japanese had routed General Jones's 51st Division (PA).[37] Two regiments of the Philippine Division had moved forward to fill the breach, but after five days and nights of effort they had been unable to restore the line. Meanwhile, more by luck than by design, the Japanese 9th Infantry Regiment had filtered around and through the 51st Division and unknowingly reached the Abo-Abo River, which flowed southeast off Mount Natib. Continuing down the river valley, the Japanease troops were now in position to get well behind the Abucay line.

On the west side of the peninsula, during the night of 21–22 January, a battalion of the Japanese 20th Infantry Regiment had managed to reach the West Road behind Brig. Gen. Fidel Segundo's 1st Division along the Mauban line. A mixed force of Philippine Army and Constabulary soldiers, Scouts of the 26th Cavalry, and American-manned M3s of the 194th Tank Battalion failed to dislodge the enemy. The 1st Division's soldiers destroyed their artillery, edged down the coast, and hiked back to the West Road south of the Japanese roadblock. This withdrawal was complete by 25 January, and Wainwright's I Corps began taking position along the western portion of the Orion-Bagac line.

General Sutherland had visited the front and already decided that the Abucay line could no longer be held. Lim was called to II Corps headquarters near Limay on the twenty-third and returned with instructions to move the division to the Pilar-Bagac road. Lim had sent Atienza to scout out the division's new headquarters along the road near kilometer marker 138. The following day, Fortier stayed at the forward CP to oversee the division's evacuation. On the evening of 24 January, the 41st Infantry Regiment filed south, followed by the 42nd, and finally the 43rd Infantry. A covering shell provided by a battalion of the 42nd remained behind, firing machine guns to disguise the retreat. It would depart unmolested by the Japanese at 2:30 A.M. on 25 January.

About 9 P.M. the next night, with most of the division gone, Fortier and two other Americans climbed into Fortier's jeep and made their way to where the Abucay Hacienda Road crossed what was known as the "back road" that led south to the small settlement of Guitol. Fortier found utter confusion: troops were pouring in "from all directions" and nothing was moving out. The pileup of men and vehicles threatened all they had achieved on the front line. Fortunately, the Japanese did not realize that the Filipino-American forces were withdrawing and did nothing to take advantage of USAFFE's exposure to enemy air and artillery; nevertheless, in the Americans' estimation the disorganized withdrawal undid the soupçon of Filipino competence that had begun to emerge in the previous weeks' action, and it was their recollections that would inform the U.S. Army's official history of the Philippine Campaign. The 41st Division history published by the Philippine Army makes no mention of that night.[38]

What price did the 41st Division pay for its success at Abucay? Given the widespread destruction of unit records at the time of surrender, historians have been reluctant to offer casualty statistics, a tone Louis Morton set in the official history: "Since there are no casualty tables for this campaign, it is not possible to state what the losses for the action along the Abucay-Mauban line were." (He was dubious of MacArthur's claim to have lost 35 percent of his entire force and as much as 60 percent of some divisions since 8 December 1941 and felt that it was "extremely doubtful that [losses at Abucay] were serious enough to force a withdrawal.")[39] Subsequent historians, Filipino and American, have not ventured to offer casualty figures for Abucay, or elsewhere on Bataan, either. Death-in-battle figures are available for American units, however, and they suggest that wartime impressions of the high human cost of Bataan contrast sharply with the actual number of losses. For example, with about 1,800 officers and men, the New Mexico National Guard's 200th Coast Artillery Regiment (antiaircraft) and its spin-off, the 515th, made up one of the larger American organizations on Bataan. "Almost the whole unit was wiped out," according to an army-authored history of the campaign written in 1946. In fact, eighteen to twenty enlisted men and no officers were killed in the Philippine Campaign, eight of them on Bataan (less than one-half of 1 percent of unit strength). To the New Mexico National Guard's official historian, this was a "remarkable" figure, given that the units "engaged in combat with the invaders several times every day for four continuous months." (Losses are relative, of course. The antiaircraft regiment of the Delaware National Guard originally earmarked for Philippine service instead spent the war in the South Pacific and did not lose a single man to enemy action.)[40] Similarly, army nurses told fellow prisoners at the University of Santo Tomas internment camp that the 31st U.S. Infantry had been "practically wiped out" in the final Japanese offensive. "Manila's Own" did pay a high price, but nowhere near as high as the nurses thought.[41]

Battle deaths in other American units were equally low. The tank group began the Philippine Campaign with eighty-five officers and 1,067 enlisted men. By the time of the surrender, six officers and 41 enlisted men had died, some in accidents and not all on Bataan.[42] Most of the air corps ground units on Bataan suffered few battle casualties. An officer of the provisional regiment estimated its losses while assigned to the Orion-Bagac line on Bataan as six killed in action while on patrol and "no more than a dozen" additional casualties from Japanese bombing. Memoirs by unit veterans note few deaths before the surrender as well.[43] There were, in addition, a few marines and sailors killed on Bataan.[44] The Philippine Scouts lost just over five hundred officers and men—about 4 percent of its enlisted force—during the campaign, all but sixty or so on Bataan.[45] Relying on data provided by U.S. Army doctors soon after the surrender of Corregidor, the Japanese, who, if anything, had reason to inflate the number of enemy deaths, calculated that 365 American officers and men had been killed on Bataan.[46] In sum, the decimation of American units in the Philippines in 1941–42 came after surrender, not fighting the Japanese in battle.

As for the Americans assigned to Lim's division, the army nurses told the other internees that losses had been high at Abucay, "especially among the American officers serving with the Philippine Army." Of the eighty or so American officers and enlisted men with the 41st Division, eight—most of them former NCOs from the U.S. 31st Infantry Regiment—are known to have been killed in action or listed as missing, two at Abucay. Statistically, Americans assigned to the 41st Division were more than twice as likely to be killed in action as those who served in any U.S. Army unit on Bataan.[47]

Determining Philippine Army losses poses significantly greater challenges.[48] No Philippine Army muster rolls survived the war. Philippine Army headquarters papers were burned at the time of surrender. The 41st Division buried its remaining records on 9 April 1942, and officers who returned to the burial site after the war saw that it had already been dug up. The documents were never recovered. Nevertheless, some casualty figures for Abucay do exist. Fortier estimated that each of the three line regiments had lost about one-third of its strength at Abucay (from 1,800 men down to 1,200). An American officer who served with the 41st Infantry Regiment gave the precise figure of 696 casualties suffered over a five-day period at Abucay. Another officer with the regiment estimated its losses as "over seven hundred" by 18 January 1942. According to an American officer attached to the 43rd Infantry, that regiment had 162 killed, 154 wounded, and about 150 missing along the Abucay line. Divisional organizations behind the line fared better. Capt. Andrew Shoemake, who served with the 2nd Battalion, 41st Field Artillery (and who would, like so many others, survive the fighting on Bataan only to die as a prisoner of war), noted that the regiment lost no officers, either American or Filipino, during the campaign, but that seven enlisted men were killed as a result of Japanese counterbattery fire on 14 January. On the same day, the 41st Engineer s lost three men killed by friendly artillery fire. If the other infantry regiments suffered losses comparable to the 43rd Infantry—and each had seen significant action in mid-January—then the 41st Division may have had about as many men killed at Abucay as did all American-manned units combined over the course of the entire Bataan campaign.[49]

Abucay established the 41st Division's reputation as the best Philippine Army division on Bataan and Lim's reputation as the best Philippine Army general—the "grand old man of the Filipino army," as he was beginning to be called; so journalist Frank Hewlett informed the readers of American newspapers during the initially heady interlude between Abucay and the calamitous enemy offensive of April 1942 that followed. Carlos Romulo sent Lim a letter from Corregidor filled with accolades: "You are *the* one Filipino general who has caught the imagination of everyone," Romulo wrote: General MacArthur "has praised you time and time again." Sutherland spoke highly of him, and President Quezon had exclaimed that Lim was "the only general we have in our army with *cojones*, and he is showing it now." Even discounting Romulo's penchant for puffery, Lim must have been pleased. Over the course of two intense weeks, the men of the 41st Division had withstood one Japanese assault after another across the length of their line. Like the much-heralded 57th Infantry Regiment (PS) on their right, they had at times bent but not broken. Unlike the Philippine Scout regiment, the 41st Division had neither history nor tradition. Unlike the 57th Infantry, the division had not had its pick of recruits, nor had it nearly a year of training before the enemy attack. It had no modern small arms, nor a cadre of long-serving NCOs, nor American officers with command authority down to the platoon level. USAFFE awarded no Medals of Honor to Philippine Army soldiers during the war, and only four Distinguished Service Crosses, the army's second-highest medal for bravery, went to enlisted men of the Philippine Army; but three of the four DSC recipients were soldiers of Lim's division. In a letter to his wife mailed from "the front line, Bataan," in February, Lim bragged that his division had "defended the biggest portion of the Abucay position" and had killed or wounded thousands of Japanese. "We are all brave," he told her, "and I do not know how I can pick the ones who are not."[50]

CHAPTER 9

"His Division, His Kingdom"

Lim on Bataan, II

Notwithstanding the Philippine Army's greater numerical presence on the peninsula and Filipino veterans' insistence that Bataan had been "a Filipino fight"—to them, Corregidor was the Americans' battle—the Americanization of Bataan began during the war itself. Within weeks of the battle's end, for example, the soldier magazine *Yank* had proclaimed Bataan to be "a Story of Courage that becomes more beautifully American with each telling."[1] In American-authored histories, at least, Philippine Army enlisted men would be largely unseen participants in the Bataan Campaign. Filipino officers would be all but invisible. Lim could not know that the Philippine Army would lose the battle for history, but thirty years of interaction had certainly sensitized him to the American tendency to discount Filipino ability. In that sense, anyway, he understood that the Japanese were only the more obvious enemy on Bataan. Thus Lim determined, as one unhappy American instructor complained in writing, that "his division [would be] his kingdom" and did not "intend for anyone to interfere with him."[2]

Inevitably, the Americanization of Bataan meant the diminishment of the Philippine Army on Bataan, and that, too, started during the war. "I can tell you about the army" on Bataan, U.S. Navy ensign George Cox is quoted as saying in *They Were Expendable*, William White's wartime classic about the navy torpedo boat squadron in the Philippines commanded by swashbuckling, Medal of Honor–winning Lt. John Bulkeley. "The front-line fighting soldiers consisted, first, of about two thousand Americans, well seasoned and good fighters. Then, about twelve hundred Filipino Scouts—equally well trained and equally good. Lastly, . . . about twenty-seven thousand Filipino trainees—young kids who had never worn a uniform until a few weeks before the war started."[3] At least Cox recognized the Philippine Army's numerical predominance on Bataan. Others did not. From intelligence officer Lt. Col. Warren Clear, who had been evacuated from Corregidor by submarine in February 1942, the American public learned that, on Bataan, "Filipino riflemen" served as a "screen" against attacking Japanese who then came up against a "murderous belt of barbed-wire tangles, foxholes manned by American regulars, [and] machine guns trained down jungle trails." In fact, the only "American regulars" who manned foxholes on the front line on Bataan were soldiers of the Provisional Air Corps Regiment assigned to sector B along the Orion-Bagac line. According to the official U.S. Army history of the campaign, the ill-equipped regiment "fell back without a fight" when Japanese tanks advanced against it on the morning of 7 April. When the unit regrouped farther to the rear, 1,000 of the 1,400 men who had begun the withdrawal had disappeared, and few of the missing men had been killed in battle.[4]

The Philippine Army took unrecognizable form in other books. Francis Miller, author of an early and popular MacArthur biography, had Filipino soldiers swinging on rattan vines through the jungles of Bataan "with the agility of Tarzans" from one "stately . . . Philippine mahogany tree" to another. A Melville Jacoby article in *Life* even included a photo of "swarthy, barking General Vicente Lim, whose soldiers say if they don't jump at his command, he'll kick them in the tail," but a diligent reader would have had to conclude that Lim commanded either American soldiers or Philippine Scouts. Jacoby made no mention of the Philippine Army.[5]

The marginalization of the Philippine Army was well illustrated—literally—by a four-photo display of the surrender on Bataan that appeared in *Life* magazine in July 1942, among the first of the event to be published in the United States. Three-fourths of Luzon Force was Filipino; three of the four photographs showed only Americans. One was of Maj. Gen. Edward King at Lamao; in a second image, resolute-appearing American soldiers confronted their Japanese captors; the third posed photo pictured an American soldier, an army helmet, and Old Glory; a final photograph showed Filipino soldiers as they "come out of their hiding place." The brief accompanying text mentioned the surrender of 37,000 American soldiers on Bataan (three times the actual number present) "after four heartbreaking months of continuous fighting." It said nothing about the Philippine Army.[6] Aware from reading the stateside press that Americans had little appreciation of the part Filipinos had played in the fighting, the Commonwealth government-in-exile stressed the Philippine Army's prominence on Bataan. In a speech prepared for delivery before the Maryland Bar Association in January 1943, for example, President Quezon intended to remind his audience that Filipino soldiers comprised the "immense majority of General MacArthur's infantry" and that "many, many, more" of them died in the campaign than did Americans. "There were approximately seven Filipino soldiers for each American soldier" in USAFFE, the government's publicity bureau emphasized, but the only literature it could recommend to interested Americans were those very same popular magazine articles that for the most part ignored the Filipino presence in MacArthur's army.[7]

Damning characterizations of the army circulated among American soldiers. General Wainwright's aide-de-camp Thomas Dooley scribbled in his diary in mid-January that Philippine Army troops "start running when the first shot is fired." "It is generally accepted," he continued, "that all Philippine Army units will not fight." Coast artilleryman Col. Paul Bunker spent the war on Corregidor, but he heard plenty about the "so-called" Philippine Army from those who had visited the front lines. One officer returning from Bataan in mid-January told Bunker that "catching sight of a few Japs," the Filipino infantry ran back through the artillery positions and fled to the rear. The engineer officer Wendell Fertig, who later gained fame as a guerrilla chieftain on Mindanao, joked that Filipino soldiers threw everything away except their mess kits, which led one wit to suggest welding their mess kits to their rifles. The Filipinos "were never soldiers. They didn't really want to fight," one veteran of the air corps regiment said. "One way or another," a second agreed, "they quit before the surrender."[8]

Negative stereotypes of the Philippine Army have so long dominated the historical literature in the United States that it is useful to recall that in 1941 few Americans knew anything about the army, and those who did, or thought they did, were as apt as not to have a positive image of it, especially the many officers who came to the Philippines in the few weeks remaining before the outbreak of war. Officers assigned to the Philippine Department had been sent to observe or instruct Philippine Army activities from its founding, but until General Grunert began encouraging garrison officers to familiarize themselves with the Philippine Army in 1940–41, there had been remarkably little interaction with the new army. There was some interest, however. One officer who returned from the Philippines in 1939 told War Plans Division officials that while the new army suffered from a lack of trained officers and adequate funding, nonetheless the recruits "look[ed] very well" and appeared to have great potential. "This may be heresy," the unnamed officer wrote, "but they look much better potentially to me than the Scouts. With well-trained leaders of small units, I think I would rather campaign with them than with the Scouts." An officer of the 31st U.S. Infantry assigned to visit a Philippine Army camp "'to observe and report' upon the mobilization test" held in May 1939 came to a similar conclusion: "These units, given thirty to sixty days training properly supervised by a few officers of experience, could be brought to a state of efficiency which would make them of great value [to the U.S. Army] in defense of the Islands."[9]

For officers in the United States, knowledge of the Philippine Army could be gleaned from occasional articles that invariably portrayed the army in a positive light, just as they did the mobilizing draftees and national guardsmen of the American army. In an illustrated piece that appeared in *The Coast Artillery*

Journal in early 1941, for example, Lt. Col. Robert Carswell, who served on the High Commissioner's staff, explained that "training for national defense" had been ongoing since 1937 and that the Philippine Army had continued to grow "in both numbers and efficiency" thereafter. Photographs of spotless barracks rooms and of armed, uniformed, and well-groomed soldiers reinforced the message: the Philippine Army was progressing along the same lines as the expanding U.S. Army. Capt. Edward Kraus had been so impressed by "the drill of a field artillery battalion in the Philippine Army maneuvers" of March 1941 that in his "subsequent recommendations [he] stated that this unit was then ready for combat" (provided, of course, that an American officer commanded it). Kraus's article was not published until the war began, but officers must have been hearing and reading this kind of thing before then, because, discussing the Philippine Army aboard a Manila-bound troopship in October 1941, Lt. Col. Hiram Tarkington and his colleagues assumed that MacArthur had already raised an army of a half million men. Their task, they agreed, would be only to put "the finishing touches" on the army's training. Soon after his arrival in Manila, Col. Bradford Chynoweth—initially assigned to command the 61st Philippine Army Division—betrayed his ignorance of local conditions by asking a senior staff officer, Col. Charles Stivers, if the Philippine Army had yet received M-1 rifles. Stivers reportedly "threw back his head and roared with laughter." It was "easy to see from that question," Stivers answered, that Chynoweth had not "been in the Islands long this time." The Philippine Army did not have the new Garands; it did not even have the older Springfields.[10]

Chynoweth at least had the excuse that he had last seen the Philippines when his army-officer father had been stationed on Mindanao early in the century. Richard Malloneé's experience was more extensive and recent, but he, too, was surprised by the Philippine Army's lack of progress. He had served in the Philippines in the late 1920s, first with the 24th Field Artillery at Stotsenburg and then as assistant operations officer at Fort Santiago. As such, he had traveled the length of the archipelago, was intimately knowledgeable about the Philippine Department's war plans, and prided himself on having stayed current on Philippine political issues. He also knew MacArthur. As recently as 1937, during MacArthur's trip to the United States with Manuel Quezon early that year, MacArthur had told him that the Philippine Army was to have "the newest and best guns" available from Europe, far superior to the United States Army's "outmoded" weapons. The reality, a stunned Malloneé learned, included obsolete guns, little or no ammunition on hand, and Filipino soldiers who had never seen an artillery piece.[11]

It was that sense of shocked surprise and, ultimately, of anger and betrayal felt by the surrendered American soldiers of Bataan that informed the official history of the campaign. Its publication in 1953 would do nothing to enhance the reputation of the Philippine Army. In *The Fall of the Philippines*, Louis Morton, himself an army veteran who had served in the South Pacific and in the Philippines, had a compelling story to tell and told it well. The Office of the Chief of Military History nominated the book for a Pulitzer Prize and Bancroft Prize and held it up as the literary standard to which authors of other volumes should aspire. Morton's was unique among volumes of the *United States Army in World War II* series in that while the authors of all the other "green books" (so-called because of the color of their original binding) described victory, Morton alone had to explain defeat. The reams of official documents that girded the other volumes (and have left them largely unread both by the public and subsequent generations of historians) did not exist for Morton's book. Instead, as Morton explained in a lengthy note on sources, "only a small number of official documents survived the campaign [and thus] unofficial records . . . are far more numerous, and, with published works, constitute the main sources" on which the volume was based. Morton "embarked on an ambitious letter-writing program, made trips to various parts of the country, and induced many officers to support his requests by letters of their own." "The response," Morton concluded, "entirely justified the time and effort spent."[12]

Naturally, the bulk of existing documents and correspondents was to be found in the United States. Morton did attempt to solicit commentary and material from the Philippines to ensure "proper recognition to the activities of the Philippine units," but nothing came of the effort. He did not succeed in developing a link to the Philippine Army's historical section. He sent copies of the completed draft manuscript to Generals Francisco and Capinpin, the only two of the five Filipino generals captured on Bataan to have survived the war. Neither responded.[13]

Since most of the soldiers on Bataan were Filipinos, much of the more detailed commentary and contributions to the official history came from American officers who had served with Philippine Army units. Bluemel offered a lengthy report on the activities of his own division as well as extensive comments on drafts of the official history. Ray O'Day sent a record of the 21st Division, to which he had been the senior adviser. Richard Mallonée, also with the 21st, shared his two-volume diary with the Office of the Chief of Military History. Malcolm Fortier responded at length to draft portions of Morton's work. Colonel Fortier intended to write a history of the 41st Division and had completed a lengthy narrative of the division's activities in Batangas and Bataan that he shared with OCMH. Another officer, Calvin Chunn of the 45th Infantry (PS), had begun interviewing officers in prison camp soon after the surrender with the intention of collecting material for a campaign history. Chunn's material was also provided to OCMH.

Of course, the Philippine Army did have the well-known problems in leadership, training, and equipment that Morton's correspondents readily identified. How could it not, given that no division had fully mobilized when the Japanese attacked? Nevertheless, Morton knew that the ill-tempered and exaggerated characterizations of the Philippine Army that he chose to repeat in the official history—most infamously Bluemel's comment that the soldiers of his division were "proficient in only two things": to "jump up and salute" when an officer appeared, and "to demand three meals per day"—were not matter-of-fact depictions of the army.[14] They reflected the disdain, even hatred, that some veterans harbored for Douglas MacArthur, feelings that went much deeper than the mere cynicism suggested by the use of phrases like "Dugout Doug" and "I have gone to the latrine, but I shall return." Naval officer Alvin Chester, in command of a gun detachment aboard a troopship returning from Australia to the United States with Philippine escapees on board, was surprised by what he heard them say about MacArthur. "The survivors," Chester recalled, "would sit for hours venting their anger about General MacArthur. . . . They hated this man with a venom I never witnessed before or after." Chester later commanded a ship that participated in the Leyte operation and had his own reasons to think poorly of MacArthur, but contemporary evidence bears out his wartime memories. Carlos Romulo's papers, for example, include a memorandum informing General Sutherland that the American journalist Annalee Jacoby had spoken to the first group of escaped nurses to leave Australia for the United States and had heard from them "the most violent attacks" against General MacArthur. One, "a certain Miss Hatchett," had a diary in which MacArthur was "bitterly criticized." The diary was said to be very well written, and Romulo feared that it would be of great interest to journalists. He urged Sutherland to be on the lookout for the nurses and intercept their biased and prejudiced writings.

Those in captivity were naturally more bitter. In a prison diary that he shared with Morton, General Brougher excoriated an unnamed commander in chief, "an arch-deceiver, traitor, and criminal, rather than a great soldier" by whom a "small group of Americans in the Philippines [had been] 'sold down the river.'" Time and perspective did not always dim such attitudes. When historian John Beck did his research in the late 1960s, one officer he interviewed acknowledged "a universal resentment against MacArthur by those he left behind in the Philippines. . . . [MacArthur] should have been more resourceful in assessing the relative capabilities and limitations of opposing forces." They had paid a heavy price for his shortcomings. Looking back on the war, this officer wrote, it was as if there were "two MacArthurs, the bumbling, senile, pompous egotist of Bataan and Corregidor, and the brilliant strategist who left his stroke of genius in military history."[15]

The brilliant strategist came later; the MacArthur they knew had bamboozled the War Department into thinking that he had raised a large army capable of defending the islands. Had authorities in Washington not been fooled by MacArthur, these men might never have been sent to the Philippines. They could not attack MacArthur openly; they could attack his creation. Morton did not have to read between the lines to know their feelings when he and other army historians gathered material for the official history in the late 1940s and early 1950s. They told him how they felt in no uncertain terms. Bluemel admitted that his uncharitable comments—he lived long enough to wish he could take them back—were not meant "to be derogatory of the Filipino soldiers but as a reflection on General MacArthur and his group who were responsible for the training of the Philippine Army before the war."[16] That many of the Americans were no better trained or prepared—facts made perfectly clear to knowledgeable Filipinos by what happened to the air corps on the first day of the war—was irrelevant. After all, there were not that many Americans, and they were mostly not on the front line.[17]

The Philippine Army field marshal and USAFFE commanding general himself made no contribution to the official history. He refused to play any part in the preparation of *Fall of the Philippines*, so many questions about the campaign remained, and will always remain, unanswered. The one person in a position to champion the Philippine Army and the Filipino officers he had allowed to command its divisions kept silent. Over a period of nearly six years, from 1946 until the manuscript was completed in November 1951, Morton "tried many times both officially and unofficially to solicit information from the general without success." MacArthur shared neither documents—he claimed he had none—nor insights with OCMH historians. General Sutherland was back in the United States by 1946, and he told Morton that "no cooperation" would be had from MacArthur's headquarters. One letter to MacArthur on this subject in 1948 drew a response from Sidney Huff that the demands on MacArthur's time were "so heavy" that he could not devote "direct personal attention to any historical matters."[18] MacArthur may not have spent his own time on historical matters, but he diverted "a large amount of [his intelligence staff's] duty time" and "considerable government funds" to the completion of a four-volume history of the Southwest Pacific Campaign and several other historical projects. A young historian who arrived in Tokyo to work on the tail end of the campaign history recalled that he "soon learned . . . that the mission basically assigned to us was . . . to 'glorify' MacArthur." Those "attractive, slick histories, in full color, prepared by Toppan in Japan, the finest of the printing houses there" were the result, but they were "not distributed to the general public."[19]

By the time the army published *Reports of General MacArthur* in 1966, their content would have been familiar to readers of MacArthur's memoirs or of the hagiographies written by the likes of Courtney Whitney and Charles Willoughby. Sentences and paragraphs lifted in their entirety from *Reports* had already appeared in MacArthur's *Reminiscences* published two years previously. Just as in MacArthur's memoirs and the works of MacArthur's sycophants, the small portion of *Reports* devoted to the Philippine Campaign of 1941–42 (thirteen or fourteen pages or so) was unrelentingly dishonest and mostly an exercise in blame shifting. MacArthur's activities from 1935 to 1941 were glossed over, as were the arrival of B-17 squadrons and other reinforcements in late 1941, the events at Clark Field on 8 December, and MacArthur's inexplicable inactivity during the early morning hours of that day. Supply and food shortages on Bataan did not result from MacArthur's failure to stock the peninsula; rather, they reflected the Japanese army's pushing of "thousands of homeless refugees" into Bataan to overwhelm the "logistics of defense." The false claims of battlefield success that filled USAFFE press releases in 1941 reappeared in the pages of *Reports.*[20]

If MacArthur had once believed the Philippine Army capable of resisting Japanese landings, the events of late December 1941 disabused him of that notion. "MacArthur," Morton wrote, "never publicly acknowledged the poor performance of the Army he had done so much to organize and train, but it was noted by every American who served with the Philippine Army units and is the central fact that emerges from a study of the first days of the campaign."[21] USAFFE communiques continued to speak of the valor of MacArthur's forces, but General Wainwright's senior aide, Lt. Col. John R. Pugh, put in his diary that MacArthur was said to have admitted that he did not expect his forces on Bataan "to hold through January." A foreign service officer with the Office of the High Commissioner on Corregidor included in a telegram to the secretary of state in mid-January what presumably was being said among staff officers and the high command: "organizing of a final stand on Bataan Peninsula is proceeding with hearty backing of both military and civilian officials at Corregidor though noticeable reluctance among many Filipino soldiers." When MacArthur's intelligence chief, then-Colonel Willoughby, visited the command post of the 57th Infantry (PS) just before the Japanese attack at Abucay, he expressed a confirming opinion: the Philippine Army was not likely to fight. What authorities in Washington had come to think of the Philippine Army—influenced by the tales brought to America by those escaping the islands, by reading between the lines of MacArthur's missives, and by WPD chief Dwight Eisenhower's deep knowledge of just how little the military mission had achieved before the war—became clear enough in early February 1942.

In response to Quezon's fervid suggestion that the islands be neutralized, that "all occupying troops, both American and Japanese be withdrawn," and that the Philippine Army "be immediately disbanded," President Roosevelt informed MacArthur that he expected the American forces would fight to the last against the Japanese, but that arrangements could be made to surrender the "Filipino elements" of MacArthur's command "when and if in [his] opinion that course appears necessary."[22]

Of course, MacArthur had no intention of doing that, and some Americans were willing to concede the obvious: the Philippine Army's shortcomings were the inevitable result of inadequate preparation for war. Criticisms of the Philippine Army could be transposed word for word with evaluations of their own mobilizing army and national guard. William White had Ensign Cox acknowledge that Philippine Army soldiers were really no different than American draftees who had had a comparable level of training—"which is to say they weren't worth a damn."[23] "Much has been said," wrote an American officer who had served with the Philippine Army, "and probably always will, about the Filipino being yellow and lacking courage. This, to my mind, is a gross injustice as the Philippine Scouts proved time and again. You just can't expect untrained, undisciplined troops to stand up to trained troops. No one, to my mind, should blame the Filipino for running. It is a surprise to me that he put up so good a fight as he did."[24] This officer, Capt. Robert Besson, had commanded a battalion of the 21st Infantry (PA) during the retreat from Lingayen and suffered the unhappy distinction of being one of the first Americans captured by the Japanese. He never made it to Bataan, but 21st Field Artillery (PA) adviser Richard Mallonée did. Americans who criticized the Filipino soldiers, Mallonée observed, were not those who served on the front lines. Under the circumstances, the Philippine Army performed well, especially by contrast to allied forces in Malaya, Singapore, Java, and elsewhere in Southeast Asia. General King's aide-de-camp Achille Tisdelle agreed: "considering their inexperience, the Filipino soldier made one of the most remarkable stands against a seasoned, well-equipped enemy, [that he] believe[d] the world [had] ever seen."[25] Even General Bluemel would write long after the war that Philippine Army soldiers on Bataan "did better than any of their critics would have." Unfortunately, as Filipino officers familiar with Bluemel's much-quoted earlier statements feared would happen, his derogatory remarks entered the public record to be quoted by successive generations of American historians. His later, more positive assessment was included in a letter reprinted in an unpublished master's thesis.[26]

As Besson emphasized, clear evidence that Filipinos made good soldiers came with the Philippine Scouts. Much as soldiers of the Philippine Army have become the Bataan Campaign's invisible men, the U.S. Army's Philippine Scouts have become its "marble men." There had been doubters. Capt. Donald Stroh served with the 45th Infantry (PS) in the mid-1930s and complained that before coming to the islands he had been led to believe that "the Filipino troops were so well trained that . . . all a company commander had to do was to sign the morning report." The reality was far different. The men answered "yes, sir" to every command, but few actually knew English. "When individual thinking is required," Stroh lamented, "most of them are completely at sea. Their initiative is much inferior to that of white men and [I] seriously doubt if they would prove satisfactory under war time conditions." Similarly, Capt. Robert Scholes had been pleased to learn that he would serve with the Scouts when he went to the Philippines in April 1941. The "native troops," he wrote to the family he left forever behind, had the reputation of being "fine soldiers [who] really get things done." Command of a company of the 57th Regiment (PS) disappointed him: "For some reason," Scholes now wrote, "these guys haven't got what it takes. They don't seem to have the driving power we have [and] have to be prodded every step." Scholes conceded that part of the problem was that for too many years their officers had treated a Philippine assignment as a "two year vacation." The Scouts remained, the soldier-poet Henry Lee would write a few weeks before the outbreak of war, "still an unknown quantity under fire." Colonel Willoughby had not only expressed the opinion that the Philippine Army would not fight but thought that "the Philippine Scouts were unlikely to fight" too.[27]

Whatever doubts had been entertained about the Scouts before the war were soon laid to rest. Time and time again the high command called upon the Scout regiments to serve as a sort of "fire brigade" on Bataan, rushing from one part of the endangered peninsula to another to pinch off a Japanese salient, repulse coastal landings, or reinforce faltering Philippine Army units at points across the front.

The way to get the most out of Filipino soldiers was to turn them into Philippine Scouts. USAFFE had considered enlarging Scout forces at the expense of Philippine Army mobilization before the war, but at that time MacArthur had considered such a policy "impolitic." Now the chief engineer, General Casey, revisited the idea. He urged USAFFE command to request congressional authorization to double the size of the Philippine Scout organization. Existing Scout units could become cadres for new battalions and regiments of soldiers from the Philippine Army. General MacArthur made no such request, but during the hiatus following the withdrawal to the Orion-Bagac line, Philippine Army soldiers were encouraged to volunteer for service with the Scouts, and several hundred of these men commenced selection courses with the 45th and 57th Infantry Regiments.[28]

The implication of American attitudes was clear: Filipinos made good soldiers—but not under Filipino officers. They fared no better than enlisted men in American-authored accounts of the fighting on Bataan. Ensign Cox told William White, neither apparently aware that dozens of American officers with the rank of full colonel on down had been assigned to work with each Philippine Army division, that "toward the end [on Bataan], it was grotesque. Tough, experienced American Regular Army privates would be giving orders to Filipino generals." An equally credulous John Toland, whose *But Not in Shame* was far more widely read in the Philippines than the official history, recounted a story an American officer of the 45th Infantry (PS) told of having met a dazed and babbling Filipino brigadier general stumbling along amidst his fleeing soldiers when the portion of the Abucay line abutting Mount Natib began to collapse in mid-January.[29]

When the Philippine Army did well on Bataan, Americans credited themselves for its success. Albert Jones, commanding general of I Corps following Wainwright's departure for Corregidor, was willing to acknowledge "the ability and confidence" acquired by Philippine Army troops who drove Japanese soldiers out of several "pockets" behind I Corps' line in February 1942. But he traced the Filipino soldiers' success to a "handful of American leaders" who pushed themselves and their troops "to victory." It was we Americans, Lt. Col. Irvin Alexander, adviser to the 1st Infantry (PA), agreed, "who set an example which, for years to come, will be the goal of the officers of the army of the infant Philippine Republic."[30] The failure of Filipino officer leadership was even highlighted in at least one medal citation: Donovan Swanton, who had known Lim at West Point, was commended for leading soldiers of the 51st Infantry (PA) against infiltrating Japanese on 21–22 January 1942 near Guitol. Swanton won the Silver Star but was seriously wounded, and the attack stalled because Filipino officers "were too inexperienced and lacking in tactical training and troop leadership" to continue the advance.[31] After the war, General Jones, now chief of the Military Advisory Group that took the place of the old military mission, emphasized that the clear lesson to be drawn from the experience of 1941–42 was "that the average Filipino must be invested with complete responsibility if he is to acquire independence of action." Americans could not make decisions for them. But during the fighting more immediate concerns trumped longer-range goals. Wainwright's aide Colonel Pugh summed up the American viewpoint at the time of Bataan's surrender: "The Philippine Army was raw, green, and untrained. It has been due to the work of the American officers that they have stood as they have."[32]

Abucay reinforced "the necessity for providing a maximum number of experienced officers for duty with combat troops." USAFFE instructed headquarters units on Bataan to keep American staff officers to a minimum. Officers were needed at the front. If "experienced officers" could not be found, less experienced would do. American civilians resident in the islands were commissioned to serve with the Philippine Army. (Lim's division got one or two such officers.) The high command also combed through American units to find noncommissioned officers suitable and willing to serve with the Philippine Army. The 41st Division received several men from the air corps in February, one of whom, William Montgomery, wrote a memoir of his service in the Philippines. Montgomery had been an airplane mechanic since joining the army in 1927 and had arrived in the country with the 7th Materiel Squadron a few weeks before the outbreak of war. He was assigned to the 41st Infantry and remained at the front until the third day of the Easter offensive, when an infected wound sent him to Hospital no. 1. He was instructed that he was not to give orders but rather to help the Filipino officers choose the correct course of action. After a few days posted at the 41st's outpost line of resistance (OPLR), Montgomery concluded that the real reason he was there was to ensure that men stayed on the line. Montgomery had no training suitable for the circumstances he now faced; indeed, Montgomery claimed that he "had never even had an army rifle in [his] hands." There were better-qualified advisers. Enlisted men from the 31st Infantry (U.S.) were assigned to teach infantry skills to Philippine Army soldiers after the withdrawal from Abucay and were offered commissions if they would agree to remain. One enlisted man, who refused the offer because he wanted to stay with his friends and doubted the "resolve and capability" of the Philippine Army, recalled that "some accepted, some did not."[33]

Filipino historians have offered a contrasting view of the Philippine Army on Bataan. At about the same time that OCMH commenced work on what would become *Fall of the Philippines*, the now-independent Philippine Army embarked on its own history-writing effort. It expected, according to the author of its earliest volume, to publish "a series of 'after action reports' of the Philippine Army divisions that had participated in the Philippine Defense Campaign of 1941–42." Like *Fall of the Philippines*, the first of these books, a history of the 1st Regular Division, appeared in 1953. A 2nd Division history followed in 1967. Authors of these division histories pushed back against the image of Filipino ineptness. If Colonel Alexander credited himself with effectively running the 1st Regiment (PA) on Bataan, the author of the 2nd Division's history, a veteran of Bataan and longtime postwar head of the Philippine Army's historical office, evaluated the American's role differently. He made only passing mention of Alexander, who, Lt. Col. Ambrosio Peña explained in a footnote, had been the quartermaster at Fort Stotsenburg. "In Bataan, he had nothing more to do with the QM, which perhaps was the consideration of this assignment."[34]

Strikingly different images of 21st Division commanding general Brig. Gen. Mateo Capinpin emerge in the division histories too. Morton underlined Capinpin's unsteady leadership of the division: he falsely reported the repelling of a Japanese landing at Lingayen and became "needlessly alarmed" during the retreat into Bataan. In Filipino-authored histories, however, General Capinpin "never lost his composure and calmness" during the retreat from Lingayen in spite of the confusion and sense of panic generated by his American superiors' conflicting orders and failure to plan adequately "for the retrograde movement." For his "masterly conduct of delaying actions under enemy pressure," the Philippine government presented General Capinpin with a Philippine Army medal after the war.[35] Similarly, American scholars have relied on the unpublished reports and recollections of General Bluemel to make his 31st Division the archetypical Philippine Army division, but Bluemel's much-repeated derogatory comments about Filipino soldiers had angered Filipino veterans. When confronted by one, Maj. Nicanor T. Jimenez, an officer in the 31st Division and student at the Infantry School in 1947, Bluemel defended himself by claiming that he was just stating the facts. Not only was it not a "fact" that Filipino soldiers were only proficient at saluting and demanding to be fed, Jimenez responded, but Bluemel had not seen reason to make known certain other facts (of which Major Jimenez proceeded to remind him) that reflected poorly on Bluemel's leadership of the division. The authors of the 31st Division's history drew on the recollections of Jimenez and other officers to recall episodes on Bataan that diminished Bluemel's stature.[36]

What then was Lim's significance on Bataan? Beyond identifying him as the 41st Division's commander, the U.S. Army's official history of the Philippine Campaign purposely had nothing to say about Lim on Bataan. What Lim did or did not do, to quote from a letter an army researcher wrote to one senior-ranking American Bataan veteran, was not "a determining or even a significant factor in shaping the course of events."[37] But what did *any* particular general officer, Filipino or American, do to shape the course of events on Bataan? Of course, the Philippine Campaign is indelibly linked to the name Douglas MacArthur. General MacArthur made the decisions that sent the army into Bataan; he had also made the decisions that left Bataan unprepared to sustain the army. Only his secretary has struck a discordant note: Paul Rogers—the sole army enlisted man evacuated with MacArthur's party from Corregidor in March 1942—thought that Richard Sutherland deserved what credit there was to be had for the Philippine Campaign. General Sutherland, wrote Rogers, "had coordinated the withdrawal from north and south Luzon. He had organized the defenses on Bataan. He had made the tactical decision[s]." MacArthur, Rogers asserted, "had watched it [all] without too much personal involvement."[38]

MacArthur's was an infrequent presence on Bataan itself. According to most accounts, only once during the two and one-half months that passed between USAFFE's withdrawal into the peninsula in late December 1941 and MacArthur's departure for Mindanao on 11 March 1942 did the USAFFE commander make the three-mile trip to Bataan from his headquarters on Corregidor. On 10 January MacArthur crossed to Cabcaben on a Philippine Army Q-boat and traveled with his entourage up the east coast road, stopping at General Parker's II Corps headquarters near Limay and the command posts of subordinate units along the Abucay line before retracing his steps to cross into the western half of the peninsula to visit General Wainwright's I Corps. Fortier confirms that MacArthur stopped at the 41st Division CP. He undoubtedly spoke to Lim, though no account of what they said exists.[39] MacArthur's much-commented-upon reluctance to face the frontline troops on Bataan earned him the sobriquet "Dugout Doug" among some American soldiers, perhaps unfairly, as he purposely and unnecessarily exposed himself to enemy fire on Corregidor; but if nothing else, his near avoidance of Bataan "did little to inspire his men," as Hanson Baldwin would write, and—more to the point—set a poor example for the other officers. They had, General Wainwright admitted, little more to offer the soldiers than morale-boosting visits. Wainwright supposedly identified the failure of "ranking officers . . . to visit troops in the front lines" as one of the "major military mistakes" made in the campaign.[40]

Wainwright meant MacArthur, of course, but in American officers' memoirs, the infrequent observance of officers on the front line is a frequent observation. James Callahan claimed that he was the only officer on II Corps' staff who regularly saw the troops. Sutherland appeared at Parker's command post sometime in January and "blatantly asked who had visited [the] front recently." No one had. Sutherland encouraged the officers to do so, but only a few did and not often. The II Corps operations officer, Fortier wrote, "never visited our C.P. or checked our lines during [the] war." A few subordinate officers—"mostly youngsters with increased promotions," in Fortier's words, who "lacked experience and judgment"—visited from corps headquarters. An officer on the 31st Division's line along the Pilar-Bagac road told an inspecting engineer one day in mid-February that he had not seen General Bluemel or any other member of the division staff in over two weeks. General Casey complained that he once walked the entire distance of the front line (after the withdrawal to Orion-Bagac) and could get not a single corps or division commander to accompany him.[41] General Jones told John Toland that one division commander in I Corps had been relieved for not visiting the front lines and that another stuck to his "impregnable" CP and "never went up front." The acerbic Major Gay commented on what might be termed Bataan's "leadership problem" in one of his weekly reports of engineering activities. "Few people are willing to put it into words," Gay wrote,

> either because of personal loyalty or fear of later discrimination, but the younger officers know that a large number of senior officers are incompetent or indifferent and that these officers who have spent years in schools and in service are not measuring up to the high standards we have been led to believe they have attained. . . . We need active aggressive leadership . . . and we are not getting it. . . . Our commanders are satisfied to sit in their dugouts and C.P.'s and let everything proceed "according to plan."[42]

Gay was not referring to Filipino generals.

Aside from MacArthur, the only "Philippine general" to escape the obscurity fated to all other general officers in the Philippine Islands in 1941–42 was Jonathan Wainwright. MacArthur's contemporary (their years at West Point overlapped), Wainwright had come almost to the end of his military career when World War II intervened to prolong it. His personnel record does not survive at NPRC to confirm or refute these conclusions, but according to a sympathetic biographer, Wainwright's age, his devotion to the outdated horse cavalry, along with his too-well-known love of the bottle had led incoming chief of staff George Marshall to mark Wainwright as one of those officers for whom an army gearing up to fight Germany had no need. The friendship of outgoing chief of staff Malin Craig had gotten Wainwright the single star of a brigadier general, but his assignment to remote Fort Clark, Texas, in December 1938 was meant to bring his career to an end. Wainwright instead was marked for Philippine service and arrived in Manila near the end of 1940 to command the Philippine Division. Wainwright took the North Luzon Force into Bataan and there became commanding general of the I Philippine Corps.[43] His officers and men thought well of him, but the high command had little confidence in either his strategic vision or his tactical sense, thus the convoluted command arrangement devised by MacArthur to keep General Wainwright under his thumb after USAFFE staff left for Australia. "Skinny" Wainwright's plainspoken, unassuming demeanor and good humor in the face of adversity made him an appealing counterpoint to the distant and aloof MacArthur. He became the sympathetic public face of the doomed garrison.

Until MacArthur's departure in March, Wainwright commanded the western half of the peninsula. He had nothing to do with Abucay. Lim's corps commander was George M. Parker Jr., who had reached the Philippines in May 1941 to become Wainwright's "infantry adviser."[44] Though Parker ended up with the more important command on Bataan—his II Corps area was the likely venue for a Japanese advance—he made little impression on contemporaries and less still on historians. Richard Marshall, head of USAFFE's forward command post on Bataan, thought that Parker "would have been an excellent commander" if only he had been "in better health and more vigorous." Officers interviewed by MacArthur biographer James typically used adjectives like "cautious" and "quiet" and "studious" (and some less respectful phrases) to describe Parker. Fortier recalled that General Parker toured the 41st Division's lines only once at Abucay and again, just one time, after the withdrawal to the Orion-Bagac line. Harold Johnson remembered that Parker "rarely visited" the front and, when he did, "never had much to say." Bluemel claimed to have been informed by Wainwright that "had the war continued," General Parker would not have remained in command of II Corps. When MacArthur published his memoirs twenty years later, he did not even remember that it was Parker who had commanded the South Luzon Force that became II Corps on Bataan.[45]

Lim, Fortier reported, thought that Parker did not like him, but in his report of his corps' operations on Bataan prepared while a prisoner of war, Parker did acknowledge that Lim "deserve[d] the highest possible commendation" for his leadership of the 41st Division at Abucay. After the war, Parker included Lim's name on a list of officers whom he recommended be awarded the army's Distinguished Service Medal. (General King removed it.) Parker saved his strongest words of praise, however, for Lim's American adviser. The division's success at Abucay, Parker asserted, was "largely due to the untiring efforts and superior military knowledge and ability of Colonel Fortier."[46]

So far as Lim's reputation on Bataan went, the division adviser proved to be something of a two-edged sword. Fortier's superior qualifications undoubtedly contributed to the division's accomplishments, but Fortier was dissatisfied with being a mere adviser while other Americans, no better qualified and arguably less able than himself, held commands. He tried to get a transfer but said that during the retreat into Bataan he had been told by USAFFE G-4 Louis Beebe that MacArthur wanted Fortier to remain with the 41st because the USAFFE commander "did not want to trust the division to Lim."[47] Fortier informed Louis Morton that MacArthur had created the instructor role in the first place because he "had all these high ranking Filipino officers on his hands and had to give them command." After his release from prison camp in 1945, Fortier waged a letter-writing campaign to have himself recognized as having been the commander in fact if not in title of the 41st Division, thereby justifying a promotion to brigadier general. Fortier wrote to Generals George Marshall, MacArthur, Wainwright, Parker, Lough, Casey, and others. His former corps commander did not agree that Fortier had been "assured" of advancement to general officer (as Fortier insisted) but did endorse Fortier's claim, as did Generals King and Lough, to have "in fact perform[ed] the functions of a division commander."[48]

As Fortier told the story, he and Lim arranged a division of labor that left the slightly younger, more physically active American officer responsible for the "tactical handling" of the 41st, while the Filipino commander took care of "administrative matters, including supply and replacement of materiel." "I kept him well informed of everything I did," Fortier wrote, "but he left the decisions up to me." "Early in the game," Fortier informed General MacArthur, Lim "told me that because of my excellent physical condition and his confidence in my military knowledge he was going to leave the active handling of the Division in my hands." Bluemel prepared a memorandum for Fortier in which he wrote that he visited the 41st command post for a period of three to four hours one day in January during which the division was "engaged in close combat with the Japanese." "I observed," Bluemel stated, "that you were receiving all orders, making all decisions and issuing all orders." General Lim "made no comments or suggestions and apparently approved all your actions and orders." And Fortier received a fuller characterization in the official history: he organized a counterattack, rounded up stragglers, and searched for a missing unit.[49]

Lim did lean on Fortier. When, for example, the division engineer met up with the commanding general near Abucay, Lim told him to report to Fortier, who would "show you the line to be organized." Philippine Army officers acknowledged Fortier's role in the division's success at Abucay. In 1948, after independence, Fortier would receive the Philippine Army's Gold Cross Medal for "personally direct[ing] the operations of the 41st Division [on 22–23 January 1942] unmindful of possible bodily harm should the enemy make a successful breakthrough."[50]

Lim was more active, however, than Fortier cared to remember. After the division withdrew to the Orion-Bagac line, Fortier claimed that General Lim "never made a single trip to [the] front lines nor to [regimental] CPs" except once to the 41st Infantry's command post, but, Fortier admitted, Lim had engaged in "constant and continuing reconnaissance" while preparing defense works in Batangas. Once on Bataan Lim himself had responded to a brief letter from Quezon (sent to all senior Filipino officers during the battle at Abucay) suggesting that he "personally talk to [his] officers and men," by writing that he had already "visited every trench or foxhole in the front line. . . . You can be sure," he informed Quezon, "that I am not a general who stays in the dugout."[51] Magtoto recalled a day in early January that Lim arrived to inspect "the organization work in our position" and then remained for a while to talk to the officers about "our forthcoming engagement" and what was known about Japanese fighting techniques meant to confuse the men. It was not Lim's first visit, because Magtoto quoted the division commander as saying that there had been "a lot of improvements in your position since the last time I was here." An American soldier, the medical officer Paul Ashton, told a story of meeting a "rather elderly" Filipino soldier while hiking toward the 41st Division's clearing station along a trail behind the Orion-Bagac line. The soldier wore no insignia on his uniform and did not identify himself but introduced Ashton to a third lieutenant, his nephew, who was accompanying him. The three continued to a nearby infantry unit, and only when the men there shouted "attention" did Ashton learn that he was with General Lim. Lim, according to Ashton, proceeded to ask pointed and knowledgeable questions about the unit's weapons and their disposition.[52] An American who served with the 41st Division, Capt. Winston Jones of the field artillery, said that there was no doubt at the time to either officers or men, Americans or Filipinos, as to who was in charge of the division, and it was not Colonel Fortier.[53] Nor did Fortier's superior officers fully accept his evaluation of his activities on Bataan. "I realize that Colonel Fortier did very good work," Wainwright would acknowledge, but "he was not actually in command of the division." Wainwright refused to endorse Fortier's request for promotion.[54]

The performance of several senior Philippine Scout officers did nothing to promote confidence in Filipino leadership. Col. Rafael Garcia, the discredited former superintendent of the Philippine Military Academy, relocated to Bataan still in charge of the 4th Military District (maintained as an administrative unit in the rear area to funnel replacements to the front line), nursed his grievances against the army, and was finally shipped to Panay. The only other Scout officer in Lim's division, Lt. Col. Amado Martelino, did not last out the campaign. Martelino, the brother of General Bluemel's chief of staff Pastor Martelino, commanded the 41st Field Artillery Regiment. His American subordinate Winston Jones remembered him as a "very fine, well respected" officer, but like several other Scout officers, he brought family members to Bataan. Martelino was "constantly worrying" about them, so much so that it affected his ability to command. He was replaced with an American officer at the end of January and sent to I Corps as a supply officer.[55] A former Scout officer who commanded a field artillery regiment on Bataan, Nemesio Catalan of the 21st, enjoyed a poor reputation at corps headquarters. The regiment's senior instructor was authorized to take Catalan's place near the end of the campaign.[56]

If there was a truly tragic figure on Bataan—in the classical sense—it was yet another long-serving Philippine Scout officer, Fidel Segundo. By no design of the high command, Segundo had the best chance of putting a Filipino stamp on the campaign. The recently promoted Philippine Army brigadier general faced the most difficult challenges of any Filipino division commander. His 1st Division had been intended to be the centerpiece of the Philippine Army's regular force, but prior to the army's mobilization it numbered fewer than 800 men and was viewed by the Philippine Department's intelligence office "essentially as a group of training cadres rather than as a combat division." In the event that the Philippine Army was mobilized, HPD contemplated withdrawing the division's battalions separately for use where needed, along with the trainees who happened to be assigned to them at the time. Whatever had been the division's intended role in the military mission's or HPA's pre–July 1941 war plans, when the Philippine Army was mobilized beginning in August 1941, its regular component was stripped of most of its personnel, assigned a caretaker commander, and shunted to the sideline.[57]

Ten days after the war began, the 1st Division was assigned what remained of Philippine Military Academy personnel. The academy's superintendent, then-Colonel Segundo, was told to bring the cadets to Manila. There, the academy classes of 1944 and 1945 (those who had entered the academy in 1940 and 1941) were sent home and the classes of 1942 and 1943 graduated and were commissioned in the regular army. Most of the young officers remained to serve with the 1st Division, which was placed under Segundo's command and inducted into USAFFE on 19 December. Even at that late date, a contingent of American officers and enlisted men was found to serve as the division's instructors and advisers. Since most enlisted reservists had long since reported for duty, the 1st Division filled its ranks with volunteers from the city and surrounding areas, including some ex-prisoners who had been released from jail on the promise that they would join the army. Almost at once Segundo led the division's 1st Regiment southeast to Tayabas, where it and the division engineers participated in the failed attempt to prevent the enemy landing at Mauban, Tayabas, on 24 December. By the end of the month, the regiment had withdrawn to southern Pampanga, rejoined the rest of the division, and begun the movement into Bataan. To Segundo's scratch division that had not even existed in USAFFE's order of battle two weeks earlier went responsibility for almost the entire western half of the initial line of defense on Bataan.[58]

Segundo seems to have been allowed more tactical control over his troops than any other Filipino general; at least, few accounts of the Bataan Campaign mention his senior adviser, Col. Albert Dumas.[59] His was a more frequent physical presence along the front line than that of any other Filipino general—and most American generals—and orders for his division were given to him directly, not through American advisers. But the 1st Division's failure to tie in with II Corps and its retreat along the coast from Mauban tarnished Segundo's reputation. Worse still, Segundo—either in uniform or out, depending on which version of the story one prefers to believe—showed up in the rear area having left his men to make their own way to safety. Those events or the inability promptly to reduce the "pockets" soon after led to his dismissal. General Segundo at least was allowed to keep his star.[60]

Segundo was the most Americanized of the senior Scout officers and the one most highly regarded by American officers before the war. His demotion crystallized American attitudes toward Filipinos: even the best of them could not bear the weight of command. Though grounded in the realities of combat performance, the American propensity to assume the worst of Filipino ability strengthened Lim's determination to keep problems within the division. He did intend to hold his men accountable, if not always in ways appreciated by his American advisers. Fortier claimed that one of the "greatest stumbling blocks" to getting more out of the 41st Division was the large number of Filipinos "completely ignorant of their jobs" yet who could not be relieved. But over the course of the campaign, Lim relieved all three of his infantry commanders (and USAFFE relieved his artillery commander). He had his doubts about some of the regimental commanders from the beginning but had paired them with, he hoped, able subordinates. In keeping with the prewar decision to give officers of appropriate rank the opportunity to demonstrate their ability, the infantry regiments had been put in the hands of long-serving Constabulary officers. Lim considered outspoken Lt. Col. Emanuel Baja to be "one of the hardest-working men in the army." Baja's 43rd Regiment had had the least amount of training when the war began, however, and at Abucay Baja proved to be nervous and "fidgety." Lim replaced him with the regiment's executive officer, Capt. Valentin Salgado, who remained in command for the rest of the war. Lim had been less enthusiastic about the 41st Infantry commander, Lt. Col. Silvino Gallardo, but that regiment's executive officer, Capt. Fidel N. Cruz, was, in Lim's view, "one of our best soldiers." Cruz took Gallardo's place after Abucay. Only the 42nd Infantry's commanding officer lasted most of the campaign. Lim thought that Lt. Col. Claro B. Lizardo would make a good regimental commander teamed with his executive officer, Capt. Bernardo Salazar. Lim would give Atienza the command of the 42nd Infantry during the enemy offensive. Magtoto, who was one of Lizardo's battalion commanders, wrote that at least it could "be said to his credit that very few regimental commanders venture beyond the main line of defense," as Lizardo did.[61]

In fairness to the Americans, they were well aware of limitations within their own ranks. More than one American officer ended the Bataan Campaign with a tarnished reputation. The Philippine Scout 57th Infantry Regiment gained a much deserved reputation for tenacity on Bataan, but the same could not be said of all of its officers. The regiment ran through a series of commanders during its first month on Bataan. William Brougher had been its prewar commander, but he had been reassigned to head the Philippine Army's 11th Division. It fell to his executive officer, George S. Clarke, to lead the regiment to war. Clarke, a World War I veteran who had begun his military career in the

Philippine Constabulary in 1912, had been assigned to duty with the Philippine Army in September but took command of the 57th after Brougher left. Clarke soon collapsed under the strain of active service. He "spent virtually all of his daylight hours in a dugout," one of his subordinates later recalled, fearful of enemy aircraft and friendly artillery. He was relieved of command in mid-January 1942 and sent back to the States. A replacement, Col. Philip T. Fry, was in poor health and lasted eight days in command.[62] The commanding officer of the 45th Infantry (PS), Col. Thomas Doyle, generated controversy when he showed up on Corregidor with a few other officers just before Bataan surrendered, having left his regiment behind.[63] He, too, was sent back to the United States. Brigadier General Selleck was relieved of command and reduced in rank. Selleck, whom Lim had known at West Point, had been unimpressive in his leadership of the 71st Division during both mobilization and the withdrawal through central Luzon. When his soldiers failed to drive the Japanese off of Quinauan Point, the high command replaced him with the 26th Cavalry's Col. Clinton Pierce.[64]

These were only the more prominent failures. Even before the 57th Infantry (PS) had moved to Bataan, a company commander had been "sent to a hospital for observation" and never rejoined the unit. One captain ordered to the regiment by II Corps to replace losses at Abucay reported for duty and then "abruptly stated that he did not like war and that this was no place for him." He quickly absconded for the rear area.[65] Two company commanders in the 31st U.S. Infantry were relieved early in the campaign, one for "misbehavior in face of [the] enemy"; the other's company had fled its first contact with the Japanese at Layac junction.[66] Several of the Americans assigned to the 41st Division fell short of expectation. When Lieutenant Montgomery and another officer took advantage of a lull in the Japanese bombardment of the front line on 3 April to begin directing men back to the reserve line, a third American officer with them refused to leave the dugout and finally had to be escorted to the rear.[67] Another experienced major, a veteran of World War I, proved "too nervous" and a "bad influence" and spent only a few weeks as an adviser before finding his niche as a supply officer. Yet another major, a reservist who regretted that he had turned down the offer of an assignment to Panama to go the Philippines instead, did not "stray far from a foxhole." Fortier lamented that the 42nd Infantry's senior adviser, Lt. Col. E. C. Atkinson, "was physically weak and did not get down in the lines like he should." Lt. Col. R. G. MacDonald took Atkinson's place just in time for the final enemy offensive. The 41st Field Artillery Regiment's senior adviser, Lt. Col. Arthur Moore, was relieved for having mispositioned the unit's guns after the withdrawal to the Orion-Bagac line. Another American, a warrant officer disgusted that his promotion to lieutenant meant a reduction in pay, proved to be "a fair paper man," Fortier allowed, but lacked tactical experience and was "the first to dive for a dugout" whenever an enemy plane appeared.[68]

But while American faults were those of individuals who failed to measure up to well-defined standards of professional behavior, the shortcomings of Filipino officers reflected what Americans saw as difficult-to-surmount cultural flaws (the same that Lim himself had railed against) that encouraged the avoidance of responsibility, favored promotion by connection rather than by merit—in Americans' memory almost every Philippine Army officer was a "political appointee"—and emphasized the prerogatives of officership over the performance of leadership. The solution to the Philippine Army officer problem was self-evident to many American officers: put Americans at the head of Philippine Army units. "If we could only command instead of advising," lamented an officer serving with a Constabulary regiment on Bataan, "we could have a crack outfit in a short time." As it was, complained Lt. Col. Irvin Alexander to USAFFE intelligence chief Charles Willoughby, "the lack of discipline is terrific" and his regiment's Filipino commander "has little force and cannot maintain discipline."[69] Fortier wrote that he had tried repeatedly to put Americans in command positions in the 41st Division. Fortier even claimed that General Parker "dallied with the idea" of relieving Lim and putting Fortier in his place. Fortier wrote that he advised against doing so "in view of the adverse effect it would have on morale" and because he and Lim "were working most harmoniously together."

Attempts to replace Filipino with American commanders rarely met with success. For one thing, doing so undermined the high command's "long range objective [of training] Filipino officers to take over when [the United States] pulled out." Nor, as Fortier acknowledged, did putting Americans in charge necessarily enhance troop morale. There was "much silent criticism" from the rank and file, the 1st Division's historian perceived, when a reorganization in early January left Filipino officers as merely "the nominal heads of the regiments and battalions," their American instructors "having been given so much leeway to run the show."[70]

An underappreciated important aspect of MacArthur's insistence on mobilizing the entire Philippine Army was that doing so nationalized the war against Japan. Had Grunert had his way, the army on Bataan would have been a smaller, more effective fighting force, but it still would have lost the war, and it would have taken on a "sepoy" cast unrepresentative of the Filipino nation. The downside of MacArthur's action, many American soldiers believed, was that it brought to Bataan hundreds of un- or underqualified Filipino officers whose very presence inhibited improving the discipline and fighting qualities of the Filipino enlisted men. Instead of becoming commanders, many Americans continued in their roles as advisers and instructors. They confronted the need not to "give orders" but to cajole, to persuade by example, to accept responsibility without commensurate authority, to keep their own fears and frustrations in check, and to do all that despite the persistent prejudice that had kept Filipinos out of Manila's Army and Navy Club and off military golf courses before the war.[71]

Racial incidents on Bataan became, at least in Filipino accounts, increasingly commonplace. "To the world it appeared that the Filipinos and Americans were palsy-walsies," wrote Manuel Buenafe, who edited a collection of veterans' stories and published a book about the war, "but beneath that propaganda were facts of discrimination." As the siege wore on, "the cleavage between Filipinos and Americans was getting more marked. Incidents there were aplenty." Filipinos (and a few Americans) peppered their recollections with such incidents: an American lieutenant who refused to obey the orders of a Filipino captain, "because he is 'a Filipino capt[ain]'"; American drivers who refused "to share a ride with Filipino soldiers"; an American officer overseeing a civilian construction crew who was told to "move my Filipinos away from [a nearby American] camp." And there was worse. "I'm ashamed to admit it," a veteran of the 31st Infantry (U.S.) told an interviewer long after the war, but some American soldiers on Bataan—even officers—openly referred to Filipino soldiers using racial slurs. Stories like this reached Quezon, who queried Lieut. Felipe (Philip) Buencamino about the "friction [that] exists between Filipinos and American[s]." John Toland repeated a tale told to him by Antonio Aquino that the young lieutenant "had swum from Bataan [to Corregidor] to warn Quezon of the increasing hostility between Filipinos and Americans at the front." Even Manzano—the Filipino Scout officer who before the war had refused to serve with the Philippine Army—was quoted as having said during the war that Filipino soldiers on Bataan "faced daily discrimination and despotism" at the hands of their American officers.[72]

Japanese propaganda embellished and played up the issue. Leaflets and broadcasts emphasized the Filipinos' subservience to the Americans and urged them to turn on their white masters. Philippine Scout officer and historian John Olson saw the first of these leaflets around 20 December. Its theme was the "massacre" of Filipinos by U.S. Army troops on Samar during the Philippine-American War. A concerned company commander "covertly" watched the men's reaction. Most officers were convinced of the Scouts' loyalty, but the regimental commander "preferred to take no chances and ordered . . . the leaflets collected and destroyed." In early January 1942 in occupied Manila, Homma's chief of staff Lt. Gen. Masami Maeda told former resident commissioner Quintin Paredes that the Americans had been treating "the Filipinos like slaves and were tying the legs of Filipino soldiers to prevent them from retreating."[73] Historian Teodoro Agoncillo wrote:

> Similar stories of American cavalier treatment of Filipino soldiers on the Bataan front circulated during the occupation, but the Filipinos took those stories as pure propaganda designed to infuriate them against the Americans. Only after the war, when many Filipino veterans began telling stories of American racial prejudice and unequal treatment of soldiers, the Japanese propaganda stories, at least some of them, were divested of their fictive character and assumed the nature of gospel truth.[74]

Such incidents, real and imagined, may not have represented the tip of an iceberg. Most Philippine Army soldiers, after all, saw few Americans. One memoir by a Filipino veteran of the war specifically refutes allegations that Americans received better treatment (in terms of food rationing, for example) or discriminated against their Filipino comrades. General Francisco told a Japanese journalist during the war that despite some isolated cases of discrimination, relations between Americans and Filipinos were generally harmonious. One veteran of the 41st Infantry (PA) remembered the two American advisers in his unit as friendly and approachable. Filipino officers by contrast, he said, tended to emphasize their status as officers. But others found the Americans aloof and unwilling to associate with Filipino officers.[75] Silvestre Tagarao, the only enlisted man of the 41st Division to have authored a book about his experiences on Bataan, mentions having seen three Americans with his division. One was Gaylor Fraser (whom he gives the name "Major Roberts"), a former company commander in the 31st U.S. Infantry and the highly regarded leader of the division's sniper platoon; the others were NCOs from the 31st Infantry who arrived to train the Filipinos in infantry tactics. Tagarao spoke well of them, but when he and his comrades got to know the two American enlisted men better, they worked up the nerve to ask a question "which [he recalled] had been in our minds from some time already": Why were there no Americans on the front line?[76]

Decades of bitterness felt by many Bataan veterans over the refusal of the American government to extend to Philippine Army soldiers the same benefits made available to MacArthur's American soldiers no doubt sharpened such long-after-the-fact recollections; however, in units that included contingents of Americans and Filipinos, contemporary evidence suggests a deteriorating relationship. Mallonée, in Capinpin's 21st Division (PA), put the matter succinctly: "The Filipino command, high and low, began to concern itself with matters extraneous to the battlefield. Political differences, food, a decoration here and none there, promotion problems, differences in pay between American and Filipino officers, criticism of tactical decisions by the American high command, fault with the conduct of individual American officers—these things, not the state of the defense, became our paramount problems."[77] "A definite Filipino [versus] American attitude" existed, Major Gay concluded of the 1st Engineer Battalion (PA) after inspecting it near the end of February 1942. The USAFFE engineer papers include another memorandum extending the same conclusion to the entire 2nd Division. The division had "published a new daily program" that it would not "let the American instructors see." In response, the American officers were "ready to quit as they can get nothing accomplished."[78] MacArthur's attempt to equalize pay only exacerbated the situation. Lieutenant Buencamino, an aide to Brig. Gen. Simeon de Jesus, who ran the Philippine Army's intelligence operations on Bataan, expressed the Filipino point of view: "There is no reason why an American should get higher pay than a Filipino doing the same job with the same rank." But American officers were less likely to concede that Filipino officers of the same rank were "doing the same job." Capt. William Osborne with the 51st Division (PA) said the talk of giving Filipino officers the same pay as Americans made the Americans "goddamn mad."[79]

The racial divide was evident enough in other divisions that toward the end of February a delegation of Filipino officers met with Lim to talk about worsening relations between American and Filipino officers. According to notes Fortier took (and later provided to Morton), these officers claimed that General Bluemel "was about crazy." He "cursed Filipino officers and treated them like dogs." A senior instructor in Capinpin's division "not only cursed hell out of Filipino officers but struck them and was drunk most of the time." (This officer was replaced by an officer from the instructor staff of the 41st Division.) Mallonée reported a similar incident in the 21st Field Artillery (PA). The American adviser to one of the regiment's batteries had several times slapped officers and men in his unit. Mallonée thought an official reprimand should close the matter; the Filipino commanding officer of the regiment thought Mallonée failed to understand how enraged the men of the battalion were toward the adviser and to grasp that his life was in danger should he remain. At Lim's request, Fortier visited the II Corps commander to express Lim's concern about a "growing feeling of hatred developing in many Filipino officers of other divisions in corps at treatment being given them by American officers."

It was not that none of this existed in the 41st Division, but the officers of the 21st and 31st Divisions approached Lim about the matter because, they said, everyone knew things were better in the 41st. Americans and Filipinos were like "brothers" in General Lim's division.[80] Perhaps here lies Lim's unexamined and unappreciated significance to the campaign. For Filipino soldiers on the front line, intense periods of fighting took place in mid-January to early

February and then again in early April. Most of their time on Bataan fell within the "lull" period in February and March. Ostensibly that time was spent training and improving the state of defenses. But there was time to visit with friends, to gossip, to grumble, to wonder why they were there and to ask whose war was it. This aspect of the "lull" period Morton chose to ignore in the official history, though his "large number of interviews and informal conversations with [American] survivors" made him strongly aware of it. It allowed ample time for episodes of "anti-Filipino" behavior to multiply and fester.[81]

Like the other generals, Lim lacked the authority to influence strategy; tactics were, for the most part, the forte of his American adviser. But no senior officer on Bataan was as respected by both Filipinos and Americans as General Lim. His presence on Bataan gave hope to his own men and encouraged his officers to do more than they might otherwise have attempted. He had gained a reputation before the war as "rough and outspoken," Atienza later acknowledged. But on Bataan he became "a father to his men," encouraging them to feel that the outcome of the battle depended on their personal endeavors. "Many who knew him before the war" might find it hard to believe, Atienza wrote, but on Bataan General Lim even showed a sense of humor. His presence ameliorated friction between soldiers of the two armies that was bound to grow during the lull period, along with hunger, sickness, and the numbing awareness that, for all but a favored few—senior officials, American nurses, pilots, supernumerary colonels ("there must have been a thousand of them in the Philippines," joked one pilot)—there would be no way out.[82]

CHAPTER 10

"You Could Have Stopped This Useless Fighting"

Bataan to Capas, February–July 1942

Not everyone was resigned to the inevitability of USAFFE's defeat. One refugee in the hills outside Manila remembered the excitement felt when a report reached his camp that the city "was in total blackout." It happened to be MacArthur's birthday; the refugees were certain the long-anticipated counteroffensive that would return Filipino-American forces to the capital had begun. On Bataan itself, buoyed by the beating the Japanese had taken at Abucay and the enemy's failure to breach the new defensive line, and confident that help was on the way from the United States, "many of the officers now greet each other with 'See you in Manila soon,'" wrote a soldier in Lim's division. Others kept spare uniforms clean to wear in the soon-to-be-held victory parade. General Lim was an important part of the perception that the war could be turned around. In Filipino-authored accounts of Bataan, Lim features prominently as the champion of a counteroffensive during the lull that followed Abucay. Teodoro Agoncillo recalled that in Manila "rumor had it that General Vicente Lim wanted to counterattack and drive the Japanese out of Bataan in order to recapture Manila, but General MacArthur allegedly dissuaded him from carrying out his plan." Atienza saw Lim daily at the time. "When the Japs withdrew from Bataan in February 1942," Atienza recounted in a speech he gave on the eighth anniversary of Bataan's fall, "General Lim recommended a full scale counteroffensive."[1]

As usual, Lim goes unmentioned in American-authored histories. Louis Morton conceded that "many officers favored a return to the Abucay position [or] wished to go even further" but mentions by name only General Bluemel, who claimed to have urged the II Corps commander to mount a "reconnaissance in force" in preparation for returning at least to Abucay. "What the proponents of a general counteroffensive failed to consider," Morton reminded readers of the army's official history, "was the fact that a local victory could not change the strategic situation in the Philippines" since the enemy "could reinforce at will."[2] Of course, the retreat-to-Bataan provisions of WPO-3 had been put into effect in the first place because of the army's inability to hold the invading forces at the beach, not in the belief that Japan could not try again should USAFFE defeat the enemy's initial attempt to invade the islands.

Along the new main line of resistance (MLR) that ran across the peninsula's waist from Orion (just south of Pilar) in the east to Bagac on Bataan's China Sea coast, "the reduced size of units, the shortage of trained combat officers, and the difficulty of communications" led II Philippine Corps to divide its half of the front line into lettered sectors, the commanders of which would report "directly to corps." Sector A (31st U.S. Infantry, soon replaced by the 31st Infantry, PA) was along part of the bay and inland for 2,500 yards; B (Provisional Air Corps Regiment, the only American-manned unit remaining along the front) continued 2,000 yards farther west; C (31st PA Division and remnants of the 51st Division) filled in the center portion of the corps' line for a distance of about 4,500 yards; Capinpin's 21st Division and then Lim's 41st Division completed the longest (6,000 yards) and westernmost portion of the corps' line. Their sector D met up with I Philippine Corps' "right sector" at the Pantingan River.[3] Perhaps it meant nothing, but the two Filipino generals would have noticed that only their divisions had been placed in a single sector over which an American general, an ex-Philippine Constabulary officer no less, had been put in charge.

Lim's new command post was located along the Catmon River about a mile and one-half south of the MLR. Fifty feet across at its widest, the Catmon flowed north off the slopes of the Mariveles Mountains to form roughly the dividing line between the 41st Division and the 21st Division to its right before crossing the east–west road and joining the Tiawir River that empties as the Talisay River into Manila Bay near Balanga. Lim had been nearer the MLR but told Atienza to find a less vulnerable location farther away for the division CP. Atienza identified an area near the conjunction of several trails but still partially hidden from aerial observation by the jungle canopy. The new command post, in place by the afternoon of 27 January, would remain until the final Japanese offensive in early April. Supply, ordnance, and engineering sections as well as Lim's headquarters could be found in well-camouflaged bamboo huts dispersed along the Catmon and farther back on the adjoining hillsides. Airplane mechanic Montgomery reported for duty to the division as a newly commissioned infantry lieutenant in early February and was immediately struck by the "rare beauty" of the setting. The division, he observed, "might not be winning" the war, but it "had picked a lovely setting in which to lose."[4]

Fighting did not cease with USAFFE's withdrawal from the Abucay line. The Japanese tried to exploit landings on several fingers of land that jutted into the sea along the southwestern coast of Bataan. In the subsequent battle of the

Points, each landing was contained and destroyed by the end of the first week in February. In the I Corps' right sector, enemy soldiers pushed through the MLR and formed two "pockets" that would not be fully extinguished until 17 February. The Japanese launched their main effort against II Corps along trail 2, a major north–south route that ran into USAFFE-held ground along the eastern edge of Mount Samat, a 1,920-foot-high peak just north of the Mariveles Mountains that "afforded excellent observation of the entire battlefield below." The area fell within the 31st PA Division's sector, but Bluemel was given two battalions of the 41st Infantry Regiment (PA) to help hold the line. By the time the exhausted enemy withdrew on 3 February, the 41st had proven itself to be "a veteran, unshakable outfit."[5] To the 41st Division's immediate front, Lim had problems of his own. A company or more of Japanese soldiers, possibly the remnant of a unit that had tried to get behind II Corps' retreat to the Orion-Bagac line, had entrenched itself along the southern bank of the Tiawir River before the division could solidify its hold on the area. "I told my two regimental commanders," Lim would tell his wife, "that if they can't drive the Japs out I would lead the fight." It cost elements of the 42nd and 43rd Infantry Regiments four days and seventy-four casualties to drive away the enemy, but Japanese losses were even higher.[6]

Japanese operations against II Corps at the end of January and into February—thwarted entirely by units of the Philippine Army—brought the first battle of Bataan to an end. Homma's decision to stop fighting and rebuild his debilitated forces led to a lull of several weeks' duration. Frontline divisions devoted themselves to training and strengthening defenses, though growing hunger and omnipresent malaria and other diseases dulled commitment to both tasks. Ultimately, MacArthur's refusal to countenance a counterattack combined with the inability to send supplies and reinforcements meant that starvation and disease would accomplish what Japanese arms could not. Food rations had been cut in half in early January and halved again in mid-March. The formal system of food distribution was more of a problem for the 41st Division than for other units because the division was at the far end of the II Corps' distribution chain. Everything moved as far as possible up the coastal road and then inland along hardly existent trails—time and distance that offered ample opportunities for pilfering. The division also suffered self-inflicted handicaps. A stunned Fortier learned that an overly fastidious supply officer had refused further issues of carabao meat after some maggot-infested quarters had been received. And much of the division's coffee supply had been left behind at Abucay, since the supply officer had considered it nonessential. For a short while, the men's resourcefulness kept hunger at bay. Foraging beyond the outpost line of resistance, into a no-man's-land largely abandoned

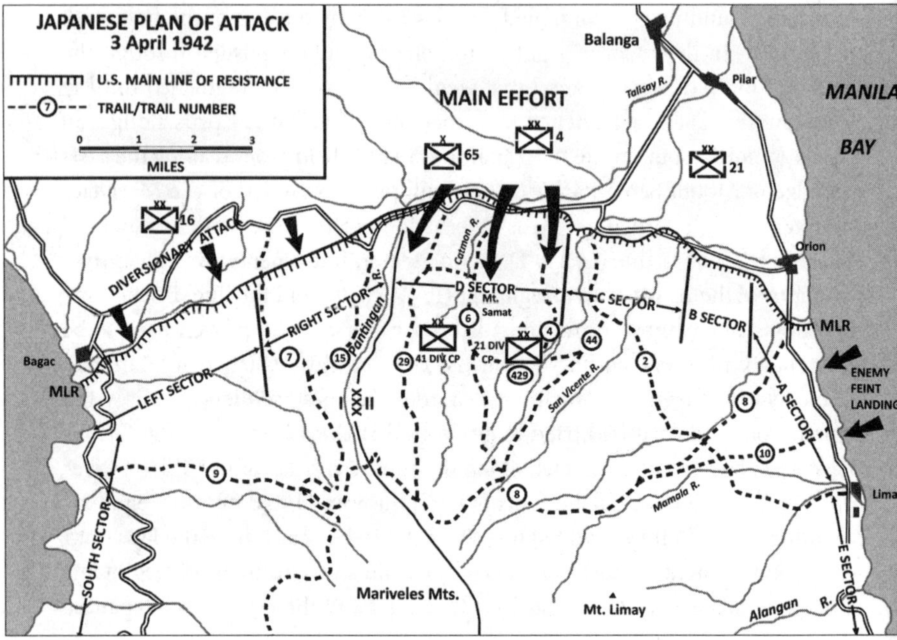

Bataan, April 1942. Copyright © 2018 by The University of Oklahoma Press, Publishing Division of the University. All rights reserved.

by the Japanese by mid-February, brought in carabao, palay, and other foodstuffs, but as February gave way to March, many men were not where they were supposed to be. They were instead, Lieutenant Montgomery observed, "wandering the hills in search of food."[7]

Of course, officers ate better than enlisted men. Medical officer Harold Glattly was of the opinion that Philippine Army officers never went hungry, and Carlos Romulo's depiction of Lim's "scarecrow body outlined against the sunset" notwithstanding, Atienza recalled that Lim's cook invariably managed to prepare appetizing meals. Lim shared these with the division staff. Nor was the general reluctant to invite others to take from his stock of cigars and cigarettes. Lim had joked that the war would end when his cigars ran out. By his estimate that would be mid-April.[8]

But even Lim could not avoid the physical deterioration to which weeks of deprivation ultimately led. He developed an infected tooth and, like many on the peninsula, suffered from recurrent malaria. The division commander, who celebrated his fifty-fourth birthday on Bataan, became less able to withstand the physically taxing inspections of the front lines after the withdrawal to the Orion-Bagac line; concern that his men would think he was "running out on them" kept him from going further to the rear or to Corregidor to seek medical aid and a respite from the difficult living conditions that existed at the front. By the middle of March, the American senior instructor with the 41st Infantry estimated "that 75 percent of the men were sick or convalescent from flu, dysentery or malaria or a combination" of the three, and he did not believe that his regiment was any worse off than others. The adviser to a battalion of the 42nd Infantry reported that the unit had 399 men on its rolls on 2 April: 125 were at the battalion aid station, and another 150 or so were sick but remained on the line. Adding to the general misery, toward the latter half of the dry season temperatures rose to highs topping 103 degrees in Manila by mid-May 1942, "an all-time record" for the city.[9]

A meeting of senior officers with General Wainwright in late March dashed whatever hope Lim may have retained about the possibility of reinforcements reaching Bataan. Lim returned to the division command post to tell his staff that the aid long expected from the United States would not arrive; what could be sent would be diverted to Australia. Lim understood the strategic necessity of building up forces in Australia rather than expending them on wasted efforts to relieve Bataan, but many of his officers were bitter and angry that America would, as President Quezon had supposedly shouted on Corregidor, "writhe in anguish at the fate of a distant cousin [Britain and its empire] while a daughter is being raped in the back room." At least, Magtoto observed, it was a good thing Lim had been elsewhere the day of the generals' meeting. The division headquarters area had been bombed by Japanese planes while Lim was away, and the division commander was known for his reluctance to seek cover during air raids. But the mood was grim. Gregorio Recio, a junior officer of the 41st Infantry who around this time passed through the division CP en route to his unit after a stay in the hospital, remembered hearing General Lim say to his staff words to the effect that there was "nothing much to do, troops demoralized, things out of control, no food or medicine."[10]

As the Philippine Campaign approached its fourth month, the Japanese did what the Americans and Filipinos could not: they brought in substantial reinforcements. Though angry at his failure to crush USAFFE by the end of January, General Homma's superiors provided him with the resources needed to bring the operation to a successful conclusion. Homma himself would be sent home in June 1942 and given no further field commands for the rest of the war, but he remained in the Philippines to direct the final offensive. Beginning in late February, troops flowed in from Japan, from China, Hong Kong, Malaya, and Singapore. The decimated 65th Brigade and 16th Division were built up to strength. A new division, the 4th, arrived, as did independent battalions of infantry and artillery. The Luzon Force commander later estimated that "at least" 50,000 Japanese soldiers confronted the Filipino and American forces on Bataan. For once in the campaign, the invaders did have about as many men as the defenders.[11]

Japanese intentions were no secret. By mid-March aerial activity had increased significantly and the front line was subjected to daily air and artillery bombardment. The enemy presence made patrolling difficult, but observers could see the growing artillery and troop strength south of Abucay. In an effort to avoid a replay of the events of January and the failure to break through along the east road, this time Homma concentrated his effort near the left of II Corps' line. This would be an area that the Americans were less likely to expect to be attacked, and, if successful, an assault would allow the quick seizure of Mount Samat, which would provide observation posts for the artillery support of the advancing infantry and tank force. II Corps expected a Japanese attack on the 41st Division's portion of the line. An officer of the 31st U.S. Infantry (held in reserve) wrote in his diary that his regiment "had already reconnoitered carefully routes to the area" in preparation for reinforcing the division, while the regiment's commanding officer had visited the regimental CPs of the 41st Division and "talked over the local situation with Colonel Fortier and General Lim."[12]

Japanese infantry began probing the Filipino line near the end of March. During the night of 30–31 March, the 42nd Infantry lost control of its outpost line of resistance. An artillery-supported counterattack failed to evict the Japanese. On the evening of 2 April, the Japanese followed up a mortar barrage with an assault on the 43rd Infantry OPLR. The regiment repelled a first wave; a second wave led by Tagalog-speaking soldiers shouting that Filipinos would not be harmed if they stayed in their fighting holes and offered no resistance penetrated the regimental line in two places. A third wave soon followed. At the division CP, Fortier listened in as Colonel Salgado directed the defense. When the regimental commander asked Fortier for instructions, the American adviser told him "to make his own decisions." He was doing fine. Continued enemy pressure forced the unit back to the MLR, but it withdrew in good order and with all of its equipment.[13]

The next day, 3 April, was Good Friday. For Lim's men, it began as most of the days in the previous week had begun. They sat in their fighting holes, "chatting or smoking, waiting for the shelling to stop." But this day the shelling did not stop. It grew in intensity and continued into the afternoon. In later years American officers who had been at the front that day would say that the Japanese gunnery was like that of a German artillery barrage along the western front. Others thought the comparison exaggerated, but in the estimation of the corps commander, the Japanese shelling was "the heaviest by far of any artillery fire in any battle to date in the Philippines."[14]

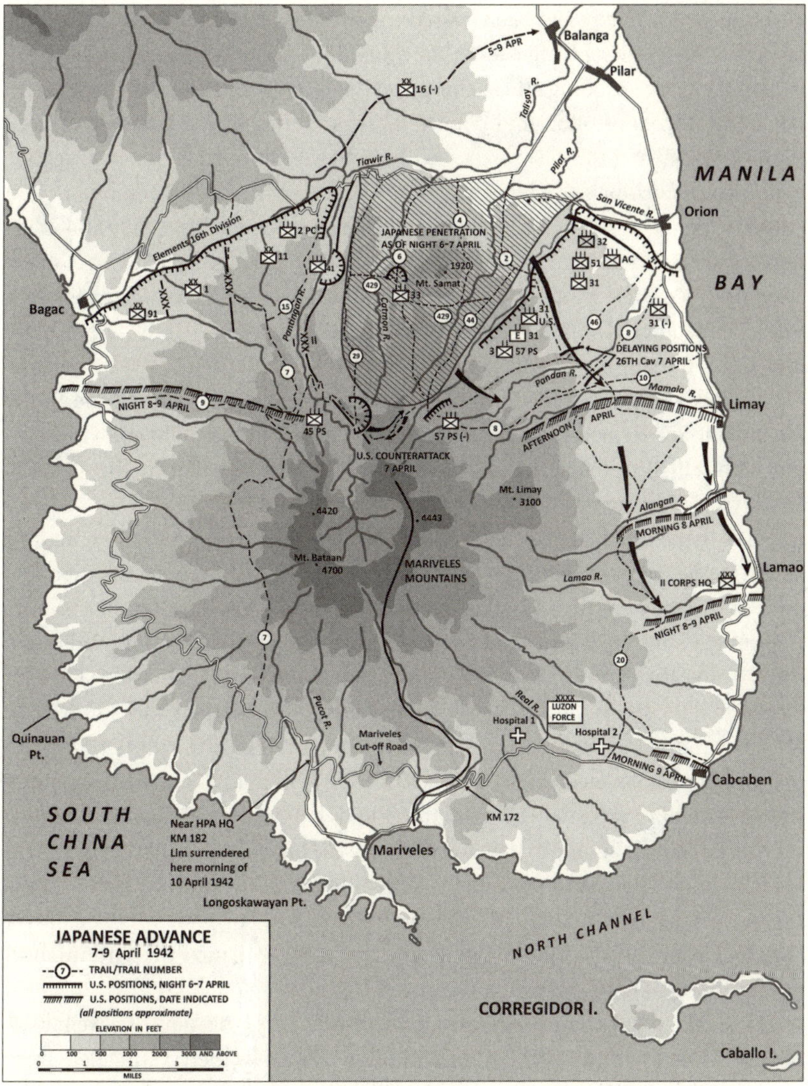

The 41st Division's 42nd and 43rd Infantry Regiments bore the brunt of the barrage. They may have lost few men throughout the daylong bombardment—Edgarto Gumban, at least, reported that his company in the 42nd Infantry had had three men killed and another five wounded that day, although he was of the opinion that the Japanese had concentrated their fire further to the rear and thus his company had been spared the worst—but the regiments soon collapsed. What General King called "the ailment of nerve fatigue" brought on by constant enemy bombing and shelling and the utter inability of the Filipino and American forces to offer any "counter activity" brought the Japanese a more rapid victory than they had expected to achieve. Philippine Army stragglers earlier in the campaign, King wrote, had "kept their arms and equipment and could be rallied and returned to the front"—but no longer. Physically and mentally exhausted, for many of the men, the artillery barrage was the final straw. They dropped their weapons and fled.[15] Fortier had considered the 42nd's main line of resistance along the steep slopes of the Tiawir River to be "impregnable," but the enemy's incendiary bombs forced the 42nd back to its reserve line. On the division's right, the 43rd Infantry faced tanks for the first time in the campaign. Fortier had expected tanks in that area, but the regiment had nothing with which to counter them. The antitank guns supplied by the 31st U.S. Infantry did not survive the opening artillery barrage.[16]

The Japanese assault was no blitzkrieg, but it was more than enough to dislodge the 41st Division. By midafternoon on the first day of the Japanese offensive, men were streaming back through Lim's command post. By the time nightfall brought a halt to the enemy advance, the Japanese had moved down the Catmon River valley to within a few hundred yards of the division's CP. Lim had to leave. Late in the afternoon, he and Fortier made their way south to an artillery command post and that evening continued east to the 21st Division command post, located on the southeast slope of Mount Samat near the junction of trails 4 and 429. They got there about 6 P.M. and informed General Capinpin and his senior instructor, Colonel O'Day, that the 41st Division was withdrawing. They had met General Lough during their journey. He was leading men of the 33rd Infantry (PA) back up trail 6, and Fortier left Lim behind at the 21st Division CP to join Lough in an attempt to reorganize the 43rd Infantry and try to put a block along the Catmon River.[17]

The division's collapse accelerated on 4 April. Later that day, Lim went back to trail 6 and together with Fortier and other officers gathered stragglers from the 42nd and 43rd Regiments at the junction of trails 6 and 8, about two miles south of his old command post.

Wainwright visited General Parker's headquarters near Lamao on Easter Sunday, 5 April, and recorded in his diary that "things are very bad with the 41st Division. It is about broken up." From the corps' perspective, the division—or at least the two right-wing regiments that remained under Lim's command—"had ceased to exist." Lim's perspective was slightly less bleak. Most of the division's officers had gathered near the junction of trails 6 and 8, and Lim ordered what remained of the two regiments placed along those trails. On the evening of the fifth, division officers managed to cobble together a force of about 330 men of the two regiments with the mission of pushing north the next morning on trail 6, which ran along the Catmon River valley perpendicular to east–west trail 8. They would attempt to delay the Japanese long enough for the 57th Infantry (PS) to come up from the south. The testimony of neither American nor Filipino officers supports the U.S. Army official history's assertion that the troops fled "at the first sign of the enemy," but they did not remain long in action. The men withstood an exchange of rifle and machine-gun fire, but a Japanese mortar barrage destroyed any semblance of unit cohesion. "Wild-eyed, pale and scared," to quote the division historians, most of the men now raced to the rear. Atienza telephoned the division CP and heard Lim tell an American general that the 41st Division had blocking positions in place across trail 6. Atienza broke in to say that only a few men remained on the trail. Soon afterward they received orders to withdraw once the 57th Infantry (PS) had relieved them. The officer in charge of Scouts at the junction of trails 6 and 44 (just north of the junction of trails 6 and 8) had ordered a machine gunner to fire over the heads of the retreating 41st Division soldiers in an attempt to get them to stay in place. When the Scouts then moved up to Atienza's location, he realized that while he thought the Scouts were arriving to relieve his men, they thought they had come as reinforcements. After "straightening things out with the American lieutenant," he herded his men south. "That was," Fortier wrote, "the last resistance of the troops of the 42nd and 43rd Regiments." So ended the existence of Lim's division as a fighting force. The 41st Regiment was still intact, and would still do damage to the enemy before the end came, but it had swung west and now formed the far right of I Corps. For what remained, in Fortier's words, "it was a succession of withdrawals to new assembly areas in an endeavor to get the men back to normal."[18]

As with Abucay, images of Lim and the events of the final offensive reflect the contrasting perceptions of the American and Filipino officers who survived to tell their tales. For the failed action on 6 April, Fortier places the American adviser, Lt. Col. Eugene Lewis (who would die as a prisoner of war), in charge of the force, while Atienza and the division history put the Filipino commanding officer of the 43rd Infantry, Colonel Salgado, at the head of the troops and make no mention of the American officer. Fortier continued the theme of Lim's dependence on his American adviser: he had guided an overanxious Lim to the 21st Division CP on the afternoon of 3 April and left him there in relative safety before returning to the sound of the guns. But in his account of that day, Capinpin made no mention of Fortier. He stated that Lim called him about 4 P.M. to confirm that the 41st Division line had collapsed. After arriving at Capinpin's CP about 6 P.M., Lim and Capinpin spoke to General Parker by telephone and at that time learned that the 33rd Infantry (PA) had been committed to support the 21st Division's left flank.

Lim's loyal subordinates place the general at the center of the action. In one of the longest recollections of Lim's actions as commanding general that he included in his memoirs, Atienza described an evening meeting on 5 April that Lim oversaw in an impromptu CP in a ravine near a bridge on trail 8. Lim calmly queried the regimental commanders about the state of their units and explained to them General Lough's orders to defend division artillery located north off trail 6. Atienza specifically mentioned the presence of MacDonald, Lewis, and Fortier, along with the division's intelligence and operations officers, Isagani Ocampo and Dionisio Ojeda. Atienza recalled Fortier's telephone call to corps headquarters to ask for tanks to support the attack and the promise of a single self-propelled antitank gun. Atienza told John Toland, whom he hoped would include the story in *But Not in Shame*, that the account of the division's "last stand" was taken from a manuscript that Atienza had written during the war and "carefully kept during the Japanese occupation." Yet in his extensive comments on a draft of *Fall of the Philippines*, Fortier claimed that he and Ojeda spent all of 5 April attempting to contact the 41st Infantry west of the Pantingan River. They did not return to the division CP until the morning of 6 April. After the war, Ojeda was cited for gallantry for having made the dangerous journey with Fortier "into enemy territory" on 5 April 1942.[19]

Except for Clifford Bluemel, the general officers commanding units along II Corps' front at the start of the Japanese offensive were no longer involved in the fighting. General Capinpin had become separated from his staff and had been captured on the afternoon of 5 April under questionable circumstances—did he inadvertently or deliberately allow himself to be taken prisoner?—that would become the subject of an inconclusive postwar U.S. Army investigation. General Lough had found himself cut off to the west; he and his staff were attached to I Corps for the final scenes of the battle.[20] Only General Bluemel, in an effort for which he would be recommended for the Medal of Honor, scrambled to organize ever diminishing numbers of hungry, weary, sick, and dispirited soldiers along the southern banks of one river line after another in a forlorn attempt to stem the collapse. By the end, he had—and wanted—only Scouts and a few Americans under his command. An officer in charge of a group of about seventy-five men of the Air Corps Provisional Regiment, among the few in that unit who had not withdrawn when the Japanese advance breached sector B on 7 April, ran into Bluemel early on the morning of 9 April and was told that the general "want[ed] only white American troops."[21] Bluemel's own Philippine Army division in sector C had avoided the worst of the Japanese artillery barrage, but when confronted by the enemy advance it had collapsed as readily as the others.

Lim played no part in the final battles of Bataan. He concluded that the division needed to get well away from the Japanese to reorganize and rebuild, assuming either could still be done. On 7 April Lim and Fortier went to Parker's headquarters to recommend that the division move further to the rear. At first resistant to the suggestion, the corps commander finally agreed. The division's soldiers were to meet about four and one-half miles to the south, at the junction of trail 20 and the Lamao River (about a mile west of corps headquarters). Lim did not believe the Lamao was far enough. On the morning of 8 April, he called his senior staff officers together to discuss continuing further to the rear. He had apparently already talked with Fortier about doing so, and his American adviser had wanted to make a stand along the Lamao. Lim thought that the men were "not fit to fight" and insisted on finding a "quiet place" for the division to reassemble. His officers agreed. Their direst threats were not stemming the flow of Philippine Army troops to the rear. Lim decided to keep moving, well beyond the Lamao River, to a site near Philippine Army headquarters northwest of Mariveles near kilometer marker (KM) 182.[22]

The greater the distance from danger, the greater was the determination to fight on. In Washington, Secretary of War Henry Stimson discussed the events on Bataan with his assistant John McCloy and the War Plans Division's Dwight Eisenhower and recorded in his diary for 8 April their agreement that fighting to "the bitter end . . . would probably be better for the cause of the country in the end than would surrender." From Australia, General MacArthur reiterated his opposition to surrender "under any circumstances." On Corregidor, General Wainwright understood what was happening to II Corps but considered himself bound by earlier no-surrender instructions. On 7 April he told General King's chief of staff, Brig. Gen. Arnold Funk, "that under no circumstances would the Luzon Force surrender."[23]

On Bataan itself, the generals responded as circumstance and inclination dictated. Lough got out of the way; Capinpin called it quits; Bluemel fought on. On the western side of the peninsula, Brougher talked of letting anyone escape who could, while he and his Philippine Scout chief of staff made for Corregidor. He spoke to Beebe, who told him, "This was not the time to desert his troops." For his part, Lim accepted the inevitability of defeat and wanted to have whatever remained of the division reorganized and intact to better withstand the rigors of imprisonment. If the Japanese were to be held at bay, others would have to do it. Lim had ordered his men to stay in their positions along the front when the enemy offensive began and as late as 6 April believed that the 41st Division, or at least what remained of it, could still play a part in stemming the Japanese onslaught. By 7 April he no longer believed so. Now, Lim made decisions without reference to his American superiors or adviser. On that day, when Fortier came back from corps headquarters to the division's assembly area, he realized that Lim had not returned and that no one knew where he was. At least, no one was willing to tell the American adviser. Magtoto reported—he was not present but his details are precise—that Lim arrived by jeep at Philippine Army headquarters later on 7 April to see General Francisco. He told the 2nd Division commander, who was the Philippine Army's senior officer still in the country (General Valdes had escaped from Corregidor with Quezon by submarine in February and had since reached Australia), that Francisco should see General King to discuss surrender. When Francisco proved reluctant to see King, Lim said that he would do so. At that point, General Francisco went to King's command post but returned without having spoken to him. King was too busy, Francisco explained, and, anyway, the time was "not propitious for surrender."[24]

By all accounts, the Luzon Force commander was a compassionate officer, deeply concerned about the suffering of the soldiers of his command. Manzano referred to General King as a "grandfatherly figure." King had completed more than thirty years on active duty when he had arrived in the Philippines on the first day of November 1940, aboard the same troopship carrying General Wainwright, for what he possibly had expected to be a pleasant twilight tour of duty in the tropics before retiring. He assumed command of Fort Stotsenburg, the same post to which he had been assigned as a young field artillery officer a quarter of a century earlier during his only other tour of Philippine duty. King had served briefly as commanding general of North Luzon Force but, to his disappointment and for reasons now unknown, was then replaced in that role by Wainwright. In a talk he gave at that time to officers assigned to work with the Philippine Army, he insisted that "there was no such thing as racial superiority" and that Filipinos made fine soldiers. On Bataan he had been the senior artillery officer, a role of sufficient obscurity that it goes almost unmentioned in published histories of the campaign, even though the artillery played a pronounced role in what successes USAFFE forces enjoyed on Bataan. King was, after Wainwright, the highest-ranking officer on the peninsula, but he was obscure enough that the secretary of war could refer to him as "Colonel King." Command of Luzon Force—that portion of the army and naval service in the Philippines trapped on Bataan—had passed to him on 21 March, when Wainwright assumed the title of commanding general of United States Forces in the Philippines (USFIP) and moved to Corregidor. General King had played no part in the decision-making process that had led to the current circumstances, but to him would fall the ignominy of capitulation.[25]

If Filipino officer Philip Buencamino's re-created diary entry is accurate—no other source recounts this event—King accepted command of Luzon Force resigned to the knowledge that it would be his fate to surrender the

Philippine-American armies. Buencamino wrote that he accompanied General de Jesus to a meeting of general officers at Wainwright's headquarters on 20 March at which Wainwright announced that he was moving to Corregidor and that King would assume command of the forces on Bataan. Buencamino quoted "Old General King" as saying at that time: "Somebody is angry with me in Washington. I am going to be given the honor of being the first American general in history to surrender the American flag."[26] King may have made the decision to surrender as early as 7 April. Certainly, he had done so by the next day. On the afternoon of 8 April, he ordered that weapons and equipment be prepared for destruction but that trucks and gasoline be saved; they would be needed to transport prisoners north. That same day, as the end of the sixth day of the Japanese offensive drew to a close, King closeted himself with his chief of staff and operations officer. Neither King nor any other senior USAFFE officer had sought the advice of the Filipino generals up to that point, nor did they now. The three agreed that no conceivable action would keep the Japanese out of Mariveles beyond the evening of the next day. Further resistance could achieve nothing beneficial to the Allied cause. King then called his staff together (one or two Filipino officers may have attended the meeting) and told them that he had decided to surrender. Two American officers, Col. E. C. Williams and Maj. M. H. Hurt, would leave within hours in an attempt to reach Japanese lines by daybreak.[27]

Given the chaotic conditions in southern Bataan, news of the surrender would for many Filipinos and Americans be rumor long before it became fact. Nor were the Japanese any better informed. Six hundred soldiers of the 41st Infantry remained in place along the Pantingan River and were preparing to take up a new defensive position on the lower slopes of the Mariveles Mountains when they received word of the surrender late in the afternoon of 9 April. The men destroyed arms and burned or buried records, but an attempt to surrender to advancing Japanese tanks later in the evening ended in disaster. The Japanese machine-gunned the assembled men and their white flags. The next day, the 41st Infantry's American instructor, Col. Loren Wetherby, rounded up a hundred or so survivors of the regiment and turned them over to the Japanese without further incident. Many men of the other regiments managed to make it to the division assembly area northwest of Mariveles, but the crowded trails and roads meant that many others could not. At the division assembly area near KM 182, Fortier heard reports that white flags were being flown by USFIP troops and learned from General de Jesus that Japanese troops had reached KM 172 on the east road (where the Mariveles cutoff road began), but not until later in the day did the division receive official confirmation that General King had surrendered Luzon Force. Officers gathered around a radio to hear Corregidor's Voice of Freedom announce the surrender of the American and Filipino forces on Bataan. General de Jesus, his aide remembered, turned away "because he did not want to show his feelings [while] General Lim wiped his eyes with a dirty handkerchief."[28]

A chronology of the division's flight from the Orion-Bagac line gives a misleading coherence to events on Bataan in early April 1942. "We had lost track of time," wrote Corporal Tagarao, who was at the front when the Japanese assault began. "All we knew was the brightness of day and the darkness of night." Manuel de Veyra, a doctor with a relatively safe job at the hospital near Philippine Army headquarters (he never saw a Japanese soldier until the surrender, though the Japanese had bombed the hospital and killed the senior officer of the Philippine Army's medical service), observed that they had no calendars and did not know one day from the next. Each passed with "depressing monotony." He was only certain the surrender came in April because hospital personnel had been paid at the end of March. For those not in the immediate path of the Japanese, routine continued even toward the end, and some remained oblivious to the approaching denouement. Colonel Alexander, adviser to the 1st Infantry (PA), professed astonishment when the Filipino regimental commander expressed surprise at the news of surrender. He did not seem to be aware, Alexander marveled, that USAFFE was losing the war. Army doctor Calvin Jackson spent two hours on the morning of 6 April at Philippine Army headquarters being "quizzed" at the court-martial of a Filipino lieutenant. Jackson thought "every Philippine gen[eral] and col[onel]" must have been there. Two days had gone by since the Japanese had collapsed the 41st Division lines a mere eight miles to the northeast.[29]

According to most accounts, not until late in the morning on 10 April did a column of Japanese troops finally appear at the 41st Division assembly area near KM 182. There, on the west bank of the Pucot River, encircled by a cordon of bayonet-wielding guards and out of hearing of the other Filipino captives, several Japanese officers and a civilian interpreter questioned Lim for about twenty minutes. What appears to be a cropped photograph of this scene, showing Lim sitting on a fallen tree trunk and facing his interrogators, was taken by the Japanese army's propaganda corps and widely disseminated, ostensibly to demonstrate the courtesy and respect accorded to captured Filipino soldiers by the Japanese.[30]

Lim was taken to Balanga. After lunch with a Colonel Nagataki, Lim, along with Generals de Jesus, Jones, and Brougher, continued to Orani, a town on Bataan's east coast road about three miles north of Mabatang. There they met General King. After three days of relatively comfortable treatment, they left by automobile for San Fernando, Pampanga, followed soon after by their staffs and aides.[31] The Filipino chief engineer of a sugar central near San Fernando reported seeing Lim at the provincial capital on 14 April. The engineer, who knew many Filipino officers by sight, saw Lim in the company of several other officers at an elementary school that served as one of the two main places of incarceration in San Fernando. Prisoners had been arriving in the city since 11 April, and he and other civilians tried to provide them with water, cigarettes, and food. The guards usually pushed the civilians away, but the unnamed engineer was able to give this group "nearly all that they were asking [for]," including hats made of palm, one of "which General Lim immediately put on."[32]

Most of the men identified by the unnamed engineer were Constabulary officers, and it is possible that he somehow confused Lim with General Francisco, the captured commanding general of the 2nd Regular Division, for there are, inevitably, competing stories of Lim's movements after the surrender. Maj. Gen. Albert Jones, Wainwright's successor as commander of I Corps, told John Toland that he and Col. William Maher were taken by truck to a "shack" where they met King, Brougher, Segundo, and Lim. The next day, Jones, King, and "one or two Filipinos" continued in a sedan car to Camp O'Donnell. Army historian Stanley Falk learned from Jones that on the evening of 12 April, King, Jones, and two unnamed Filipino generals "were packed tightly into a car" and driven from Orani to Camp O'Donnell.[33] Lim's aide Ernesto Santos testified after the war that Lim and an orderly had traveled to San Fernando in a Japanese truck transporting horses. Lim was then incarcerated with many other prisoners of war in the town cockpit—the second principal place of incarceration—and, according to yet another account, subjected to abuse by Japanese interrogators. "You could have stopped this useless fighting weeks ago!" they supposedly shouted at Lim.[34]

Lim and the other senior Filipino officers could have suffered far worse along what became known as the Bataan Death March. Bluemel and Col. Kearie Berry, who had succeeded Segundo in command of the 1st Division (PA), hiked much of the distance to the march's terminus at San Fernando. So too did Brig. Gen. Maxon Lough and Luther Stevens, the American general in the Philippine Army who commanded the 91st Division. Bluemel, Lough, and Stevens were beaten by their captors along the way. General Stevens was "almost dead and with hardly any clothes on his back" when he arrived at Camp O'Donnell, where he "was left on the floor of the foul hospital to die in his own feces." Along the march, a marine officer captured on Bataan witnessed an unidentified army brigadier general and senior staff officers forced to "run through a gauntlet of enemy privates" who slapped and beat them and robbed them of their possessions. One captured army officer claimed to have watched an *American* army private punch in the face an unnamed general officer during the March.[35]

Japanese behavior could be as arbitrary as it was brutal. Beatings, hunger, and the knowledge that to falter along the way meant death was the lot of many prisoners of war, American and Filipino; yet a few POWs rode to San Fernando or O'Donnell and witnessed little or nothing of the horrors attested to by others. The surrendered soldiers of the 41st Division underwent a similar array of experiences. A junior officer of the 43rd Infantry captured with some of his men on the first day of the Easter offensive, 3 April, rode in a truck all the way to Capas.[36] Those who made it to the division staging area near Mariveles enjoyed another week of freedom but faced the farthest distance to cover to get to San Fernando and a reduced likelihood of getting there unscathed. Unlike General Lim, most had to walk. Least fortunate of all was a group of four hundred or so junior officers and NCOs, mostly from the 91st and 71st Divisions but including at least one officer, Reynaldo Perez, from the 42nd Infantry Regiment, bound together and methodically bayoneted on 12 April along a ravine leading into the Pantingan River. Only a few of the men survived to tell the story. The Japanese told their victims that they were being punished for not having surrendered earlier, but a story later emerged that the soldiers of the 65th Brigade who carried out the slaughter were seeking retribution for the killing of comrades caught sleeping in their bivouac by an advancing Philippine Army unit, not far from where the massacre later took place. The Japanese thought the 91st Division had been involved, but it had been a portion of the 41st Infantry Regiment that had staged the counterattack early on the morning of 6 April. The regiment had seized an area near where the Pantingan River crossed the Pilar-Bagac road in an effort to support an unsuccessful advance down the river by the 45th Infantry (PS).[37]

Many soldiers surrendered but then fled the march and successfully eluded the Japanese. At least one of the 41st Division's American officers managed to do so. Near Bataan's border with Pampanga in the vicinity of Layac, Capt. Winston Jones ran into the tall grass along the highway and crawled into a ravine. Later, Filipino farmers helped Jones and other Americans who had done the same make their way farther north.[38] Still others did not surrender. Henry Harris and Murl Schrock, the American advisers to the engineer battalion, remained hidden near Balanga until early 1943, when they were captured and eventually joined POWs at Cabanatuan. Neither man survived the war.[39] Filipinos could far more easily avoid capture or escape along the march out of Bataan. Sgt. Alfredo Morada of the 43rd Infantry surrendered with a few other men in his signals platoon. He thought that almost all of them managed to disappear once the marchers entered Pampanga. The former artillery commander, Lt. Col. Amado Martelino, never surrendered. He, his brother Col. Pastor Martelino (chief of staff of the 31st Division), and a third brother (a reserve officer) managed to get back to Manila with their families. They did not turn themselves in to Japanese authorities until September 1942. Fidel Ongpauco, the officer who kept the prison camp muster rolls at Capas, estimated that about 12,000 Filipino soldiers had probably escaped along the route. Those who did not, however, arrived at San Fernando in an emaciated condition, having taken four or five days to cover the sixty-mile distance from Mariveles. At San Fernando, the closest railhead to Bataan, the prisoners found themselves crowded into small freight cars of the Manila-Dagupan Railroad and taken north to Capas, Tarlac. From there, one last march took them to the prison camp at O'Donnell. Already, more Filipino and American soldiers had died since the surrender than had been killed during the fighting.[40]

The long journey out of Bataan ended in a far corner of the vast Stotsenburg army reservation that straddled Pampanga and Tarlac Provinces to the north of the besieged peninsula, at a place called Camp O'Donnell. The unlikely name reflected the presence in the Philippines of a mid-nineteenth-century descendant of a seventeenth-century Irish Catholic refugee family in service to the Spanish crown, and Barrio O'Donnell had been one of the few areas partially exempted from military control when Stotsenburg had been enlarged to encompass nearly 200,000 acres in 1908. Local folklore held that landowners in the barrio had been "given enough time" to show prior ownership of their property, but few had done so, believing that the Yankees could not "carry their lands to America." Whatever the truth of the matter, Barrio O'Donnell was reduced in size to about half of what it had been before the expansion of Stotsenburg but lent its name to a new camp built in the area in 1941, when USAFFE established a cantonment for recently mobilized Philippine Army divisions and an engineers' training site there. The planned facilities had never been completed, but the Japanese decided that in addition to being fairly close to Bataan and to their line of communications, "so many buildings were already there" that O'Donnell would make a good site for a prison camp. As prisoners arrived, the Japanese separated them into two streams: the Americans to the north, the far larger number of Filipinos to the south and west of the American compound. General King's remonstrations could not keep the Philippine Scouts from being ordered to the Philippine Army side of the camp. Narcisco Manzano pointed out to the Japanese that though in the United States Army he was a Filipino and was sent to the Philippine Army enclosure; Mississippi-born Philippine Army general Luther Stevens and blond-haired Philippine Army lieutenant Albert McMicking stayed with the Americans. For many Japanese, as for many Americans, the color of one's skin trumped the source of one's commission.[41]

A few hundred American POWs would remain in the Philippines throughout the war, either to be liberated by the advancing American forces or slaughtered by the retreating Japanese; but for most of the Americans captured on Bataan, Camp O'Donnell was but the first stop on a long, torturous journey that led eventually to transport to Japan or occupied China aboard the notorious "Hellships." For more than a few, O'Donnell was the last stop. The emaciated condition in which many arrived, poor and insufficient diet, lack of medicine, disease, and the cruelty or indifference of the Japanese guards contributed to the deaths of more than 1,500 men (17 percent of the 9,000 American prisoners) at Camp O'Donnell, until July 1942 when survivors began moving to a camp further east near Cabanatuan, in Nueva Ecija Province.[42]

Conditions in the Filipino compound were even worse. Before the year was out, Camp O'Donnell would be the burial site for half or more of the Filipino soldiers who had surrendered on Bataan in April 1942. An estimated 44,000 to 50,000 Filipino prisoners, of the official total of 66,304 Filipino troops (including Philippine Scouts) on Bataan on 3 April 1942, had reached Capas by mid-April. Philippine Scout officer John Olson, who came to serve as adjutant of the American prisoners at O'Donnell, wrote that "the rumor was" that some 22,500 Filipinos had died by the end of June 1942. Just before he left for Cabanatuan in July, Olson managed to learn the Philippine Army group adjutant's statistics: Nemesio Catalan had recorded "somewhat over 19,000" deaths. Olson thought the figure low and concluded that some 25,000 Filipino soldiers died at O'Donnell between 11 April 1942 and the camp's closure on 20 January 1943. Catalan put the number at 26,000 when he testified at Homma's war crimes trial after the war. The chief of the Philippine Army's casualty division, Maj. Basilio Hernandez, gave a figure of 27,169 deaths by early August 1942. Volume 2 of the Veterans Federation of the Philippines' six-volume compilation of World War II reports and rosters lists the names of 25,803 Philippine Army soldiers who died at O'Donnell in 1942 and whose remains were reinterred in the Philippine military cemetery in Manila after the war.[43]

There are lower estimates. A Japanese medical officer thought Filipino totals far too high. He offered a figure of 18,000 deaths. Fidel Ongpauco, who possessed some of the surviving camp muster rolls, stated that the number of Filipino dead reported to the Japanese was inflated to cover escapees. He estimated a minimum of 15,000 dead by 25 July 1942 and a maximum of 21,000 "died or escaped" by that date.[44] Whatever the precise number, the end result was that more Filipinos died at Capas in 1942 than did American prisoners of war at all camps in Southeast Asia, China, Korea, Manchuria, Japan, and Taiwan or aboard the "Hellships" combined from 1942 to 1945.

Subjecting Filipino and American prisoners of war at Camp O'Donnell to "systematic cruel, barbarous and uncivilized treatment" was one of the charges General Homma faced in his postwar trial. Several Philippine Army officers were called on to testify to the hellish conditions at the camp: the crowded barracks that facilitated the spread of disease; blankets for only some of the sick; water not safe for drinking, but not enough containers or wood for boiling and purifying it; meals that consisted of a little rice and salt and a plant "with edible leaves [found] in the camp"; the Japanese keeping for themselves fruit and clothing and other donated items.[45] The most affecting testimony came from a man who had not been a prisoner of war. A Philippine Red Cross physician named Romeo Atienza had accompanied an ambulance into the camp in mid-July 1942 to pick up seven POWs left behind "during the first release [of prisoners] because they were reported to be very, very, ill." The stench of the camp struck him at once; in the hospital barracks where they went in search of the seven POWs, Atienza saw sick prisoners soaked in feces and urine, "with flies all around in their bodies and all around the room." As he further recounted:

> [T]here was no medical attention, no medicine and no nursing care given to the prisoners who were there. . . . When we were loading the four patients into the ambulance [the other three had died], my attention and my driver's attention were attracted by the coming of about thirty litters, bamboo litters; there were two to three half-naked almost skin and bone cadavers of Filipino prisoners of war on each one, on their way to the cemetery. . . . [E]ven without any relative there, my driver and myself could not help but shed tears when we saw that very, very pathetic scene.[46]

There was a school of thought, a hint of which came out at the Homma trial, that held that the high number of deaths among the Filipino prisoners was partly of their own making, that the indifferent discipline and disengaged officer leadership observed on Bataan continued in the prison camp with devastating effect. A prisoner on the American side of Camp O'Donnell wrote in his wartime diary that "the high death rate among the Filipinos is greatly their own fault, or rather, [their] lack of training and that's our fault."[47] That senior officers made too-little effort to improve conditions at the camp is a recurring theme in POW memoirs. The real "criminals" at O'Donnell, wrote a 2nd Division veteran, were not the Japanese but high-ranking Filipino officers and doctors who controlled the supply of food and medicine and took all for themselves as others died. He remembered that while enlisted men starved, officers from major to general received afternoon snacks of fried *camote*, hot cakes or donuts, and coffee or tea. Men loitered around the officers' kitchen waiting to devour discarded *camote* peelings. Venicio Jalandoni, a company commander in the 72nd

Infantry, suffered from malaria but like many others discovered that prisoners without money or influence were often unable to get treatment. Army doctors, he claimed, sold the medicine they were supposed to have prescribed. Only after his well-known uncle, Lt. Col. Rafael Jalandoni of the 4th PC Regiment, learned of his presence in the camp did he begin to receive more food and medicine. Teodoro Agoncillo interviewed "scores of enlisted men and officers" who had been at O'Donnell and told of Filipino group leaders beating prisoners, of officers ordering privates "to fan them while they slept" and keeping "the best of the rations" for themselves while the men made do with gruel "or a mouthful of rice and a pinch of salt." Medicine sent to the POWs "by people of Manila through the Red Cross," wrote Father Juan Labrador, who had spoken to a number of released prisoners, was "channeled by unscrupulous doctors to the black market, or sold to the prisoners at prohibitive prices." Recalling the conduct of some army doctors at Capas, "[when] I meet some of them now," one captain told Agoncillo twenty years later, "I feel like murdering them for what they did at Camp O'Donnell in 1942."[48]

Maybe some of this was exaggerated and unfair (at least that is what Catalan said at the Homma trial), and leadership on the American side of the camp had its shortcomings too. The most senior American officers were not kept long at Capas. The Japanese took the generals and senior colonels, such as Fortier, to Tarlac in May 1942 and transported them by ship to Taiwan in August. Their absence was sorely felt. Not long after the war ended, Harold Johnson of the 57th Infantry (PS), who had endured just about the worst the prisoner-of-war experience had to offer—the Death March, O'Donnell, Cabanatuan, the Hellship *Oryoku Maru*—wrote an article reflecting on "the breakdown in discipline and leadership among the American prisoners." He tried to get it published in an army-sponsored journal, but the editor rejected it. The article was too hard-hitting, the editor explained, and, anyway, some things were better left unsaid.

Like Johnson, Philippine Scout engineer officer Maximiano Janairo thought something needed to be said. He was so disturbed by the situation in the Filipino camp and the senior officers' apparent indifference to it that he feared they might all be called to account after the war. He complained to General Francisco and minced no words: "A large percentage of our deaths and most of the agonies and other miseries of the Filipino prisoners of war in this camp had been caused by the criminal negligence, indifference and 'to hell with them' attitude" of Filipino officers. Janairo enumerated a damning list of misbehavior on the part of some officers, ranging from "looting of personal property and food" of enlisted men, to beatings (both of enlisted men and of junior by senior officers), to profiteering and the unfair distribution of food.

Manzano painted an equally sorry picture of leadership at O'Donnell, and he named names. He singled out "the despicable behavior of two high-ranking Filipino officers: Gen. Capinpin and Col. [*sic*] Segundo," who "treated their men worse than the Japs." The surviving documents do not suggest Janairo's criticisms achieved much other than that when the camp was reorganized and the number of groups and subgroups into which the Japanese had organized the prisoners was reduced in mid-July 1942, Janairo was the only lieutenant colonel commanding a subgroup who lost his position. No one's surviving recollection identifies Lim as one of those who treated the men in the group he commanded with harshness, but little in the record suggests he achieved much in alleviating the poor conditions at O'Donnell either. Manzano identified the groups and subgroups of prisoners put under the charge of West Point graduates and pointedly wrote of them that Janairo commanded the "only decently ran [sub]group."[49]

Notwithstanding General Francisco's claim that many prisoners of war slept in "the open, on bare ground [including] general officers," the captive generals did not suffer at Capas, at least not physically. Lieutenant Ongpauco's role as historian and illustrator of the Filipino prison camp earned him a seat at what he referred to as the "Little Inn," a dining place where the senior officers enjoyed ample quantities of rice, beef soup, and other "delicacies" prepared by Philippine Scout cooks. Ongpauco was certain that the "everyday lunch" with "our four generals" had allowed him "to stay alive in that starvation-and-disease-ridden camp." Lim himself had a small hut of his own at O'Donnell and invited several nephews, junior officers who had served on Bataan in the 41st or other divisions, to stay with him. Through outside contacts he obtained sufficient food, medicine, and even cigars, which, as he had on Bataan, Lim shared with those around him. But he mainly thought of getting out. Lim wrote letters to his relatives telling them to contact prewar Japanese business associates to see if they could secure his release from Capas.[50]

Driven in part by the high death rate among Filipino prisoners, the Japanese began releasing survivors at the end of June 1942. That tens of thousands of Filipino soldier-prisoners would trudge out of Bataan had been unexpected, and the Japanese were not inclined toward sympathy. Not that the Japanese were a significant presence in the camp. Guerrero wrote that "it was possible to stay in O'Donnell without seeing a single Japanese [since] [t]he guards seldom ventured far from their headquarters or from the sixteen towers raised on bamboo stilts" that overlooked the camp. Rather, "the Japanese murdered the USAFFE simply by doing nothing." They not only provided their captives little in the way of food, medicine, and clothing, but also tried to prevent sympathetic Filipinos from aiding the prisoners. Doctor Atienza later testified that the Red Cross had made repeated efforts to gain access to O'Donnell but did not succeed until mid-July. Lim's friend George Vargas, head of an executive commission formed in January 1942 to cooperate with the Japanese army's administration of the occupied Philippines, had even ordered that "no person, including officials of the central Administration Organization, regardless of their rank, should visit the war prisoners' concentration camps or exert efforts to intercede in behalf of any prisoner." But rumors about the dire straits of the prisoners spread rapidly, and many relatives and other concerned Filipinos ignored Vargas's admonition. If General Homma is to be believed, in response to reports of the poor conditions at Capas and the high death rate among Filipino prisoners, he attempted to obtain additional food and medicine for the prisoners and requested permission from army headquarters in Tokyo in early May, within days of Corregidor's surrender, to begin the release of Filipino prisoners of war. He did replace the camp commander, a reserve officer named Yoshio Tsuneyoshi, who, in the understated words of one Japanese witness at Homma's trial, "did not handle matters well" at O'Donnell. All of the ex-POW Filipino officers (though not the enlisted men) called to testify at Homma's trial agreed that conditions improved at the camp with the arrival of the new commander, Lt. Col. Shiro Ito.[51]

Homma testified that some prisoners were let out of Capas in May 1942, but not until 22 June did the army announce the forthcoming "provisional release" of war prisoners. Their release, read the "Proclamation," was the "special favor of the Imperial Japanese Army, to promote the happiness and welfare of the Filipino people, and also to reciprocate their sincere cooperation and contribution they have shown under the Military Administration of the Imperial Japanese Army." That the Japanese allowed thousands of men who had so recently borne arms against them out of imprisonment may speak less to their sympathy for cooperating Filipinos than to their contempt for them as soldiers, but not just any prisoner would be allowed to leave. Active assistance to the Japanese by one's family provided one means of release. Illness, real or feigned, provided another. For the rest, a "rejuvenation" or "reeducation" course of two to three weeks' duration either at Camp O'Donnell or Camp Dau at Stotsenburg was followed by the expectation that they would work actively toward the attainment of Japanese goals in the Philippines—that is, to join a reconstituted Bureau of Constabulary, serve with antiaircraft batteries (the worst fate, because those men had to wear Japanese army uniforms), or agree to accept positions in government agencies and programs whose ostensible raison d'être was to facilitate Japanese pacification of the islands and provide raw materials and foodstuffs for the Co-prosperity Sphere. In short, they were to collaborate.[52]

Of course, the demand roiled the camps, but if there was strong resistance to acquiescing, it does not emerge in the limited sources that exist on the topic. Most of the prisoners saw no alternative. The late Mariano Villarin, who was atypically candid about this subject in the part memoir/part history he had published decades later, quoted a fellow prisoner as making a "sensible remark[:] 'Let's get the hell out of O'Donnell first, then we'll worry about how to get out of the [Bureau of Constabulary] later.'" The American historian Alfred McCoy interviewed several Philippine Military Academy graduates who saw things the same way. The "quickest way to escape [Japanese] control" was to join the constabulary and then see what happened: "Never mind those oaths and swearing," said one, "that's only a piece of paper." Whatever motivated them, it was a decision about which most of those who survived—and "collaboration" was no guarantee of that—preferred to remain silent. No one got out of jail free: all at some point had to sign oaths "solemnly pledg[ing]" themselves to do nothing hostile toward Japan and to "do [their] best" to support the objectives of the Japanese Military Administration.[53]

Of the Philippine Army's general officers, only the chief of staff and the two Americans escaped the collaborationist issue entirely untainted. Probably no senior officer from Corregidor had visited "the front" more often than had General Valdes. He had wanted to join the troops on Bataan but inevitably had agreed to accompany President Quezon to the United States. Valdes would return to the Philippines with the liberating forces in October 1944. Luther Stevens had survived the Death March to be taken along with the U.S. Army generals to Taiwan and later Manchuria, where they were freed at the end of the war. Brig. Gen. Guy Fort surrendered what remained of the 81st Division (PA) in the Lanao District of Mindanao in May 1942 but had then been killed in November 1942 for refusing "to help in the pacification campaign." The general felt, according to a historian of the wartime resistance movement on Lanao, that obeying Brig. Gen. William Sharp's order to surrender his command "did not include any [further] obligation to cooperate with the Japanese." In a late 1960s survey of fifty-four retired general officers of the Philippine Armed Forces, most of whom had gone on active duty in the Commonwealth period, only one respondent named a prewar Philippine Army officer in answer to the question, "Which military leader . . . has influenced or impressed you the most?" and that retired officer named General Fort.[54]

The other generals found or placed themselves on a different path. Soon after the occupation of Manila, even as USAFFE fought the Japanese army to a standstill on Bataan, retired Maj. Gen. Jose de los Reyes agreed to take charge of the Japanese-sponsored Bureau of Constabulary (BC). He later served as chairman of the government Amnesty Board, a "propaganda agency" established to persuade guerrillas to surrender. General Francisco headed a reeducation camp at Dau and took Reyes's place as director of the BC in April 1943. Francisco also served as vice minister of Home Affairs and chairman of the National Advisory Board on Public Security. His saving grace, wrote the authors of Francisco's OSS wartime profile, was that "in August 1944, when American attacks on the Philippines began, he was replaced [as constabulary chief]," a development that perhaps indicated "a lack of confidence on the part of the Japanese in Francisco's loyalty to them." The most junior of the generals captured on Bataan, Brig. Gen. Simeon de Jesus, led a Japanese army–sponsored Employees' Training Institute, which was to teach the Japanese language to government employees and build support for the idea of the Co-prosperity Sphere. He was then chief of the public assistance and rehabilitation division of the Bureau of Public Welfare until being appointed director of a newly created veterans bureau in August 1944.[55]

In some ways the most admirable soldier in the prewar army, retired Maj. Gen. Paulino Santos now stood apart from the rest. When interviewed in 1945 about the collaboration issue by an agent of the Federal Bureau of Investigation, future Philippine president Manuel Roxas expressed frustration at American attempts to portray as disloyal those men who, like himself, had merely used what influence they had to protect fellow citizens from ill treatment at the hands of the Japanese. If the Americans wanted an example of an authentic collaborator, they should consider the behavior of General Santos. Roxas labeled him "the chief traitor."[56]

The outbreak of war had found Santos in Cotabato, still overseeing the Coronadal settlement scheme that he had established in 1939. Though given no official military role, he met often with American officers to arrange the delivery of food and other supplies to USAFFE on Mindanao. In late March 1942, Roxas met Santos in Cotabato and stressed to him the importance of the Coronadal project to providing foodstuffs for both soldiers and civilians on Mindanao and in the Visayas. Santos was also put on notice about the high command's expectation of government officials who found themselves unavoidably put into contact with the Japanese. When Santos finally met with enemy soldiers in mid-May 1942, their "military courtesy and marked Japanese hospitality" impressed him. They shared his concern about Muslim attacks on Christian settlers in Cotabato. They wanted to seize firearms and reestablish law and order; naturally, so did General Santos. Within the week, Santos was writing letters urging unsurrendered soldiers to turn themselves in; by early June 1942, he was making pro-Japanese speeches. In an exchange of letters with guerrillas in early 1944, Santos described himself as neither "anti-American nor pro-Japanese"; nonetheless, he was clearly supportive of "the mighty and benevolent benefactor nation" that had liberated "a people that for more than four centuries were the subjects of white domination." From the time he "surrendered to the Japanese," according to a wartime OSS evaluation based on "a reliable interview source," Santos was "an active and whole-hearted collaborationist."[57]

In February 1944 Philippine president Jose Laurel appointed Santos to be commissioner for Mindanao and Sulu; in August Santos replaced Francisco at the head of the constabulary to make it a more effective tool in stamping out guerrilla activity as the American forces drew nearer. In January 1945 Santos would retreat north with the Japanese forces—really their captive, according to a sympathetic account of Santos's last days compiled by the general's son-in-law soon after the war—where he died of starvation at the end of August in a village in Mountain Province's remote Asin River valley, the last redoubt of the remnants of the Imperial Japanese Army in northern Luzon.[58]

The Philippine Scout officers faced the same pressures and mostly made the same decisions as their ex-Constabulary colleagues. After completing a course at Dau, General Capinpin became the Filipino head of the rejuvenation camp for ex-USAFFE soldiers at O'Donnell. He later made public appeals for guerrillas to surrender and joined General de los Reyes on the Amnesty Board in late 1943. In December 1944, when on Japanese insistence Jose Laurel and much of his administration joined the Japanese army's flight north, Capinpin—long a "compadre" of the president of the wartime republic—was among those accompanying Laurel to Baguio and part of the group that later flew to Japan. After Japan's surrender, Laurel noted "General Capinpin's peculiar situation as an officer of the United States Army [and] made arrangements for him to go to Tokyo. Days later, Capinpin was flown to Manila by the U.S. Army."[59]

Upon his release from Capas in October 1942, at Vargas's request Brigadier General Segundo directed a "recuperative camp" at Los Baños where unemployed ex-USAFFE soldiers were sent to be taught vocational and agricultural skills. Segundo's "individual deceased personnel file" contains numerous affidavits attesting to his continued loyalty to the United States and Commonwealth governments, but his reputation as a severe, even brutal, disciplinarian grew and probably put paid to whatever chance there had been of his postwar rehabilitation. At Capas, he had ordered erected a wire cage in his section of the camp in which recalcitrant—or just unlucky—POWs could find themselves confined after being stripped and beaten; at Los Baños he had "installed and frequently used a whipping post." The camp closed in October 1943 and Segundo thereafter refused offers of employment under the Japanese military or Philippine government.[60]

Lesser-ranked Scout officers found employment in a plethora of programs or projects at least nominally under the control of the Japanese Military

Administration. They were really more like sinecures, so some would argue after the war, created for no other purpose than to give ex-officers make-work alternatives to serving with the constabulary. Victor Gomez worked for de Jesus at the rehabilitation division in the Bureau of Public Welfare. Bienvenido Alba "engaged in the control of prime commodities." The Martelino brothers surrendered to the Japanese after hiding for several months in Manila. Pastor Martelino then spent ten months "compelled to serve in the puppet government" until getting a doctor to provide him with a diagnosis of tuberculosis. Amado Martelino and Juan Moran joined Rafael Garcia in the price control division of the Bureau of Commerce. Eustaquio Baclig worked for the Toyo Menka cotton firm, which had been given a large grant of land for a cotton-growing farm in Laguna Province. "[We] had to do what the Japs wanted," Amado Martelino would insist to an American correspondent after the war. Not to do so would have placed their families in danger.[61]

Having taken the precaution of putting his own family beyond reach, for the time being Lim avoided the issue by the commonplace if unheroic expedient of pleading poor health. Lim walked out of O'Donnell on 2 July, one in a group of one thousand POWs released on the first and second days of the month. He recuperated for several weeks at Doctors Hospital in Manila and then visited relatives in Calamba. Lim lived for a while with his brother-in-law Clemente Hidalgo in Manila and finally moved into a room in the Cancer Institute at the Philippine General Hospital. The hospital dated to 1910, but the Cancer Institute, "an imposing two-story concrete building" on the hospital grounds, had opened only the year before, in October 1941. In addition to charity wards, the institute included five private rooms. It was presumably in one of these that General Lim spent much of his time until escaping the city in June 1944.[62]

Lim was indeed in poor health. Like almost every soldier who had served in Bataan, he dealt with dysentery and recurring bouts of malaria, and he continued to suffer from high blood pressure. His doctor routinely provided health certificates to the Japanese verifying and embellishing Lim's heart problems and recommending complete rest. But Maximo Kalaw saw him often at this time and thought that Lim's "greatest trouble" was that he was "going through a terrible mental strain." General Lim was continually pressed to take an important governmental post and was "troubled by the constant preoccupation that sooner or later he would be forced finally to accept or definitely reject an offer of a position [with the government or constabulary]. Then in the later part of 1942 . . . he finally told me very convincingly and with his characteristic vigor that he would not under any circumstances accept any position. He would welcome death even." From that point he got better and commenced thinking seriously about resisting the Japanese and preparing for the return of the Americans.[63]

CHAPTER 11

Guerrillero

The Final Frustration, 1942–1944

Lim had begun thinking about a resistance movement while on Bataan. One of his regimental commanders, Col. Claro Lizardo, revealed that once it became obvious that USAFFE could not win and that each day's delay of the inevitable surrender only contributed to the deterioration of the health and discipline of the Filipino soldiers, Lim wanted to end the fighting in order to husband resources for the underground battle that was sure to follow.[1] USAFFE itself had done nothing to lay the groundwork for guerrilla warfare in the Japanese-occupied Philippines. When approached about allowing soldiers to escape Bataan to "continue the struggle" elsewhere in the islands, General MacArthur refused to go along, because he feared the consequences for the civilian population. The issue was recast as one of conducting "harassing operations" behind enemy lines, and the high command agreed. Philippine Scout engineer officer Narcisco Manzano—from whose unpublished narrative, "Anti-Jap[anese] Activities [on] Luzon," this brief summary is taken—remembered that all manner of ideas were suggested and there was no end of volunteers prepared to attempt even the most desperate of schemes. He identified the engineer staff of General Casey as the source of the proposal that eventually sent Maj. Claude Thorp, the former provost marshal at Fort Stotsenburg, and twenty or so American and Philippine Scout military policemen along with thirty civilian baggage carriers north in mid-March 1942. They ambushed a Japanese convoy on the way out of Bataan and eventually established themselves at Camp Sanchez, a prewar vacation site located on the China Sea trail that ran west from Stotsenburg along the slopes of Mount Pinatubo. Near the end of 1942, the Japanese tracked down, seized, and later executed Thorp and several of his lieutenants, but others readily took their place.[2]

From distant Australia, MacArthur's Southwest Pacific Area (SWPA) command struggled first to inform itself about the extent and nature of guerrilla activity in the islands and then to assert authority over the disparate groups. In July 1942 SWPA drew on the existing resources of the Australians, British, and Dutch to create an Allied Intelligence Bureau that would "obtain and report information of the enemy in the Southwest Pacific Area[,] . . . weaken the enemy by sabotage and destruction of morale . . . and render aid and assistance to local efforts in the same end in enemy-occupied territories."[3] By early 1943 a Philippine subsection of the AIB had succeeded in inserting a representative with reliable radio contact—the Philippine Army Air Corps hero Capt. Jesus Villamor—onto Negros Island in the central Philippines and had begun to build up the authority and resources of Col. Wendell Fertig. A reserve officer who had been directing engineering projects on Mindanao when General Sharp had ordered the surrender of USAFFE forces there, Fertig was the most senior of the officers who had instead "taken to the hills." SWPA refused to acknowledge Fertig's self-promotion to brigadier general but in February 1943 designated him to command the 10th Military District. Farther to the north, on the large island of Panay, few Filipino officers and men of the 61st Division had surrendered to the Japanese, and a sizable guerrilla army under the command of Lt. Col. Macario Peralta denied the Japanese control of much of the countryside. As 1943 progressed, resistance leaders on the larger Visayan Islands earned SWPA's endorsement, but Luzon remained largely terra incognito. Not until well into 1944 would MacArthur's headquarters establish reliable radio contact with any guerrilla force on Luzon. In the capital city itself, Manzano described a chaotic scene: "hundreds of units were conducting or claiming to conduct anti-Jap activities," with none, not even the "well-intentioned" ones, having any idea how to carry out underground activity.[4]

Ultimately, the Americans would define "recognized" opposition to the common enemy. When in October 1944 MacArthur redeemed his pledge to return to the Philippines, he did so with resources unimaginable when he had fled the islands in March 1942. General Valdes joined the Leyte invasion force at Hollandia Harbor in New Guinea and marveled at the "ships of all kinds—hundreds of them" that covered the bay, while "airplanes [flew] over continuously." It was, he recorded in his diary, "a magnificent display of force [that] shows what the U.S. can do when she gets started."[5] The 6th Army's appearance at Lingayen Gulf the following January rivaled Operation Overlord, at least in the weight of American troop strength thrown ashore. In the context of such overwhelming power, a "recognized guerrilla" was essentially someone who had served as an infantry auxiliary to the liberating American forces. Successful claimants to recognized status had to have taken the field in a unit that fought the enemy on a sustained basis, had to have contributed "materially to the eventual defeat" of the Japanese, and had to be able to substantiate a record of service "by sufficient acceptable evidence." Formal recognition could be the basis for integration into the regular forces and came with back pay. There would be many who sought recognition.

Once in 1946 and again, twice, in 1947, U.S. Army officers conducted investigations into claims put forward by individuals who thought they deserved the status of recognized guerrillas as a result of their association with General Lim during the occupation. The investigating officers interviewed dozens of people who served with "General Lim's Guerrillas" and evaluated affidavits and other records of service. The officer who conducted the final evaluation, Capt. John O. Keider, spoke to other prominent resistance leaders as well. His evaluation came to the same conclusion as the others: that General Lim's guerrilla organization "be not favorably considered for recognition." Nevertheless, these investigations generated a thick file of reports and affidavits, without which little would be known today of Lim's wartime ambitions.[6]

Lim could not know that the aging general who had escaped Corregidor in a cramped motor torpedo boat with his wife and child and a handful of soldier-companions would return little more than two and one-half years later at the head of an avenging host. Despite the confidence many Filipinos had in MacArthur, the campaign of 1941–42 had made clear the difficulty of projecting military and naval power in the Far East in the face of a first-class opponent. It might take many years for the United States to fight its way back to the western Pacific. Nor did the defeat of Japan necessarily require returning to the Philippines. In the meantime, open defiance of the Japanese by Lim would lead only to incarceration, or worse; flight to a remote part of the archipelago would not only severely limit opportunities to shape opposition to the Japanese but also probably lead to punitive expeditions while contributing nothing to the war effort.

At Camp O'Donnell, Lim "sounded out a few of his trusted officers on the subject of an underground organization, should they be released by the Japanese." Lim began cautiously building a framework for resistance around officers of the 41st Division. Lt. Col. Juan Chioco, the division's G-4 officer, left Capas the same day as Lim and became the general's "chief of staff." He would serve as an intermediary to operatives who gathered information about Japanese military activities, shared news from American and British radio broadcasts, or carried messages to other resisters. Division officers who found themselves in the BC, like Colonel Lizardo and Tomas Domaoal, Lim encouraged to seek assignments that would put them in positions to organize guerrilla bands or turn BC detachments against the Japanese. Another of Lim's regimental commanders, Valentin Salgado, served as an aide to President Laurel and so became Lim's "chief operative in Malacañan." Lim also drew on the support of relatives. His nephew Bienvenido Rillo continued to assist him; his brother-in-law Eduardo Quisumbing arranged contacts with agents of other guerrilla leaders and claimed to have been sent to various parts of Luzon to observe Japanese troop dispositions.[7]

This, at least, was the story sketched to the army's postwar investigators by those who claimed to have been part of Lim's network. Of course, statements by those who served in the BC or other government positions to the effect that they did so with Lim's blessing might be self-serving. Among the guerrillas Captain Keider spoke to was Peralta, the onetime guerrilla leader on Panay who had by then risen to brigadier general and deputy chief of staff of the Philippine Army. He expressed the opinion that Lim "had never commanded a guerrilla unit"; rather, a "group of people was taking advantage of the shadow of the prestige of a deceased general officer to advance their claims." Nevertheless, the U.S. Army's investigators accepted that "Lim had a long-range plan of unifying all guerrillas on Luzon, and he had a tentative cadre of high ranking Philippine Army men who were to constitute the backbone for a planned division. . . . He planned either an overthrow of the puppet government, or to have a disciplined group of men on hand to assist the liberating forces on their arrival; he prepared for both plans, and he intended to employ whichever was opportune."[8]

Additional evidence of Lim's attempts to exert influence over Luzon guerrillas comes from a number of American officers who had been contacted by people purporting to represent Lim, though often they had no way of verifying the bona fides of these emissaries. A man named Lorenzo Cabreira told army investigators that Lim had "authorized him to organize guerrilla units." Cabreira and his adoptive mother, Mrs. Petronila Cabreira, traveled throughout central Luzon collecting money and meeting with guerrilla leaders. One contact was Robert Lapham, the military police officer who had left Bataan with Thorp and subsequently established himself in Pangasinan, Nueva Ecija, and northern Tarlac Provinces. Lapham told the army that he had "arrested [the Cabreiras] as possible spies and investigated the possibility that they were working for unification [of guerrilla units on Luzon] under Gen[eral] Lim." Lapham eventually agreed to assist them but then became suspicious at Cabreira's assumption of high rank, "promotions and recruit[ment] of unarmed civilians," and failure to bring written authority from Lim for his rank (he claimed Lim had made him a colonel) and activities. Lapham also said that he had sent a message to Lim "requesting that he join him in Nueva Ecija where he could be kept beyond the reach of the Japanese" but received no response. Bernard Anderson said that "he had been contacted by operatives representing Col. Edmond P. Ellsworth (supposedly a nom de guerre of Gen[eral] Lim)" but had ordered his men "to have no liaison with these operatives because he did not know their objective and viewed their activities with suspicion." "He had heard of Lim's guerrillas," Anderson recalled, "but he heard of no accomplishments."[9]

Edwin Ramsey wrote that General Lim had contacted him directly. An officer of the 26th Cavalry (PS) who had escaped Bataan at the time of the surrender, Ramsey had been appointed by Thorp as deputy to Capt. Joseph Barker, whom Thorp had designated to take charge of the East Central Luzon Guerrilla Area. When Barker was captured in early 1943 (he would be executed near the end of the year), Ramsey took over Barker's area of authority that, in Ramsey's words, encompassed "the entire plain from Lingayen Gulf to Manila and including Bataan." Ramsey's subsequent depiction of himself as the leader of a Luzon-wide network of guerrilla outfits is a picture other ex-guerrillas have claimed not to recognize—of Ramsey's "professed" exploits, Lapham wrote that "a lot of it I never heard about and none of it affected me," while Manzano (who had a low opinion of most American-led guerrillas) expressed the opinion that "as far as [he] could find out, Ramsey's unit was more concerned with self-propaganda than in doing anything constructive"—but SWPA accepted that Ramsey "had excellent contacts and might have done more if support had been given earlier." Ramsey stated that in November 1943 he "received a message" from Lim, who wanted to meet Ramsey but was too closely watched to journey to the provinces. Ramsey was in turn keen to meet Lim: General Lim "had the reputation, prestige and skill to coordinate the resistance and to put an end to dissension within the movement."[10]

Other accounts associate Lim with Lt. Col. Hugh Straughn's organization that operated to the east and south of Manila, in Rizal Province. One of those enlisted men who had been commissioned in the Philippine Scouts just before World War I, Straughn had been the provost marshal at Fort McKinley when he retired from the army in 1935. Straughn had organized a guerrilla unit "from a handful of Philippine Scouts and some civilians who were his former neighbors" that became known as the Fil-American Irregular Troops (FAIT). SWPA believed Straughn had made considerable success toward uniting "various central Luzon guerrillas," but other sources reported that many of the elderly officer's "troops" had joined other guerrilla factions by the time the Japanese captured Straughn in August 1943 and dispersed his remaining men. Lim had some connection to Straughn. Chioco singled out "the late Miss Remedios Filoteo" for her assistance to General Lim, and Quisumbing confirmed that she carried messages from Straughn and other guerrilla leaders to Lim. Journalist Adalia Marquez identified a Miss Filoteo, whom she saw incarcerated at Fort Santiago in mid-1944, as having established contact between Lim and Straughn. The anonymous author of the army's official report on the guerrilla recognition program concluded that FAIT "fell to pieces" after Straughn's capture, though "several Filipino leaders, notably General Lim," tried to "hold it together." Lim supposedly took charge of reorganizing FAIT using the name Edmond (or Elliot or Lincoln) P. Ellsworth. SWPA had information that identified Ellsworth as an American officer claiming to have been sent from Australia (SWPA knew of no such person), that made Ellsworth "the brains behind the reorganization of FAIT," that identified Ellsworth as an alias for Lim, and that confirmed Lim's denial that he was Ellsworth.[11]

Each claim confronts a counterclaim. Marquez recognized Filoteo as a "home economics expert who knew the ins and outs of the different islands in the Philippines for she had traveled them extensively demonstrating the different ways of cooking foods," but the name Remedios Filoteo, a 1916 graduate of the training school for nurses at the Philippine General Hospital, is also included in a published list of Filipino nurses who died in World War II. (Filoteo was sentenced to death in the same trial as General Lim.) Petronila Cabreira told the army's investigating officers that she was the one who had thought up the idea of using the alias of Edmond Ellsworth for General Lim when contacting other guerrilla units, but within a couple of months others had begun claiming that "Ellsworth" had authorized them to collect money for anti-Japanese activities. Lim told the Cabreiras to stop using the name and told others that he was not Ellsworth. But others credited Eliseo P. Estaniel of Straughn's unit with having come up with the name Edmond P. Ellsworth. Lorenzo Cabreira stated that he had originally been associated with Straughn's FAIT, and Straughn had "once mentioned General Lim in Manila," which had led Cabreira to approach Lim about organizing Luzon guerrilla units. The well-known journalist Armando Malay identified guerrilla colonel "Lorenzo Cabrera" as someone who went around after the war offering to add your name to his guerrilla roster to get benefits from the Americans.[12]

Postwar attempts by still others to attach Lim's blessing to their enterprises further muddy the water. The army's guerrilla recognition files include a statement by a "Major General" Bonifacio Araullo that Lim had "sent for" him to be designated as his chief of staff. That, Araullo claimed, was on 25 June 1944, a date by which Lim was already incarcerated in Fort Santiago. Another claimant, Alfredo David, visited Lim at the Cancer Institute and watched the general sign documents that designated David as his successor. He even presented a letter dictated by "Col. Edmond P. Ellsworth" (David thus knew that Ellsworth and Lim were one and the same) making "Colonel David" Lim's "personal representative invested with the full responsibility of carrying on to the last the noble policy of my predecessor Col. Straughn." When the interviewer asked why "Ellsworth" would include a serial number after his signature if, as David had testified, he was trying to disguise his identity, David said he did not know.

Chioco confirmed that Lim had designated Lorenzo Cabreira to be his representative to other guerrilla units, since using a civilian for that purpose lessened the chance of close scrutiny that would have confronted any 41st Division officer given the task. But no one believed that Lim (with, as Rimando put it, "his well-known consciousness of rank") had promoted a civilian to the rank of colonel. Petronila Cabreira stated that both Lim and Chioco had refused to put any appointment in writing. Quisumbing agreed that his brother-in-law had been "very secretive and very prudent" and "appointed or designated his operatives verbally."[13]

Lim's determination ultimately to command a "home army" capable of wresting control of Manila and central Luzon from the occupying Japanese pushed him toward the islands' political leadership, and by late 1943 Lim had gotten involved with Manuel Roxas, future president of the postwar republic and the most controversial "collaborator" to emerge from the wartime Philippines. By the time World War II began, Manuel Roxas—"a man of brilliant intellect and powerful personality," as Joseph Hayden had characterized him—had been prominent in Philippine political affairs for two decades. With Quezon's support, he had become Speaker of the House of Representatives in 1922. He later joined forces with Sergio Osmeña, and the two led the mission to Washington that brought back the original version of the Philippine Independence Act (the Hare-Hawes-Cutting Act) in 1933. Having fallen out with his onetime patron, Roxas left government to establish a lucrative law practice. He returned to public service as secretary of finance, and the last prewar election had sent him into the Philippine Senate. By then, with Quezon ailing and Osmeña aging, the younger Roxas had become the inevitable president. Lim was not a friend. Lim's published prewar letters include two mentions of Roxas, neither flattering. Roxas, Lim opined in a letter to his son in July 1941, was politically powerful "and by education and experience no doubt . . . the best man . . . next to Quezon," but Roxas was also "not honest either intellectually, morally, or financially. I know his record." Roxas numbered among those "brainy crooked men" who were bound to run a free Philippines into the ground.[14]

Roxas had obtained an army commission upon completing a reserve officers' training course in 1936, and when the war began—to follow mostly his own account of his activities—he was called to active duty on 15 December 1941. He was an aide to General MacArthur and a liaison officer between USAFFE and the Philippine government. Lim met him on Bataan at least once. When Quezon left Corregidor, he gave Roxas "full authority, to act for and in his behalf in all matters of government." About this time Wainwright advanced Roxas to brigadier general. In mid-March 1942 Roxas made his way to Mindanao ostensibly expecting to accompany Quezon to Australia. When the two met, Quezon agreed that Roxas should remain in the Philippines for a while longer "to carry on the fight" and join him later in exile. Quezon granted to Roxas "practically all the powers" of Commonwealth president.[15]

As Roxas told the story, he never surrendered, exactly. He worked in "close cooperation" with the American commander in the southern Philippines, Brig. Gen. William Sharp, provided funds for relief activities to provincial governors, and "did everything in [his] power to maintain morale" and encourage faith in eventual victory. He "went to the hills" when Corregidor fell, but when the Japanese, angry that so few Filipino soldiers on Mindanao had given themselves up, threatened reprisals, Roxas snuck into the prison camp at Malaybalay to consult with General Sharp. The Americans persuaded him to remain with them.[16] Later Roxas was put in charge of the Filipino section of the prisoners' camp and finally, in November or December 1942, brought to Manila. It was Roxas's good fortune to have been captured on Mindanao. Because he was not formally paroled or released from prisoner-of-war status as the POWs at Capas had been, he apparently did not have to sign the oath by which ex-prisoners agreed to cooperate in Japan's administration of the Philippines.

In Manila Roxas was—like Lim, only more so—under close observation and constant pressure to assist the Philippines' Japanese military rulers. For months Roxas feigned illness and kept to his home "under strict instructions not to receive visitors and not to leave the premises without permission." Roxas fended off attempts to have himself made president of the Japanese-sponsored republic in October 1943, but he did help write a new constitution and later, in early 1944, became chairman of the Economic Planning Board and head of the board of directors of the Bigasang Bayan, an agency that had the responsibility for the "production, supply and distribution of rice and other cereals." He agreed to the appointment, Roxas wrote, only because "the food situation in Manila [had become] very acute" and only after consulting "a few of my friends, including General Lim," all of whom urged him to accept the position "in order to save the people from hunger" and give himself greater freedom of movement.

Along with other members of President Jose Laurel's administration, Roxas would be taken north with the retreating Japanese army in December 1944. Roxas remained in the vicinity of Baguio, and when government officials began making their way into American lines in April 1945, Roxas and Jose Yulo and their families were led to safety by an Igorot guide; but while Yulo and the other "puppet officials who fell into American hands" were taken into custody, Roxas was declared to have been "rescued." When asked by Sergio Osmeña what the distinction between these men was, MacArthur said that the others were being detained because their wartime records as collaborators suggested that "they are potential threats to the military security of our armed forces." Roxas, however, he had known for many years and knew personally was no threat: "Therefore we are not detaining him," MacArthur was quoted as having said. Later, from Tokyo in 1946 soon after the election campaign in which Roxas defeated Osmeña to become the republic's first president, MacArthur went further. He revealed that Roxas "not only was instrumental in providing me with vital intelligence of the enemy, but was one of the prime factors in the guerrilla movement." Outside MacArthur's inner circle, American observers were uniformly condemnatory. To most, Roxas was "a wily Filipino politico" adept at playing "both ends against the middle and coming out with first prize." Roxas's claim "to have been in touch with the guerrillas and even to have been their leader" was disparaged as unsupported by any evidence; MacArthur's assertion that Roxas had provided "vital intelligence" was dismissed as equally fraudulent.[17]

MacArthur was mostly repeating what Roxas himself had begun to assert. Roxas claimed that he had "formed a group in Manila that was to become the center of espionage in this area." Lim was part of this group, as were prominent political figures and other Scout officers, such as Manzano, Pastor Martelino, and Juan Moran. Roxas assigned these men various tasks: some were to assist POWs and civilians interned at Santo Tomas; others were "to watch troop and supply movements." Manzano he told to "make plans of all Japanese airfields in Luzon" and Martelino he instructed to "watch coastal defense installations." Roxas did not just direct the operations of his own guerrilla organization. He "was in contact with practically all the heads of the guerrilla units in Luzon and with most of those in the Visayas." He gave them "all the information that they desired and encouraged them in their activities and helped maintain the morale of their men." It would be "very long and tedious," Roxas summed up, "to relate my activities in this connection."[18]

Inventing or embellishing a personal guerrilla history was something of a cottage industry in the Philippines at the time. "For every patriot," as the unnamed, but clearly disillusioned, author of the guerrilla recognition history put it, "there flocked to the colors hundreds who desired to cover up their past collaborationist activities." Of course, some of the men Roxas mentioned were dead by war's end and not in a position to challenge his version of events; survivors might seek to benefit from (or at least see no value in confronting) Roxas's postwar status as the Philippines' leading political figure. MacArthur himself has been accused of mimicking Roxas's assertions in order to ensure Roxas's silence about Quezon's large payments to the field marshal and other members of the military mission while on Corregidor. If either MacArthur or any of his subordinates who claimed to know with certainty that Roxas was a source of intelligence during the war could point to a single specific item of valuable information obtained from Roxas or his agents, they never bothered to do so.

There is evidence from reputable sources to bolster at least some of Roxas's story. Narcisco Manzano did not have an especially high opinion of what he referred to as "the Roxas Group"—he thought it was "initially organized" mostly to find a bolt hole for Roxas, and he was appalled by its members' inability to keep secrets—but he identified himself as the "military member" of its "Board of Directors" and confirmed that it engaged in collecting military intelligence and passing, or at least attempting to pass, that information to Australia. And he puts Lim in the picture. Manzano wrote that toward the end of 1943 he learned that Roxas had designated Lim to take his place as the "military member." Though unhappy at the "underhanded way" he had been supplanted, when he visited Lim at the Cancer Institute he accepted a commission "to carry on with [his] intelligence work." (Not unknown to the Japanese but far less prominent than Lim, Manzano was relatively free to come and go, and family wealth gave him the resources to avoid accepting a government position.) In "Brief Summary of the Activities of Manuel Roxas during the Japanese Occupation" (there is no longer version), Roxas wrote of Lim only that he had designated the general "to take charge of the Fil-American guerrillas" left leaderless with the capture of Straughn, but in another document he claimed that he intended to unify guerrilla activities "into one command" under General Lim.[19]

When these revelations of wartime activity were made public after the war, Lim could not speak for himself, and others obviously harnessed his reputation—or put themselves in his place—to buttress their own claims. Lim no doubt overestimated his ability to shape the future. As the most prominent soldier in the Philippines and the only senior Filipino officer not to cooperate with the Japanese, Lim was an all-too-obvious focus of resistance. His doctor said that the many visits of ex-USAFFE officers to Lim's room at the Cancer Institute drew Japanese suspicion, so Lim established a "downtown office" at a hotel on Avenida Rizal. Lim had some freedom of movement, at least for a while. He could visit relatives and once managed to attend a reunion with 41st Division officers at Malabon, Rizal. But at other times the Japanese were much more watchful, so much so that Rillo would take Lim's place in bed to allow the general to meet with his agents.

Lim, as his research papers completed at army schools in the late 1920s underline, had a deep interest in Philippine history. He may have imagined that the return of the Americans might replicate the circumstances of 1898, when Commodore George Dewey's victorious squadron had found itself without the land forces needed to finish off the enemy. Then would be the time for well-organized and coordinated guerrilla units to unearth their weapons and emerge under the leadership of General Lim to destroy the enemy's army, to play again the role of Filipino forces in the war with Spain. Lim did not envision the massive force that MacArthur would command in 1944 nor the reinforcements the Japanese would pour into Luzon that would have made a guerrilla uprising difficult.

Nonetheless, as a second year of Japanese occupation neared an end, Lim's "long-range plan of unifying all guerrillas on Luzon," to quote again army investigators, and of either overthrowing the puppet government or having "a disciplined group of men on hand to assist the liberating forces on their arrival" remained largely that—just plans. Nor had he completely avoided doing Japan's bidding. Though postwar interviews and affidavits shed almost no light on the episode, MacArthur's headquarters had been the recipient of several messages in 1943 that mentioned Lim's release from a "Los Baños prison camp" in March of that year. A later radio message from Villamor, dated 20 September 1943, and the response to a request from Quezon earlier in September asking to know "favorable or unfavorable news about [Lim]" explained that the "Japs [had] caught on" to General Lim's exaggerated claims of poor health "and picked him up for 'rejuvenation.'" Lim got out, according to a Tokyo broadcast, just a few weeks before the first anniversary of the Japanese defeat of USAFFE on Bataan.

April 1943 saw "celebrations"—to quote from Father Juan Labrador's diary—"of the usual fare: display of Japanese flags in all public buildings, parade and program at the Luneta, hymns and Japanese marches, salutes and bowings in the direction of the Imperial Palace." The big event followed in early May, on the first anniversary of Corregidor's surrender, with an unannounced but highly publicized visit to Manila by "General Tojo himself, the Prime Minister and Chief of State." The pressure to make some gesture supportive of the new order grew too great to resist. All the general officers were reported to have made anti-American statements. In a radio broadcast from Tokyo (datelined Manila, 5 April 1943), Lim was quoted as having said that American soldiers lacked the conviction to win the war. On Bataan they had kept to the rear and allowed Filipino farmers "to take bullets" meant for themselves. Lim and the other senior Filipino officers had urged General King "to give up the unequal fight," but King refused and later was the "first to surrender to the Japanese when the Bataan stronghold finally became untenable."[20]

At her home in Los Angeles, Pilar Lim had already gotten a brief message from Quezon revealing that news "had recently been received" that Lim had "taken the oath of allegiance to the Japanese government" and as a result might be "considered by the Government of the United States as automatically depriving him of all his rights as an officer of the Philippine Army." The context for the wartime correspondence between the Commonwealth government-in-exile and Pilar Lim (at least that which survives in the Quezon Papers) was not General Lim's reputation but Mrs. Lim's allotment from the general's army pay, and Quezon dispatched a letter to Secretary of War Stimson noting that Lim had taken such an oath "and even went to the extent of making publicly serious charges against the conduct of American officers on Bataan." Quezon asked if, in light of these revelations, "in the opinion of the War Department," he should "no longer consider General Lim as an officer of the Philippine Army" and stop paying Pilar Lim?

Quezon's papers include no copy of a reply from the War Department, but Pilar shot back with a strongly worded defense of her husband. She obviously had some idea of the circumstances under which prisoners considered themselves to have been let out of Capas. That Lim and other POWs, she wrote, "might have been paroled and freed" and to have "promise[d] under oath" to cause no trouble while "enjoying the freedom of paroled war prisoners" hardly amounted to taking "an oath of allegiance" to Japan. And she did not disguise her wonderment at Quezon's readiness to accept unsubstantiated enemy propaganda rather than place confidence in the many testaments—some prominently made by Quezon himself—to her husband's "bravery and skill" in battle against the Japanese on Bataan, especially since he was not now in a position to defend himself. Taken aback by the accusative and disdainful tone of the letter, Quezon responded that as a "loyal friend" he had only wanted her to be prepared should the "Government of the United States" take any action against Lim, which of course could not "be ignored by the Government of the Commonwealth." For his part, Quezon assured her, he assumed the loyalty of those Filipinos who might "look to us as giving aid to the enemy." Their actions, he supposed, were "being done in good faith as, in their opinion, being to the best interest of our people." He enclosed a copy of the transcript of one of Lim's purported anti-American radio broadcasts, so that she would "be fully aware" of what had disturbed him.[21]

It is difficult to know what to make of this today, just as it was at the time. Neither MacArthur in Australia nor Quezon in the United States had complete or accurate knowledge about things taking place in the Philippines. The information they did have often lacked context. The Japanese could put words into anyone's mouth. So Roxas, for example, claimed that despite having refused to cooperate with the Japanese, on Mindanao they "printed a leaflet purported to have been signed by me asking all USAFFE personnel to surrender." Later, they made changes to and published a speech he had given to POWs.[22] Guerrilla radio messages might reflect rumor rather than fact (as evidenced by the many reports of Lim's death received months before his execution) or the personal agenda of a guerrilla leader who happened to have radio contact with MacArthur's headquarters. Lim did make at least one radio address critical of the United States. Rimando, drawing on a statement to Philippine Army investigators in July 1945 made by an otherwise unidentified "Mr. Magtira" (the same Cirilo T. Magtira who later gave a statement to the U.S. Army about Lim's activities during the war), wrote that Lim "read the prepared message in a garbled voice so as to make it hardly intelligible or he omitted portions which he did not like to broadcast."

What MacArthur's headquarters interpreted as confirmation of Lim's release from prison and oath taking was probably an event that took place at Malacañan Palace on 16 March 1943 at which some 2,770 "ex-USAFFE servicemen" who, like Lim, had been provisionally released from Capas due to illness or who had not surrendered but had later made themselves known to the authorities, were now required to take "an oath of loyalty to Japan." Lim was there. The *Manila Tribune*, which gave the ceremony prominent coverage, reported that he "responded on [the POWs'] behalf." It did not repeat his response, but according to the newspaper the men "pledged their loyalty to the Imperial Japanese Army and resolved to work with greater determination for the reconstruction of the new Philippines." They were now "regularly released prisoners of war." Manzano was there too, and he wrote in his memoirs that he took the oath "with my fingers crossed behind my back."[23]

According to biographer Carlos Quirino, during the war Quezon chafed at his inability to know what was going on in the occupied Philippines and wanted to send an agent to check on the activities and loyalties of "his former henchmen." He eventually settled on Emigdio Cruz, a medical doctor and army reserve officer who had been on Bataan. From the United States, Cruz went to Australia and from there proceeded by submarine to the Philippines. After Cruz had returned to Washington, Quezon sent a note to Pilar Lim telling her, in the strictest confidence, that he had obtained "personal information about people and affairs" in the Philippines and had been assured that he could have "absolute confidence in those whom I have trusted." He would tell her more "should [she] come this way again."[24]

The inauguration of the "Second Philippine Republic" under Laurel's presidency increased the pressure to cooperate with Japan's agenda in the Philippines. Even in an isolated prison camp in Taiwan, the former commanding general of the 11th Division (PA) William Brougher had a sense of what "independence" might mean for the Filipino officers who had fought on Bataan. "Poor Moran [Brougher's chief of staff], Lim, Capinpin et al.," he wrote in his diary when he learned on 14 October 1943 that the Philippines had been "given independence today." "What are they going to do? Obviously, this is to put the Philippines on the spot where the puppet government will have to declare war on the United States and resist the U.S. Forces when they land."[25] A Japanese staff officer tasked with preparing a chapter on "Philippine Defense Plans" in 1943–44 for MacArthur's postwar *Reports* explained that, from the Japanese perspective, the purpose of granting independence to the Philippines at this time was "to win increased Filipino cooperation" in the war effort. By late 1943, with Japan now on the defensive and attempting to hold "'an absolute defense zone' embracing areas west of [the] Marianas-Carolines-Western New Guinea line," the Philippines was becoming a rear area base of operations, an "assembly and staging area for troops and supplies." The Japanese needed a more tractable population amenable to contributing foodstuffs and manpower to the war effort. Lim fell under closer scrutiny at this time. When Edwin Ramsey went to Manila in December 1943, by his own account he met frequently with informants and socialized extensively but dared not approach Lim, who was under constant surveillance.[26]

Ramsey's fear of contacting the man he had come to Manila specifically to see encapsulated Lim's frustration at failing to coordinate guerrilla organizations on Luzon and the increasing difficulty of resisting pressure to work openly with the Japanese-sponsored republic. Moreover, it was simply getting harder to subsist in Manila. The spectacle of streets filled with starving people and of corpses collected off the sidewalks and carted away each day would not come until later in 1944, but already during Lim's last months in the city "star" meat ("rats" spelled backward) was being sold in the markets, and homes in the better neighborhoods were being searched for hoarded food stocks. A typhoon in mid-November 1943, more devastating than any the older citizens could remember, left most of the city under water, destroyed much of the rice crop in the surrounding provinces, and drove food prices beyond the reach of many. A growing number of Japanese soldiers compounded the hardships. They "teemed in streets, plazas, stores and restaurants," Father Labrador confided in a diary entry of 3 December 1943, with rumors circulating "that more than half a million more were coming to fortify the country and eat up the little food supply that we had." It came as no surprise when early in 1944 the minister of agriculture warned that "Manila should be depopulated to avoid starvation."[27] Lim continued to encourage cooperation between guerrilla units, but, by the end of 1943, he was also contemplating escape.

Maximo Kalaw wrote that in late December 1943 or early January 1944 Lim asked him to journey to Mindoro to sound out the local guerrilla chieftains about the possibility of accepting Lim as "a guerrilla leader" on the island. Mindoro was close enough to Luzon that Lim might still enjoy some possibility of influencing events in the capital, while the island was large and undeveloped enough to avoid easy detection by the Japanese, or so he may have hoped. (He knew of the island's terrain firsthand as it was a popular hunting site before the war.) Mindoro was also a part of the 4th Military District from which the 41st Division had drawn a portion of its men, and presumably Lim would find there a willingness to accept his authority. The politically prominent Kalaw had been about as successful as Lim in avoiding being pressed into service by either the Japanese or the Laurel administration; more pertinently, he owned a farm on Mindoro, which gave him a ready excuse to make the trip. Once there, Kalaw and several companions slogged for hours through mud "almost knee deep" to reach the camp of Maj. Ramon Ruffy, an unsurrendered Philippine Constabulary officer, and Esteban Beloncio, a high school teacher who had taken up arms against the Japanese. They greeted Kalaw courteously enough, showed him new weapons they had received from Australia, and bragged about their link to General MacArthur; but their response to his message from General Lim "astounded" Kalaw: they had orders to accept "no surrendered prisoner of Bataan" into their units. They did concede that Lim might be a special case.[28]

Kalaw shared this story with American army investigators in 1946; others the army interviewed, however, made no mention of Kalaw. Those familiar with Lim's attempt to reach Mindoro claimed that in January 1944 Capt. Alberto Abeleda and Sgt. Pedro Melgar, both Bataan veterans of the 42nd Infantry Regiment, had gone to the island specifically to contact the American officer Maj. Lawrence H. "Merc" Phillips, who had led a radio communications team to Mindoro in late 1943. Kalaw wrote that he made the trip accompanied by a Lt. Pedro Kalalo, a member of Lim's staff on Bataan. He mentions Abeleda's trip to meet Phillips but dates it several weeks later, after Lim grew "nervous" when no answer had come from the guerrillas in response to Kalaw's mission.[29]

Phillips had direct radio communication with Australia and represented the first real opportunity for Lim to contact MacArthur with some certainty that messages would, in fact, reach the former military adviser and thus learn—by SWPA's silence if nothing else—what MacArthur really thought of him. The Philippine Regional Section (PRS) of AIB, created in late May 1943 and put under the command of Col. Courtney Whitney, had inserted Phillips's team of nine American and Filipino officers and enlisted men—code-named ISRM (for "I Shall Return, MacArthur")—onto Mindoro to act as a coast watching station and serve as a conduit for intelligence collected from sources in Manila. The team had set up its transmitter on Mount Calavite on the island's northwest corner, from where it could report on ships entering and leaving Manila Bay, sixty miles to the northeast.

ISRM's commander was a thirty-seven-year-old army reserve officer, a native Californian who had spent several years on Mindanao with the Philippine Packing Corporation. J. K. Evans, who had served on Grunert's HPD intelligence staff, described Phillips as a "dynamic personality, physically hard and active," but Phillips was also too little appreciative of the need to take precautions. His presence was widely known, radio security was poor, and he ran afoul of the disintegrating relationship between the island's rival guerrilla factions. Robert Kramer, an officer of the 14th Engineers (PS) who was hiding in Batangas Province across the narrow Verde Island Passage that separates Mindoro from Luzon, wrote in his memoirs that "toward the end of November 1943" he had heard that there was an American officer on Mindoro "who was supposed to have a communications set-up." Kramer and his traveling companions, another engineer officer and an enlisted man in the coast artillery who had fled a prisoner-of-war work detail at Nasugbu, were wary—if they had heard of an American officer with a radio on Mindoro, surely the Japanese had?—but wanted to meet him. Like Lim, they thought he might arrange to have them taken to Australia by submarine. Kramer found Phillips to be cocky and careless, and in late February 1944 they were ambushed by the Japanese. Kramer and the enlisted man fled into the jungle and eventually made their way to Australia, but Phillips was later killed and his team dispersed.[30]

Not long after Kalaw and Abeleda went to Mindoro, Narcisco Manzano left for Mindanao at Lim's and Roxas's behest with the ultimate goal of reaching Australia in order to explain the guerrilla situation on Luzon to MacArthur and return with the authority and resources that would allow "the Roxas Group" to coordinate effectively all guerrilla activities. Manzano never reached his destination. It took him nearly two months to get to Wendell Fertig's headquarters, and once there, he spent the next few months doing, in his own words, "practically nothing of value."[31]

Manzano did get Fertig to radio PRS about Lim, though Lim would hardly have approved of the message Fertig transmitted. Roxas and Lim, Fertig told SWPA, were "interested in maintaining control of both political and military authority." Advancing the Allied cause "may be secondary" to their own interests. "An intelligence agency to work with them but to maintain its direct connection with you will give best results," Fertig advised. If he was merely repeating a suggestion from Manzano, who saw himself as a suitable contender for the intelligence-agent intermediary, Manzano did not say so in his memoirs. With no response from Australia, in April Manzano pressed Fertig again to ask SWPA's "attitude toward Lim and his organization." "Lim, with approval of Roxas," Fertig now radioed, "is coordinating activities of anti-Jap elements in Luzon. . . . Can he be assisted with funds and supplies?"[32]

The radio communiques from Fertig must have perplexed PRS, because Phillips had also transmitted messages to SWPA concerning Lim and Roxas, and they contained an entirely different theme. The two did not want help organizing an intelligence-gathering network on Luzon; they wanted out. One message from Phillips on 9 January 1944 informed PRS that Lim and other high-ranking officers had contacted Major Ruffy (this was undoubtedly Kalaw's trip) for help in moving to Mindoro to "avoid Nip cooperation." A second message reflected the arrival of Lim's "special agent" (Captain Abeleda) later in January. Phillips now signaled that "all arrangements [had been] made" to move Lim, Roxas, and several family members to Mindoro.

In response to these queries, PRS finally acted. Whitney drew MacArthur's attention to the latest message from Fertig and surveyed the others that had been received from PRS operatives concerning Lim since the beginning of the year. Whitney, always inclined to think the worst of Filipinos (or so was his reputation, so much so that Quezon once wrote to MacArthur asking that Whitney be relieved of duty), believed that Manzano's query should be "guardedly answered." Its purpose, he suggested, was at least in part calculated to give Lim a "clearance" from MacArthur.

Later, after American forces had returned to the Philippines and as paroled Filipino soldiers had begun reporting for duty, MacArthur took the position that having signed the release oath to get out of Capas would not be a bar to reintegration in the Philippine and American armies. The oath came perilously close to "being an oath of allegiance to the Japanese," but having learned more about the circumstances under which it had been given, MacArthur had "taken the stand . . . that that parole was not binding, given with reservations, given to keep them from dying and was of no real effect." But in early 1944 the SWPA chief's policy was "to treat General Lim and other ranking Filipino officers" who they assumed had signed the Japanese release oath to gain freedom from prison camp "with considerable reserve." Whitney admitted that PRS had "no specific knowledge" that Lim had signed the oath, but it understood that Roxas was the only general officer of the Philippine Army who had "refused to do so." And if Roxas had appointed Lim "to unify guerrillas in Luzon," Whitney pointed out, he must have done so very recently, since Phillips's messages indicated that "Lim has been endeavoring to escape from Luzon." Whitney proposed a draft message confirming SWPA's commitment to assisting "any individual or group" resisting the Japanese but specifically reserving judgment about Lim and other senior officers until learning the "full circumstances" surrounding their release from POW camp. MacArthur, however, penned "Do Not Reply" on the cover of Whitney's report. That was toward the end of April 1944. Around the same time, Lim contacted Bernard Anderson, the American air corps officer leading a guerrilla force to the east of Manila, and asked to join him. Anderson queried PRS, affirming that Lim was loyal and not cooperating with the Japanese. According to the card index of guerrilla and coast watching station radio messages now found in the National Archives, this was the only radio message sent to SWPA from the Philippines that mentioned Lim to which there was a response. The reply, received in mid-June 1944, was that Lim was "undoubtedly under close enemy observation" and should be avoided. By then, Lim had already attempted to escape from Manila.[33]

Several sources claim that Lim had tried to rendezvous earlier with a submarine off Batangas or Mindoro in February 1944. The completest and most-cited version of the episode comes from an account provided by U.S. Navy reserve officer Charles Parsons, who played a prominent role in SWPA's effort to establish and supply resistance groups and coast watching stations in the Philippines via submarine from Australia in 1943 and 1944. If nothing else, it stands as an unsurpassed example of the challenges to knowing exactly what happened in the Philippines during the war even in well-documented episodes involving Americans.

The Lim-tried-to-escape-by-submarine story is also a good example of how fact and fantasy can be difficult to untwine in the "Chick" Parsons saga. A native of Tennessee, Parsons had lived in the Philippines as a boy and had returned to the islands around 1920. He married the daughter of a Philippine-American War veteran, worked as a stenographer for Leonard Wood, and tried his hand at a variety of businesses. By the 1930s he was a much valued employee of the prosperous Luzon Stevedoring Company. In the early 1930s he obtained a commission in the naval reserve. In late December 1941 he was, along with a few other "reserve officers who wished to remain in Manila" when naval forces withdrew to Corregidor, apparently given an "informal release" from service. He was living as a civilian in Manila and passed himself off as the Panamanian consul when the Japanese took the city in January 1942. Repatriated to the United States with his family on the *Gripsholm* in mid-1942, Parsons then joined MacArthur's headquarters in Australia in January 1943. "Because of his wide and intimate knowledge of the Philippines," a history of the guerrilla movement reads, he "was selected to lead a secret fact-finding mission to Mindanao and carry in cipher materials and token supplies." Thereafter, "the real and highly meritorious place of Comdr. Parsons in the Philippine guerrilla and intelligence picture is connected with his expert organization of the heavily increased submarine supply movement."[34]

Parsons's parallel effort to nourish a spy network based on his contacts in Manila and elsewhere was, as one officer involved in AIB's activities wrote after the war, "obscure to say the best." When MacArthur was queried in 1946 by Lorenzo Tañada, the Philippines' solicitor general tasked with prosecuting wartime collaborators, about Parsons's testimony supporting a high-profile defendant's claim to have been active in Parsons's guerrilla activities, Courtney Whitney responded that he had "read the testimony of Commander Parsons with considerable astonishment." Whitney labeled Parsons's suggestion that he (Parsons) "was the head of General MacArthur's pre-invasion intelligence organization" as false: "Parsons' primary job was rounding up the supplies which were sent in by submarine, and his official connection was with G-4 section, not the G-2 section."[35] But whether officially sanctioned or not, PRS had to know that Parsons's actions went beyond those of a supply officer. Parsons explained in a June 1943 "Report on Conditions in the Philippine Islands" (he was on Mindanao at the time) that in early 1942 he had organized a "group of interested reserve officers" in Manila—he called it the "Manila Intelligence Group"—to gather information useful to USAFFE. It had been unable to get the intelligence to Bataan or Corregidor before the surrender but had "continued to function with the idea that sooner or later" useful information could be placed in the hands of American forces. He made clear that from Mindanao he had renewed contact with this group and had devised means of communicating with it in Manila. "This group," a guerrilla history asserts, "was the object of Parsons' Philippine activities after he was attached to GHQ, but little information eventually reached G-2 from this particular source." Furthermore, when Parsons escorted the Phillips party to Mindoro in October 1943, he took it upon himself to "put the party in at Paluan" rather than follow the original plan of landing the men "on an isolated coast" because he wanted "to contact a friend whom he had spotted there before leaving the Philippines in 1942." The friend could serve as a conduit to Parsons's agents in Manila. After the war, Parsons claimed he had even made his way into Manila.[36]

Parsons had brought with him to Australia "a handwritten letter from President Quezon to General MacArthur" that read, Parsons recalled to an interviewer decades later, "Please, whatever you do, please conserve Roxas for posterity to the Philippines." Before leaving on his first submarine voyage to Mindanao (in February 1943), Parsons said he raised the issue on his own initiative when "in discussing with General MacArthur the matters not mentioned in my written directive which I thought might develop in the course of my trip to the Philippines, I asked whether I should do anything about the repatriation of General Roxas."[37] At that time, MacArthur thought Roxas could be of greater value to the war effort by remaining in Manila. Parsons nevertheless followed up, in a June 1943 report on conditions in the Philippines, with the recommendation that Roxas be repatriated "when deemed advisable." In early August 1943 Parsons (through Whitney's PRS) raised the issue again. Sutherland replied that MacArthur did not think Roxas could be successfully evacuated and the matter was to be dropped. Parsons responded at the end of the month with yet another appeal to Whitney in which he wrote that he had just received a message from Roxas asking to be evacuated and again expressing his conviction that they should make every effort to get Roxas out before he was compelled to take a position in the puppet government. Sutherland responded to Whitney's memorandum passing along Parsons's latest missive with a brief letter stating that MacArthur had been "amazed" to learn that Parsons had "established communication with Roxas without reporting the fact to General Headquarters." MacArthur wanted "full information" about Parsons's actions. MacArthur must have been satisfied with whatever Whitney had to say (the report was verbal), because a few days later he authorized a message to Roxas that read: "Understand you desire evacuation. If it can be done without too great a hazard I believe it a wise step."[38]

The turnabout coincided with the SWPA chief's awareness that Roxas was playing some part in writing the constitution for the Japanese-sponsored Philippine republic that would be established in October 1943 under Jose Laurel, whom MacArthur considered untrustworthy and pro-Japanese.[39] Despite his supposed message to Parsons, if Emigdio Cruz is to be believed, Roxas himself was not overly concerned about escaping at that time. Cruz had reached Manila on 22 October 1943 and three days later met with Roxas. Cruz reported that when he told Roxas of Quezon's desire that he come to America, Roxas refused to leave but told Cruz that he would like to be evacuated a few weeks before MacArthur's invasion of the islands. The same month, leaving Australia on 23 October, Parsons accompanied the Phillips party to Mindoro and recalled that Phillips "was advised . . . of *the possibility* that [Roxas's] repatriation might be at some time attempted."[40]

Phillips's executive officer, Capt. Ricardo Galang, wrote that he had been told by Phillips that they "had a deep secret mission" to rescue Roxas, and in February 1944 Roxas made an attempt to escape Manila or at least contemplated doing so at that time. Presumably he intended to meet the submarine *Narwhal*, which was scheduled to rendezvous with Phillips on Mindoro in late February. Whitney's files include a memorandum (dated 29 January 1944) explaining that the *Narwhal* would leave on a fourth trip to the Philippines and asking permission for Parsons to accompany it. The memorandum outlined in some detail the submarine's mission. It said nothing about rescuing Roxas, but a memorandum two weeks later (dated 13 February) noted the commander in chief's directions "that he be kept closely informed of developments having any bearing on the Roxas escape attempt" and passed along the information that Phillips had reported a Japanese patrol in his area. This message does not explicitly state that the *Narwhal* would play a role in Roxas's escape, but that seems a logical inference. A further memorandum on 17 February confirmed that the *Narwhal* had left Darwin the day before and restated its mission, again saying nothing about picking up Roxas or anyone else. At the end of the month, PRS informed Sutherland that the submarine had failed to contact Phillips. It had remained the night of 26–27 February off Mindoro "without observing security signals."

Again, there was no mention of Roxas. However, according to Parsons, Roxas did leave Manila at that time, remained for a week or so near Cape Santiago, Batangas, "where he expected to be picked up," but "when the submarine did not appear" went back to Manila. Roxas's biographer relied heavily on Parsons for this episode but nonetheless did not claim that Roxas left Manila—only that he "made preparations" to do so.[41]

Parsons is the source of almost every published account of Roxas's attempt to rendezvous with a submarine in February 1944, but his own role is opaque. Lichauco, as well as some other tellers of this tale, believed that Parsons was awaiting Roxas on Mindoro or aboard the submarine. In his compilation of guerrilla-related records, Willoughby included the erroneous information that Parsons left Australia on a "supply run" to Phillips on 16 February. "The submarine was expected to pick up important papers from Mindoro, and later it seems as though General Vicente Lim and others were to have made the rendezvous." This put Parsons on the scene but aboard the submarine, not waiting for it on Mindoro. Though Whitney's PRS memoranda from January and February 1944 suggest that Parsons was aboard the *Narwhal* on its fourth mission, they do not explicitly say so, and Parsons's name is not included on the passenger list found in the *Narwhal* log. Whitney later provided a chronology of Parsons's movement—at odds with the chronology published in the GHQ-authored history—which included the statement that "Parsons was in Australia from January to April 1944." Parsons himself wrote to a contact in the Philippines, in a letter dated 15 February 1944, confirming that he would not be aboard the submarine, and in his 1945 "Recital" describing the event, Parsons made no claim of either being on the submarine or on Mindoro. In Australia with AIB at the time, Allison Ind wrote that a submarine already on mission was diverted to make the rendezvous.[42]

Where did Lim fit into the Pasons saga? Ricardo Galang agreed that Phillips's "deep secret mission" included rescuing General Lim. Furthermore, in a postwar affidavit, Emigdio Cruz claimed that he had received "specific instructions" from MacArthur "to get General Lim out of Manila so that he could be made overall commander of all the guerrillas of the Visayas and Mindanao." This cannot be true, however. In an earlier, more complete report of his journey to Manila, Cruz said nothing of having been told by MacArthur of a desire to arrange Lim's evacuation, nor did he claim to have raised the topic with Lim. All he said of Lim was that the general "had succeeded in pretending to be more sick than he really was and was waiting for a chance to escape and join the guerrillas." Parsons knew that Roxas had wanted to include Lim in the escape but that MacArthur felt that as a regular army officer who had signed the Japanese "amnesty agreement securing his release" from imprisonment, Lim might be subject to court-martial. "I was at GHQ while this was under discussion," Parsons wrote, and MacArthur did not want Lim evacuated. Parsons thought that Lim must have decided to join one of the rendezvous parties anyway, and to try to clear his name in Australia, even at the risk of being court-martialed.[43]

Sergeant Melgar, who had accompanied Captain Abeleda to Mindoro in January 1944, confirmed that he had returned to the island in early February, having been told by Abeleda that Lim and Roxas planned to escape with Phillips's help. He was now to tell Phillips that Roxas refused to leave unless family members could accompany him. Phillips agreed and arranged for Melgar to return to Manila with a sailboat, the *Doña Juana.* When he got back to Manila on 18 February, Melgar learned that his contact, Colonel Chioco, had left the city; Abeleda had gone to Lubang Island expecting to follow Melgar to Mindoro. Melgar had never met either Lim or Roxas, and through another officer he learned that there was no safe way to approach them. Soon, word came from Mindoro that "Japanese soldiers were zoning Paluan and the neighboring towns" and searching for a boat called the *Doña Juana.* Melgar left for Cavite and then made his way to Abeleda on Lubang. He had no further involvement in the affair. Chioco expressed familiarity with Roxas's and Lim's efforts to arrange an escape from the Philippines through Phillips on Mindoro but stated that they never actually acted on the plan. Phillips was then killed and Lim "undertook to make his own arrangement in reaching Australia."[44]

Parsons's story continues that it was precisely because of Lim's involvement in the February 1944 rendezvous attempt that Roxas was able to avoid arrest—and quite possibly execution—by the Japanese. "According to our reconstruction" of the episode, Parsons wrote, Roxas had divided the escapees into "two or three sections," some members of which went ahead to meet the submarine while Roxas waited to be rescued on Batangas. Meanwhile, in Manila, a Japanese agent named Franco Vera Reyes had infiltrated and betrayed Parsons's Manila Intelligence Group (MIG). The Japanese had seized "almost the entire membership." Roxas may have been familiar with the group but bluffed his way through questioning by the Japanese. The enemy knew from Reyes that "a high-ranking official was to be among the escapees." Lim, Parsons continued, was aware of the submarine rendezvous and "joined one of the parties heading for it. He was captured." Their interrogation of members of the Manila Intelligence Group satisfied the Japanese "that General Lim was the individual for whom the repatriation attempt was to be made": a "miracle," Parsons concludes, had saved General Roxas. Since the chronology of events clearly undermines the story, the posthumous role assigned to Lim in the disaster that befell Parsons's MIG seems to be that of scapegoat. The aborted submarine rescue attempt took place in late February 1944; the arrests occurred in early February; Lim remained unmolested in Manila for another three months.

As for Roxas? In his "Brief Summary," Roxas himself says nothing about abandoning the Philippines during the war. However, only two days before Quezon's death on 1 August 1944 at Saranac Lake, New York, the Commonwealth president had sent another message to MacArthur urging him to rescue Roxas. MacArthur had replied that that would be "very difficult to do." In early December Anderson radioed MacArthur the information that Roxas had "requested evacuation to your headquarters." The SWPA chief repeated his "strong doubts that [Roxas] could be successfully evacuated," but, if Roxas insisted, MacArthur would "do all in [his] power to assist." That was the last GHQ heard of Roxas until "he came through American lines" in northern Luzon in April 1945.[45]

Lim made his escape in June 1944. According to a published account of Lim's last fateful departure from Manila, in May an agent sent by Villamor on Negros met Lim at the Philippine General Hospital and told him of Villamor's request that Lim "consolidate all Luzon guerrillas and act as over-all chief thereof." Many of the details in the article, which was written by a Philippine Army officer and published in an army journal four years after the war's end, can be verified by official documents and other testimony but not this detail. Villamor could not have sent any such message; he had left Negros months before, in October 1943. Nor had MacArthur authorized him to contact Lim. At any rate, by that time Lim had just the opposite in mind. Attempts to unify the Luzon guerrillas had met with no success, and there was an increasing likelihood that the Japanese would put an end to Lim's efforts to do so. Lim was convinced that his arrest and that of other senior officers was imminent. He was disappointed that his efforts to arrange an escape through American agents on Mindoro and Mindanao had not borne fruit and was now resolved to make the attempt on his own with a small party of associates. He reportedly told the AIB agent that he had his own important message for SWPA: "Ranking officers will be taken hostage. Request rescue by submarine."[46]

Lim intended to seek out SWPA agents or guerrillas off Luzon and make further arrangements. An officer who had been involved on the margins of Lim's activities stated after the war that Lim intended to go to Mindoro, where he expected to contact the same submarine that had brought the communications team that had replaced Phillips. But that team, led by Lt. Cmdr. George Rowe (like Phillips, a reserve officer who had lived in the islands before the war), did not establish itself on Mindoro until July 1944. Lim's former aide Ernesto Santos thought that Lim was trying to reach Marinduque, a small island just east of Mindoro. Another report claimed that their immediate destination, if not their final one, was Samar. Presumably Lim and his party expected to make further plans once they were safely away from the Japanese and had joined up with guerrillas. His ultimate goal, one member of his team would later confirm, was to reach Australia.[47]

Over the previous few months, Lim had made repeated trips to Calamba to habituate his Japanese watchers to his doing so. Meanwhile, in April 1944 Lim had asked either Maximo Kalaw or Maximo's nephew Teodoro (their postwar statements about the matter are irreconcilable) to start gathering prewar Philippine currency for him and was later given 700 or 750 pesos. Maximo Kalaw visited Lim in the Cancer Institute and found him packing. When he mentioned that he wanted the general to be a sponsor at Teodoro's wedding a few days later, Lim replied that he did not expect to be in Manila. Teodoro stated that Lim had asked him to start saving money in April, had requested the money at the end of May, and that Teodoro had given it to him on his next visit to the hospital, in early June. When asked if Lim would be a sponsor at Kalaw's upcoming wedding, Lim advised Teodoro to get his uncle Maximo to sponsor him instead, since Lim planned to leave soon.

On the pretext of visiting his hometown once again, Lim left the hospital on 2 June 1944. This is the story his nephew and companion Bienvenido Rillo told of what happened next: Lim was to be joined outside the city by Antonio Escoda, the prewar journalist who, with his wife, Josefa Llanes, had long been involved in anti-Japanese activities. But when Rillo, who was supposed to escort other members of the party to where Lim was waiting in Parañaque just south of the city, arrived at Escoda's home that morning, he found that several of their traveling companions were not yet there. Emilio Borromeo was there but without the radiomen who were supposed to have accompanied him. Finally, Rillo, Escoda, Borromeo, and Victor Baltazar joined up with Lim, and the party proceeded south. At Mataas na Kahoy, near the south shore of Lake Taal, they met a man named Pedro Manalo (probably the officer of the same name who had served with the 42nd Infantry on Bataan). The party continued to Talaga, in Batangas Province, from where Borromeo returned to Manila in search of the radio mechanic and operators. The others sailed to nearby Maricaban Island. Borromeo and the radiomen (Jose Mariano, Pedro Villena [or Villona or Villiana], and Ramon Roque) joined them, and on the evening of 4 June, they resumed the journey south.[48]

Only a few hours of freedom remained to them. In his published diary, Lichauco repeated what was apparently a rumor that later spread in Manila, that the Japanese had learned of Lim's flight and were methodically searching every boat found in the waters between Batangas and Mindoro. Perez's version of Lim's capture, however, seems to be based on statements made by Baltazar, and Perez wrote that the next morning the men spotted a Japanese patrol boat that seemed likely to miss them until a shift in the wind brought it to Lim's batel. (Rillo said simply that after breakfast they "saw a Jap patrol boat on its routine patrol of the sea.") A Japanese soldier found the pistol that Borromeo had placed in his valise (or, by other accounts, pushed under a sack of rice) and then the radio. A Japanese intelligence report dated 21 June 1944 confirmed the capture of "a group of bandits in a sailboat" (it put the size of Lim's party at fifteen or sixteen) and added that "strict surveillance of the high-ranking Filipino officers who are graduates of America's West Point military academy" was necessary. Lim had made no attempt to disguise his identity.[49]

By 1944 the Japanese military police, the Kempeitai, had established a network of jails and interrogation sites across the city, and various accounts of their arrest put Lim and his companions at one place of imprisonment or another, but Rillo and Baltazar, the only two to survive the war, testified that the group was taken on 10 June 1944 from Mindoro directly to Fort Santiago, which had by then a fearsome reputation. An American civilian who had been hauled off to the old fort in July 1942 to be asked about his assistance to escaped POWs said at the Homma trial that "from the first reference of Fort Santiago after the occupation of Manila by the Japanese it was considered . . . one-way traffic. If you went in you wouldn't come out alive." Some did come out—obviously this man did—but they tended to keep their mouths shut about their experiences, which only heightened the terror invoked by Fort Santiago's name.[50]

At the 1949 war crimes trial of Lt. Gen. Shigenori Kuroda, the commanding general of the Japanese army in the Philippines at the time of Lim's capture, Rillo would testify that he had been rigorously interrogated continuously for three weeks. He was forced to kneel for hours while holding a weight above his head as the interrogator whipped him with a leather strap. If he collapsed, he was kicked and beaten. Baltazar was subjected to the water cure and clubbed "all over [his] body" with a lead pipe. Rillo saw Escoda bleeding from the mouth and nose, having been worked over by two guards using a stick or pole. Borromeo, he knew, had been deprived of sleep for two days (guards patrolled the cell and hit those who seemed to be falling asleep). Baltazar heard Pedro Manolo say that he had had "sharpened small bamboo pieces" stuck between his fingernails, and Ramon Roque had been subjected to electric shock. Lim fared no better, though after a few weeks, he was provided with a mattress so that he would not have to sleep on the bare cement floor. The mattress was soon soaked by an overflowing toilet to the front of the general's cell. Baltazar was certain the mattress had been authorized by a visiting officer, because "that fellow who was torturing us was incapable of ever treating anybody decently."

Sometimes during "so-called rest periods" he would "stick a lighted cigarette butt on you, because he just felt like doing it."[51]

A guerrilla-authored report written a few days before Lim's court-martial reported that Lim was said to have told the Japanese that he was bound for his "hacienda" at Boac, but after being tortured—"all of them were," the report reads—Borromeo "began to spill the dope" and revealed that they hoped to reach Australia. He also acknowledged "connections with [a] certain guerilla unit." The confession "made it tough for Gen. Lim." Lim then admitted that he wanted to see his family in America. Beyond that? Rillo said that he had "heard General Lim tell the guard that he could inform the captain to kill him, if he wanted to, but he could not admit what the captain desired him to admit because that was not true."

As word of his arrest spread, people involved in Lim's activities fled the city or went into hiding. His chief of staff, Chioco, seems to have left at once. The Cabreiras were picked up by the Kempeitai but not until several months later, in September, and for reasons that had nothing to do with any interaction they may have had with Lim. SWPA had begun receiving word of Lim's death in early August—that he was executed either on Mindoro or within a few weeks of his arrival at Fort Santiago. But Bernard Anderson told Parsons that Lim had been visited at Santiago by his brother-in-law Clemente Hidalgo on 20 September. Rillo last spoke to Lim about 7 October.[52] The men were eventually moved to larger cells, and other prisoners or visitors to the fort reported seeing or hearing of him as the year wore on and the Americans drew nearer. It was at this time that Adalia Marquez expressed surprise at seeing General Lim, since she had thought him to be long dead.[53] Claire Phillips, an American who passed herself off as an Italian and ran a nightclub in Manila that allowed her to inveigle information from Japanese officers (which led to her arrest), claimed to have witnessed a number of horrors in Santiago, including having seen Colonel Baja, the former commanding officer of the 43rd Infantry Regiment, "spread-eagle[d] and flogged unmercifully with a thick rubber hose wrapped with barbed wire, while his wife and four children were forced to watch." She did not see Lim but heard about his presence at Santiago and shared a cell with several women who were incarcerated and tortured for having carried money and messages between Lim and other guerrillas.[54]

The Philippines had been a military backwater since the defeat of USAFFE, but the approach of American forces led the Japanese to build up the strength of the occupying 14th Area Army and, by August 1944, to make reinforcing the archipelago their "first priority." In September, lackadaisical, luxury-loving General Kuroda was sent home to be replaced by Tomoyuki Yamashita, the "Tiger of Malaya." That same month, American aircraft reappeared over

Philippine skies. New Guinea–based army bombers blasted Japanese airstrips at Davao on the first day of September; carrier-based naval aircraft followed up a few days later with attacks on enemy installations on Mindanao and in the Visayas. The official army history's bald statement that, finally, on 21 September 1944 naval aircraft "directed their attention to the Luzon area" hardly evokes the emotion of those who watched below. Father Juan Labrador began the day's diary entry with the exclamation "They have arrived!" Gladys Savary, an American whose marriage to a French national had left her uninterned in Manila throughout the war, recorded that the American attack was "the most wonderful sight I have ever seen and the most welcome." Her Filipino neighbors, she continued, "seem elated[—][a] little too pleased openly for everybody's good." The Laurel government found itself pressed to "declare war" on the United States; Laurel responded, one day after the aerial assault on Manila's harbor and airfields, with a semantic sleight of hand by which he proclaimed that a "state of war" existed between the Philippines and the United States and its British ally. Laurel was anxious to propitiate the Japanese, whom he feared wanted his government to implement military conscription; the cabinet minister who was said to have recommended the wording thought the Japanese unlikely to notice the distinction between declaring war on another country—what the Japanese wanted—and simply acknowledging the reality that a state of war existed. (The distinction tended to be lost on Americans too.) Less than a month later, on the afternoon of 20 October, Gen. Douglas MacArthur and Commonwealth president Sergio Osmeña waded ashore at Leyte.[55]

In October 1944, prisoners could still get out of Fort Santiago. Rillo and Baltazar were released in the middle of that month. Rillo reported that Lim had told him that he did not expect to be released but might be sentenced to a term in the New Bilibid Prison at Muntinlupa, with which "he would be satisfied." Rillo then learned from Clemente Hidalgo that Lim was transferred to Old Bilibid (in Manila) on 16 October. They worked to free him. Rillo had had a chance to talk to Josefa Escoda (whom the Japanese had imprisoned in August and would later kill), and she had said that Laurel was trying to help Lim. Hidalgo contacted one of Lim's prewar Japanese business partners, who agreed to try to assist Lim but could accomplish nothing. As for the possibilities of escape, Ojeda stated that in November 1944 some of Lim's officers met in Malabon, Rizal (just to the north of Manila), to discuss the Leyte landings. "We were all advised . . . particularly those of us who were with the constabulary and had men under our commands," Ojeda recalled, to be alert and ready for instructions. "Colonel Cruz told me to be ready at any time with my men in Rizal province to rescue General Lim . . . when he gives me the order and the signal." Not long after that, however, the Japanese began rounding up ex-USAFFE officers who might threaten their preparations to meet the impending American invasion of Luzon. Cruz, Domaoal, Ojeda, and others were arrested at this time. Ojeda alone survived the war.[56]

Rillo told his aunt that he had expected to see Lim freed from Bilibid at the time of the Liberation. He was not, but there was as yet no confirmation of Lim's fate. Numerous persons told Rillo that they had seen Lim taken north with the retreating Japanese. Rillo looked into the stories but wrote that he could get no "credible information." In fact, Lim had long since been tried, convicted, and executed. The American army sergeant Richard Sakakida, who successfully passed himself off as a civilian Nisei interpreter after the Japanese captured him on Corregidor and spent the occupation years working as a clerk and translator in the Japanese army's judge advocate's office at Fort McKinley, attended many of the courts-martial of those accused of being guerrillas. He probably attended Lim's too. "All trials held during the occupation of the Japanese army" were, in his view, "kangaroo trials." Appearance before the military court was a formality at which a predetermined finding based on a military police investigation—almost always one of guilt—was announced. Whether or not the prisoner could make a statement depended on who presided at the court. Usually, the charges were read, the prisoners confirmed that they were the ones named in the indictments, the presiding officers recessed for a few minutes, and then reappeared to pronounce sentence. Each "trial" lasted about five minutes. Prisoners to be executed were not told their fate. They were removed from the court and several days later taken to Manila North Cemetery and put to death by shooting, bayonet, or beheading.

Eventually, the Japanese dispensed with even these few formalities. "Prosecutors, judges, clerks and everything composing a complete court-martial" gave way to a single prosecutor who pronounced judgment on groups of prisoners. Many of the accused said nothing at all. Guards packed those to be executed—the vast majority—into trucks and took them to North Cemetery. Lim and the others captured with him had gone through this process in November. That month, the Japanese staged four mass trials of nearly 700 suspected guerrillas and those accused of other crimes. On 4 November, 163 guerrillas were sentenced to lengthy prison terms or death. A trial the next day dispatched another 330 prisoners; and a third, on 20 November, 58 more. The fourth court-martial, on 24 November 1944, brought 132 prisoners before the military court. Three—Lim, Escoda, and Borromeo—were convicted of treason and sentenced to death. Manalo, Roque, Mariano, and Villena were convicted at the same time of guerrilla activities and also received death sentences. Lim and Borromeo (Escoda was already dead) made the fateful trip to anonymous graves in Manila North Cemetery a few days later. Lim's remains were never identified;

the day of his death was never determined with certainty. Sakakida may have witnessed the execution by decapitation, but if so, he found it impossible to speak of the matter when queried by one of General Lim's sons after the war. The American army conducted no formal investigation into the death of General Lim as it did for Segundo and other Philippine Scout officers. As far as the War Department was concerned, Vicente Lim was not on active duty with the United States Army during World War II.[57]

Epilogue

Had Vicente Lim survived World War II, he might at last have achieved his ambition of becoming chief of staff of the Philippine Army. Quezon had never intended to appoint him to the post, but he had died during the war, replaced by the long-suffering Sergio Osmeña. The two Chinese mestizos had very different backgrounds and temperaments, but Lim was more or less Osmeña's army equivalent: the best-credentialed candidate who never got what he deserved. Osmeña inherited General Valdes as chief of staff, but Valdes wanted to see combat and was made commanding general of a division ostensibly slated to take part in the invasion of Japan. Manzano met Osmeña on Leyte in late 1944 and claimed he was offered the army's senior post, but MacArthur's headquarters objected. The Philippine president tentatively appointed to the army's senior positions two recovered Filipino Scout officers who had served with the Philippine Army on Bataan. Frederick Worcester, a naval reserve officer in Manila at the time, thought the appointments a cynical ploy to immunize the government from having to push charges of collaboration against the rest of the officer corps.[1]

The collaboration issue dominated the immediate post-Liberation period. As had often been the case in Philippine-American affairs, distance conferred both superior moral judgment and ignorance of local realities. Washington officialdom thought the matter clear-cut: anyone who had worked with the Japanese or the Japanese-sponsored Philippine Republic was a collaborator and would be punished. Under American pressure, the Philippine Army issued general orders that forbade the reintegration into the army of any soldier who had served the Japanese in any way. If enforced, Manuel Roxas pointed out, the order meant that there could be no Philippine Army, since almost all officers had participated in some form of government employment during the occupation.[2]

That included the Filipino officers of the Philippine Scouts, though not all survived to confront the consequences. Pastor Martelino, chief of staff of Bluemel's 31st Division, was dead. So, too, was Brougher's 11th Division chief of staff, Col. Juan Moran. The army later determined that Moran along with Lim's chief of staff, Tomas Domaoal, and 41st Infantry commander Fidel Cruz and several other officers had been executed at about the same time the Americans had landed at Lingayen. As far as the army could learn, they went through no form of trial, not even the shadow of a court-martial described by Sakakida.

The War Department never learned in any detail what happened to Eustaquio Baclig (USMA 1918) or Alejandro Garcia (USMA 1923), though both were known to be dead at the hands of the Japanese by the end of 1944. General Segundo had removed his wife and two of their children to Ilocos Norte in June 1944, but had himself remained in Manila with his eldest son. Amado Martelino wrote that he tried to get Segundo and several others to leave the city when he did early in December 1944, but they had said that they had plans of their own. Japanese military police seized the general and his son at their home in Santa Ana on 16 December. Several people told army investigators that they had seen Segundo, beaten and unable to walk without aid, at one or another Kempeitai holding site in early January. The army concluded that General Segundo had probably been executed at North Cemetery about 7 January 1945 (possibly at the same time as Colonel Moran), but one informant insisted that Segundo and other captives had "been slaughtered by the Japanese" at a house in Manila, their remains left for dogs to feast upon.[3]

Those who did survive appeared before a board of American officers to confirm their employment by the Japanese Military Administration or the "puppet" Philippine government, both prima facie reasons for dismissal from the army. A brief account of one such hearing survives in the Philippine Archives collection of documents in the U.S. National Archives. Salvador Reyes (the same Osmeña had thought to appoint chief of staff), a 1917 graduate of West Point who had served on Bataan as chief of staff of the 71st Division, said that the Japanese had pressured all the high-ranking Filipino officers to perform some kind of government service. He admitted that he had worked briefly with the military administration and then had accepted a position with the Philippine Cotton Growers' Association. He supervised ex-POWs working on an experimental farm. The association had been set up under the JMA to increase cotton production to meet Japan's and the Philippines' domestic needs and help ensure the self-sufficiency of the Greater East Asia Co-prosperity Sphere. The program was anything but successful. The "total failure of the scheme," one historian concluded, "sharpened anti-Japanese feeling among the Filipino people during the Occupation." Even had they known that, it would have been of no relevance to the officers of the loyalty board. Reyes was found to have "abandoned loyalty" and was recommended for discharge from the army, as were Scout officers Bienvenido Alba, Pio Caluya, Emmanuel Cepeda, Victor Gomez, Santiago Guevara, Amado Martelino, Ricardo Poblete, and Pacifico Sevilla. The loyalty board not only found Rafael Garcia and Jose Olivares to have abandoned loyalty; it also recommended that they be court-martialed.[4]

Documentation on this issue is sparse, but these were only recommendations, which the army ultimately did not accept. An officer who forwarded Reyes's case to the judge advocate for review noted that both Segundo and Pastor Martelino had been determined to have been loyal, even though both had "apparently accepted employment with the Puppet government." Segundo had been "helpful [to the Allied cause] while in [the] employ of the Japanese puppet government," and Martelino had "engaged in underground activity." The Japanese had killed Segundo and Martelino, but if exceptions could be made for them, why not for the others who happened to have lived?

That line of thinking benefited Scout officers under investigation. Their service to the Japanese, the army concluded, had been modest and coerced, and they had, or claimed to have had, contributed in some way to supporting guerrilla activities. Most of those found to have "abandoned loyalty" remained in the army. With the approaching demise of the Scout organization in 1949, Congress approved a bill authorizing officers of the Philippine Scouts "who are or become citizens of the United States" to accept in-grade appointments in the regular army. The law accommodated the native officers of the prewar Scouts who remained on active duty, only one of whom, by that date, had not become an American citizen. Nine continued to serve in the U.S. Army into the 1950s and early 1960s, at which time they retired as colonels or lieutenant colonels. The last to do so was Lieutenant Colonel Cepeda, who retired from the army in July 1963. Upon his graduation from West Point in 1933, Cepeda had been the last Filipino to be commissioned in the prewar Philippine Scouts.[5]

Lim took a hard line toward those actively helping the Japanese. Maximo Kalaw remembered that Lim's "policy on collaborators as he expressed [it] to me was a mo[st] drastic one. He spoke of the elimination of quite a number of people." Hernando Abaya, a journalist who joined the Free Philippines resistance group, wrote that Lim "condemned his colleagues who collaborated with the Japs. And he was for 'purging' the army after liberation. 'Let the heads roll,' he used to tell friends." The collaboration issue was symptomatic of a souring Philippine-American relationship. From the United States, Carlos Romulo reported to Osmeña that America was beset by so many important issues that it was rapidly losing interest and sympathy with the Philippines. "We've liberated you at the cost of our boys' lives [he quoted Americans as saying]—isn't that enough?" Collaboration only made matters worse. "Things are coming to such a pass here in the United States," Romulo told another correspondent, "that unless we are careful Bataan and our three years of resistance will be forgotten and completely over-shadowed."[6]

Those American soldiers who knew the Philippine Army best put the country behind them. Field Marshal MacArthur did. "It is customary to believe," his wartime secretary Paul Rogers observed, "that MacArthur had deep and abiding roots in the Philippines." Rogers assumed so, but one day when he commented that MacArthur would no doubt come back to Manila once the war was over, MacArthur gave a surprising response: "Rogers, I will go to Japan and I will never return to the Philippines again." The next year, in late 1946, Chief of Staff Eisenhower took it upon himself to ask MacArthur's opinion about the wisdom of keeping army posts in the now-independent Philippines. Eisenhower thought it a bad idea. The presence of American soldiers was "almost certain to engender friction, intensify bad feeling, and keep us constantly in hot water." Eisenhower did not make an explicit comparison to the situation in 1935, when the two men had arrived in Manila to commence building a Filipino army, but the parallel Eisenhower drew would have been immediately apparent to MacArthur. The United States would not keep enough forces in the Philippines to hold the islands without help and that would require the assistance of a "well organized and intensely loyal ally." To anyone who shared their experiences in the Philippines, Eisenhower reminded MacArthur, that expectation was "beyond . . . logic."[7] The observation was unjust to the Filipino soldiers who had followed their American commanders into the maelstrom of Bataan, and to the many who had stood by the Americans under the most difficult circumstances during the war. But perhaps he had in mind Lim's opposition to the military mission a decade earlier.

Lim would not have appreciated the irony, but MacArthur's arrival in the Philippines in 1935 had saved him from the professional dead end the Philippine Scouts proved to be. No Filipino officer of the prewar Philippine Scouts remained with the Philippine Army after the war. Quezon's embrace of the military system introduced by MacArthur and the military mission proved to be of short duration, but during that interlude Lim solidified his reputation as the preeminent Filipino soldier. The unpalatable alternative would have been to make peace with the Constabulary, and he had burned far too many bridges to have done that successfully and without appearing to be opportunistic. Despite Lim's frustration at American dominance of the army-building enterprise, had there been no MacArthur, there would have been no 41st Division and no Bataan in Lim's future. In sharp contrast to the other senior-ranking Philippine Army officers, Lim's reputation emerged from the war singularly untainted and enhanced by his leadership on Bataan and his resistance to the Japanese. Surveying the behavior of the generals who remained in the islands during the occupation, Worcester characterized Lim as "the only member of this group whose loyalty remains unquestioned and whose reputation is without blemish." The resistance movement was "conspicuous for the absence of top ranking army officers," journalist Abaya agreed.

Only "one name stood out"—Vicente Lim, whom death had finally graced with the heroic stature among his countrymen that he had long sought but never quite achieved in his long, frustrating struggle to put his mark on the military history of his country.[8]

Abbreviations

ACS	Assistant Chief of Staff
AEF	American Expeditionary Forces
AGO	Adjutant General's Office
BAHC	*Bulletin of the American Historical Collection*
BIA	Bureau of Insular Affairs
BHL	Bentley Historical Library, University of Michigan
CGPD	Commanding General Philippine Department
CMH	Center of Military History, United States Army
CMTC	Citizens Military Training Camps
EPL	Eisenhower Presidential Library, Abilene, Kansas
FHC	Family History Center
GHQ	General Headquarters (SWPA)
GO	General Orders
HPA	Headquarters Philippine Army
HPD	Headquarters Philippine Department
HPNG	Headquarters Philippine National Guard
IDPF	Individual Deceased Personnel File (held at NPRC)
JAG	Judge Advocate General
JMA	Japanese Military Administration
LOC	Library of Congress
MC	Morton Collection
MID	Military Intelligence Division
MMA	MacArthur Memorial Archives, Norfolk, Va.
NA	U.S. National Archives
NCO	noncommissioned officer
NPRC	National Personnel Records Center, St. Louis, Missouri
OCMH	Office of the Chief of Military History
OTAG	Office of the Adjutant General
PA	Philippine Army

PC	Philippine Constabulary
PMS&T	professor of military science and tactics
PMT	Preparatory Military Training
PNA	Philippine National Archives, Manila
PNG	Philippine National Guard
PNL	Philippine National Library, Manila
PROTC	Philippine Reserve Officers' Training Corps
PS	Philippine Scouts
RG	Record Group
ROTC	Reserve Officers' Training Corps
SO	Special Orders
SWPA	Southwest Pacific Area
TAG	the adjutant general
UP	University of the Philippines, Diliman, Quezon City
UPDA	University of the Philippines, Diliman, Archives, Quezon City
USA	United States Army
USAMHI	U.S. Army Military History Institute, Carlisle, Pennsylvania
USMA	United States Military Academy
USNA	United States Naval Academy
USAFFE	United States Army Forces Far East
WCD	War College Division
WPD	War Plans Division

Notes

Introduction

1. "Vicente Lim," *Assembly* 7, no. 4 (1949): 12–13; Eisenhower, "Personal Estimates," McCann Papers; *Philippines Herald*, 23 Sept. 1937; Eligio B. Ortega, "Thrice I Met General Lim," *Philippines Free Press*, 27 Feb. 1960.
2. John O. Keider, "Report on Headquarters, Combat and Intelligence Battalion, General Lim's Guerrilla Unit (Independent)," box 273, RG 407, Philippine Archives, NA.
3. G. R. Perez, "General Lim's Last Days," *Philippine Armed Forces Journal*, June 1949, 12–13.
4. International Military Tribunal for the Far East, *Tokyo War Crimes Trial*, 6:12502–6.
5. People of the Philippines v. Kuroda, 4 Mar. 1949, 31:1139–55, Japanese War Crime Records, PNA.
6. Marquez, *Blood on the Rising Sun*, 163.
7. Morison, *United States Naval Operations*, 3:150.
8. Petillo, *Douglas MacArthur*, 66–78, 151–53; James, *Years of MacArthur*, 1:88–90, 107; Blunt, "Very Confidential, Post of High Commissioner: Conversation with Vice-Governor J. R. Hayden," 24 Aug. 1935; Blunt to Adrian Holman, 4, 22 Nov. 1935, FO 371/18764, reel 3, Onorato Collection.
9. H. W. Baldwin, "Bitter Road to an Epic Defeat," *New York Times*, 27 Dec. 1953.

Prologue

1. Franklin, "History of the Philippine Scouts," 1–3. The interest in the Philippine Scouts may have been related to the passage of the Philippine Independence Act in 1934, which pushed the army to consider the Scouts' future status, or to a recent Supreme Court ruling defining the Scouts as members of the regular army for retirement purposes.
2. Sexton, *Soldiers in the Sun*, 141; *Annual Report of the War Department, 1900*, pt. 2, *Report of the Lieutenant-General Commanding the Army*, 209. Batson's 4th Cavalry assignments are from "Returns from Regular Army Cavalry Regiments," reel 46, microfilm series M744, NA.
3. LeRoy, *Americans in the Philippines*, 1:200; Foreman, *Philippine Islands*, 446; Sonnichsen, *Ten Months a Captive*, 155.
4. Franklin, "History of the Philippine Scouts," 3–4. Otis is quoted in a paper Batson wrote in 1908 titled "The Scout" (copy in box 2, Batson Papers).
5. Sexton, *Soldiers in the Sun*, 181, 200–203; Linn, *Philippine War*, 154; Franklin, "History of the Philippine Scouts," 44, 155–57; *Annual Report of the War Department, 1900*, pt. 4, *Report of the Lieutenant-General Commanding the Army*, 126.
6. Woolard, "Philippine Scouts," 77–82.
7. *New York Times*, 14 Dec. 1901; Edward M. Coffman, "The Philippine Scouts, 1899–1942: A Historical Vignette," *ACTA*, no. 3 (1978): 71.

8. "Letters of Major Matthew A. Batson, USA, Ret., Cuban and Philippine Campaigns, 1898–1901," box 3, Batson Papers.
9. Taylor, *Philippine Insurrection*, 1:62–63, 71–72, 77–78, 262–66; 2:17–18, 24–25, 32.
10. Faust, *Campaigning in the Philippines*, 142.
11. Woolard, "Philippine Scouts," 56–58; Franklin, "History of the Philippine Scouts," 8–10; and Twichell, *Allen*, 106–8. For an account of service with Lowe's Scouts, see O'Reilly, *Roving and Fighting*, 111–53. On the Ilocano Scouts, see Linn, "Guerrilla Fighter," 13.
12. Lawton to Otis, 19 Nov. 1899, quoted in *Report of Major-General E. S. Otis, U.S. Army, September 1, 1899, to May 5, 1900*, 265–66. The Ganley Papers include a 1920s-vintage chart showing the ethnic makeup of the Scouts: Macabebes made up 0.2 percent. Casualty figures are from Millett and Maslowski, *For the Common Defense*, 653.
13. Batson to TAG, 29 Mar. 1900, AGO 318980, RG 94, NA; Root, *Military and Colonial Policy*, 368; Woolard, "Philippine Scouts," 8–9, 13, 225.
14. *An Act to Increase the Efficiency of the Permanent Military Establishment of the United States, U.S. Statutes at Large* 31 (1901): 757; "No Filipinos in Army," *Washington Post*, 7 Jan. 1901; Fletcher, *America's First Black General*, 24–27.
15. Woolard, "Philippine Scouts," 226–28; Ochosa, *Tinio Brigade*, 131–32; *Boston Transcript*, 30 Sept. 1920; C. G. Lawrence (a Scout officer in 1905–8) to Ganley, 10 Mar. 1959, and Capinpin questionnaire (undated), Ganley Papers. On Patajo, see also *New York Times*, 10, 12 July, 9 Aug. 1903; and *Washington Post*, 19 July 1925. Bell's statement can be found in the latter, written at the time of Patajo's death. General Bell had arranged to have Patajo brought to Fort Leavenworth. Patajo was advanced to captain in 1908; Abelino was made first lieutenant. A 1908 law allowed for promotion of Scout officers to captain.
16. Quoted in Elliott, *End of the Military Regime*, 505.
17. Pringle, *William Howard Taft*, 1:169–70.
18. Berthoff, "Taft and MacArthur," 197n10.
19. Young, *General's General*, 207; Stanley, *Nation in the Making*, 77–78.
20. Taylor, *Philippine Insurrection*, 2:275; Taft to Root, 30 July, 11 Aug., 13 Sept., 16 Oct. 1900, 24 May 1901, reel 19; and Taft to Charley [Charles P. Taft], 2 Oct. 1900, reel 18; 15, 30 Nov. 1900, reel 19, Taft Papers.
21. Taft to Bellamy Storer (U.S. minister to Spain), 6 Jan. 1902, reel 34; Taft to Roosevelt, 18 Oct. 1907, reel 604, Taft Papers; Taft, *Special Report*, 14–15.
22. House of Representatives, *Hearings before the House Committee on Military Affairs . . . 1908–09*, 60th Cong., 1st Sess. (1908), 243–45; *Congressional Record* 42, pt. 7, 60th Cong., 1st Sess., 6984–86; Rosenfeld, *Richmond Pearson Hobson*, 170.
23. *Army and Navy Journal*, 15 Feb. 1908; Crowder to Taft, 19 Sept. 1912; and Taft to Crowder, 21 Sept. 1912, reel 400, Taft Papers.
24. Ambrose, *Eisenhower*, 39; Smith, *Lucius D. Clay*, 33.
25. *Manila Daily Bulletin*, 31 July 1917.
26. Aguinaldo was a student at Phillips Academy at Andover, Mass., when he was appointed second alternate after writing former governor-general W. Cameron Forbes to express an interest in attending the military academy. The principal and first alternate then failed the physical examination. Aguinaldo was unprepared for West Point's curriculum, was turned back to repeat his first year, and withdrew

in 1924. See the correspondence in Emilio Aguinaldo Jr., BIA name file, box 10, RG 350, NA; and Forbes's letters to Secretary of War Weeks and to Gen. Emilio Aguinaldo in the "correspondence from notable persons" files, Forbes Papers, Houghton Library, Harvard.

27. Lim took the army exam (specially written for Filipino applicants) in September or October 1908. With the inauguration of the Commonwealth government in 1935, the candidate for West Point would be selected from among top cadets at the Philippine Military Academy.
28. TAG to BIA, 3 July 1908, BIA 11685-7, RG 350, NA; *Army and Navy Journal*, 1 Aug. 1908. From 1910, applicant numbers can be found in the *Annual Report of the Bureau [later, Director] of Civil Service to the Governor-General of the Philippine Islands.*
29. Bureau of Education, circular no. 81, series 1911, and circular no. 93, series 1912, BIA 11685, RG 350, NA; *Cablenews-American*, 22 June 1911.
30. *Annual Report of the Bureau of Civil Service* (FY 1913), 8; *Annual Report of the Bureau of Civil Service* (FY 1914), 3–4; *Army and Navy Journal of the Philippines*, 19 July 1913.

Chapter 1

1. On Lim's childhood, see the biographical introduction by Edilberto C. de Jesus in Lim, *To Inspire and to Lead*, 13–14; *Philippines Herald*, 29 Apr. 1936.
2. Capinpin questionnaire, Ganley Papers; Janairo questionnaire (author's collection).
3. Garcia to Charles E. Walcutt Jr., 17 Oct. 1915, BIA name file, box 224, RG 350, NA.
4. Bureau of Insular Affairs, *Pronouncing Gazetteer*, 574; Lim, *To Inspire and to Lead*, 13–14. On Calamba and the friar controversy, see Coates, *Rizal*, 5, 138–41, 184–85; and Roth, *Friar Estates of the Philippines*, 15–23. On economic trends in the mestizo community and for an explanation of Chinese family names, see Wickberg, *Chinese in Philippine Life*, 32, 134–35, 149, 172.
5. Lim, *To Inspire and to Lead*, 14; Nichol to Ganley, 15 Sept. 1960, Ganley Papers.
6. Lim, Original Letters, 13 Sept. 1938; Lim application form, USMA Archives; *Discurso leído en la inauguración del Liceo de Manila, por su presidente D. Leon Ma. Guerrero el 29 de junio de 1900* (Manila, 1900), 8. The authors of an unpublished history of Lim's World War II division wrote that Lim's hometown was either Calamba or Tanauan, "for he was born in one and grew up in the other" (author's collection).
7. *Census of the Philippine Islands, 1903*, 3:664; Maniago, "First Peace Corps," 210–15; *Philippine Normal School*, 10; Cornejo, *Commonwealth Directory*, 1885; *Manila Times*, 13 June 1914.
8. Rimando ("Vicente Lim," 45) was told that a teacher named "Beatty" encouraged Lim to enter West Point. G. W. Beattie was the school superintendent until 1908.
9. Smith to Secretary of War, 9 Sept. 1908, BIA 11685-12, RG 350, NA. The name of the candidate is given as Villar in some sources. That Lim "failed to pass the finals" was public knowledge (see, e.g., *Cablenews-American*, 22 June 1911). Most of the early Filipino cadets failed the civil service exam but were deemed "promising candidates" and allowed to proceed with the West Point exam. These included Anastacio Ver (see BIA 11685-22), Luis Salvosa, Rafael Garcia (BIA 11685-33), and Fidel Segundo (BIA 11685-40, 11685-60)—all in RG 350, NA.

10. The army had recently changed the reporting date from June to March on a trial basis. The experiment was not a success, and the date reverted to June. Rimando ("Vicente Lim," 64–65) learned that the civil register of births at Calamba had been destroyed during World War II and that the records of San Juan Bautista church in Calamba failed to show Lim's baptismal date. (The bound church records are available on microfilm through the Family History Center of the Church of Jesus Christ of Latter-Day Saints, and they reveal that thirty pages from early 1888, covering the time Lim would have been baptized had he been born in Calamba in February, are missing. See FHC microfilm 1084021, "Bautismos, 1887–1891.") Lim's widow told Rimando that Lim had given a false date of birth to the army "to escape some West Point practices."
11. *New York Times*, 24 Dec. 1911.
12. See Barry's testimony in House of Representatives, *Hearings before the House Committee on Military Affairs . . . 1913*, and his comments in the *Annual Report[s] of the Superintendent, United States Military Academy.* See also Nye, "Educational Reform," 93–96.
13. Forman, *West Point*, 165–66; Nye, "Educational Reform," 83–84.
14. Hancock, *Life at West Point*, 49; James, *Years of MacArthur*, 1:68–71; Ambrose, *Eisenhower*, 44; Forman, *West Point*, 171.
15. *New York Times*, 24 Jan. 1910; Lim, *To Inspire and to Lead*, 192. Selleck, Lim wrote, "took care of me during my first year" at West Point. Since Selleck graduated on 15 June 1910, Lim must have been referring to Beast Barracks.
16. U.S. Military Academy, *Howitzer, 1914*, 69; Vicente Lim Jr. interview, Manila, 19 Jan. 1994. Some later Filipino cadets did have white roommates. A letter by Miguel describing his experiences is printed in *Philippines Herald*, 30 Aug. 1924.
17. See Swanton's letters of 7 July 1912, 12 Mar. 1913, and Dec. 1914, Swanton Papers.
18. Dauncey, *The Philippines*, 191.
19. Ben Cailles Unson, "Vicente P. Lim: His Life and Labors," *Manila Times Daily Magazine*, 8 Apr. 1959; Hancock, *Life at West Point*, 67, 126–27; "The Court martial of Capt. Rufo C. Romero," pt. 4, *Kislap-Graphic*, 19 Aug. 1959.
20. Lim, Original Letters, 8 Oct. 1938.
21. Lim, *To Inspire and to Lead*, 15; U.S. Military Academy, *Howitzer, 1914*, 69.
22. Nye, "Educational Reform," 80–82; Forman, *West Point*, 167–68.
23. Lim, Original Letters, 3 Nov. 1939.
24. The quote is from Walton Williams, "Filipino a Graduate of West Point," published in the *Lexington Herald*, 5 Aug. 1914, and other papers. For Quezon's description of the ceremony, see *Filipino People* 2, p. 23; and "The Manuel L. Quezon That I Know," *Philippines Free Press*, 27 July 1929, an anonymously authored article by someone who accompanied Quezon to Lim's graduation.
25. Ridgway, *Soldier*, 27.
26. Collins, *Lightning Joe*, 6; Eisenhower, *At Ease*, 4.
27. Quezon's quote is from his *Filipino People* article. The authors of the appreciation of Lim that appeared in *Assembly* 7, no. 4 (1949) wrote that Lim was in Berlin when the war began (12). Lim, *To Inspire and to Lead*, 15; and Cornejo, *Commonwealth Directory*, 1885, place him in Russia, which seems more probable.
28. Meixsel, "Army Policy," 56–67.

29. Returns from U.S. Army Posts, Fort San Pedro, Oct. 1910 to Oct. 1917, reel 1116, microfilm series M617, NA.
30. Blair and Robertson, *Philippine Islands*, 49:40–41; Rich, "Fort San Pedro 22," 5–6; Kumai, *Blood and Mud*, 34.
31. Description based on "Military Reservation and Post, Fort San Pedro, Iloilo, Panay, P.I.," Office of the Department Quartermaster, Sept. 1914, map no. 37 in "Military Stations, Philippine Islands," RG 77, NA.
32. Commanding Officer to Robert C. Davis, 6 Mar. 1915, doc. 11221; Lt. Col. F. R. Day, "Annual Inspection of Post," 20 Oct. 1915, doc. 11227; TAG to Commanding General, 27 May 1916, doc. 11451, File 1166, RG 395, NA.
33. 18th Infantry regimental return for June 1901, reel 198, M665, NA; Halsema, *E. J. Halsema*, 191–92. On Speth, see also Memo. for Officer in Charge, HQ CIC Area no. 12, re Major E. Speth, 1 Dec. 1945, box 184, RG 65, NA.
34. Lim to Sullivan, 29 Dec. 1927, BIA 1877–147, RG 350, NA; Lim, *To Inspire and to Lead*, 192.
35. For Lim's school assignments, see SO 47, Headquarters Ft. San Pedro, 10 Sept. 1915; and GO 30, Headquarters Ft. San Pedro, 11 May 1916—both in Ft. San Pedro Special and General Orders, 1910–16, RG 395, NA.
36. Alfred W. McCoy, "A Queen Dies Slowly: The Rise and Decline of Iloilo City," in McCoy and de Jesus, *Philippine Social History*, 326.
37. Philippine Commission of Independence, *Beautiful Philippines*, 66; Hamm, *Manila and the Philippines*, 89–91; Worcester, *Philippine Islands and Their People*, 223–29; Gilbert, *Great White Tribe*, 64–65; Dauncey, *The Philippines*, 61; Boyce, *United States Colonies and Dependencies*, 345–48.
38. Unson, "Vicente P. Lim: His Life and Labors," 8 Apr. 1959; *Iloilo Enterprise-Press*, 3 Nov. 1914; Vargas to Kalaw, 8 Dec. 1914, reel 53, Quezon Papers (2).
39. Coffman, *Regulars*, 66–67; "A New Military Policy for the United States in the Philippines," 22 June 1911, reel 4, Bandholtz Papers.
40. Lim to Quezon, 27 Nov. 1914, reel 50, Quezon Papers (2); Unson, "Vicente P. Lim: His Life and Labors," 8 Apr. 1959.
41. Harrison, *Cornerstone of Philippine Independence*, 143–57; John H. Parker, "Memories of the Service," 130, Parker Papers. See also Gleeck, *Manila Americans*, 246–47; and Halsema, *E. J. Halsema*, 104–5.
42. Davis, *Autobiography*, 4, 27, 36, 44, 57–58, 69.
43. Charles Ivins, "The Monkeys Have No Tails in Zamboanga," 30, Ivins Papers.
44. "Philippine Scouts (Native Born)," undated [mid-1935] evaluation, RG 18, MMA.
45. "Senior Officers Debriefing Program: Conversations Between Lieutenant General Edward M. Almond and Captain Thomas G. Fergusson," 40–41, Almond Papers; Ivins, "Zamboanga," 46.
46. Sulit to Quezon, 6 Oct. 1918, series 7, box 520, Quezon Papers (1); Manzano, "Memoirs."
47. Lim, Original Letters, 30 July 1941. At that time, regular army captains commanded PS battalions with the temporary grade of major. No personnel file for Morton exists at the NPRC, and the Ft. San Pedro general correspondence file makes no mention of this episode. It may be significant that the first general order issued by Chamberlain after taking command, GO 4, 2 Feb. 1916, stated that no officer could leave the post between midnight and noon without the commanding officer's permission.

48. For Lee's court-martial, see SO 22, Ft. San Pedro, 6 May 1916, "Ft. San Pedro Misc. Letters and Reports," and for the addendum concerning Lim, see file 1116, #11368—both in RG 395, NA.
49. O'Reilly, *Roving and Fighting*, 163.
50. Clark, *Chronicle of Aunt Lena*, 38–39. For the air service and Brereton, see Meixsel, *Clark Field*, 3–4; and Roger G. Miller, "A 'Pretty Damn Able Commander': Lewis Hyde Brereton," *Air Power History* (January 2000): 4–27.
51. SO 214, War Department, s. 1916, cited in Fort Mills post return, October 1916; Maximo Kalaw to Quezon, 2 Aug. 1916; and Quezon to Kalaw, 3 Aug. 1916, series 7, box 59, Quezon Papers (1).
52. Lim to Quezon, 6 July 1915, and Quezon to Lim, 10 July 1915, reel 50, Quezon Papers (2).
53. Twichell, *Allen*, 115–46; Willis, *Our Philippine Problem*, 122.
54. The law required "that officers who had not served two years of the previous six with a troop, battery or company should immediately be returned to troops." There were exceptions but service with the Philippine Constabulary was not among them. See Ganoe, *History*, 444–45.
55. Meixsel, "Army for Independence?," 239–44.
56. *Annual Report of the Governor-General of the Philippine Islands, 1916*, 14. For officer and enlisted strength figures for the PC from 1901 to 1926, see Forbes, *Philippine Islands*, 1:227. On the retirement act, see Gleeck, *American Half-Century*, 183; and Onorato, *Brief Review of American Interest*, 14.
57. *Report of the Philippine Commission to the Secretary of War* (1912), 12; *Manila Times*, 31 Mar. 1911; *Cablenews-American*, 12 Apr. 1911; "Troops in the Philippines," *New York Tribune*, 14 Nov. 1910; and Governor-General to BIA, 17 Oct. 1916, BIA 2275-29; Secretary of War to Governor-General, 22 Nov. 1916, BIA 2275-31; and BIA to TAG, 13 Jan. 1917, BIA 1877-88, RG 350, NA.
58. *Report of the Philippine Commission to the Secretary of War* (1909), 138; *Report of the Philippine Commission to the Secretary of War* (1915), 35; *Journal of the Philippine Commission*, 8:469, 675–76; *Journal of the Philippine Commission*, 9:358–62, 560, 809–10; Elliott, *End of the Commission Government*, 175–76; "Philippine National Army," *Cablenews-American*, 5 July 1912.
59. *Cablenews-American*, 14 Sept. 1912; *Manila Times*, 11 Aug. 1917; Rimando, "Vicente Lim," 78–79; Pilar Lim to Georgia Williams (Philippine Pensionado Agent), 26 June 1928, Vicente Lim BIA name file, box 360, RG 350, NA; A. S. Lardizabal, "Pilar Hidalgo Lim," in de Guzman, *Women of Distinction*, 183–86. Pilar Hidalgo, born 24 May 1893 in Boac, was the sixth child of Luis Hidalgo and Eulalia Lardizabal.

Chapter 2

1. Quezon, "The Control of the Constabulary," *Filipino People* 2, no. 11 (1914), copy included with letter, Bandholtz to Taylor, 2 Dec. 1914, reel 10, Bandholtz Papers; Clements, *Presidency of Woodrow Wilson*, 106–7; Cooper, *Woodrow Wilson*, 75–76; Salamanca, *Filipino Reaction to American Rule*, 141–46; Stanley, *Nation in the Making*, 179–80; Golay, *Face of Empire*, 171; *Cablenews-American*, 12 Nov. 1912; *New York Times*, 7 Oct. 1913. See also Kalaw, *Case for the Filipinos*, 195–203. On Quezon's belief that the Constabulary might soon become a Philippine army, see

his exchange of correspondence with Maj. Henry Knauber, 14 Mar., 12 May 1916, box 59, series 7, Quezon Papers (1).

2. Quezon to Osmeña, 24 Apr. 1914; Quezon to Harrison, 28 Apr. 1914, and Quezon to Harbord, 15 June 1914, GLMR film 35934, Onorato Collection.
3. Gleeck, *American Half-Century*, 215; Harrison to BIA, 27 Oct. 1916, BIA 2275-29, and Baker to Harrison, 22 Nov. 1916, BIA 2275-31, RG 350, NA. The Militia Act is included in Philippine Legislature, *Laws of the Fourth Philippine Legislature*, 1:194–212.
4. *Manila Times*, 14 July 1917.
5. "Present status of the proposed Philippine National Guard," 6 Sept. 1918, WCD 9136-58, RG 165, NA.
6. *Manila Times*, 26, 28 June 1918. Evans's recall to active duty is not shown in the *Army Register*, and nothing of his personnel file remains.
7. Harrison to Hartigan, 6 Apr. 1918, BIA 2275-116, RG 350, NA.
8. Woolard, "Philippine Scouts," 173–74. The War Department responded that there was "no provision in law" for the existence of Scout regiments. See memo., William Graves to TAG, 9 Jan. 1918, WCD 9136-29, RG 165, NA.
9. Harrison, *Cornerstone of Philippine Independence*, 161; Perley to Ganley, 21 Apr. 1960, Ganley Papers. On Landon, see Quezon to de Veyra, 8 July 1918, GLMR film 35934, Onorato Collection.
10. *Decorations, United States Army*, 701. See also Tierney to Ganley, 1 Mar. 1959, Ganley Papers.
11. Per Ramee to Ganley, 11 May 1959, and Perley to Ganley, 21 Mar. 1960, Ganley Papers.
12. "Notes for General Staff," 15 Apr. 1918, and Hartigan to Harrison, 24 Apr. 1918, BIA 2275-119, RG 350, NA; de Veyra to Quezon, 28 Feb. 1918, box 373, series 7, Quezon Papers (1). Philippine Constabulary files include a translation of Roa's article, which appeared in *La Vanguardia*, 15 May 1918, in PNG Records, film 1716507, FHC. See also James Tierney to Ganley, 1 Mar. 1959, Ganley Papers.
13. Alejandrino, quoted in *La Nacion*, 5 Feb. 1918, PNG Records, film 1716507, FHC. For a list of Filipinos who died while serving with the army in World War I, see *Philippines Herald*, 26 May 1921. Ayres, *War with Germany*, 23, gives a figure of 255 Filipinos in the army in 1917–18, but Franklin, "History of the Philippine Scouts," 43, puts the number of individuals claiming the Philippines as their place of residence who served in the army during the war at 21,480, including a Philippine Scout force of 8,268. On navy recruitment, see *Manila Times*, 19, 25 June 1918.
14. For dates of the national guard's service, organization, and commanders, see *Order of Battle of the United States Land Forces*, 3, pt. 2:674–75.
15. Hill, "Philippine Army," 60. Claudio, from Moron, Rizal, was living in Nevada when he enlisted in the army. He died on 29 June 1918, of wounds received while serving with K Co., 28th Infantry Regiment, 1st Division.
16. Williams, *United States and the Philippines*, 179–80.
17. Jose, "Philippine National Guard," 281, 292–93; *Cablenews-American* 11, 23, 29 Oct., 7 Nov. 1918; Gleeck, *Laguna in American Times*, 60, 69; Jamias, *University of the Philippines*, 21; Ben Cailles Unson, "Vicente P. Lim," *Manila Times Daily Magazine*, 11 Apr. 1959. See also Pobre, *History of the Armed Forces*, 122–54.

18. See, for example, the comments of Ralph Jones, "Memorandum for Governor-General: Need of Systematic Cultivation of Interest of the Educated Filipinos in the National Guard Division," 20 June 1918, GLMR film 35934, Onorato Collection.
19. *Manila Times*, 6 July 1918; Kalaw, *Self-Government*, 62; Harrison, *Origins*, 106; Quezon, *Good Fight*, 165. A copy of Campos's statement, dated 10 May 1939, can be found on reel 2, RG 1, MMA.
20. For Lim's assignments in 1917, 1918, and 1919, see *Roster and Directory*, and Robinson, *Cullum's Biographical Register, 6B, Supplement, 1910–1920.*
21. Nier and Menke, *Gleim Medal Letters*, 27.
22. SO 203, HPD, 6 Sept. 1918; SO 291, HPD, 20 Dec. 1918; GO 66, HPNG, 9 Oct. 1918; GO 69, HPNG, 12 Oct. 1918.—copies filed with PNG Records, film 1716187, FHC. The undated handwritten evaluation of national guard officers is filed with other PNG-related papers in the Quezon Papers (1). Lim's personal data card, which records his regimental assignments, is in PNG Records, film 1716519, FHC. There was a second Vicente Lim in the guard as well, a private serving in an engineer company.
23. Adjutant General to Provincial Governors, "Recruiting Men for Federal Service," 20 Aug. 1918, PNG Records, film 1716507, FHC.
24. Manzano, "Memoirs."
25. For several years before World War I, enlisted men with at least two years of service and civilians who were citizens of the United States or the Philippines could take PS commissioning examinations, offered each November in the United States and in the Philippines. The names of those who took the exam were listed in order of test score, and those at the top were offered commissions. Pedro D. Dulay took the exam in the United States in 1911, and Vincente R. Barros, a PC officer, tested in the Philippines. Both were commissioned in 1912. Esteban B. Dalao took the exam in 1912 and was commissioned in 1913. Application and examination records for Dulay and Barros are filed under AGO 968510, RG 94, NA. Dalao's army career is sketched in *Philippines Herald*, 1 Oct. 1935. He is the "Major Ladao" character in Daroy, *Nobody Gathers Seashells*, 40–42, a collection of stories based on her life as a soldier's daughter on Corregidor.
26. Frank Stoner to Ganley, 9 Mar. 1959, and Alan Jones questionnaire, 1 Dec. 1958, Ganley Papers. Stoner was a failed West Point cadet who accepted a Scout commission in 1917 as a preliminary to a regular commission, which he received in 1920. Jones was an army regular assigned to the Scouts in 1921–23. See also Lt. Frank S. Ross, 45th Infantry (PS), testimony in trial of Pvt. James Vandevender, 15th U.S. Infantry, Aug. 1924, CM 162930, Records of the Office of the Judge Advocate General, RG 153, NA; *Army and Navy Journal*, 3 Nov. 1917; and Harrison, *Cornerstone of Philippine Independence*, 150–51. Taylor's comments are found in Memo. for the Secretary of the General Staff, "The use of native military forces in the Philippine Islands," 26 Mar. 1918, WPD 9136-40, RG 165, NA.
27. *Annual Report of the War Department, 1920*, 1:256; *National Defense Act of 1920*, Public Law 66-242, *U.S. Statutes at Large* 41 (1920): 759.
28. Philippine troop strength through 1926 can be found in Forbes, *Philippine Islands*, 1:192. In 1926 Americans numbered 4,946 and Scouts 7,170. In the 1930s the Scout organization was smaller, with about 6,400 enlisted men, but there were several hundred fewer American soldiers in the garrison.

29. [Munson], *Psychology of the Filipino*. The nine-page "conversation" appended to the booklet consists of an interview with Wood conducted by Edward P. Bell, reprinted from the *Chicago Daily News*. The original report, with Edward Munson's name attached, dated 21 Aug. 1924, is filed as WPD 2903, RG 165, NA.
30. Prosser to Maj. J. J. Bain, 4 Sept. 1924, MID 10582-59/12, RG 165, NA; Ward to Ganley, 7 June 1960, Ganley Papers.
31. Lim, *To Inspire and to Lead*, 18.
32. Ibid., 230.
33. *Philippines Herald*, 13 June 1923.
34. Lim to Cabrera, 18 July 1922, and Quezon to Lim, 22 July 1922, box 520, series 7, Quezon Papers (1); W. M. Wright, "Elimination of Major Vincente R. Barros, Philippine Scouts," 5 Sept. 1922, Barros personnel file, NPRC.
35. Quezon to Isauro Gabaldon, 13 Mar. 1922, BIA 1877-123; Department of Justice to Secretary of War, 28 Mar. 1922, and William Patterson to Gabaldon, 24 June 1922, BIA 1877-124, RG 350, NA; Lim to Quezon, 8 Apr. 1922, box 520, series 7, Quezon Papers (1).
36. Eugene Ganley, "Bloodless Mutiny," 6, Ganley Papers; *New York Times*, 30 Mar. 1924. For a more detailed account of the event, see Meixsel, "American Exceptionalism in Colonial Forces?," 171–94.
37. Maj. Walter Prosser, "Mutiny of July 7–8, 1924, in Philippine Division, Fort William McKinley, P.I.," 24-25, 1 Oct. 1924, MID 10582-59/18, RG 165, NA.
38. Meixsel, "American Exceptionalism in Colonial Forces?," 182.
39. Lim's comments can be found in trial testimony, 818–21, CM 162932, Records of the Judge Advocate General, RG 153, NA.
40. Prosser, "Mutiny," 23; U.S. Senate, *War Department Appropriation Bill for 1938*, 21–22.
41. *Manila Daily Bulletin*, 21 July 1924; Potts, "1914 in the Philippines," 31. I could find no official statement of Lim's billets in the 1920s. A department directory was not published in the mid-1920s. Aside from a few World War I–era pay slips, Lim's personnel record no longer exists. The relevant volume of *Cullum's Biographical Register* of West Point graduates shows only that Lim was assigned to the 57th and 45th Regiments (PS) to 1926, when he left for the United States. Several publications state that Lim commanded the 3rd Battalion, 45th Infantry, for several years in the mid-1920s, apparently after returning from Japan in 1923. See *Manila Daily Bulletin*, 4 July 1936; *Volunteer* 5, no. 2 (1936): 15; and *Khaki and Red*, Nov. 1927, 2.
42. *Philippines Herald*, 7 Jan., 7 Mar., 3 Apr., 4, 6 May, 28 June 1923. See also Camilo Osias, "Warmer Friendship between Japan and the Philippines," *Philippines Herald*, 17 June 1923. Lim and Osias traveled together to Osaka.
43. Coffman and Herrly, "American Regular Army Officer Corps," 67–68.
44. Statistics compiled using the 1973 *Register of Graduates and Former Cadets* and the 1938 *Army Register*.
45. Lim, with his wife and three sons (seven-year-old Luis; Roberto, age 6; and Vicente, age 3), arrived in the United States aboard the *Thomas* on 5 June 1926.
46. The army normally required a two-year separation between graduation from Leavenworth and attendance at the war college. It obviously made an exception for Lim, but the relevant War Department file in the National Archives includes no correspondence concerning Lim's selection for the school. *Philippines Free Press*,

19 Oct. 1929, states that Rafael Garcia and Pedro Dulay were completing a course at Fort Benning and that both expected to follow in Lim's footsteps to Leavenworth and Washington; neither did so.

47. *Washington Post*, 14 May, 28 June 1929; Guevara to Quezon, 29 Sept. 1928, reel 13, Quezon Papers (2). For the "wallow," see *New York Times*, 4 Dec. 1928, *Washington Post*, 9 Dec. 1928, 11, 17 Feb. 1929; and *Philippines Herald*, 3 Apr. 1929.
48. "Disposition of Philippine Scout Officers," 8 June 1928, WPD 1785-9, RG 165, NA.
49. F. Parker, BIA Chief, to Albert J. Bowley, Assistant Chief of Staff, G-1, 7 Feb. 1930, BIA 1877-153, RG 350, NA; Leon F. Punsalan telephone interview, 10 Apr. 1991. Although later Filipino graduates of West Point would be commissioned directly into the Philippine Army, Punsalan received his commission through the intervention of the resident commissioner and the military adviser's office. He became a U.S. citizen after the war and retired from the U.S. Army in 1963.
50. Manzano, "Memoirs"; Villa-Real interview, Quezon City, 23 May 1994; Mallonée, "Bataan Diary," 1:11, Mallonée Papers.
51. *Philippines Herald*, 5 Oct. 1929.

Chapter 3

1. House Committee on Military Affairs, *Hearings before the Committee on Military Affairs . . . 1908–09*, 60th Cong., 1st Sess. (1908), 40.
2. Army War College, Session 1914–15, Part III, "Blue and Orange Series, and Blue and Black Series," vol. 55, 123–40. In these pages, McFarland analyzed Map Problem No. 30, Defense of the Philippine Islands, AWC Files, USAMHI. For the controversy over the fortification of Subic Bay, see Braisted, *United States Navy in the Pacific*, 119–24, 216–23.
3. Meixsel, "Major General George Grunert," 306.
4. Hagood to Booth, 23 Jan. 1932, Hagood Papers; TAG to CGPD, "Report of a Joint Army and Navy Board, Philippine Department," 14 Mar. 1921, filed with "Records of the Joint Board, 1903–1947," reel 4, microfilm series M1421, NA.
5. Meixsel, "Army for Independence?," 75–77.
6. Ibid., 89–93; Linn, *Guardians of Empire*, 185–89.
7. See Chief of Staff, HPD, to TAG, 23 June 1923, and Read to TAG, 27 Dec. 1923, AG, Formerly Classified, Philippines, RG 407, NA.
8. *Philippines Herald*, 6 Dec. 1921, 1 Apr. 1923; *Cablenews-American*, 7 Dec. 1912; H. Gamboa, "U.P. First Institution to Organize ROTC Unit," *Citizen Army*, Mar. 1941, 9, 11, 25; *Philippine Collegian*, 11 Aug. 1922, 15 Aug., 30 Oct. 1923, 25 Mar. 1941; McCoy, *Closer than Brothers*, 21–22; Raphael Palma to Secretary of War, 22 Mar. 1924, BIA 28003-11/A, RG 350, NA. Cadet numbers can be found in "Basic Plan—Brown, Philippine Department, 1923" and "Papers pertaining to proposed 1926 revision of Basic Plan, Special Plan Brown," box 88, Special Projects, Harbor Defense, Philippines, RG 407, NA.
9. ACS/WPD memo. for the Chief of Staff, 1 Sept. 1923, and memo. for TAG, 6 Mar. 1925, WPD 331-4, RG 165, NA.
10. Meixsel, "Army for Independence?," 80–82.
11. Pershing to J. M. Wainwright, 8 May 1924, Pershing Papers; Pershing to Wright, 23 May 1922, and Wright to Pershing, 16 Aug. 1922, WPD 331-2, RG 165, NA.
12. Wood to Weeks, 5 Feb. 1923, WPD 532-5, RG 165, NA.

13. Wood diary, 14 Mar. 1924, Wood Papers; Weeks to Wood, 27 Aug. 1923, WPD 532-6; memo., acting ACS/WPD to Chief of Staff, 6 Nov. 1923, WPD 532-8—both in RG 165, NA.
14. Sladen to TAG, 26 Mar. 1928, AG, Formerly Classified, Philippines, RG 407, NA.
15. Morton, "War Plan Orange," 232–34.
16. Summerall, *Way of Duty, Honor, Country*, 197–98, 203; *New York Times*, 24 Aug. 1928.
17. *Philippines Herald*, 27 Oct. 1927; Stimson to Summerall, 27 Jan. 1928, and Lassiter to Summerall, 8 Feb. 1928, Lassiter personnel file, NPRC; Stimson to Lassiter, 20 Jan. 1928, and Stimson to Summerall, 15 July 1928, Stimson Papers.
18. *Manila Daily Bulletin*, 21, 23 Apr. 1928. To improve army housing may really have been why a general officer was making a special trip to Manila, since doing so was one of Summerall's pet projects. See Summerall, *Way of Duty, Honor, Country*, 199–201.
19. Lassiter to Summerall, 6 July 1928, AG, Formerly Classified, Philippines, RG 407, NA.
20. TAG to Lassiter, 30 Jan. 1928; Summerall to Stimson, 6 Feb. 1928; TAG to MacArthur, 6 Feb. 1928; Summerall to Lassiter, 11 Feb. 1928—all in Lassiter personnel file, NPRC.
21. On Stimson's attempt to keep MacArthur at home, see Summerall to General Wahl, "Relief of General Lassiter," 9 May 1928, Lassiter personnel file, NPRC; Stimson to Summerall, 3 May 1928, reel 75, and Summerall to Stimson, 16 June 1928, reel 76, Stimson Papers; and Petillo, *Douglas MacArthur*, 145, 269n100.
22. Summerall to Lassiter, 11 Feb. 1928, Lassiter personnel file, NPRC.
23. Meixsel, "Army for Independence?," 110.
24. MacArthur to TAG, 19 Oct. and 1 Dec. 1928, AG, Formerly Classified, Philippines, RG 407, NA; ACS/WPD memo. for Chief of Staff, 6 Nov. 1928, WPD 3251, RG 165, NA; Carpenter, "Philippine National Security Capability," 48–51.
25. Summerall to Lassiter, 6 Aug. 1928, copy in box 9, AG, Formerly Classified, Philippines, RG 407, NA; Simonds memo. for TAG, 28 Feb. 1929, WPD 3251, RG 165, NA; James, *Years of MacArthur*, 1:305–6, 314–16.
26. *Khaki and Red*, Dec. 1929, 8; *Philippines Free Press*, 26 Oct. 1929; *Manila Daily Bulletin*, 8 Jan. 1930.
27. *Philippine Collegian*, 31 Mar. 1936.
28. *Khaki and Red*, Oct. 1930, 29; MacArthur to TAG, 19 June 1929, and Frank LeJeune Parker to TAG, 28 June 1929, BIA file 28003, RG 350, NA.
29. A. J. Malay, "Notes for 'The Rushing Years: An Autobiography,'" 2:105, Malay Papers; Galang, *Leaders of the Philippines*, 179–80.
30. Meixsel, *Clark Field*, 31, 93; "Summary of statement made by General Hagood in Reference to Disaffection among Native Troops in the Philippine Islands," 13 Aug. 1924, WPD 1799-2, RG 165, NA; "Philippine Scouts (Native Born)," RG 18, MMA; *Philippines Herald*, 29 Apr. 1936.
31. G-1 annex of the 1931 Philippine Defense Project so characterized the Letran program. It had some connection to the army, since an article in the *Philippines Herald*, 17 Dec. 1927, mentioned that Letran's "model cadet company" had visited San Fernando, Pampanga, under a "Lt. Ramsey of the U.S. Army." This was the program Lim found in place. Lim's comments are found in *Letran 1931–32*, the school annual.

32. Vicente H. Lim Jr. interview, Manila, 19 Jan. 1994; *Volunteer* 5, no. 2 (July 1936): 15, copy in Quezon Papers (1).
33. Baja, *Philippine Police System*, 90.
34. *Khaki and Red*, July 1926, 18; *Khaki and Red*, Apr. 1927, 3.
35. *Khaki and Red*, Apr. 1927, 8–9; June 1927, 25; Nov. 1928, 11; Jan. 1929, 8; Mar. 1932, 29. On the range of Constabulary duties, see U.S. Army, *Civil Affairs Handbook*, "Section 14: Public Safety," 19–20.
36. *Philippines Herald*, 23 Feb. 1930.
37. For details of Crame's career, see GO 1, Headquarters, Philippine Constabulary, 3 Jan. 1927; *Philippines Herald*, 4 Jan. 1927; Elarth, *Philippine Constabulary*, 150; Berlin, *Before Gringo*, 9n11; and McCoy, *Policing America's Empire*, 234.
38. "Gov. Wood Faces Battle with Filipinos on Constabulary," *Chicago Daily Tribune*, 5 Jan. 1927; *Progress*, 27 May 1934. This Cebu newspaper did a special feature on Francisco when he was named to be Constabulary chief of staff. *Tayo* is the first-person plural. When doubled (*tayo-tayo*) it denotes inclusion-exclusion: just us/only us/we are the only ones. (My thanks to Prof. Joseph McCallus for his explication of the phrase.) See also Friend, *Between Two Empires*, 27–28.
39. *Annual Report of the Governor General of the Philippine Islands, 1925*, 13–14; James Harbord (army deputy chief of staff) to Frank McIntyre (BIA chief), 30 Nov. 1921, BIA 4600-345, RG 350, NA.
40. Four more Americans joined the PC in 1928, but at the same time five of those who had accepted appointments the previous two years quit. See *Annual Report of the Governor General of the Philippines Islands, 1926*, 12–13; and *Official Constabulary Register* for 1927, 1928, and 1929.
41. Henry Stimson, "Memorandum of Personnel in the Philippines for Governor-General Davis," 27 May 1929, reel 78, Stimson Papers; Marshall to Pershing, 28 June 1929, in Bland, *Papers of George Catlett Marshall*, 1:343–44.
42. *Manila Daily Bulletin*, 19 Mar. 1927; *Philippines Herald*, 7 Jan. 1927; *Khaki and Red*, Feb. 1933, 2.
43. *Manila Daily Bulletin*, 14, 18 Apr. 1932; memo. for Chief of Staff from Brig. Gen. Creed Cox, 23 Jan. 1934, AGO Central Files, Philippines, 1926–39, RG 407, NA.
44. *Khaki and Red*, July 1932, 18; *Philippines Herald* editorial reprinted in *Khaki and Red*, Feb. 1933, 13. See also "Digest of Confidential Information Furnished the Department Commander during the Month of August, 1931," 1 Sept. 1931, MID 10582-90/1, RG 165, NA.
45. Governor-General to BIA, 8 Feb. 1933, and BIA to HPD, 17 Feb. 1933, in Lim BIA name file, box 360, RG 350, NA.
46. Memo., ACS/WPD to Chief of Staff, 31 Jan. 1934, AGO Central Files, Philippines, 1926–39, RG 407, NA.
47. *Khaki and Red*, Apr. 1934, 2; Fine, *Frank Murphy*, 113.
48. *Khaki and Red*, Oct. 1930, 29; Williams, *United States and the Philippines*, 304; Cornejo, *Commonwealth Directory*, 1802.
49. TAG to HPD, 15 Aug. 1930, AG, Formerly Classified, Philippines, RG 407, NA.
50. Embick to Booth, 19 Apr. 1933, included with Booth to TAG, 25 Apr. 1933, WPD 3251-15, RG 165, NA; Schaffer, "General Stanley D. Embick," 89.

51. Basic Document, Philippine Defense Project (1931 Revision), 1 Oct. 1932, Special Projects—War Plans "Color," 1920–48, RG 407, NA.
52. "G-3 Estimate of the Situation—Philippine Department, First Phase, Plan Orange, 1934" and "Harbor Defenses, First Phase, Plan Orange, 1934," in Special Projects, War Plans "Color," 1920–48, RG 407, NA.
53. Memo., Kilbourne to TAG, 17 Nov. 1933, WPD 3251-14, and memo., Kilbourne to Chief of Staff, 21 Apr. 1934, WPD 3251-17, RG 165, NA.
54. Morton, "War Plan Orange," 240–41; Miller, *War Plan Orange*, 183; Embick interview, 21 Apr. 1948, box 12, MC.
55. See, for example, Brig. Gen. George Simonds memo. for Chief of Staff re hearings on Philippine independence, 5 May 1930, box 3065, Records of the Army Air Forces, Philippine Department, RG 18, NA; and Malcolm, *Commonwealth of the Philippines*, 272.
56. "Digest of confidential information furnished the Department commander during the month of December 1932," 1 Jan. 1933, MID 10582-90/6, RG 165, NA; *Congressional Record* 75, pt. 9, 72nd Cong., 1st Sess. (1932), 9526–28; Vicente Albano Pacis, "Army Held Ready to Quit Philippines," *Washington Post*, 10 June 1934; Vicente Villamin, "Philippine Scouts," *Washington Post*, 13 Apr. 1932; *New York Times*, 11, 12 Apr. 1932, 13 Apr. 1933. See also Robert Aura Smith, "Cost of Defense Shocks Filipinos," *New York Times*, 15 May 1932. A copy of the 1932 HPD Plan Brown is filed with Special Projects, War Plans "Color," 1920–48, box 87, RG 407, NA. Villamin was the husband of Pilar Hidalgo's older sister, Ursula. For his attitude toward independence, see "Filipino Opposes Island Self-Rule," *New York Times*, 13 May 1926, in which Villamin remarked "that he had been repeatedly burned in effigy in Manila because of his campaign against independence," and *Philippines Free Press*, 6 July 1940, which characterized Villamin as having "been arguing against Philippine independence since time out of mind."
57. The Philippine Commonwealth and Independence Law, sec. 2, para. 12, in Hayden, *The Philippines*, 809.
58. "An Act to authorize an increase in the enlisted strength of the Philippine Constabulary," Act 4188, approved 8 Dec. 1934, in *Public Laws Enacted by the Philippine Legislature*, 30:333–34; *Philippines Free Press*, 15 Dec. 1934; *Manila Tribune*, 11 Nov. 1934; *Philippines Herald*, 3 Dec. 1934; Fine, *Frank Murphy*, 113–14; Lim to Quezon, 14 Dec. 1934, reel 18, Quezon Papers (2). A copy of the bill including Murphy's veto message is filed with WPD 3251-1, RG 165, NA. Vice Governor Joseph Hayden's unflattering analysis of the bill—it makes no mention of Lim—can be found in box 10, Hayden Papers. See also the survey of press articles in Carpenter, "Philippine National Security Capability," 149–68, 209–15.
59. Sandoval was married to Lim's wife's younger sister Concepcion Hidalgo. A photograph of Lim, Rafael Garcia, and Fidel Segundo testifying in favor of the bureau act can be found in *Manila Tribune*, 30 Sept. 1934.

Chapter 4

1. Meixsel, "Military Mission," 255–56 (emphasis added). See also Eisenhower, *Prewar Diaries*, 98; and Harrison, *Origins*, 170–71.
2. On the authorship of Quezon's memoirs, see Harrison, *Origins*, 152.

3. Eisenhower, *Prewar Diaries*, 286–88; Davis to Jorge Vargas, 29 Feb. 1936, Davis Papers.
4. Quezon comments before National Defense Council (undated but ca. 18 Nov. 1935), box 71, series 8, Quezon Papers (1).
5. Meixsel, "Army for Independence?," 119–22.
6. Quezon to Secretary of War, 19 Nov. 1934, reprinted in *Khaki and Red*, Feb. 1935, 7–8; Parker to TAG, 1 July 1935, and MacArthur to TAG, 2 July 1935, RG 18, MMA; James interview with Ned Moore, box 11, James Papers; Brig. Gen. E. T. Conley to Parker, 18 Sept. 1935, RG 1, MMA; Fine, *Frank Murphy*, 187.
7. Eisenhower, *Prewar Diaries*, 289–90, 293–94.
8. *Washington Post*, 31 Jan. 1938; *Army and Navy Journal*, 5 Feb. 1938; Hoge, *Engineer Memoirs*, 64; "Interview with Brig. Gen. William L. Lee," 9 Dec. 1970, 94, 179, EPL Oral History Program.
9. NPRC has no record for Ord. These details come from "Biographical Sketch of James Basevi Ord, Major of Infantry," Adjutant General's Office, 10 Apr. 1928, MID 2550-129, RG 165, NA. See also Meixsel, "Army for Independence?," 43–52.
10. Eisenhower, *Prewar Diaries*, 410.
11. "Memorandum for chief clerk," 2 Nov. 1934, RG 18, MMA; Challener, *Nation in Arms*, 137–46, 156–57, 178–80, 222. On opposition to the one-year length of training, see Bankwitz, *Maxime Weygand*, 84–85.
12. Challener, *Nation in Arms*, 73–74, 177.
13. Eisenhower, *Prewar Diaries*, 413 (emphasis in original).
14. Hayden, *The Philippines*, 469–73.
15. The National Defense Act established six military districts in the Philippines: three on Luzon; one in the Visayas; and two on Mindanao. In mid-1937 the country was reorganized into ten military districts: five on Luzon; four in the Visayas; and one on Mindanao. For a discussion of the uncertainty over how many men were to be trained, see Meixsel, "Military Mission," 271n33.
16. Ord and Eisenhower had originally expected there to be 1,500 officers and 19,000 enlisted men, but money was not available to support so many regulars. The "ultimate strength of the Professional element" given in MacArthur, *Report on National Defense*, 21, was to be "930 officers and approximately 10,000 enlisted men." Eisenhower, *Prewar Diaries*, 295, set the latter figure at 7,000. Actual strength at the end of 1936 was 444 officers and 7,012 enlisted men—and that included the Constabulary. See *Annual Report of the Chief of Staff of the Philippine Army . . . 1936*, 21.
17. "Notes of an address by Field Marshal Douglas MacArthur delivered to a group of officers today, Aug. 3, 1936," RG 1, MMA (emphasis in original); MacArthur, *Reminiscences*, 104; Eisenhower, *Prewar Diaries*, 294; A. R. MacKechnie, "Our Two Years in the Philippines," 59, Harrison Collection.
18. G-1 Appendix to 1924 Basic Project, 16, AG 1917–1925, Formerly Classified, Philippines, RG 407, NA.
19. Committee Report no. 25, in "Laurel on the Constitution," 1:117–25, Laurel Papers. The provision became Article II, Section 2, of the 1935 constitution. See also Hayden, *The Philippines*, 45–49. Quezon referred to the Spanish *quintos* system, "under which one man out of every five was compelled to serve as a soldier," and denounced "some fools" who were claiming that the Commonwealth government

was reviving the practice. See Quezon, "Government cooperation and national defense," 28 Feb. 1936, *Messages of the President*, 2, pt. 1:50.

20. Rostker, *I Want You!*, 3; James, *Years of MacArthur*, 1:375–78; *Philippine Forum* 1, no. 7 (1936): 52–57; Magtoto, "Rock of Bataan," 68–69; Francisca T. DeBenitez, "Why not something like the R.O.T.C. for our girls," *Character Education* 1, no. 2 (1939): 41, 72. Quezon's speech is reprinted in Ghormley, *Military Order of the Carabao*, 83–89. See also "Military training camps as fields of instruction for democracy," in *Messages of the President*, 5, pt. 1:119–20. The other quotes are from *Philippines Herald*, 10 Mar., 16 Apr. 1936, 18 Jan. 1937, 5 July, 20 Sept. 1939, and *Manila Tribune*, 26 Aug. 1936.
21. Cooling, "Dwight D. Eisenhower at the Army War College, 1927–1928," 26–36. Various claims are made about Lim's papers: the unidentified author of "Vicente Lim: Symbol of Loyalty," a sketch of Lim's life that appeared in the AFP civil affairs magazine *Today* (Oct.–Nov. 1954), wrote that Lim's paper at Benning was titled "Philippine Defense in Case of Japanese Invasion." Presumably the author meant Leavenworth because *Infantry School News*, 26 Nov. 1926, states that Lim gave a final presentation at Benning titled "Philippine Insurrection from February 1899 to include the capture of Aguinaldo."
22. Lim to Quezon, 1 Sept. 1919, box 376, series 7, Quezon Papers (1).
23. The radio addresses were reprinted in the following days' *Philippines Herald*: 9, 23 Feb., and 2 Mar. 1930.
24. *Manila Tribune*, 6 Feb. 1934.
25. Lim, "Discipline and Nationalism," *Khaki and Red*, Sept. 1939, 8–9, 14; Lim, "National Discipline," *Citizen Army*, Aug.–Sept. 1940, 5, 23, 26. *Philippine Scouting* 4, no. 8 (Oct. 1940), provides historical data and membership numbers. See also Lim, *To Inspire and to Lead*, 61–62. Brevet Maj. Gen. Emory Upton was an army reformer whose ideas for strengthening the nation's military—one of which was to rely on a Prussian-like system of conscription and reserves—found a wide following among army officers in the late nineteenth and early twentieth centuries but not Congress or the public. See Millett and Maslowski, *For the Common Defense*, 272–74.
26. Memo. for the High Commissioner, "National Defense Bill proposed by the United States Military Mission," 10 Dec. 1935, and "Proposed National Defense Bill," 12 Dec. 1935, reel 25, Murphy Papers; Eisenhower, *Prewar Diaries*, 295; MacArthur to Murphy, 28 Nov. 1935, box 8, James Papers; Murphy to Secretary of War George Dern, 8 May 1936, included with WPD 3251, RG 165, NA.
27. *Philippines Herald*, 26 Nov. 1935, included a copy of the proposed act. A slightly different version dated 12 December as well as the approved version can be found in Philippine National Assembly, *Diario de sesiones*, 1:160–71.
28. Osias to Quezon, 11 Aug. 1930, series 6, box 25, and Carlos Romulo to Quezon, 15 May 1935, series 5, box 101, Quezon Papers (1); *Philippine Forum* 1, no. 3 (1936): 69.
29. A copy of the speech is in series 8, box 95, Quezon Papers (1). Sinco, *Government of the Commonwealth*, 234.
30. Eisenhower, *At Ease*, 219.
31. Morison, *United States Naval Operations*, 3:150; Eisenhower, *Prewar Diaries*, 292, 294.
32. Hayden to Reeves, 29 Sept. 1935 (with additions dated 7, 12, 21 Oct. and 7 Nov.), box 41, Hayden Papers; Hayden, *The Philippines*, 737–50. For a fuller statement of this argument, see Meixsel, "Military Mission."

33. Vicente Lim, "The Philippine Islands—A Military Asset," 29 Apr. 1929, AWC Curricular Archives, USAMHI.
34. Vicente Lim, "Preparing a Defense for the Philippines," *Philippines Herald*, 23 Feb. 1930; Vicente Lim, "The Philippines," *Infantry Journal* 38, no. 1 (1931): 32–35.
35. MacArthur to O'Laughlin, 9 Dec. 1935, O'Laughlin Papers.

Chapter 5

1. Eisenhower, *Prewar Diaries*, 387; Lim, *To Inspire and to Lead*, 33; *Manila Daily Bulletin*, 18 Dec. 1936; Wyatt Smith to Secretary of State for Foreign Affairs, 15 Aug. 1938, FO 371/21541, reel 6, Onorato Collection.
2. *Philippine Magazine*, Jan. 1935, 4–5.
3. War Department, General Staff, Personnel Division, G-1, Memo. for the Chief of Staff, "Philippine Scouts," 1 Apr. 1936, OTAG Central Files, 1926–39, AG 093.5 P.I., RG 407, NA.
4. Eisenhower, *Prewar Dairies*, 295–96.
5. Baja, *Philippine Police System*, bk. 2:104; *Manila Daily Bulletin*, 28 July 1939. For an exchange of correspondence in 1917–18 dealing with hostility between Scouts and Constabulary, see BIA 1877-90, RG 350, NA.
6. *Philippines Herald*, 2 Jan. 1936. Comparative pay scales can be found in Jose, *Philippine Army*, 228.
7. Lim, *To Inspire and to Lead*, 35–40; *Philippines Herald*, 29 Sept., 3, 7 Oct. 1938; undated memorandum for the chief of staff, series 6, box 19, Quezon Papers (1).
8. Eisenhower, *Prewar Diaries*, 439–40.
9. *Philippines Herald*, 2 Jan., 29 Apr., 15 May 1936; Harrison, *Origins*, 26, 57; McCoy, *Policing America's Empire*, 366. The "Vargas Scrapbook for February–May 1936," Vargas Museum, UP Diliman, has a copy of the commencement program. Lim retired on the basis of "disability incident to service." He had heart problems and high blood pressure. Several sources claim that Lim also gave up American citizenship at this time. I filed a Freedom of Information Act request with the U.S. Department of Homeland Security, U.S. Citizenship and Immigration Services, asking that its naturalization records be searched for any references to Vicente Lim and was informed that it had no record that Lim had applied for citizenship.
10. Quirino, *Quezon*, 289; Steinberg, "Interviews of Prominent Filipinos," 376–77; J. Jimenez Burgos, "Doctor Turned Soldier," *Filipiniana Reference Shelf* 1, no. 1 (1940): 18–20.
11. *Manila Tribune*, 16 May 1936; Eisenhower, *Prewar Diaries*, 296–97, 305–6.
12. Foulds to Anthony Eden, 31 Aug. 1936, FO 371/19824, reel 4, Onorato Collection; Cornejo, *Commonwealth Directory*, 2123–24; "Paulino Santos Appointed Chief of Staff of Army," *Khaki and Red*, May 1936, 2–6; *Philippines Herald*, 16 May 1936.
13. Hurley, *Jungle Patrol*, 375–76; Elarth, *Philippine Constabulary*, 118.
14. *Cablenews-American*, 19 Oct. 1918; *Report of the Governor-General of the Philippine Islands, 1920*, 20; *Khaki and Red*, Dec. 1930, 10; Wood diary, entries for 9, 31 Jan., 26, 27 Feb. 1924, Wood Papers.
15. *Annual Report of the Governor-General of the Philippine Islands, 1930*, 24; *Annual Report of the Governor-General of the Philippine Islands, 1931*, 234, 236; Foulds to Anthony Eden, 12 June 1936, PRO 371/19823, reel 4, Onorato Collection.
16. Harrison, *Origins*, 100.

17. Baja, *Philippine Police System*, 164–65, 280; Dr. Rosa Santos Munda interview, Manila, 2 Mar. 1994; *Philippines Herald*, 15 May 1936; Harrison, *Origins*, 89; *Philippines Free Press*, 13 Nov. 1937; B. Ayonet [Jose Alejandrino], "Discontent in the Army," *National Review* 1, no. 18 (1936): 10; Jose, *Philippine Army*, 93–94. "Discontent in the Army?," *Khaki and Red*, May 1936, 16–17, offered a point-by-point refutation of "B. Ayonet's" criticisms of Santos. Apparently in an effort to strengthen Santos's credentials, the government chose this time (November 1935) to award him the Medal for Valor for the incident that had taken place in 1917.
18. *Philippines Herald*, 3, 18 Jan. 1936; *Khaki and Red*, Jan. 1936, 2.
19. Eisenhower, *Prewar Diaries*, 305; *Manila Bulletin*, 18 Jan. 1936; Harrison, *Origins*, 42. Dosser's comments are found in "The Dosser Story: Life in the Philippines," a bound collection of newspaper articles that appeared in a Baguio newspaper, *The Mountaineer*, in 1958–59 (copy in the American Historical Collection at Ateneo).
20. *Philippines Herald*, 4, 5 May 1936. Santos's daughter, who was old enough to have worked as his secretary in the late 1930s, was certain that MacArthur had been instrumental in naming her father chief of staff (Dr. Munda interview). Eisenhower's words also strongly suggest that MacArthur wanted Santos to be chief of staff, and Lim claimed (*To Inspire and to Lead*, 90) that in response to criticism of Santos, MacArthur admitted that "Gen. Santos was my creation." However, Segundo wrote in his diary (7 Sept. 1938) that he had been told by Santos that MacArthur had really wanted Valdes for the job.
21. *Army and Navy Journal*, 21 Sept. 1935; Buencamino, *Memoirs of Victor Buencamino*, 201–2. Admittedly, Buencamino could be recalling late 1938, when Quezon was choosing a replacement for Santos. On the popular perception that Lim was "the man most called for" to be chief of staff, see Gaston Montero, "Politics in the Army?," *Philippines Free Press*, Jan. 1936. Lt. Col. Esteban Dalao, commissioned by examination in 1913 and the longtime commander of the penal battalion on Corregidor, was the ranking Filipino Scout officer in 1935. He either had no interest in serving with the Philippine Army or was not asked to do so.
22. I. J. Nichol to Ganley, 10 Feb. 1959, 15 Sept. 1960, Ganley Papers; "Philippine Scouts (Native Born)," undated memo., RG 18, MMA. The Carnival episode is described in *Manila Daily Bulletin*, 21, 22 Feb. 1930, and the students' resolution is in *Philippines Herald*, 28 Feb. 1930, a copy of which made its way into Lim's BIA file.
23. Eisenhower, *Prewar Diaries*, 301.
24. Accounts of registration week are from *Philippines Herald*, 2, 3, 6, 8 Apr. 1936; *Manila Tribune*, 7, 9 Apr. 1936; the Bacolod English-language weekly *Commoner*, 9 Apr. 1936; and the Cebu Spanish-language daily *La Revolucion*, 1 Apr. 1936. The instructions to army officers are from Bulletin 6, HPA, 11 Feb. 1936, RG 350, NA. A U.S. Army document, "First Registration for Military Service," 1 July 1936, filed with MID's Philippine Army file #6200, in MID Regional Files: Islands: Philippines, RG 165, NA, states that HPD G-2 estimated 135,000 men would register for the draft; HPA estimated "not over 110,000." More or less complete collections of prewar Philippine Army orders and bulletins are held by the U.S. National Archives (RG 350), LOC, and USAMHI.
25. Quezon to Roy Howard, 15 May 1936, Howard Papers.
26. Bulletin 20, HPA, 30 Apr. 1936.
27. Figures are of those who registered during the designated registration periods. Adjusted totals for 1936 to 1941 are provided in Bulletin 85, HPA, 24 June 1941.

Predicted registration numbers are found in "Vital statistics concerning the annual registration of young men, 1936–1945," an attachment to Bulletin 111, HPA, 30 June 1938.

28. *Census of the Philippines, 1939*, 2:10, 13, 53, 112, 115, 133.
29. Foulds to Anthony Eden, 8 July 1936, FO 371/19823, reel 4, Onorato Collection; Bulletin 111, HPA, 30 June 1938; Bulletin 64, HPA, 1 June 1940.
30. Malvar interview, Quezon City, 25 Apr. 1994.
31. Morada interview, Pasig, Rizal, 2 Mar. 1994.
32. Bias interview, Pililla, Rizal, 30 Oct. 1993; Millante interview, Barangay Buenavista, Presentacion Municipality, Camarines Sur, 23 Feb. 1994. Bias served with the 41st Infantry Regiment on Bataan. Millante trained with the 2nd Sorsogon Cadre, Bulan, in 1939, and served with the 52nd Infantry.
33. "History of Moises Padilla," Negros Occidental Historical Commission Office, Bacolod; *La Vanguardia*, 3 Sept. 1936; *Philippines Herald*, 18 Jan. 1937; *Commoner*, 21 Jan. 1937; *Manila Tribune*, 17 Apr. 1937; "Minutes of the City Council of Bacolod," sessions of 16 Feb. and 13 Mar. 1939, Bacolod City Hall archives.
34. Bulletin 64, HPA, 1 June 1940.
35. I am grateful to attorney Ildefonso M. Villanueva Jr. and his staff for providing me with copies of the criminal cases filed in the Court of First Instance, Bacolod, from 1936 to 1939, for violations of the registration provisions of the National Defense Act.
36. Eisenhower, *Prewar Diaries*, 424.
37. For the 1937 training periods, about 27 percent of registrants in Manila and each province were ordered to report for military training. The exception was Cotabato, Mindanao, where 34 percent of registrants were called to service. These figures were similar to those in Japan, where in the 1930s about a quarter of annual registrants were drafted for army service. See Drea, *Service of the Emperor*, 78.
38. *Commoner*, 22 Apr. 1937.
39. "Memorandum on the increase of Military Science requirements in the University of the Philippines," Gonzales Papers.
40. Joaquin Sanchez, "Selection of Army Registrants," *Khaki and Red*, Oct. 1936, 11–12; Joves interview, Fort Bonifacio, Makati, 19 Mar. 1994. Joves commanded a battalion of the 22nd Infantry Regiment on Bataan.
41. *Camp Dau Journal*, 15 Aug. 1939; *Philippines Herald*, 29 Aug. 1938; *La Revolucion*, 8 Apr. 1937; *Khaki and Red*, Mar. 1937, 4–6, 28.
42. Lope C. Garcia interview, Tondo, Manila, 17 July 1994. According to Garcia, he and some friends, all ex-trainees, were waiting in line to enlist when he noticed the presence of white officers. Only when he asked who they were did he learn he was joining the U.S. Army, not the Philippine Army.
43. *Philippines Herald*, 28 Nov. 1940; Lee diary, 22 Apr. 1937, Lee Papers; Bulletin 170, HPA, 29 Oct. 1937. Jose, *Philippine Army*, 74–79, details the problems besetting the cadres in 1937.
44. Morton, "Philippine Army," 103–7.
45. Eisenhower, *Prewar Diaries*, 309, 429–30; undated memo. for General MacArthur, "The Philippine Defense Plan as amended 1939," box 1851, MID Regional Files: Islands: Philippines, RG 165, NA.
46. Meixsel, "Military Mission," 272.

47. *Philippine Forum* 1, no. 7 (1936): 13–14.
48. *Manila Tribune*, 31 Mar. 1937; Lim memo. for Chief of Staff, 29 Apr. 1937, box 8, James Papers.
49. F. J. Monaghan to Lim, 26 Oct. 1936; Monaghan to Cox, 27 Oct. 1936; and TAG to CGPD, 18. Jan. 1937, OTAG Central Files, 1926–1939, AG 093.5 P.I., RG 407, NA.
50. Meixsel, "Military Mission," 277–90.
51. Eisenhower, *Prewar Diaries*, 487; Bulletin 54, HPA, 28 Mar. 1938.
52. Lim, Original Letters, 1 Feb. 1939; Lim, *To Inspire and to Lead*, 59.
53. Eisenhower, *Prewar Diaries*, 342, 357, 485; Eisenhower, "Personal Estimates," McCann Papers; Ord to Eisenhower, 17 Aug. 1937, box 87, Pre-Presidential Papers, Principal File, 1916–52, EPL.
54. Craig to Watson, 17 May 1937, Woodring Papers; Eisenhower, *Prewar Diaries*, 363, 377; Harrison, *Origins*, 136; James, *Years of MacArthur*, 1:484. On Quezon's surprise that he had agreed to pay for meals too, see the exchange of correspondence between T. J. Davis and Vargas in Feb. and Mar. 1936, box 1, Davis Papers.
55. *Philippines Herald*, 11 Oct. 1938.
56. Eisenhower, *Prewar Diaries*, 411, 420; Eisenhower, *Mrs. Ike*, 150, 156; Lee diary, 14 Dec. 1937 and 19 Feb. 1938, Lee Papers.
57. Garcia to Quezon, 10 July 1918, series 7, box 374, Quezon Papers (1).
58. Eisenhower, *Prewar Diaries*, 456; Vargas to Chief of Staff, Philippine Army, 14 Feb. 1940, Davis Papers; Eisenhower to "Pete" [Maj. Francis G. Bonham], 25 Jan. 1939, Casey Papers; Eisenhower to Vargas, 16 Dec. 1939, Vargas Museum, UP Diliman.
59. Eisenhower to Martelino, 28 July 1951, in Eisenhower, *Papers of Dwight David Eisenhower*, 12:443–45; "Philippine Scouts (Native Born)," RG 18, MMA; S. Wyatt Smith to Halifax, 29 June 1939, F.O. 371/22801, box 7, Onorato Collection.

Chapter 6

1. Friend, *Between Two Empires*, 194; Eisenhower, *Prewar Diaries*, 381; *Philippines Herald*, 14 Feb. 1940; GO 4, HPA, 8 Jan. 1940; "Oral Reminiscences of John H. Chiles," box 11, James Papers; Eisenhower, *Crusade in Europe*, 5.
2. Sayre, *Glad Adventure*, 208; Meixsel, "Army for Independence?," 329; Friend, *Between Two Empires*, 193–94; Lim, *To Inspire and to Lead*, 97. See also Jose, *Philippine Army*, 137–39.
3. Eisenhower, *Prewar Diaries*, 423–24, 438; Lim, *To Inspire and to Lead*, 54–57.
4. Memo., Field Marshal MacArthur and Maj. Gen. Basilio Valdes to Quezon, 8 Dec. 1939, reel 2, RG 1, MMA; Lim, Original Letters, 3 Nov. 1939.
5. Lim, *To Inspire and to Lead*, 58, 89; *Philippines Herald*, 19 Sept. 1940.
6. Bulletin 74, HPA, 13 June 1939; Bulletin 84, HPA, 5 July 1940; Bulletin 148, HPA, 5 Oct. 1940; and Bulletin 57, HPA, 26 Apr. 1941.
7. The service requirement for fourth-year high school students would be suspended in late 1941; see "Quezon Stops High School Cadre Service," *Manila Tribune*, 27 Nov. 1941.
8. Bulletin 57, HPA, 26 Apr. 1941. Camp Murphy, built in Quezon City in 1936 and named for the then High Commissioner, is now known as Camp Aguinaldo.
9. Sturtevant, *Popular Uprisings*, 48–49; Alfred W. McCoy, "Quezon's Commonwealth: The Emergence of Philippine Authoritarianism," in Paredes, *Philippine Colonial Democracy*, 138–39.

10. Larkin, *Sugar*, 230–31; McCoy, "Quezon's Commonwealth," 139–40. For more sympathetic interpretations of Quezon's social justice program, see Sturtevant, *Popular Uprisings*, 248–51, and Gopinath, *Manuel L. Quezon*, 71–106.
11. *Philippines Free Press*, 11 Dec. 1937; memo., Lt. Col. Simeon de Jesus to Lim, 7 Feb. 1940, series 8, box 19, Quezon Papers (1).
12. Taruc, *Born of the People*, 52–53. General Tan (interview, Camp Aguinaldo, 23 May 1994) supervised acceptance boards in central Luzon and stated that no thought was given to the fear that trainees from these areas might turn on the government.
13. "Laurel on the Constitution," 1:119, Laurel Papers; Harrison, *Origins*, 73; Bulletin 36, HPA, 26 Feb. 1938.
14. Quoted in Helen N. Mendoza, "Looking Back: Days of War," in Constantino, *Under Japanese Rule*, 133. Bulletin 23, HPA, s. 1941, cited in *Citizen Army*, Sept. 1941, 26, amended ROTC participation rules.
15. "Minutes of the Board of Regents of the University of the Philippines," 16 Oct. 1941, UPDA. Student and ROTC enrollment figures can be found in the annual *Report of the President of the University of the Philippines to the Board of Regents.*
16. Details of Santo Tomas's cadet program are taken from *The Varsitarian* (school newspaper), 1940–41, *Thomasian* (school annual), 1937–41, and the unpublished "*Cronica de la Real y Pontificia Universidad de Santo Tomas*," 1936–40—all found in the University of Santo Tomas Archives, Quezon City.
17. Bulletin 61, HPA, 21 May 1940; Bulletin 166, HPA, 30 Oct. 1940; Jesus Albano, "Military Notes," *Philippine Collegian*, 25 June 1940. This was but a precursor to implementing a mandatory four-year program in 1941.
18. Nelson and Herradura, *Scientia et Fides*, 42–43.
19. *Philippines Herald*, 9 Mar., 10 May 1939; Eisenhower, *Prewar Diaries*, 472.
20. Santos, "Problems Which Confront Young Officers," *Khaki and Red*, Aug. 1938, 4–6; Meixsel, "Army for Independence?," 252–54; Quezon to Valdes, 6 July 1934, Valdes to Quezon, 7 July 1934, and Quezon to Charles Livingston, 16 Jan. 1936, series 7, box 62, Quezon Papers (1).
21. Eisenhower, *Prewar Diaries*, 430. Lim put names to specific "instances." See Lim, *To Inspire and to Lead*, 51, 58, 70, 73, 85, 89; and Jose, *Philippine Army*, 123–24, 158–59.
22. "The Philippine Defense Plan, as amended, 1939," box 1851; "Philippine Loyalty" file, anonymous report, 25 Aug. 193_, box 1852, MID Regional Files: Islands: Philippines, RG 165, NA; Lim, *To Inspire and to Lead*, 56.
23. Eisenhower, *Prewar Diaries*, 380; James, *Years of MacArthur*, 1:535–36; Lim, *To Inspire and to Lead*, 63, 85; Blesse, "Filipino Fighting Man," 6. "I am not one of those who attempt to ascribe to the Filipino any racial defect which would make it impossible for him ever to become a good officer," Eisenhower avowed (*Prewar Diaries*, 332), but other Americans were. See, for example, HPD, "Monthly Intelligence Report," 1 July 1939, MID 10641-374/15, box 1853, MID Regional Files: Islands: Philippines, RG 165, NA.
24. Presidential press conference, 3 Nov. 1937, series 8, box 79, Quezon Papers (1); *Manila Tribune*, 26 Aug. 1936.
25. Bulletin 123, HPA, 4 Oct. 1939.
26. Eisenhower, *Prewar Diaries*, 369, 419; "Wings Plucked," *Philippines Free Press*, 18 Dec. 1937.

27. *Philippines Herald*, 14 May 1938; "Talk of Major General Paulino Santos, Chief of Staff, Extemporaneously delivered before the officers of Camp Murphy, Rizal, on February 1, 1937," in Santos, "Speeches," 73; A. V. H. Hartendorp, "The Hartendorp Memoirs," *BAHC* 7, no. 4 (1979): 52; GO 5, HPA, 3 Jan. 1939.
28. Lim, Original Letters, 28 Nov. 1938, 27 Nov. 1939; Buencamino, *Memoirs of Victor Buencamino*, 201–2; Bernstein, *Philippine Story*, 183; Valdes diary, 12 Feb. 1942. General Marshall explained that Valdes had "no technical military training. He is actually a doctor whom President Quezon found very valuable in handling the matter of the development of the Philippine Army" ("Memorandum for General McNair," 8 Feb. 1943, in Bland, *Papers of George Catlett Marshall*, 3:538). Marshall ordered McNair to devise a training program that would help General Valdes "prepare himself for a combat opportunity." On Santos's relief, see also Lim, *To Inspire and to Lead*, 35–40.
29. Gwekoh, *Quezon*, 24–25, 34–38; Harrison, *Origins*, 215.
30. Quezon, *Good Fight*, 52, 55–56. For Hara's career, see Enosawa, *Quezon*, 14–16.
31. Quezon's statement is included in *Congressional Record* 48, pt. 8, 62nd Cong., 2nd Sess. (1912), 8095.
32. "Speech on the occasion of the taking of oath of office by Brigadier General Vicente Lim as Deputy Chief of Staff of the Philippine Army, at Malacañan, on May 17, 1939," *Messages of the President*, 5, pt. 1:121–24; Lim, *To Inspire and to Lead*, 61–63; Segundo, "Diary," 17 May 1939. An account of Quezon's "plain speaking" was given to the British consul-general by Lt. W. J. Given, an officer on the military mission. See R. A. Finlay to Halifax, 19 May 1939, F.O. 371/22801, British National Archives.
33. Harrison, *Origins*, 113; Eisenhower, *Prewar Diaries*, 453–55; Lim, *To Inspire and to Lead*, 62; *Philippines Herald*, 15, 19 May, 16, 17 Oct. 1939; HPD G-2, "Monthly Intelligence Report, January 1940," MID 10641-374/23, box 1854, MID Regional Files: Islands: Philippines, RG 407, NA.
34. *Philippines Herald*, 31 Oct., 1, 3 Nov. 1939.
35. *Philippines Herald*, 17 May 1939; H. C. McLean, "Formation of Department of National Defense," HPD G-2, 1 Nov. 1939, MID 2802-4, RG 165, NA; Lim, *To Inspire and to Lead*, 92.
36. *Philippines Herald*, 4 May 1939.
37. *Manila Bulletin*, 16 Dec. 1939; Meixsel, "Army for Independence?," 321–23.
38. Harrison, *Origins*, 171.
39. Office of the U.S. High Commissioner to the Philippines, "March 1940 Review of Events," 23 Apr. 1940, box 1841, MID Regional File, 1922–44: Islands: Philippines, RG 165, NA.
40. *Philippines Herald*, 2 Jan., 2, 23, 29 Mar. 1940; *Manila Bulletin*, 9 Mar. 1940; Lim, *To Inspire and to Lead*, 113.
41. Eisenhower, *Prewar Diaries*, 423; Segundo, "Diary," 16 July 1940; Lim, *To Inspire and to Lead*, 113–15; Friend, *Between Two Empires*, 193.
42. *Philippines Herald*, 1 May 1940. Cuenco couched his criticism in terms of national defense needs, but his concern may have been more parochial. Much against the national trend, Cebu's registration figures had rebounded in April 1940. The 8th Military District (Cebu and Bohol) led the Philippines in registrants that year with several thousand more than any other military district, so, therefore, a decline in the number of trainees could have a negative impact on Cuenco's legislative district.

43. Meixsel, "Army for Independence?," 325–29; Office of the U.S. High Commissioner, "March 1940 Review of Events," 23 Apr. 1940; "July 1940 Review of Events," 8 Aug. 1940, box 1841, MID Regional Files: Islands: Philippines, RG 165, NA. Publicly Segundo's transfer was ascribed to routine reassignments of general staff officers or possibly a "strategic move" to strengthen the army's presence in Mindanao, but ex-governor Harrison was told by Andres Soriano that Quezon had "disciplined" Segundo by exiling him to Parang. See Eisenhower, *Prewar Diaries*, 482, 501; Jose, *Philippine Army*, 159, 173; *Manila Daily Bulletin*, 13 Sept. 1940; and Harrison, *Origins*, 164.
44. *Annual Report of the President of the Philippines to the President and the Congress of the United States . . . 1937*, 19–20.
45. Meixsel, "Major General George Grunert," 304–5.
46. M. V. Fortier, "What About Japan," speech dated 19 Mar. 1951, Fortier Papers.
47. Blesse to Maj. Gen. Charles R. Reynolds, 4 Nov. 1938 (author's collection).
48. Meixsel, "Major General George Grunert," 312n21.
49. Ibid., 308–11.
50. Watson, *Chief of Staff*, 414, 417–19.
51. Grunert to Marshall, 2 Nov. 1940, and Memo. for the Chief of Staff, 20 Nov. 1940, approved 13 Dec. 1940, WPD 3251-39, RG 165, NA; Watson, *Chief of Staff*, 422–23.
52. Memo., Acting ACS/WPD to Chief of Staff, 26 Dec. 1940, approved 6 Jan. 1941, WPD 3251-39, RG 165, NA.
53. Acting ACS (Gerow) memos. for Chief of Staff, 26 Dec. 1940, WPD 3521-39, and 5 Feb. 1941, WPD 3251-42, RG 165, NA; Watson, *Chief of Staff*, 423; James, *Years of MacArthur*, 1:551–52.
54. *Philippines Herald*, 14 May 1938; *Philippines Free Press*, 2 Nov. 1940; *Manila Tribune*, 13 Aug. 1941; Meixsel, *Clark Field*, 28, 95; Jacobsen, *We Refused to Die*, 36–43.
55. L. S. Harrison, "Interview with Romero Family," Capas, Tarlac, 1 Apr. 2001, Romero Papers.
56. *Philippines Free Press*, 26 Oct. 1940; Lim, *To Inspire and to Lead*, 133.
57. Romero's account of his life in the army was published as "The Court Martial of Capt. Rufo C. Romero, as told by Capt. Rufo C. Romero to Celso Al. Carunungan," in twenty weekly installments, of two to four pages each, in the magazine *Kislap Graphic*, from 22 July to 2 Dec. 1959.
58. Manzano, "Memoirs"; Lim, Original Letters, 17 Oct. 1940; *United States* v. *Rufo C. Romero*, CM 215630, 4:565, RG 153, NA. For the testimony concerning the army's earlier suspicions of Romero, see CM 215630, 3:270–71, 284.
59. Lim, Original Letters, 5 Oct. 1940; Lim, *To Inspire and to Lead*, 133; *Philippines Herald*, 14 Dec. 1940.
60. Lim, Original Letters, 4 Dec. 1940.

Chapter 7

1. *Philippines Herald*, 19 Sept. 1940.
2. *New York Times*, 17 Apr. 1941; "Oral Reminiscences of Milton A. Hill," 9, box 12, James Papers.
3. Meixsel, "Major General George Grunert," 314–15; *Philippines Herald*, 3 Feb. 1941. The newspaper makes no mention of MacArthur's participation in the plan to recruit reservists, but Hunt writes that it was made "with the full approval of General MacArthur" (*War against Japan*, 6).

4. Harrison C. Browne, "Report of Operations of the Philippine Division," in Ancheta, *Wainwright Papers*, 4:4–5; *Philippine Scouts*, 153; Edward Kraus, "How They Did It," *Field Artillery Journal* 32, no. 6 (1942): 421–22.
5. Exhibit "H" to "Journal for June 1940," reel 3, RG 1, MMA; *Philippines Herald*, 11, 12, 18 Mar. 1941; *Manila Daily Bulletin*, 12 Mar. 1941. Philippine Army coast artillerymen usually trained at Fort Wint in Subic Bay, a U.S. Army fort that had been in caretaker status for many years until refurbished by the Philippine government in 1938. See "Philippine Army Coast Artillery," *Coast Artillery Journal* 81, no. 4 (1938): 310.
6. *Philippines Herald*, 8, 10 Mar. 1941; "Ten Days Active Duty," *Citizen Army*, Mar. 1941, 4–5, 14; Teofilo Sison, "Philippine National Defense," *Filipiniana Reference Shelf* 1, no. 5 (1941): 86.
7. Lim, *To Inspire and to Lead*, 163; Magtoto, "Rock of Bataan," 23.
8. *Philippines Herald*, 1 July 1941.
9. M. L. Quezon, "Philippine Loyalty to America," *Filipiniana Reference Shelf* 1, no. 7 (1941): 126.
10. *Philippines Herald*, 16 June 1941; Lim, *To Inspire and to Lead*, 165–66. Delaying the semiannual intake of trainees was the "certain decision" to which Lim was referring in this letter.
11. Porter, *Crisis in the Philippines*, 112.
12. Quoted in Meixsel, "Major General George Grunert," 316.
13. Vicente Lim, "The Unconquerable Spirit," *Filipiniana Reference Shelf* 1, no. 8 (1941): 149–50, 162.
14. Lim, *To Inspire and to Lead*, 175.
15. Ibid., 89–90.
16. Lim, Original Letters, 28 May 1941; "Philippine Collaborationists," 25 Nov. 1944, Research and Analysis Branch, Office of Strategic Services, in United States, *Japan and Its Occupied Territories* (hereafter cited as OSS); Eisenhower, *Prewar Diaries*, 423; Eisenhower, "Personal Estimates," McCann Papers.
17. Meixsel, "Major General George Grunert," 317–18. This may have been Grunert's sixtieth birthday. He had his personnel record amended during the war to show that he was born a year later than he had long thought (Grunert personnel file, NPRC).
18. Sayre, *Glad Adventure*, 209. Hill arrived in the Philippines in October 1937 and began serving with the military mission in 1938 (see James's interview for his statement). On Speth's relationship with Quezon, see Memo. for the Officer in Charge, HQ CIC Area no. 12, re Maj. E. Speth, 1 Dec. 1945, box 184, RG 65, NA.
19. *Philippines Herald*, 27 Jan. 1941.
20. Meixsel, "Major General George Grunert," 320; Lim, Original Letters, 28 May 1941.
21. Watson, *Chief of Staff*, 411–40; Morton, *Strategy and Command*, 97–98. Figures from Watson, *Chief of Staff*, 416; and Morton, *Fall of the Philippines*, 24, 49.
22. Watson, *Chief of Staff*, 425–26; Stimson diary, 21 May 1941, reel 6, Stimson Papers; Lim, *To Inspire and to Lead*, 180. See also Meixsel, "Major General George Grunert," 319n38. Marshall's letter to MacArthur, dated 20 June 1941, is reprinted in Watson, *Chief of Staff*, 435–36. Marshall wrote that the decision to place MacArthur in command of army forces in the Far East had been made "about three months ago."

23. Sayre, *Glad Adventure*, 209. The War Department later apologized for not having told Quezon "at the proper time" about the recall of MacArthur and mobilization of the army. See Elizalde to Quezon, 27 July 1941, reel 20, Quezon Papers (2).
24. Hunt, *War against Japan*, 1–2; Hunt, *Untold Story*, 208–10; Whitney, *Rendezvous with History*, 3–4; Manchester, *American Caesar*, 211. The quotes are from the third edition of the *Sunday Tribune*, 27 July 1941. It is true that the article appears near the bottom left corner of the paper's front page under the heading "late bulletins," but, in this edition at least, there is a two-line headline above the paper's masthead that reads "Roosevelt Orders P.I. Army into United States Service."
25. Lim, *To Inspire and to Lead*, 173–74.
26. See, for example, the 26 July 1941 issues of the *Philadelphia Bulletin* and the *New York Sun*. The *New York Herald Tribune*, 27 July 1941, ran two articles on the mobilization of Commonwealth forces on page 2, one of which identified MacArthur as the head of the mobilized troops; the other named Grunert.
27. Lim, *To Inspire and to Lead*, 175, 193. Sison was replaced by Serafin Marabut on 16 July 1941. Quezon appointed Valdes to be defense secretary, in addition to continuing as army chief of staff, in late December 1941.
28. Lim, *To Inspire and to Lead*, 161–65; Vicente Lim Jr., BIA name file, box 360, RG 350, NA.
29. Lim, *To Inspire and to Lead*, 181–82. Lim's original letters provide the details of Garcia's relief, most of which were excised from the published version of the letters.
30. *Manila Tribune*, 11, 13 Sept. 1941; Magtoto, "Rock of Bataan," 21; Lim, Original Letters, 14 Aug. 1941, a portion of which is reprinted in *To Inspire and to Lead*, 183–85 (misdated 19 August).
31. King to Elizabeth King, 27 July 1941, box 1, King Papers.
32. Meixsel, "Major General George Grunert," 320–22; *Manila Tribune*, 3 Sept., 4, 16, 20 Oct., 1 Nov. 1941; "Order of Battle, U.S. Army in World War II, The War Against Japan, Chapter II: First Philippine Campaign," 4, box 1481, RG 407, Philippine Archives, NA; "Remarks by Maj. Gen. Grunert, Commanding General Philippine Department, to Officers' Conference, August 22, 1941"; Grunert to George Moore, 6 Sept. 1941; and Grunert to Dr. C. K. Young, 6 Oct. 1941, in Grunert Papers.
33. Lim, *To Inspire and to Lead*, 192; Lim, Original Letters, 8 Aug. 1941; *Manila Tribune*, 24 Sept., 25 Nov. 1941.
34. *Manila Tribune*, 3 Sept. 1941.
35. Lim, Original Letters, 21 Aug. 1941; Catalan, *History of the 81st Division*, 18.
36. Mallonée, "Bataan Diary," 1:14–15, Mallonée Papers; Lim, Original Letters, 17 Nov. 1941.
37. PNG Adjutant General's undated report, series 5, box 376, Quezon Papers (1); Eisenhower, "Personal Estimates," McCann Papers; James Tierney to Ganley, 1 Mar. 1959, Ganley Papers; Lim, Original Letters, 3 June 1941; Navarro, *Beds of Nails*, 19–20. A biographical sketch of Capinpin can be found in *Philippines Herald*, 5 May 1936.
38. For dates of service, see *Philippine Army Official Register, April 1, 1941*, box 1551, RG 407, Philippine Archives, NA. Stevens held an army reserve commission in the 1920s and 1930s (in intelligence because he lacked the professional qualifications for the infantry commission he had sought) but was required to resign his commission when the PC became the PA. See Stevens personnel file, NPRC; and Wood diary, 23 Aug., 9 Dec. 1924, Wood Papers.

39. Lim, Original Letters, 7, 11 July, 5, 8 Aug., 16 Sept. 1941; Lourdes de Leon interview, Manila, 24 Mar. 1994; Magtoto, "Rock of Bataan," 83. Segundo's 1940 diary entries make very clear his unhappiness with Lim (e.g., 23 Sept., 13, 17 Oct., 2 Nov., 20 Dec.). Segundo calls Lim by a slur referring to the fact that Lim had smallpox in his youth.
40. Eisenhower, "Personal Estimates," McCann Papers; Lim, Original Letters, 12 Nov. 1941.
41. Details of Fortier's career are based on Fortier's *Life of a P.O.W.* and on information provided by his niece, who accompanied the Fortiers to the Philippines in 1940. Fortier's original personnel file no longer exists. His re-created file at NPRC consists mostly of a photocopy of Fortier's medical record.
42. Magtoto, "Rock of Bataan," 28.
43. Mallonée, "Bataan Diary," 1:1–2, Mallonée Papers; Lt. Col. Roy Hilton to Wainwright, 12 Nov. 1945, box 6, Wainwright Papers; Whitehead, *Odyssey of a Philippine Scout*, 133.
44. Quinn, *Love Letters to Mike*, 129, 259, 335.
45. Ashton, *Bataan Diary*, 22.
46. Chynoweth claimed that he was "one of a small group of colonels designated as suitable for promotion to general officer" and sent to the Philippines in November 1941. "I did *not* want to go." See "Written statement, Brig. General B. G. Chynoweth," 24 Feb. 1947, Chynoweth personnel file, NPRC (emphasis in original).
47. Chynoweth, *Bellamy Park*, 186.
48. *Manila Tribune*, 23 Oct. 1941; Leonico Tan, "Organization and Operations of the 11th Division, Reserve, PA," box 1478, RG 407, Philippine Archives, NA. Bluemel told James that he "ran" the school (interview in box 11, James Papers); Albert Jones told Toland that he had "laid out [the] courses" and was the school's most-experienced instructor (second interview, box 81, Toland Papers). Clyde Selleck wrote that he joined the staff at the school about 1 November (*War Diary*, 7).
49. *Manila Tribune*, 25 Sept., 23 Oct. 1941; Lim, Original Letters, 7 Nov. 1941; Lim, *To Inspire and to Lead*, 194.
50. F. S. Lagman, untitled paper, ca. 15 July 1943, box 620, RG 496, NA; Lim, Original Letters, 19 Oct., 2 Nov. 1941.
51. *Manila Tribune*, 25 Sept. 1941; Lim, *To Inspire and to Lead*, 201; Lim, Original Letters, 5 Aug. 1941; [R. Atienza,] "General Vicente Lim: Hero of Bataan," box 82, Toland Papers.

Chapter 8

1. Malcolm Fortier, "Notes," 14, box 4, MC; "Diary of Arthur L. Shreve, Lt. Col., FA GSC," 2, box 4, MC; Atienza, *Time for War*, 3; Magtoto, "Rock of Bataan," 68.
2. Lim, *To Inspire and to Lead*, 200; Leonico Tan interview, Camp Aguinaldo, 1 Dec. 1993; Calvin Chunn, "Notebooks," 29, box 3, MC; Jubal and Asturias, *History of the 41st Division*, 24; Atienza located this "Command Post . . . in a cowshed" in Nasugbu, where the division's advance CP was to be found (*Time for War*, 13).
3. Magtoto, "Rock of Bataan," 98; Jubal and Asturias, *History of the 41st Division*, 18–19; Fortier, "Operations of the 41st Div. (P.A.)," 14 May 1946, box 17, MC; Chunn, "Notebooks," 29, box 3, MC. The terrain of the Nasugbu-Tagatay area is described in Smith, *Triumph in the Philippines*, 222–26.

4. Pogue, *George C. Marshall*, 121–24.
5. *Manila Times*, 9 Oct. 1923; Charles Drake, "The Philippine Maneuvers," *Infantry Journal* (1926), reprinted in *Philippine Scouts*, 49–53; *Manila Daily Bulletin*, 7, 9, 10, 11 Jan. 1930.
6. Lichauco, *"Dear Mother Putnam,"* 2; Gunther, *Inside Asia*, 310.
7. Atienza, *Time for War*, 5–8, 212–13; Tagarao, *All This Was Bataan*, 3–5; William A. Gay, "Report on Road Block Mission," 13 Dec. 1941, Casey Papers.
8. Drea, *Service of the Emperor*, 14–25; Allan R. Millett, "Assault from the Sea: The Development of Amphibious Warfare between the Wars," in Murray and Millett, *Military Innovation*, 64–70.
9. Morton, *Fall of the Philippines*, 127–32; Smith, *Triumph in the Philippines*, 31.
10. Parker, "Report of Operations of South Luzon Force," in Ancheta, *Wainwright Papers*, 1:99.
11. *Reports of General MacArthur*, 2, pt. 1:82; *Philippine Operations Record*, 28.
12. Walter Edmonds, "Interview with Lt. Gen. R. K. Sutherland," Manila, 4 June 1945, Edmonds Papers; James, *Years of MacArthur*, 2:27–28. Quezon puts his meeting with MacArthur on 12 December (*Good Fight*, 194–98); the USAFFE Diary reads 10 December (RG 2, MMA).
13. Fortier, "Notes," 49, box 4, MC. See also the statement of Lt. Col. Jacobo Zobel, 22 May 1947, box 1566, RG 407, Philippine Archives, NA, which describes how vehicles were obtained to move the division.
14. Atienza, *Time for War*, 14–15.
15. León Ma. Guerrero, "Passion and Death of the USAFFE." This was the opening paragraph of a sixteen-part essay published in the *Manila Evening News* beginning on 9 April 1947.
16. Miller, *Bataan Uncensored*, 77. Morton estimated the strength of the Philippine Army at about 120,000 men, a figure that included the Constabulary and units formed after the war had started (*Fall of the Philippines*, 27). John R. Vance wrote that his office thought the size of the Philippine Army to be about 125,000 men, not including a Constabulary of about 6,000 men ("Report of Operations by the Finance Officer, USFIP," in Ancheta, *Wainwright Papers*, 4:184). Army MID files give a smaller figure (for all islands): ten Philippine Army divisions totaling 87,000 men plus three PC regiments totaling 3,000 men. See "Strength of Principal units in the Philippines, as of Dec. 20, 1941," MID 10641-374/63, box 1851, MID Regional Files: Islands: Philippines, RG 165, NA. U.S. Army strength as of 30 November 1941 was 31,095 American and Filipino officers and men (Morton, *Fall of the Philippines*, 49). Karig and Kelley estimated the number of naval service personnel in the Philippines, who eventually fell under USAFFE command, at "more than 3500" (*Battle Report*, 304). George Moore gave a total of 3,765 marines and sailors on the fortified islands in mid-April 1942 ("Report of Operations of the Harbor Defenses," in Ancheta, *Wainwright Papers*, 2:102–3).
17. Morton, *Fall of the Philippines*, 230; Golay, *Face of Empire*, 525n68.
18. Morton, *Fall of the Philippines*, 478n2, 529.
19. For air corps personnel as of 30 November 1941, see Morton, *Fall of the Philippines*, 49–50. He adds in a footnote that the figure had grown to 7,460 by 7 December, but that was the size of the air corps in Hawaii, not the Philippines. For air corps strength on Bataan, see Floyd Marshall, "Report of G-1," in Ancheta, *Wainwright*

Papers, 1:175, 178. "History of the 5th Air Force and Predecessors," 1:36 (in Edmonds Papers), puts air corps personnel "permanently assigned to the Mindanao Force" as 100 officers and 1,034 enlisted men (not including "the group of several hundred awaiting evacuation"). William Sharp gave a figure of 898 air corps personnel on Mindanao ("Historical Report on Visayan-Mindanao Force [in the] Defense of the Philippines," in Ancheta, *Wainwright Papers*, 3:47). How many got out? Maj. J. H. M. Smith wrote that 140 of the 19th Bomb Group's 210 officers were evacuated from the Philippines along with 240 of 1,300 enlisted men. See Smith, "Historical Information Concerning 19th Bombardment Group (H)," 2 Nov. 1943, reprinted in Fields, *Kangaroo Squadron*, 146.

20. Morton put the total number of troops on Bataan at "almost 80,000" but noted that after taking command of Philippine forces in late March, Wainwright informed the War Department "that he had 90,000 men on Bataan alone" (*Fall of the Philippines*, 254, 401). In *Strategy and Command*, 183, Morton accepted the latter figure as more accurate.
21. HPD G-2, "Military Handbook of the Philippines," Nov. 1923, 2:471–79, box 1876, MID Regional File, 1922–1944: Islands: Philippines, RG 165, NA.
22. *National Almanac and Guide of the Philippine Islands* (Manila: Sugar News Press, 1926), 344; HPD DP-G4, Special Plans, Color, RG 407, NA; HPD WPO-3, G-4 Annex, box 89, Special Plans, Color, RG 407, NA; Lewis, *Intercept Station C*, 9.
23. Guerrero, *Waiting for the Enemy*, 116–17; Collins, *Lightning Joe*, 65–72; Meidling, *Engineers of the Southwest Pacific*, 2:4.
24. Olson, *Anywhere-Anytime*, 13–18.
25. Morton makes the argument for why the War Department could believe that the Japanese would not attack until later (no earlier than March 1942) and possibly not at all given the growing strength of American forces in the islands (*Strategy and Command*, 99–100).
26. *Reports of General MacArthur*, 2, pt. 1:79, 81n11; Swinson, *Four Samurai*, 34–35, 45–49.
27. Stories of Japanese officers disguising themselves as servants and merchants have a long pedigree. An English governess recalled in her memoirs hearing Kaiser Wilhelm tell of an "English naval captain who had had a Japanese cook serving in the galley of his ship." Later, the captain visited a Japanese battleship and learned that his "cook" was a senior officer aboard the warship. That was in 1902. See Topham, *Distant Thunder*, 221–22. For similar tales about Japanese officers in the Philippines, see Beebe, *Prisoner of the Rising Sun*, 45. Lydia N. Yu-Jose concluded that "there were indeed spies among the Japanese community in the Philippines" (among whom was said to be Maeda) "but they were only a handful" ("World War II and the Japanese in the Prewar Philippines," *Journal of Southeast Asian Studies* 27, no. 1 [1996]: 73–74).
28. Toland, *But Not in Shame*, 149; Morton, *Fall of the Philippines*, 261–62; ACS, G-2, USAFFE to ACS, G-2, War Department, 12 Feb. 1942, "Summary of Identifications, up to present date, of Japanese units in the Philippines," box 1855, MID Regional Files, RG 165, NA; "Distinguished Officer from Japan Is Taking Advanced Class Here," *Infantry School News*, 24 Sept. 1926. Lim was quoted by Frank Hewlett in the *Washington Post*, 2 Mar. 1942, as remembering Nara to have been "a strange fellow," without elaboration.

29. Fortier, "Operations of the 41st Div. (P.A.)," 14 May 1946, box 17, MC.
30. Young, *Battle of Bataan*, 33–34; Jubal and Asturias, *History of the 41st Division*, 27; Magtoto, "Rock of Bataan," 134; Whitman, *Bataan*, 97; Morton, *Fall of the Philippines*, 266, 273–74; Atienza, *Time for War*, 29–30.
31. Magtoto, "Rock of Bataan," 146–47; Tagarao, *All This Was Bataan*, 20–21. Sources differ in the dates assigned to specific incidents. Jubal and Asturias, *History of the 41st Division*, 33–34, has Pvt. Pascual Donio return with the officer's sword on 4 January; Gumban, *Bataan Company Commander*, 21–24, dates Donio's patrol to 9 January.
32. Fortier complained of the poor quality of junior PA officers and stated that "many of them had defected on the front line, in face of enemy" (to Morton, 10 Jan. 1952, box 17, MC). But in an earlier document ("Operations of the 41st Div. (P.A.)," 14 May 1946), he wrote that the Japanese made numerous appeals "to our men to turn on us and come over to them. They had little effect." Wetherby claimed to know of "only four or five desertions" (to Ward, 4 Mar. 1952, box 2, MC). Chunn includes this statement, referring to the 42nd Infantry: "3 deserters [at Abucay] from 1 Co. No others later" ("Notebooks," 28).
33. Morton begins the battle on 9 January, citing a 65th Brigade report (*Fall of the Philippines*, 265). Whitman writes that "first blood was drawn" when several men of the 41st Infantry, on the division's right, were killed on the afternoon of 8 January, citing the reports of American officers (*Bataan*, 156). Jubal and Asturias agree that the division "had its baptism of fire on 8 January" but place the action on the left, held by the 43rd Infantry, citing two Filipino officers (*History of the 41st Division*, 34–35).
34. In "The Operations of the 41st Infantry Regiment (Philippine Army)" (Fort Benning, Advanced Infantry Officers Course, 1949–1950), William E. Webb describes the counterattack by C Co., which he commanded for this action. In *Anywhere-Anytime*, Olson makes no mention of the 41st Infantry's role in assisting the 57th Infantry. This is in keeping with the late Colonel Olson's view that the 41st Division was not reliable—"a swinging gate," he called it (personal communication with author). Webb thought the 57th Infantry's "demonstrated lack of faith in the ability of the 41st Infantry Regiment (PA) to stand up under fire" made operations less effective than they might otherwise have been. An inspecting officer reported having been told by Lim that "had it not been for him the 57th Combat Team would have been forced into the bay. (It is believed [this officer added in parenthesis] that this statement is somewhat exaggerated.)" See Lt. Col. Frank Carpenter Jr., "Memorandum for G-4, USAFFE, Fort Mills, P.I., 'Report of Inspection Trip, 13 Jan. 1942,'" box 6, OCMH Background Papers, RG 319, NA.
35. Whitman, *Bataan*, 159–60; Morton, *Fall of the Philippines*, 275–77, 285–86.
36. Atienza, *Time for War*, 59–60. Jubal and Asturias obtained from the division signals officer a slightly different version of the story (*History of the 41st Division*, 49–50). Toland shares Atienza's account of the incident but dates it to 21 January (*But Not in Shame*, 163–64).
37. Fortier, "Operations of the 41st Div. (P.A.)," box 17, MC.
38. Fortier, "Notes," 55–59, box 4, MC; Miller, *Bataan Uncensored*, 156–57; Morton, *Fall of the Philippines*, 293; Magtoto describes the actions of the covering force, which he commanded ("Rock of Bataan," 202–6).

39. Morton, *Fall of the Philippines*, 290–91n61.
40. Ancheta, *Triumph in the Philippines*, 83. For 200th and 515th Coast Artillery casualties, see Matson, *It Tolled for New Mexico*, 18–19; Cave, *Beyond Courage*, [410–11]; Jolly, *New Mexico National Guard*, 77. On the Delaware unit, see Kushner, *Bogged Down in Bora Bora*.
41. The nurses' impressions are found in Hartendorp, *Japanese Occupation of the Philippines*, 1:179. The 31st Infantry's wartime morning reports were buried on Bataan, but, while at Cabanatuan prison camp, Lt. Col. Jasper Brady, the last regimental commander, and Maj. Marshall Hurt, the regimental adjutant, prepared a roster noting what could be learned about the status of every soldier who had served with the regiment from December 1941 to April 1942. The roster was recovered in 1945. The army made copies and returned the original to Brady's widow, who further annotated it. In preparation of a history of the 31st Infantry, the late regimental association historian, Col. Karl Lowe, USA, Ret., calculated the regiment's losses based on the prison camp roster and other data. He determined that 135 members of the regiment had been killed in action in the Philippines.
42. McElhenny et al., *Armor on Luzon*, 49. On losses in the tank group, see also J. R. N. Weaver, "Report of the Operations of the Provisional Tank Group," in Ancheta, *Wainwright Papers*, 2:159.
43. Chunn, "Notebooks," 49–52. John Poncio, an enlisted veteran of the 91st Bomb Squadron, a component of the 27th Bomb Group and of the air corps regiment on Bataan, guessed that his squadron had "about five men [killed] and only a few wounded" (Poncio and Young, *Girocho*, 50). Another member of the regiment, Clarence Larson, mentioned the death of one comrade, killed in an aerial bombardment (*Long March Home*, 41). Mary Cathrin May lists two enlisted men (and no officers) of this squadron killed before 9 April 1942 (*Steadfast Line*, 178–81). Known dead prior to 9 April for other units of the 27th are the following: headquarters squadron, six killed (five on Bataan); 16th Bomb Squadron, no confirmed deaths; 17th Bomb Squadron, one possible death; 48th Materiel Squadron, three dead. Another twelve men in the bomb group are listed as dead or missing (and possibly dead) on 9 April. Of the 18 officers and 211 enlisted men assigned to the 34th Pursuit Squadron, which fought at Quinauan Point, four died on Bataan. See the roster in Oatman, *Only the Beginning*, 341–43. Bartsch put the 21st Pursuit Squadron's losses on the west coast action at "six killed and an undetermined number wounded" (*Doomed at the Start*, 302). Another veteran who served with the 20th Pursuit Squadron on Bataan, Gene S. Jacobsen, included a unit roster with his memoir of Philippine service; according to him, once the unit withdrew into Bataan, it lost three men killed in action prior to the surrender, two pilots shot down, and one enlisted man killed at Mariveles in March 1942 (*We Refused to Die*, 263–68). Bartsch wrote that no one in the 20th Pursuit was killed "during its west coast [of Bataan] tenure," though one man was injured in an accident (*Doomed at the Start*, 321). Two officers, but no enlisted men, in the 17th Pursuit Squadron were also killed in action fighting along the west coast (Chunn, "Notebooks," 49). One veteran of the 803rd Aviation Engineers who had been pressed into service as an infantryman recalled that "except for the airplanes, we hardly saw Jap troops during the battle for Bataan." See John Zubay, "We Ate the Rice, Bugs and All," in Wissolik and Killen, *There Was a War*, 509.

44. Condit and Turnbladh, *Hold High the Torch*, 240, and Hough, Ludwig, and Shaw, *Pearl Harbor to Guadalcanal*, 200, 395, state that the marines lost a total of 331 men (killed in action, died of wounds, or missing and presumed dead) in the Philippine Campaign, the "great majority" on Corregidor. However, Morton, citing a history of the navy medical department in World War II, gave a figure of 89 marines and 339 sailors killed in action or died of wounds in the Philippines from 7 December 1941 to 6 May 1942 (*Strategy and Command*, 586). This figure is also accepted by Miller, in *From Shanghai to Corregidor*, 42.
45. Scout losses are listed in *Philippine Scouts*, 486–95. Casualty figures for the 57th Infantry can also be found in Olson, *Anywhere-Anytime*, 191, 221–31; and those for the field artillery in Rosen, *Philippine Scouts Field Artillery*, Annex H. William Jones, an officer who served with the 14th Engineers in the late 1930s, compiled a list of those killed in that regiment up to the surrender of Bataan: no officers; thirty-three enlisted men, twenty-two of them from 5 to 9 April 1942. Copy in Harrison Collection.
46. *Philippine Operations Record*, 242. USAFFE losses are categorized as "American Army" and "Philippine Army" and divided into the Bataan Peninsula period (9 January–9 April) and the Corregidor period (10 April–4 May). Ancheta reads that "from the beginning of January until the 9th of April, more than 2100 Americans and Filipinos were killed in Bataan. Of these, about 600 were American" (*Triumph in the Philippines*, 94). The Statistical and Accounting Branch of the Office of the Adjutant General, in *Army Battle Casualties and Nonbattle Deaths in World War II, Final Report* (1 June 1953), 95, ultimately calculated that 1,909 officers and men of the U. S. Army (including Philippine Scouts) had been killed in action in the Philippines from 7 December 1941 to 10 May 1942. That figure includes losses on Corregidor and in the southern islands and also includes deaths of prisoners of war, since the army counted as killed in action many soldiers who died while prisoners. On the army's definition of killed in action, see Memo. re case of Rufino Tagarino, PS, from commanding officer, Military Personnel Records Center, to chief, Comptroller Division, Office of the Adjutant General, Records Management Section, 24 May 1954, box 1536, RG 407, Philippine Archives, NA. By way of example, the Armored School calculated that 47 soldiers in the tank group had been killed in action prior to 9 April 1942; an additional 164 had been killed in action as POWs (McElhenny, "Armor on Luzon," 49). The Philippine Archives, box 20, RG 407, NA, holds a "Casualty listing of enlisted men who were in the Philippine Islands area as of 7 December 1941." This machine-generated list includes 28,066 names of Americans and Philippine Scouts. Box 6 holds an "Alphabetical casualty listing of officers who were in the Philippine Islands area as of 7 December 1941" of 2,992 names. The lists contain obvious errors. General Grunert's name, for example, is on the officer list. Many of the Philippine Scouts are shown as missing in action. A name-by-name count of these lists resulted in the identification of 383 American enlisted men killed in action, 448 enlisted PS killed in action, and 184 officers killed in action.
47. These Americans killed while serving with the 41st Division on Bataan were Thomas Spears, Lee Louderback, Allen Estep, Lloyd Balt, John Rossick, Newton L. Mathews Jr., Clyde Smock, and Gaylord Fraser. Whitman notes the death of another American assigned to the division, Lt. Col. R. G. MacDonald (*Bataan*, 481); however, MacDonald died as a POW. Guerrero tells of the death of Capt.

Lawrence Smarr, an artillery officer who joined the 41st Field Artillery near the end of the campaign (*Waiting for the Enemy*, 439–40). Guerrero, a reserve officer in the Philippine Army, had served with Smarr in the 88th FA (PS) and was told that Smarr had been killed on 3 April 1942, but Smarr survived Bataan, only to die on the *Enoura Maru.* Major Fraser, a reserve officer who had commanded D Co., 31st Infantry (U.S.), before the war, achieved legendary status among Filipino veterans of the 41st Division. He was killed by a combination of rifle and mortar fire while leading a specially trained sniper platoon forward of the Orion-Bagac line on 25 February 1942. On the formation of the platoon and Fraser's death, see Fortier, "Notes," 71–73, box 4, MC; Jubal and Asturias, *History of the 41st Division*, 70–72; and Magtoto, "Rock of Bataan," 239–41.

48. In *Fall of the Philippines*, 586, Morton concluded that the lack of clerical personnel, illiterate senior NCOs, and the scarcity of paper on Bataan meant that combat units—that is, most units in the Philippine Army, which had little logistical or administrative "tail"—"even if they had wished to do so, could not have complied with [recordkeeping] regulations." That "many first sergeants and company clerks could neither read nor write" was a claim made by General Sharp ("Historical Report on Visayan-Mindanao Force," in Ancheta, *Wainwright Papers*, 3:9). This was not likely to be true in the 41st Division, because Philippine Army assignment policy sent many ROTC cadets into the NCO ranks (only the top graduates got commissions); however, there was at least one American soldier, a Private Workman from the Coast Artillery, assigned to the 41st Division as a clerk. Presumably he maintained records concerning the Americans assigned to the division.
49. See Chunn, "Notebooks," 31 (for 43rd Infantry casualties); and Wetherby to Orlando Ward, 4 Mar. 1952, box 2, MC, and K. C. Emerson, "The Operations of the II Philippine Corps on Bataan, 10 January–8 April 1942," box 81, Toland Papers (for 41st Infantry losses). Henry Harris (in Chunn, "Notebooks," 33) dated the friendly fire incident to about 13 January and gave the figure of six killed, but Lim complained that Scout artillery had killed three men in his division and wounded five more (see Carpenter, "Report of Inspection Trip 13 January, 1942"). Former governor-general Harrison was told either by Quezon or by members of his party who had escaped from the Philippines in early 1942 that "there were not very many [American and Filipino enlisted men] killed" on Bataan but that losses among officers had been higher (Harrison, *Origins*, 145, 147).
50. *New York Times*, 2 Mar. 1942; *Los Angeles Times*, 2 Mar. 1942; Lim, *To Inspire and to Lead*, 205, 210. Aside from a handful of PA medals authorized by Quezon mostly to officers involved in guerrilla activities, Philippine Army soldiers received U.S. medals during the war. However, when in the 1990s the army evaluated nonwhite DSC holders for possible receipt of Medals of Honor, it decided that PA soldiers were ineligible for the higher award. See James C. McNaughton, Kristen E. Edwards, and Jay M. Price, "'Incontestable Proof will be Exacted': Historians, Asian Americans, and the Medal of Honor," *Public Historian* 24, no. 4 (2002): 22, 26–27, 31.

Chapter 9

1. "Homage to Bataan," *Yank*, 8 July 1942, 8–9.
2. Quoted in Dod, *Corps of Engineers*, 99; "Inspection trip of Lt. Delamore," 11 Feb. 1942, Casey Papers.

3. White, *They Were Expendable*, 73.
4. *Reader's Digest*, July 1942, 1–4, 155–68; Morton, *Fall of the Philippines*, 444; Ancheta, *Triumph in the Philippines*, 78; Whitman, *Bataan*, 528–31; Coleman, *Bataan and Beyond*, 58. See also the remarks of Capt. Mark Wohlfeld in Knox, *Death March*, 99–101, and Larson, *Long March Home*, 41–43.
5. Miller, *General Douglas MacArthur*, 237; Melville Jacoby, "MacArthur's Men: Bataan War Produces a Crop of Fabulous Fighters," *Life*, 16 Mar. 1942, 14–23.
6. *Life*, 20 July 1942, 34–35.
7. Office of Special Services, Commonwealth of the Philippines, "The Epic of Bataan." Quezon spoke extemporaneously at the meeting rather than use his prepared address. See Harrison, *Origins*, 204, and Manuel L. Quezon, "The Undying Spirit of Bataan," *New York Times*, 4 Apr. 1943.
8. Dooley diary, 16, 22 Jan. 1942, RG 135, MMA; Bunker and Barlow, *Bunker's War*, 29, 127; Fertig, "Diary, 1942," box 8, RG 53, MMA; James Cavanaugh, 28th Bomb Squadron, quoted in Knox, *Death March*, 58–59; Larson, *Long March Home*, 45.
9. Office of the Chief of Staff to ACS/WPD, 31 July 1939, box 1851, MID Regional Files: Islands: Philippines, RG 165, NA; Mackechnie, "Our Two Years in the Philippines," 55–57, Harrison Collection.
10. Robert M. Carswell, "Philippine National Defense," *Coast Artillery Journal* 84, no. 2 (1941): 121–24; Edward Kraus, "How They Did It," *Field Artillery Journal* 32, no. 6 (1942): 421; Tarkington, "There Were Others," 8–10, box 5, MC.
11. Mallonée, "Bataan Diary," 1:1–7, Mallonée Papers.
12. A. C. Smith to Carl Ackerman, 13 Nov. 1953, and Kent Greenfield to Bancroft Prize Committee, 10 Nov. 1953, box 8, RG 319, NA; Morton, *Fall of the Philippines*, 585–601.
13. Morton to Colonel Badger, 12 Mar. 1948, box 2, MC; Morton memo. for CMH, 31 Jan. 1952, box 8, RG 319, NA.
14. Morton, *Fall of the Philippines*, 30.
15. Romulo memo. for Chief of Staff, 29 May 1942, box 1, Romulo Papers; Chester, *Sailor's Odyssey*, 136–37; W. E. Brougher, "The Battle of Bataan," box 3, MC; Morris L. Shoss to Beck, 28 Sept. 1969, quoted in Beck, *MacArthur and Wainwright*, 283n27.
16. Bluemel to George Groce, 15 June 1948, box 3, MC; Bluemel to Lilly, 1 Apr. 1963, Lilly Papers; Bluemel to D. Clayton James, 14 Aug. 1972, box 14, James Papers.
17. Vance wrote that, on Corregidor, Filipinos were the only ones who would speak freely about the war and that some wanted "the officers responsible for the destruction of the air corps at Clark and Iba Fields on December 8 court-martialed and shot" (*Doomed Garrison*, 90).
18. Morton to Hanson Baldwin, 18 Nov. 1953, Baldwin Papers; Baldwin, "Bitter Road to an Epic Defeat," *New York Times*, 27 Dec. 1953; Sutherland interview, 12 Nov. 1946, box 2, MC; Huff to Morton, 4 June 1948, box 6, RG 319, NA.
19. James, *Years of MacArthur*, 3:668–69; Coox, *Unfought War*, 9.
20. *Reports of General MacArthur*, 2, pt. 1:107, 110. Willoughby told James that *MacArthur, 1941–1951* was "a digest of the four volumes of 'The Reports of General MacArthur'" ("Oral Reminiscences of Charles A. Willoughby," box 13, James Papers). For a discussion of the similarity of MacArthur's various memoirs and reports, see James, *Years of MacArthur*, 3:671, 683–85.

21. Morton, "Decision to Withdraw to Bataan," in *Command Decisions*, 164. This article was taken almost entirely from the text of *Fall of the Philippines*, with the quoted sentence added.
22. Pugh, "Diary," 9 Apr. 1942, quoted in Beck, *MacArthur and Wainwright*, 196–97; Cabot Coville [second secretary in the Office of the High Commissioner] to Secretary of State, 11 Jan. 1942, in *Foreign Relations*, 1:884; for Willoughby's statements, "Oral Reminiscences of Harold K. Johnson," box 11, James Papers. Quezon's message, dated 8 Feb. 1942, is reprinted in *Foreign Relations*, 1:894–95; Roosevelt's response to MacArthur, dated 9 Feb., is found in Eisenhower, *Papers of Dwight David Eisenhower*, 1:104–5. The editors add that Eisenhower authored the message and that his original text read "the Filipino troops could be placed by you under the command of a Filipino officer who would conduct actual negotiations with the enemy" (106n2). See also James, *Years of MacArthur*, 2:94–97, and Friend, *Between Two Empires*, 218–23, for a discussion of the context in which Quezon's suggestion was made.
23. White, *They Were Expendable*, 73.
24. Anselmi, "Colonel Robert Besson," 19–20. This is an edited version of Besson's wartime diary.
25. Mallonée, *Battle for Bataan*, 120; Mallonée, "Bataan Diary," 2:6–7, Mallonée Papers; Maj. A. C. Tisdelle Jr., "Story of Bataan Collapse," Baldwin Papers.
26. Bluemel's letter is reprinted as an appendix in Masi, "MacArthur's Defense."
27. Stroh, "Letterbook," 159, 166–67; Scholes to family, 11 Apr. 1941 and [no day] Aug. 1941, Harrison Collection; Lee, *Nothing but Praise*, 77; Sorley, *Honorable Warrior*, 45–46.
28. Morton, *Fall of the Philippines*, 34; Casey to CG USAFFE, "Increase in Philippine Scouts," 9 Feb. 1942, Casey Papers; *Philippine Scouts*, 320, 328; Olson, *Anywhere-Anytime*, 154–55; Browne, "Philippine Division," in Ancheta, *Wainwright Papers*, 4:28.
29. White, *They Were Expendable*, 73; Toland, *But Not in Shame*, 160–61. The division history places General Capinpin in the area at that time. See Cariño, *History of the 21st Division*, 128–29.
30. A. M. Jones to Groce, 29 Sept. 1949, box 6, RG 319, NA; Alexander, *Surviving Bataan and Beyond*, 119–20.
31. GO 49, Forward Headquarters 51st Division, 24 Jan. 1942, handwritten citation included with A. M. Jones to King, 19 Feb. 1946, box 2b, King Papers.
32. Chief, USMAG to CINC Far East, included in "Report by the Joint Staff Planners to the JCS on Joint U.S. Military Advisory Group to the Republic of the Philippines," 14 Oct. 1947, box 74, RG 165, NA. Pugh, quoted in Beck, *MacArthur and Wainwright*, 196.
33. "American officers with combat troops units," 3 Feb. 1942, box 29, RG 496, NA; Montgomery, "I Hired Out to Fight," 38–39, Montgomery Papers; Rutledge, *My Japanese POW Diary Story*, 19.
34. Alexander, *Surviving Bataan and Beyond*, 119–20; Peña, *Bataan's Own*, 112.
35. Morton, *Fall of the Philippines*, 107, 224; Cariño, *History of the 21st Division*, 99; Catalan and Calderon, *History of the 51st Division*, 85; Baclagon, *They Served with Honor*, 6.

36. Copies of the letters exchanged between Bluemel and Jimenez can be found in box 82, Toland Papers. Portions of Jimenez's letters are reprinted in Pestaño, *History of the 31st Division*, 67–68.
37. George Groce to K. L. Berry, 23 Jan. 1950, box 2, MC.
38. Rogers, *Bitter Years*, 241–42.
39. Fortier, "Notes," 80, 107, box 4, MC; Morton, *Fall of the Philippines*, 268; Beck, *MacArthur and Wainwright*, 66–68; and James, *Years of MacArthur*, 2:52–53, offer similar descriptions of the trip.
40. Baldwin, *Great Mistakes of the War*, 73; Wainwright, quoted in Toland, *But Not in Shame*, 268.
41. Callahan, "Boys Letter," 5:18–19, Callahan Papers; Fortier, "Notes," 80, box 4, MC; T. H. Delamore, "Inspection Trip of Lt. Delamore, 2-9/10-42," 11 Feb. 1942, and Casey to Col. W. F. Heavey, 15 Oct. 1946, Casey Papers.
42. "Second interview with Albert Jones," box 81, Toland Papers; Gay, "Inspection of Major Gay, 2-1-42 to 2-3-42," 3 Feb. 1942, Casey Papers.
43. Schultz, *Hero of Bataan*, 35–42.
44. "Infantry adviser to the C[ommanding] G[eneral] [of the Philippine Division]" was Parker's designation in the 16 July 1941 issue of the Philippine Department directory. The billet does not exist in earlier directories.
45. Morton, "Interview with Maj. Gen. R. J. Marshall," 7 Apr. 1948, box 2, MC; Bluemel to King, 2 Aug. 1946, box 2b, King Papers. Bluemel stated that "Wainwright had already committed himself on the matter" of Parker's relief. Bluemel expected to be the new corps commander. See also the "Oral Reminiscences" of James V. Collier and H. K. Johnson, box 11, and Joseph L. Chabot, box 13, James Papers; and MacArthur, *Reminiscences*, 113.
46. King to Parker, 23 Jan. 1946, box 2a, King Papers; Parker, "Report of Operations," in Ancheta, *Wainwright Papers*, 1:115.
47. Fortier to Wainwright, 14 Nov. 1945, Fortier Papers.
48. Fortier to Morton, 10 Jan. 1952, box 17, MC; Parker to Fortier, 10 Jan. 1946, Fortier Papers; Parker to King, 13 Jan. 1946, box 2a, King Papers.
49. Fortier to Wainwright, 4 Oct. 1945; Fortier to MacArthur, 5 Nov. 1945; and Bluemel to Fortier, 17 Dec. 1956, Fortier Papers. Lim and Fortier are indexed four times each in *Fall of the Philippines*, but the references only identify Lim as the 41st Division commander. Fortier is first identified as the division's senior instructor on a fifth, unindexed page (251n26). Even when Fortier provided Morton with documentation noting Lim's participation in some event (e.g., at 286, describing a meeting of senior officers at the 41st Division CP on 18 January), Morton left Lim's name out of the text.
50. Atienza, *Time for War*, 25; Jubal and Asturias, *History of the 41st Division*, 50.
51. Fortier, "Memorandum to General Wainwright," 14 Nov. 1945; and Fortier to Maxon Lough, 17 July 1955, Fortier Papers; Fortier, "Notes," 18–19, box 4, MC; Quezon to Lim, 15 Jan. 1942, and Lim to Quezon, 23 Jan. 42, Hall Collection.
52. Magtoto, "Rock of Bataan," 136–37; Ashton, *Bataan Diary*, 127.
53. Winston Jones telephone interview, 20 July 1996. Jones, who died in 1996, is believed to have been the last surviving American to have served with the 41st Division.
54. Wainwright's comments comprise the fourth endorsement of Fortier's promotion request, dated 11 Jan. 1946, Fortier Papers. See also Fortier to Wainwright, 1 Jan. and

13 Apr. 1946, and Wainwright to Fortier, 16 Apr. 1946, box 8, Wainwright Papers. Fortier retired from the army in 1950 and suffered a fatal heart attack while playing golf in Seattle, Washington, in 1958. He had persisted in trying to interest senior officers and politicians in his case but was never advanced to brigadier general.

55. On Garcia see Gay, "Report of Incident with Colonel Garcia," 6 Jan. 1942, Casey Papers; Underbrink, *Destination Corregidor*, 145–46; and Chynoweth, *Bellamy Park*, 230. On the transfer of officers—"some of them are excellent and some are no good"—from Bataan and Corregidor to Panay, see Sutherland to Chynoweth, 19 Feb. 1942, in Rogers, *Bitter Years*, 313–14. On Martelino see Fortier, "Notes," 77, box 4, MC; and Chunn, "Notebooks," 32, box 3, MC.

56. Mallonée, *Battle for Bataan*, 113–16.

57. HPD G-2, "Philippine Army—Composition and Combat Estimate," 26 Mar. 1941, MID 2802-9/1, RG 165, NA; Peña, *1st Regular Division*, 10–11, 31.

58. Peña, *1st Regular Division*, 17–20; Rio, *Rays of a Setting Sun*, 40–41. Rio was Segundo's aide. See also R. T. Jose, "Beach Defense: The First Regular Division at Mauban, December 23–26, 1941," *BAHC* 17, no. 2 (1989): 7–24; and McCoy, *Closer than Brothers*, 79–85.

59. Peña, *1st Regular Division*, 38, 99–100; and Young, *Battle of Bataan*, 177 (citing Peña), are the exceptions. Dumas survived the war but did not contribute to the official history. His personnel record at NPRC includes no mention of his assignment to the Philippine Army.

60. "Someone had to shoulder the blame for the rupture of the M[ain] L[ine of] R[esistance]," wrote Peña, *1st Regular Division*, 99. Magtoto was also of the opinion that Segundo had been relieved as a result of his division's failure to prevent Japanese penetration of the new line of defense ("Rock of Bataan," 212–13). Both officers must have known that Segundo had already fallen into disfavor because of the incident that had taken place when his division had been cut off above Mauban. While preparing the official campaign history, army historian George Groce was told that after the Japanese had blocked the West Road, Segundo "put on civilian clothes and took off" (Groce to K. L. Berry, 23 Jan. 1950, box 3, MC; Berry to OCMH, 11 Jan. 1952, box 8, RG 319, NA). Conrado B. Rigor, who served on the division staff, wrote (in Peña, *1st Regular Division*, 133) that while trapped north of the roadblock, Segundo "pointed out that the craggy western shoreline was the only possible avenue of exit [and then] showed up alone and unescorted at GHQ in blue denim outfit [a Philippine Army uniform normally worn by enlisted men] without insignia." General Segundo's daughter stated that she had been told by the general's aide that they (General Segundo and his chief of staff, Santiago Guevara, who was also relieved of duty) had removed their uniforms in order to pass themselves off as fishermen during the escape (Lourdes de Leon interview, Manila, 24 Mar. 1994). Magtoto explained that Segundo put on the denim uniform so that Japanese snipers would not recognize him as an officer as he made his way back "to his command post along the coastline" ("Rock of Bataan," 200). Years later, in *Filipinos at War*, 209, Carlos Quirino included an insulting anecdote about Segundo that seems to have reflected what many Bataan veterans had come to think about the episode (author's interviews with Quirino and other former officers). See also Buencamino, *Memoirs and Diaries*, 51, 99.

Former governor-general Harrison was told by Andres Soriano, who made his way to Washington from Corregidor, that Segundo "was always uncertain

[and] should not have fallen back at the first day's battle at Morong [Moron]." See Harrison, *Origins*, 164. See also Brig. Gen. C. Bluemel, USA, Ret., comments on "Fall of the Philippines," box 2, MC; and Houston Houser to Morton, 18 Mar. 1947, box 12, MC. These two sources emphasize Segundo's failure to make contact with forces east of Mount Natib. Edwin Ramsey, an officer with the 26th Cavalry (PS), claims to have witnessed Wainwright berate Segundo for having withdrawn troops from Moron, a coastal village to the north of Mauban, prior to the Japanese attack on I Corps. See Ramsey and Rivele, *Lieutenant Ramsey's War*, 64; and "Oral History Transcript, Edward [*sic*] Price Ramsey," California State Military Museum (at www.militarymuseum.org/Ramsey.html), 28, 32. In his diary, Wainwright makes no mention of Segundo's relief, which he later wrote was done on MacArthur's orders (see "Certificate for K. L. Berry," 6 July 1946, box 7, Wainwright Papers). Colonel Berry took Segundo's place as division commander on 9 February 1942. Segundo remained a lieutenant colonel in the U.S. Army, the rank to which he had been promoted in 1940. His general officer rank came from the Philippine Army. See GHQ AFP, Military Personnel Status Board, "Memorandum for Record," 31 Jan. 1956, Segundo personnel file (recreated), NPRC.

61. Fortier to Morton, 10 Jan. 1952, box 17, MC; Lim, *To Inspire and to Lead*, 201; Magtoto, "Rock of Bataan," 154, 161, 258.
62. Olson, *Anywhere-Anytime*, 19, 78, 139; Col. Edmund J. Lilly Jr., "Notebook #19," 2, Lilly POW Papers; Collier, "Notebooks," 3:27, box 13, MC; Sorley, *Honorable Warrior*, 45–48. On the problems of command in the 57th Infantry (PS), see also H. K. Johnson, "Diary," box 7, MC. In a letter to Carlos Romulo, 8 Feb. 1944 (box 2, Romulo Papers), Clarke claimed to have seen much of Lim—a friend of long standing—on Bataan. Magtoto opined that it was Lim's report to II Corps of his "observation of the 57th Infantry and its regimental commander" that led to Clarke's replacement ("Rock of Bataan," 153).
63. The 45th Infantry was ordered to Corregidor but was unable to make its way to Mariveles at the time of surrender. Callahan wrote that when Doyle received the order to move the 45th to Corregidor, he "sought safety in flight" ("Boys Letter," 5:25–27, Callahan Papers). One of those Doyle brought with him was his medical officer, William Donovan, who claimed that MacArthur had ordered that Doyle be evacuated from the Philippines. See Donovan, *P.O.W. in the Pacific*, 34–38, and the comments in Vance, *Doomed Garrison*, 125–26.
64. Morton, "Interview with Maj. Gen. R. J. Marshall," 7 Apr. 1948, box 2, MC; Morton, *Fall of the Philippines*, 304–5; Olson, *Anywhere-Anytime*, 124; Whitman, *Bataan*, 139–40, 274–75; Collier, "Notebooks," 3:15–17, box 13, MC; Wainwright diary, 4, 18 Dec. 1941, box 3, Wainwright Papers; Christensen telephone interview, 30 Dec. 1996; Sorley, *Honorable Warrior*, 45–48. After the war, Selleck unsuccessfully petitioned the army for the return of his general's rank and remained forever embittered toward MacArthur and Sutherland. When James asked for an interview, Selleck responded that he could not talk about "these two men whom I hate so much" (transcript of telephone conversation, 22 June 1971, box 13, James Papers). See also Wainwright to Selleck, 14 Dec. 1945, and Wainwright memo. for Wade Haslip, 28 Feb. 1946, box 11, Wainwright Papers.
65. Whitman, *Bataan*, 145; Olson, *Anywhere-Anytime*, 77; Lilly, "Notebook #19," 8, 12, Lilly POW Papers.

66. Whitman, *Bataan*, 81, 86; 31st U.S. Infantry roster, RG 15, MMA.
67. Montgomery, "I Hired Out to Fight," 64, Montgomery Papers.
68. Chunn, "Notebooks," 28–29, box 3, MC; Fortier, "Notes," 74, 77, 81, box 4, MC; Magtoto, "Rock of Bataan," 73, 77, 99–100. On Moore see also Groce interview with Lt. Col. Charles E. N. Howard, 14 June 1948, box 2, MC. Disciplinary records were apparently not among the documents evacuated from Bataan or Corregidor, but one officer told his family, in a letter sent from Bataan in late February, that he "had been handling a number of general and special courts-martial." Quoted in Heisinger, *Father Found*, 159.
69. Alexander to Willoughby, 24 Feb. 1942, box 1, Romulo Papers.
70. Fortier, "Memorandum to General Wainwright," 14 Nov. 1945; and Fortier to Maxon Lough, 17 July 1955, Fortier Papers; Fortier, "Notes," 78, box 4, MC; Gay, "Inspection I Corps, 2-28-42," 1 Mar. 1942, Casey Papers; Peña, *1st Regular Division*, 69.
71. Edward Alcorn questionnaire, 27 Aug. 1999, Harrison Collection. Alcorn was on Corregidor in 1940–42 and helped train Philippine Army coast artillerymen before the war. "A number of times I observed American servicemen both drunk and sober being abusive to Filipinos," Alcorn wrote; ". . . I have never heard a Filipino talk disrespectful to an American." On racial incidents and attitudes in the immediate prewar period, see also the comments of Lichauco, *"Dear Mother Putnam,"* 31; of Thomas Hayes about the army's treatment of Col. Manuel Olympia, PA, in Hayes, *Bilibid Diary*, 9–11; and of Paul R. Hawley, in "The Probable Effect on the Natives of Luzon, P.I., of an Exclusively Close-in Defense of Corregidor," Army War College study for the 1938–39 class, copy in AWC Curricular Archives, 7-1939-69, USAMHI.
72. Buenafe, *Wartime Philippines*, 97–98; Toland, *Rising Sun*, 266; Buencamino, *Memoirs and Diaries*, 38, 49; Sevilla, *Bataan Odyssey*, 65; Thomas, *As I Remember*, 109; Houston Turner questionnaire, n.d., Harrison Collection; Christensen telephone interview, 30 Dec. 1996. Manzano is quoted in Molina, *Dusk and Dawn*, 83. Quezon's son, Manuel L. Quezon Jr., also mentioned a complaint by a priest visiting Corregidor from Bataan just before the Quezons' escape "of the American treatment of the Filipino soldiers." On Aquino see the longer account in Toland, *But Not in Shame*, 187–88 (in which Toland clarifies that Aquino took a boat most of the way to Corregidor and swam the remaining distance) and the comments of Mallonée in *Battle for Bataan*, 91–92.
73. Olson, *Anywhere-Anytime*, 44; Friend, *Between Two Empires*, 213.
74. Agoncillo, *Burden of Proof*, 21.
75. Questions posed to G. B. Francisco by Masaru Ogawa, copy in Francisco Papers; Gloria, *All the Way*, 53–54; Bias interview, Pililla, Rizal, 30 Oct. 1993; Casillan, *My Life and Times*, 38; Jalandoni, *Silent Sacrifice*, 8. Casillan served with the 31st Division (PA) in a regiment commanded by an American; Jalandoni was recalling the commander of his unit, the 72nd Infantry (PA), during its prewar training period. For a claim that American advisers did receive better rations, see the Filipino-authored "History of the 21st Division (PA)," 41, box 17, MC. Mallonée agreed that Americans did get an "extra issue" of a few items that gave "a small luxurious taste of American-type food" though did little, he thought, to improve their physical condition ("Diary," 2:11, Mallonée Papers).
76. Tagarao, *All This Was Bataan*, 83, 108. See also the comments of Sevilla in *Bataan Odyssey*, 66.

77. Mallonée, *Battle for Bataan*, 113.
78. Gay, "Inspection of I Corps, 2-28-42," 1 Mar. 1942; and T.H.D., memo re "Telephone Call Major Barrett," 1 Mar. 1942, Casey Papers.
79. Buencamino, *Memoirs and Diaries*, 49; Osborne interview, box 85, Toland Papers. MacArthur's recommendation was brought to the troops' attention in GO 31, USAFFE HQ, 22 Feb. 1942. See also the comments on this issue by General Marshall, in "Memorandum for the President," 10 Mar. 1942, in Bland, *Papers of George Catlett Marshall*, 3:125–26.
80. Fortier, "Notes," 80–82, box 4, MC; Mallonée, *Battle for Bataan*, 115; "Inspection Trip of Lt. Delamore," 11 Feb. 1942, Casey Papers (for a comment about an unhappy American officer in the 41st Division). Staff officer Arthur Christensen wrote of Bluemel that he "was hot tempered and often turned on anyone near him with harsh and often obscene language. . . . If the Filipinos thought [Bluemel] was anti-Filipino, most Americans thought that he was anti-them" (Christensen questionnaire, 15 Oct. 1996, author's collection). See also the comments in Bruce Moore, "Strong to Endure: The Story of Capt. George Moore during World War II," *BAHC* 28, no. 2 (2000): 50–51. Moore joined the 45th Infantry (PS) in 1940, then under Bluemel's command.
81. Morton, *Fall of the Philippines*, 389n104.
82. [R. Atienza,] "General Vicente Lim: Hero of Bataan," box 82, Toland Papers; Dyess, *Dyess Story*, 49, 65. Ed Dyess was an aviator who had insisted on staying behind with his men, while so many other officers elected to fly south.

Chapter 10

1. Go, *Hour Had Come*, 50–51; Magtoto, "Rock of Bataan," 232–33; Agoncillo, *Fateful Years*, 160; Pobre, *History of the Armed Forces*, 290–91; [Atienza,] "General Vicente Lim"; Baclagon, *Philippine Resistance Movement*, 54n9.
2. Morton, *Fall of the Philippines*, 351–52.
3. Ibid., 326–27, 329.
4. Atienza, *Time for War*, 74–75; Montgomery, "I Hired Out to Fight," 40, Montgomery Papers; Fortier, "Notes," 60, 62, box 4, MC; Fortier to Morton, 10 Jan. 1952, box 17, MC.
5. Morton, *Fall of the Philippines*, 326; Whitman, *Bataan*, 340.
6. Lim, *To Inspire and to Lead*, 205; Fortier, "Notes," 63, box 4, MC; Jubal and Asturias, *History of the 41st Division*, 60–65; Atienza, *Time for War*, 81–86.
7. Montgomery, "I Hired out to Fight," 59, Montgomery Papers; Fortier, "Notes," 65, box 4, MC.
8. Lee, *They Call It Pacific*, 214; Glattly to George Groce, 11 Feb. 1949, Fall of the Philippines, Records of the Office of the Chief of Military History, box 6, RG 319, NA; Romulo, *I Saw the Fall*, 268; Atienza, *Time for War*, 96–97; and Rimando, "Vicente Lim," 320–22. Senior American officers did not starve either. General Jones told John Toland that Wainwright's CP served "delicious meals [and] wine" (box 81, Toland Papers).
9. Fortier, "Notes," 71, box 4, MC; Wetherby to Orlando Ward, 4 Mar. 1952, box 2, MC; Chunn, "Notebooks," 28, box 3, MC. The higher-than-normal temperatures are noted in Hartendorp, *Japanese Occupation of the Philippines*, 1:112; and Labrador, *Diary of the Japanese Occupation*, 89, 103.

10. Atienza, *Time for War*, 128–30; Quezon, quoted in Willoughby, *MacArthur*, 56. For Recio's comment, see his interview in box 81, Toland Papers.
11. Swinson, *Four Samurai*, 64–69; Morton, *Fall of the Philippines*, 413–14; King, "Report of the Luzon Force," in Ancheta, *Wainwright Papers*, 1:173.
12. Notebook of Capt. William E. W. Farrell, 31st Inf. (author's collection).
13. Fortier, "Notes," 11, box 4, MC.
14. Parker, "Report of Operations," in Ancheta, *Wainwright Papers*, 1:131; Morton, *Fall of the Philippines*, 421–22; Jones telephone interview, 20 July 1996.
15. King, "Report of Operations of Luzon Force," in Ancheta, *Wainwright Papers*, 1:164; Gumban, *Bataan Company Commander*, 111. Magtoto wrote that during a lull in the artillery barrage on 3 April, he surveyed his battalion area and saw "scores of our men" dead and many others seriously injured ("Rock of Bataan," 279), but Atienza reported speaking to Magtoto on the early afternoon of 3 April and being told that his unit had suffered "so far, few" casualties (*Time for War*, 154). An American adviser with the 42nd Regiment remembered "many casualties" on 3 April (Chunn, "Notebooks," 29, 31, box 3, MC).
16. Fortier, "Notes," 12–13, box 4, MC.
17. O'Day, "21st Division History," 40–41, box 17, MC; Fortier, "Comments on the Fall of the Philippines," 9–12, box 17, MC.
18. Morton, *Fall of the Philippines*, 430, 435–37; Fortier, "Operations of the 41st Division," 14 May 1946, and Fortier to Morton, 10 Jan. 1952, box 17, MC; Jubal and Asturias, *History of the 41st Division*, 88–90; Chunn, "Notebooks," 29, box 3, MC; Atienza, *Time for War*, 178–85.
19. Mateo B. Capinpin 201 File, box 1890, SCAP Legal Section, Manila Branch, RG 331, NA; Atienza, *Time for War*, 177–80; Atienza to Toland, 15 Mar. 1960, box 82, Toland Papers; Fortier to Morton, 10 Jan. 1952, box 17, MC; Wetherby confirms meeting Fortier at the regimental CP on 5 April ("Activities of 41st Infantry," box 2, MC), as does Magtoto ("Rock of Bataan," 287). Ojeda's medal citation is reprinted in Baclagon, *They Served with Honor*, 116–17.
20. Morton, *Fall of the Philippines*, 443. On Capinpin, see the testimony in Mateo B. Capinpin 201 File, box 1890, SCAP Legal Section, Manila Branch, RG 331, NA.
21. Mark Wohlfeld, quoted in Knox, *Death March*, 110; General King to TAG, 31 Jan. 1946, Bluemel personnel file, NPRC.
22. Fortier, "Notes," 15–16, box 4, MC; Atienza, *Time for War*, 196–97; Jubal and Asturias, *History of the 41st Division*, 92; Rimando, "Vicente Lim," 364–66.
23. Stimson diary, 8 April 1942, reel 6, Stimson Papers; Morton, *Fall of the Philippines*, 455–56.
24. Leonico Tan, "A Brief History of the Organization and Operations of the 11th Division (Res.), PA," box 1478, RG 407, Philippine Archives, NA; Fortier, "Notes," 15–16, box 4, MC; Ben Cailles Unson, "Vicente P. Lim: Days in Bataan," *Manila Times Daily Magazine*, 10 Apr. 1959; Magtoto, "Rock of Bataan," 294–95; and [Atienza,] "General Vicente Lim."
25. Manzano,"Memoirs"; *Philippines Herald*, 1 Nov. 1940; King to wife, 1 Nov. 1941, box 2a, King Papers; Morton, *Fall of the Philippines*, 366; Stimson diary, 9 Apr. 1942, reel 6, Stimson Papers; Mallonée, "Bataan Diary," 1:4, Mallonée Papers. See also Whitman, *Bataan*, 453.
26. Buencamino, *Memoirs and Diaries*, 99. The meeting took place on 28 March.

27. Morton, *Fall of the Philippines*, 457–59. Baclagon claims that two officers of the 41st Division staff, Capt. Isagani Campo and Lt. Jose Crisol, were "directed to precede" the American officers "and went ahead with a white flag to contact the nearest Japanese commander" (*Last 130 Days*, 231). I know of no other account of the surrender that mentions the involvement of these officers.
28. Fortier, "Notes," 16, box 4, MC; Wetherby, "Activities of the 41st Infantry," box 2, MC; Chunn, "Notebooks," 31, box 3, MC; Buencamino, *Memoirs and Diaries*, 167; Ojeda interview, Quezon City, 21 Jan. 1994.
29. Tagarao, *All This Was Bataan*, 118–19; De Veyra, *Doctor in Bataan*, 55; Alexander, *Surviving Bataan and Beyond*, 116–17; Jackson, *Diary*, 35, 46.
30. Atienza, *Time for War*, 208–9; Lim, *To Inspire and to Lead*, 207. For a different depiction of the scene, see Alejandro Capitulo, "The Surrender of Gen. Lim," *Sunday Tribune Magazine*, 11 Apr. 1943.
31. Brougher places Lim in Balanga early on 11 April and with the other generals in Orani for two or three days after being taken there on the afternoon of the eleventh ("When the 11th Division, PA, 'Tried to' Surrender," box 17, MC).
32. The contemporary diary covering the period 11–23 April 1942 is reprinted in Chunn, *Of Rice and Men*, 120–27. Some of the names may be incorrectly transcribed. "Major Baylor," for example, probably should be Maj. Gaspar Baylon, executive officer of the 4th PC Regiment.
33. Falk, *Bataan*, 65, 80–82; Toland, *But Not in Shame*, 318–19.
34. Rimando, "Vicente Lim," 392–93. In *"Dear Mother Putnam,"* 37, Lichauco tells of the abuse by Lim's guards. At least some Japanese were aware that Francisco and not Lim was the "commandant of the Filipino forces" on Bataan. Francisco was identified as such in "Greater East Asia War Bulletin," 14 Apr. 1942, reprinted in Japanese Military Administration, *Official Journal*, 3:234.
35. Toland, *But Not in Shame*, 316, 321; Falk, *Bataan*, 131, 150–51. On Bluemel see also the testimony of Captain Castro in Masaharu Homma, *Before the Military Commission Convened by the Commanding General, United States Army Forces, Western Pacific, United States of America v. Masaharu Homma*, 1945, microfilm, RG 153, NA (hereafter cited as "Homma Trial"), 1153–54. For the marine officer's statement, see Miller, *From Shanghai to Corregidor*, 43; for the army officer, see Boyt, *Bataan*, 129. On Stevens see Brougher, *South to Bataan*, 71.
36. Domingo G. Gabitan (B Co., 1st Bn., 43rd Infantry) interview, Manila, 19 Mar. 1994.
37. The story of the massacre is told in Falk, *Bataan*, 95–99, Villarin, *We Remember*, 175–79, Ongpauco, *They Refused to Die*, 90–102, and Ancheta, *Triumph in the Philippines*, 96–98. "The Military History of the 71st Infantry Division, PA, USAFFE" (unpublished compilation by veterans of the division; author's collection) asserts that most of those killed were in the 71st and 72nd Infantry Regiments. Perez's story is found in Buenafe, *Voice of the Veteran*, 13–17. Abraham gives more details about the claim that the 41st Infantry's actions were the provocation for the massacre (*Oh God Where Are You?* 547–48).
38. Jones interview; Lapham and Norling, *Lapham's Raiders*, 37–38; "Affidavit of Winston Anson Jones," in "Homma Trial," 1970–71.
39. Chunn, "Notebooks," 34–35, box 3, MC.
40. On the Martelinos, see Amado Martelino to Maj. Gen. Edward King, 15 Feb. 1946, King Papers; and Amado Martelino to Col. James G. Monihan, 11 Feb. 1946, Ganley

Papers. Estimates of the number of prisoners who died on the Death March or escaped from it vary considerably. General Homma ("Homma Trial," 30) was charged with having caused "approximately 1,200 American and approximately 16,000 Filipino prisoners of war [to become] missing and dead" as a result of the Death March and other atrocities. In "Report of Operations of Luzon Force," in Ancheta, *Wainwright Papers*, 1:175–78, Floyd Marshall, the assistant chief of staff, G-1, of Luzon Force, estimated the size of the Philippine Army at about 59,000 just before the final Japanese offensive. Basilio Hernandez, the postwar head of the Philippine Army's casualty division, stated that 53,000 Philippine Army soldiers surrendered on Bataan. See Prosecution document no. 2879, exhibit no. 1449, reprinted in International Military Tribunal for the Far East, *Tokyo War Crimes Trial*, 6:12596–99. Falk concluded that around 44,000 to 50,000 Filipino prisoners of war reached Capas, including Philippine Scouts (*Bataan*, 174–75). The difference between the number surrendered on Bataan and the number arrived at Capas suggests the number dead or missing. Falk himself estimated that "between 5,000 and 10,000 Filipinos" had died on the march. Accepting either figure underlines that far more Filipinos died on the march than in combat. Ongpauco's figure is found in *Bataan and Corregidor*, 21.

Like American deaths in combat on Bataan, American deaths along the march seem to have totaled less than often thought. Falk put the number at 600 to 650 (*Bataan*, 173). M.Sgt. "Abie" Abraham, a Bataan veteran of the 31st Infantry (U.S.) who was assigned to recover soldiers' bodies from Bataan after his liberation from Cabanatuan in 1945, stated "emphatically" to historians James and William Belote that Falk's estimate of American dead was "much too high." See notes, interview with Abraham, 2 May 1964, Belote Papers. John Toland considerably confused the issue by reporting that about 2,330 Americans died on the Death March, a much-repeated figure that, according to Toland, reflected "a consensus of responsible survivors." Using Toland's figure of 12,000 captive Americans, this equals almost 20 percent of the American soldiers who surrendered on Bataan. No other account of the ordeal suggests that one in five surrendered Americans died on the march out of Bataan or that American deaths counted for one-fourth to one-third of the total. (Toland estimated total deaths along the march at 7,000 to 10,000.) In a later book about the Pacific war, Toland made significant changes to his account of the Death March but repeated the same casualty figures (*Rising Sun*, 300). Toland seems to have included the number of American hospital patients left on Bataan after the surrender (estimated by Falk as "at least 1,500") in his total of deaths on the march out of Bataan.

41. Meixsel, *Clark Field*, 101, 150–51n6; Dizon, *East of Pinatubo*, 89; Fortunato Tiglao et al., "The History of the Barrio of O'Donnell," 21 Apr. 1953, Historical Data Papers, PNL; Moriya Wada testimony, "Homma Trial," 2675; Olson, *O'Donnell*, 50; Manzano, "Memoirs."
42. Condon-Rall and Cowdrey, *Medical Service in the War against Japan*, 365–66.
43. Olson, *O'Donnell*, 74, 81, 155–56; *The Last Journey* (Manila: Veterans Federation of the Philippines, 1994); "Homma Trial," 1472, 1539. Condon-Rall and Cowdrey give a figure of "about 22,000 Filipinos" dead from 15 April to 10 July (*Medical Service in the War*, 366). The total deaths given in the army's official history is 29,180 (Army Historical Division, *History of the Philippine Army*, 207). The Manila

cemetery (*Libingan ng mga Bayani*) was established adjacent to the Manila American Cemetery. "The bulk of those buried there," the historian Ricardo T. Jose writes, were POW dead of World War II. See Jose, "Remembering World War II," 121.

44. Shusuke Horiguchi testimony, "Homma Trial," 2887; Ongpauco, *They Refused to Die*, 342.
45. Catalan and Federico Oboza (camp supply officer) testimony, "Homma Trial," 1459–97.
46. Atienza testimony, "Homma Trial," 1514–32.
47. Quinn, *Love Letters to Mike*, 14. A similar comment was made by Collier, who said that the same observation could be made of air corps personnel ("Notebooks," 4:60–61, box 13, MC).
48. Gloria, *All the Way*, 101–3; Jalandoni, *Silent Sacrifice*, 61–62; Agoncillo, *Fateful Years*, 229–33, 236n77; Labrador, *Diary of the Japanese Occupation*, 119; Hartendorp, *Japanese Occupation of the Philippines*, 2:301; Verzosa, *What Price Valor*, 30–31; Paul A. Marinas, 26th Cav., "Description of activities since 7 December 1941," 17 Apr. 1945, box 2, Pierce Papers.
49. "Homma Trial," 1491; Sorley, *Honorable Warrior*, 63; M. S. Janairo, "Memorandum for General Francisco," 12 July 1942, Guillermo Francisco File, People's Court Papers; Ongpauco, *They Refused to Die*, 340–41; Manzano, "Memoirs." The Japanese organized the Filipinos into four "groups" of prisoners, each further divided into two or three "subgroups." A general officer was put at the head of each group. Capinpin had been the first commander of the Filipino prisoners at Capas. When Francisco arrived at the camp, he took over as chief of the Filipino group. Lim commanded prisoners' group four, in which most of the 41st Division staff officers could be found.
50. Francisco to ex-PC officer John Inglesby, 21 Sept. 1950, Inglesby Collection, South Carolina Historical Society; Ongpauco, *They Refused to Die*, 177–78; Rimando, "Vicente Lim," 395–98.
51. Guerrero, "Passion," *Manila Evening News*, pt. 16; Vargas to Secretary of Justice, 9 May 1942, cited in Steinberg, *Philippine Collaboration*, 56; Takeji Wachi testimony, "Homma Trial," 2487–88, 2513–14, 2557.
52. For Homma's testimony see "Homma Trial," 3117–18, 3144–45, 3230–31. See also "Proclamation Concerning the Provisional Release of Wounded or Sick Filipino War-Prisoners," 22 June 1942, and "Notification Concerning the Provisional Release of Wounded or Sick Filipino War-Prisoners," 23 June 1942, reprinted in Japanese Military Administration, *Official Journal*, 5:11–13; *Manila Tribune*, 29, 30 June, 1 July 1942; Hartendorp, *Japanese Occupation of the Philippines*, 1:221–23.
53. For the prisoners' comments see Villarin, *We Remember*, 222; McCoy, *Closer than Brothers*; and Jose, *Captive Arms*, 6.
54. De Vera, *Zero Hour*, 110–17; Mallillin-Jamboy, *Resistance Movement in Lanao*, 34; Elarth, *Philippine Constabulary*, 154, 178; Quintin R. De Borja, "Some Career Attributes and Professional Views of the Philippine Military Elite," *Philippine Journal of Public Administration* 13 (October 1969): 406.
55. Steinberg, *Philippine Collaboration*, 189n48; "Philippine Biographies, Assemblage No. 46," OSS; *General and Flag Officers*, 117, 144; *Manila Tribune*, 18, 30 Aug. 1944.
56. F. G. Tillman to J. Edgar Hoover, 11 July 1945, re interview with Roxas by Special Agent Finley on 22 June 1945, Roxas file, box 1, RG 65, NA.

57. "Diary of General Paulino Santos Excerpts," January–August 1942, Hoover Institution Archives; "Philippine Biographies, Assemblage No. 46," OSS. The quoted portions of Santos's letters are from Jose, *Book on the Japanese Occupation*, 193–200.
58. *Manila Tribune*, 3 May 1943, 30 Aug. 1944; Santos name file in "Who's Who," box 590, RG 496, NA; Munda, *Last Days of General Santos.*
59. *Manila Tribune*, 3 Sept. 1942; Agoncillo, *Fateful Years*, 825–36; Agoncillo, *Burden of Proof*, 74–89; Laurel, *War Memoirs*, 46.
60. Segundo IDPF; Agoncillo, *Fateful Years*, 232. The *Manila Tribune*, 10, 22 Sept. 1942, describes the camp and announces Segundo's appointment.
61. Victor Gomez testimony, 26 Mar. 1946, Capinpin 201 File, box 1890, SCAP Legal Section, Manila Branch, RG 331, NA; Mariano Ma. Ganaden, "Ex-Servicemen Collaborate Actively," *Sunday Tribune Magazine*, 11 Apr. 1943; Baclig IDPF; Moran IDPF; "Pastor Martelino," *Assembly*, October 1946, 15–16; "Enemy Radio Digest," vol. 2, no. 148, 30 July 1943, bound copy in the Laurel Memorial Foundation. On Pastor Martelino, see also Manikan, *Guerilla Warfare on Panay Island*, 386. A chronology of Garcia's employment in 1942–44 can be found in "Loyalty status case of Col. Rafael L. Garcia," 4 May 1946, Garcia personnel file, NPRC. Martelino's statement was made to James G. Monihan, 11 Feb. 1946 (copy in Ganley Papers). According to Martelino, the Japanese killed the wife and children of Lt. Col. Melecio Santos because Santos dropped out of sight. General Francisco also told an American inquisitor after the war that he feared the Japanese "might take action against his family" if he did not cooperate with them (see R. E. Gleason, CIC investigation case file 52-747, 28 Aug. 1945, Francisco File, People's Court Records).
62. Rimando, "Vicente Lim," 398–99; "Statement of Dr. Pedro T. Lantin," 11 Oct. 1947, box 273, RG 407, Philippine Archives, NA. Lim's name can be found in a list of 1,086 soon-to-be-released prisoners published in the *Manila Tribune*, 1 July 1942. For a history of the Cancer Institute, see *Golden Jubilee Book of the Philippine General Hospital* (Manila, [1960]), 72. Lim, *To Inspire and to Lead*, 206, reads that Lim lived with the Hidalgos upon release from Capas and moved to the Cancer Institute in May 1944. Other sources indicate that he was there considerably longer.
63. Kalaw, "My Activities Under the Japanese Regime," box 273, RG 407, Philippine Archives, NA.

Chapter 11

1. Lizardo, "Underground Movement during Japanese Occupation," 8 June 1947, box 273, RG 407, Philippine Archives, NA.
2. Manzano, "Anti-Jap Activities, Luzon," 4–11, box 46, RG 15, MMA. Manzano covers much of the same ground in his unpublished memoirs, providing the real names of persons given pseudonyms in the original narrative. For Thorp's mission, see Lapham and Norling, *Lapham's Raiders*, 13–22.
3. Ind, *Allied Intelligence Bureau*, 9–13.
4. For a summary of these actions, see *Reports of General MacArthur*, 1:300–302. Manzano's statement comes from his 20 Sept. 1944 letter to Hugh Casey, reel 338, RG 16, MMA.
5. Valdes diary, 13 Oct. 1944.

6. "Report on the 'Combat and Intelligence Bn.' of General Lim's Guerrillas, Manila Unit," by Adelbert T. Weber, and "Report on Headquarters, Combat, and Intelligence Battalion, General Lim's Guerrilla Unit (Independent)" and a separate report on the "Skeleton Organization" of "General Lim's Guerrilla Organization (Independent)"—both prepared by John O. Keider, box 273, RG 407, Philippine Archives, NA. Keider explained that after Weber's report a second evaluation of these claims had been made by 1st Lt. Kenneth H. Neubauer based "on a study of affidavits and certificates in the files of the Guerrilla Affairs Division" of Headquarters AFWESPAC. Neubauer rendered a negative finding, whereupon Keider was ordered to complete a more thorough evaluation.
7. Juan O. Chioco, "Guerrilla Unit of Brigadier-General Vicente Lim"; Eduardo Quisumbing affidavit, 16 Apr. 1947; Dionisio S. Ojeda, affidavit, 14 Aug. 1947; and Amado N. Bautista, "Information on Brigadier General Vicente Lim," 17 Mar. 1947, box 273, RG 407, Philippine Archives, NA.
8. "Report on General Lim's Guerrillas," "Report on General Lim's Guerrilla Unit," and report on "General Lim's Guerrilla Organization," box 273, RG 407, Philippine Archives, NA (see n. 6).
9. Ibid.
10. Lapham and Norling, *Lapham's Raiders*, 63; Manzano, "Anti-Jap Activities," 169–72; Willoughby, *Guerrilla Resistance Movement*, 205; Ramsey and Rivele, *Lieutenant Ramsey's War*, 111, 182–83.
11. Mojica, *Terry's Hunters*, 351–52; Willoughby, *Guerrilla Resistance Movement*, 459, 461; Marquez, *Blood on the Rising Sun*, 187–88; HQ, Philippines Command, United States Army, "U.S. Army Recognition Program of Philippine Guerrillas," ca. 1949, available at https://research.archives.gov/id/6921767.
12. *The Filipino Nurse* 17 (1947): 78; Willoughby, *Guerrilla Resistance Movement*, 612; Malay, "The Rushing Years," 3:149–50, UPDA; G. R. Perez, "General Lim's Last Days," *Philippine Armed Forces Journal*, June 1949, 12–13.
13. Capt. Leo. S. Wortman Jr., "Report on Headquarters, FAIT (Araullo)," 9 Sept. 1945, box 300; Sabino J. Aguila, Claims Investigator, interview of Alfredo David [Justiniano Estrella], 20 Apr. 1948, filed with "General Information, Markings FAIT," in box 258; and Petronila B. Cabreira, statement [re Gen. Lim], n.d., box 273, RG 407, Philippine Archives, NA.
14. Hayden, *The Philippines*, 334; Hartendorp, *History of Trade and Industry*, 235–36; Quirino, *Quezon*, 291; Lim, *To Inspire and to Lead*, 170.
15. Roxas, "Brief Summary," 238–58; Tillman to Hoover, 9 July 1945, Roxas file, box 1, RG 65, NA; Atienza, *Time for War*, 120.
16. Roxas, "Brief Summary," 242–43.
17. Agoncillo, *Fateful Years*, 522; Steinberg, *Philippine Collaboration*, 107; Friend, *Between Two Empires*, 234, 240–41; Roxas, "Brief Summary," 250; Hartendorp, *Japanese Occupation of the Philippines*, 2:635–36; Bernstein, *Philippine Story*, 203–8; Thorpe, *East Wind, Rain*, 159–60; Tillman to Hoover, 12 July 1945, Roxas file, box 1, RG 65, NA; Rosinger, "Philippines—Problems of Independence," 86–87.
18. Roxas, "Brief Summary," 255–57.
19. Manzano, "Memoirs"; "Certificate of Brig. Gen. Manuel A. Roxas (PA), 27 May 1945," Juan Moran IDPF.

20. Vicente Lim card file in "Who's Who," GHQ SWPA AIB Philippine Regional Section, box 592, RG 496, NA; Quezon to MacArthur, 5 Sept. 1943, RG 16, MMA; MacArthur to Quezon, 8 Sept. 1943, reel 50, Quezon Papers (2); General Vincente Lim radio card file, MMA; Labrador, *Diary of the Japanese Occupation*, 156–58. A complete copy of the 5 April 1943 radio broadcast can be found on reel 21, Quezon Papers (2). The Lim guerrilla file in the Philippine Archives, box 273, includes a statement by Magtira, dated 31 Dec. 1948, identifying his home in Ermita as a meeting place for Lim and his comrades.
21. Quezon to Pilar Lim, 26 Mar. 1943; Quezon to Stimson, 8 Apr. 1943; Lim to Quezon, 17 Apr. 1943; and Quezon to Lim, 30 Apr. 1943, reel 21, Quezon Papers (2). The final draft of this last letter reads that the enclosed broadcast copy is dated 18 March 1943; however, the broadcast copy that follows is dated 5 April. GHQ SWPA's radio name file includes a synopsis of a different broadcast dated 18 March. According to stateside newspapers (e.g., *Christian Science Monitor*, 22 Dec. 1942; *Chicago Daily Tribune*, 23 Dec. 1942), nothing had been heard of Lim since the fall of Bataan until his wife received a Red Cross message saying he was "safe and well" on 21 December 1942.
22. Roxas, "Brief Summary," 243, 244.
23. *Manila Tribune*, 17 Mar. 1943; Rimando, "Vicente Lim," 402, 427n32; Manzano, "Memoirs."
24. Quirino, *Quezon*, 364–67; *Manila Tribune*, 17 Mar., 16 June 1943; Quezon to Lim, 29 Nov. 1943, reel 21, Quezon Papers (2). Some damage to Lim's reputation was done. A subsequent compilation of prominent political and military figures in the occupied Philippines compiled by the Office of Strategic Services recorded that Lim was "now reported [to be] pro-Jap[anese]." The source for the statement, found in "Philippine Biographies," 15 Sept. 1944, OSS, is given as "O-66," which is identified as coming from "Publication S-3082, Far Eastern Diplomatic Lists." I was not able to find a copy of this document. The information was clearly out of date: by September 1944, Lim had been a prisoner in Fort Santiago for several months.
25. Brougher, *South to Bataan*, 93.
26. *Reports of General MacArthur*, 2, pt. 1:309–10; Ramsey and Rivele, *Lieutenant Ramsey's War*, 200.
27. Doeppers, *Feeding Manila*, 324–27; Labrador, *Diary of the Japanese Occupation*, 179–81.
28. Kalaw, *Fighting Filipinos*, 118–22.
29. Ibid., 118, 122. Army investigators also obtained information about Lim's plan from Juan Chioco, Ricardo Galang, and Alberto Abeleda. For the history of Phillips's mission, see Willoughby, *Guerrilla Resistance Movement*, 152–56. In *Secret Mission*, 54–55, Galang recounted the arrival of "Captain Tugo Abeleda" in the company of a journalist named Johnny Orendain. Abeleda said that he had come to arrange Lim's escape. Phillips then asked about Roxas and Abeleda replied that "Roxas will be ready, too."
30. *Reports of General MacArthur*, 1:304; Willoughby, *Guerrilla Resistance Movement*, 152–56; Galang, *Hammer and Anvil*, 128–34; Ongpin, *Philippine Packing Corporation*, 9, 11, 14; Baclagon, *Allied Intelligence Bureau*, 118–20; J. K. Evans, "Violation of Security in SWPA (re Parsons), memo for Chief, MIS [Military

Intelligence Section]," 25 Oct. 1944, RG 3, MMA; Kramer, *One Out of Eleven*, 61–64; Phillips IDPF. Galang wrote that Phillips had heard about the Americans' presence on Batangas and had asked them to come to Mindoro with the promise that they would be evacuated by submarine (*Secret Mission*, 59).

31. Manzano to Col. LeGrand A. Diller, 5 July 1944, and to Brig. Gen. Hugh J. Casey, 20 Sept. 1944, reel 338, RG 16, MMA. In his memoirs and in his letter to Diller, Manzano wrote that he had left Luzon at Roxas's behest; in the letter to Casey, he wrote that he had been delegated by Roxas and Lim to try to reach SWPA.
32. Fertig to MacArthur, radio message no. 796, 25 Mar. 1944, and no. 964, 22 Apr. 1944, box 273, RG 407, Philippine Archives, NA.
33. AIB Info. Report No. 2080, 23 Apr. 1944, reel 383, RG 16, MMA; Baclagon, *Allied Intelligence Bureau*, 102; "Minutes AFWESPAC Conference on the Philippine Army Held at HQ AFWESPAC," Manila, 15 Nov. 1945, box 1551, RG 407, Philippine Archives, NA. This policy had been announced in MacArthur to Chief of Staff, Philippine Army, 8 Dec. 1944, "Status of members of the Philippine Army," which read that "any 'parole' or 'oath' signed by such personnel [members of USAFFE who had surrendered in 1942] as a condition of release by the enemy from prisoner of war status will be considered as having been signed under duress and as of no validity." Reprinted in *Congressional Record* 99, pt. 10, 83rd Cong. 1st Sess., A2147. Quirino characterized Whitney as "notoriously anti-Filipino even before the war" (*Quezon*, 364). See also Sutherland to Quezon, 15 Feb. 1944, reel 21, Quezon Papers (2), and J. R. Hayden, "Summary of Principal Matters discussed with President Quezon," Mar. 1944, box 8, James Papers.
34. *Reports of General MacArthur*, 1:301; Willoughby, *Guerrilla Resistance Movement*, 170–72. The standard accounts of Parsons's activities are the "as told to" book by Ingham, *Rendezvous by Submarine*, Wise's *Secret Mission*, and Quirino's *Chick Parsons*. Ind also gives a lengthy rendition of Parsons's work (*Allied Intelligence Bureau*, 159–88). For an entirely different perspective on Parsons's activities, see Rear Adm. Arthur McCollum's comments about a Lt. Cmdr. "Powers," in Mason, *Pacific War Remembered*, 148. McCollum was the director of Allied Naval Intelligence in SWPA. For additional biographical material, see Peter Parsons, "Special Mission Subs in World War II," *BAHC* 31, no. 1 (2003): 41; Peter Parsons, "Me and the AGOM," *BAHC* 35, no. 4 (2007): 58–59; and Charles Parsons's 1981 interview with John T. Mason Jr., RG 32, MMA. The details of Parsons's military career vary from source to source. Apparently, he obtained a reserve commission in 1932, let the commission lapse, and rejoined the navy about the time the war started. Whitney (letter to Lorenzo Tañada, 5 Aug. 1946, copy in RG 110, MMA) drew attention to conflicting accounts—all offered by Parsons himself—of Parsons's experiences in December 1941.
35. Maj. E. A. Williams, "Parsons' Activities in the Philippines, 1942–1945," 8 Oct. 1945, Parsons file, box 582, RG 496, NA; Whitney, "Testimony of Commander C. Parsons"; F. L. Worcester, "Memorandum to Mr. Nathaniel P. Davis," 6 July 1946, RG 110, MMA. Whitney acknowledged, in a PRS memorandum dated 9 Aug. 1943 (reel 345, RG 16, MMA), that while most of his work was related to PRS's supply effort, Parsons was nevertheless "technically assigned to G-2."
36. According to the compiler of the official history narratives, "Landing at Paluan was probably the party's initial mistake [because] the Japanese [also] had an agent in

Paluan." Willoughby, *Guerrilla Resistance Movement*, 152–56, 170–73, 335–67 (for the June 1943 report). On the issue of where the Phillips party landed, Parsons wrote that "we arrived quietly in the bay where Phillips and his party were to be dropped" (letter to Whitney, 14 Nov. 1943, reel 384, RG 16, MMA). On Parsons's possible trip to Manila, Whitney wrote that despite claims to the contrary, "Parsons never entered Manila between June 1942 and February 1945" ("Testimony of Commander C. Parsons"). For an argument that Parsons—"looking for Roxas [or] just plain bored"—did go to Manila, see Peter Parsons's review of the evidence in "Chick Parsons in Occupied Manila: Should He Have Been Court-Martialed?," *BAHC* 36, no. 1 (2008): 8–48.

37. Parsons, interview with John Mason; C. Parsons, "Recital of Participation in the Philippine Resistance Movement Especially with Relation to General Manuel Roxas," copy in RG 58, MMA. Friend cited this document (or a draft of it) and dated it to 1945 (*Between Two Empires*, 250n11). PRS (Whitney) to G-2 (Willoughby), 5 Aug. 1943, notes that Parsons claimed he had been told by MacArthur to investigate the possibility of evacuating Roxas (copy on reel 383, RG 16, MMA).

38. Parsons to Whitney, 30 Aug. 1943; PRS to Chief of Staff, 30 Aug. 1943; Sutherland to Whitney, 31 Aug. 1943; and Sutherland to AIB, 8 Sept. 1943, reel 383, RG 16, MMA. See also Sutherland's letter of 4 Aug. 1943 in Roxas 201 file, box 583, RG 496, NA. Parsons stated in his 14 Sept. 1943 letter to Quezon (on reel 345) that "MacArthur has recently advised General Roxas that his evacuation may be arranged provided it does not appear to be too hazardous. Developments may be expected along these lines in the not too distant future." Since MacArthur made corrections to this long letter (which he had instructed Parsons to write in lieu of returning to the United States to brief Quezon in person) but not to this portion, presumably he was in accord with what Parsons wrote. See MacArthur to Quezon, 31 Aug. 1943, reel 50, Quezon Papers (2).

39. On MacArthur's suspicion of Laurel, see his marginal notes on Parsons to Quezon, 14 Sept. 1943, reel 345, RG 16, MMA.

40. "Personal Narrative of Lt. Col. Emigdio C. Cruz, PA, sent to Gen. C. A. Willoughby," 30 July 1946, box 1, RG 23 B, MMA; Parsons, "Recital" (emphasis added), RG 58, MMA.

41. PRS to chief of staff, 13 Feb. 1944, reel 345; and PRS to chief of staff, 29 Jan., 17, 28 Feb. 1944, reel 384, RG 16, MMA; Lichauco, *Roxas*, 186–92. The submarine entered Paluan Bay at 12:34 A.M., 27 February; the deck log reads simply: "mission not accomplished." See the "Log of the United States Ship *Narwhal* SS 167," box 6154, Deck Logs, *Narwhal*, Oct. 1943–July 1944, RG 24, NA.

42. Willoughby, *Guerrilla Resistance Movement*, 171, 173–74; Whitney, "Memorandum concerning testimony of Commander C. Parsons," included with letter to Lorenzo Tañada, 5 Aug. 1946, RG 110, MMA; Parsons to "Pep" (Jose Ozamis), 15 Feb. 1944, box 1, RG 58, MMA; Ind, *Allied Intelligence Bureau*, 184. The *Reports of General MacArthur*, 1:305—which relied on the same documentary evidence later compiled in book form by Willoughby—reads that "in February 1944, Commander Parsons conducted still another supply run to Mindanao, Tawi Tawi, and Mindoro." The *Narwhal* passenger list for 16 February 1944 is found in box 6154, Deck Logs, *Narwhal*, Oct. 1943–July 1944, RG 24, NA. In his 1981 interview with John Mason (RG 32, MMA), Parsons said that he had been on Mindoro the day Phillips was

killed, had destroyed Phillips's equipment to prevent its seizure by the Japanese, and had later met the submarine that was supposed to have extracted Roxas. About eighty years old at the time, Parsons appears to have conflated several trips he had made with stories he had heard from others. He was not at Phillips's camp.

43. Galang, *Hammer and Anvil*, 134; Cruz, "Certificate" [re meeting with General Lim], 19 November 1947, box 273, RG 407, Philippine Archives, NA; "Personal Narrative of Lt. Col. Emigdio C. Cruz," in Willoughby, *Guerrilla Resistance Movement*, 397; Parsons, "Recital," RG 58, MMA.
44. Pedro T. Melgar statement, 29 Jan. 1946; and Chioco, "Guerrilla Unit of Brigadier-General Vicente Lim," box 273, RG 407, Philippine Archives, NA.
45. Parsons, "Recital," RG 58, MMA; Harrison, *Origins*, 239; MacArthur to Quezon, 1 Aug. 1944, reel 21, Quezon Papers (2). Willoughby is therefore in error in stating that "Lim was intercepted en route to Mindoro [in February 1944]" and in his implication that it was Lim's capture that led to the arrest of "almost all" the members of Parsons's "Manila net" (*Guerrilla Resistance Movement*, 173–74). On the late 1944 communications about Roxas, see the series of radio messages exchanged by Anderson and MacArthur, dated 5–9 Dec. 1944, in boxes 16 and 24, RG 16, MMA. The sorry saga of Franco Vera Reyes—reliable details of which seem to be beyond recovery—is best told by Roces, *Looking for Liling*, 224–36, 342–43. Roces includes in his account an incident in which the Philippine Army officer Capt. Vicente Gepte, a 1940 graduate of West Point, asks Lim if he could vouch for Reyes (since Reyes had earlier bragged about having met with "Ellsworth") and Lim eventually tells Gepte that Reyes was "okay." (The original story is found in Navarro, *Beds of Nails*, 85–86.) Kalaw, in "My Activities Under the Japanese Regime" (box 273, Philippine Archives, NA), stated that he had asked Reyes "for his credentials and [Reyes] said that General Lim and General Roxas knew about it. But I could not get confirmation from either General Roxas or General Lim."
46. G. R. Perez, "General Lim's Last Days," *Philippine Armed Forces Journal*, June 1949, 12–13. The messenger's name was Jose Concha, identified in Baclagon, *Allied Intelligence Bureau*, 80, as a member of a Manila-Laguna unit of the AIB under the command of Capt. Buenaventura Villanueva, who, according to Perez, transmitted the message from Lim to Villamor.
47. Testimony of Bienvenido Rillo, People of the Philippines v. Kuroda, 4 Mar. 1949, 31:1141, Japanese War Crimes Papers, PNA; Ernesto V. Santos interview, Manila, 13 Dec. 1993; Amado N. Bautista to Adjutant General, Philippine Area Command, 17 Mar. 1947, box 273, RG 407, Philippine Archives, NA.
48. Rillo to Pilar Lim, 15 Nov. 1945, reprinted in Lim, *Pushing the Envelope*, 130–39; Rimando, "Vicente Lim," 413–17 (based on interviews with Rillo but with different details); Teodoro Kalaw Jr., affidavit, Manila, 10 Nov. 1947, and Maximo Kalaw, "My Activities Under the Japanese Regime," box 273, RG 407, Philippine Archives, NA. Rimando makes no mention of the Kalaws but writes that Lim directed his nephew Ben Rillo "to go to Colonel Rufino to get the money General Lim had arranged with him." This corresponds with what Rillo told Pilar Lim; and Rufino, the 41st Division's assistant supply officer on Bataan, stated that he had given Rillo funds to help Lim escape ("Statement of Ernesto Rufino," 27 Feb. 1946, box 273, RG 407, Philippine Archives, NA). Manzano deliberately gave Borromeo a wide berth. He wrote that Borromeo was "the most prominent claimer of direct radio

contact with GHQ" in Manila and that "Lim himself was for some time in the belief that he had found a sure way of contacting MacArthur through Borromeo's radio" ("Anti-Jap Activities," 122–23). (If Borromeo possessed a radio, it lacked the capacity to transmit to Australia.) This Emilio Borromeo was apparently a junior reserve officer, but I could not further identify him. [Infante,] *Golden Anniversary*, lists a Maj. Pedro T. Manalo, Executive Officer, 3rd Bn., 42nd Infantry Regiment, from Mataas na Kahoy. Magtoto further identifies Manalo as a retired Philippine Scout NCO ("Rock of Bataan," 176), but his conviction order (in Willoughby, *Guerrilla Resistance Movement*, 612) gives his age as thirty-two. Possibly he was one of those Scout NCOs who held a reserve commission in the Philippine Army.

49. Lichauco, *"Dear Mother Putnam,"* 172; "Watari Group Intelligence Report B No. 155, 1–10 June 1944," filed with Enemy Publications #359, 28 Apr. 1945, ATIS, SWPA, Guerrilla Warfare in the Philippines (microform 10 EP 359). The document includes a map showing the location of Lim's capture. Rimando adds that Lim gave his real name to the Japanese who inspected the batel; it meant nothing to them, which suggests that they had not been told to be on the lookout for General Lim.
50. Nelson Sinclair testimony, "Homma Trial," 530–31.
51. People of the Philippines v. Kuroda, 4 Mar. 1949, 31:1139–55, 1167–74, Japanese War Crimes Papers, PNA.
52. "Report to the Commanding Off. of East Central Luzon Guerilla Unit, Subject: Case of Gen. V. Lim," 19 Nov. 1944 [handwritten; no author], box 501, RG 407, Philippine Archives, NA; "Andy" [Bernard Anderson] to Parsons, 21 Oct. 1944, RG 58, MMA; "Re Report of Execution of General Lim," 30 Aug. 1944, Lim file, RG 496, NA. SWPA had received a message from Peralta on 29 August passing along another rumor that Lim was dead, and the author of this one-page memorandum speculated that the enemy was "fearful and suspicious of the leading figures" and had killed Lim to demonstrate the penalty for failing to cooperate. What specific evidence the Japanese used as a basis for Lim's conviction is not known. Keider had interviewed Rillo and thought him "purposely vague when questioned as to why he was released and the others held, but believed it was because the Japanese had nothing to link him with an underground resistance movement." In a brief 1994 interview (transcript provided to the author by Prof. Ricardo T. Jose), Rillo stated that he "was not tortured, but slapped during investigation. The others were tortured." But in a 1973 interview with Rimando, Rillo described experiences at Fort Santiago similar to what he had stated at Kuroda's trial. Rillo told Rimando that Lim had said to him (in Tagalog) aboard the boat taking them from Mindoro to Manila to tell the Japanese that the large sum of money found with Lim was intended to buy land at Boac and that Rillo successfully stuck to that story under interrogation.
53. Marquez, *Blood on the Rising Sun*, 163.
54. Phillips and Goldsmith, *Manila Espionage*, 193, 198–99, 203. Rillo said in the 1994 interview that Baja's family was let out of Fort Santiago the same day that he was.
55. *Reports of General MacArthur*, 2, pt. 1:312, 317, 330; Cannon, *Leyte*, 42–43, 49–50; Labrador, *Diary of the Japanese Occupation*, 221; Savary, *Outside the Walls*, 129–30; Agoncillo, *Fateful Years*, 783–86; Hartendorp, *Japanese Occupation of the Philippines*, 2:377–81; Hartendorp, *History of Trade and Industry*, 143; James, *Years of MacArthur*, 2:553–55. See also Steinburg, *Philippine Collaboration*, 96–98.

56. Ojeda affidavit, 14 Aug. 1947, box 273, RG 407, Philippine Archives, NA. Rimando identifies the business associate as E. Namikawa ("Vicente Lim," 420). This is mining engineer Eijiro Namikawa, who had been in the Philippines for two decades and was president of the Pacific Mining Company. In *To Inspire and to Lead*, 185, Lim identified him as one of "my [prewar] Japanese associates in iron."
57. For Sakakida's testimony see "Transcript of Public Trial, 1945: U.S. v. General Tomoyuki Yamashita," NA Microcopy NNG 73-1223, reel 3, 2253–2302; and "Transcript of Testimony, United States of America versus John David Provoo, U.S. Court of Appeals for the Second Circuit," 13 Nov. 1952, stenographer's minutes, 317–18, 398–99, 1039–40, Case files, Records of the U.S. Courts of Appeals, RG 276, NA Northeast Region, New York City. See also Roces, *Looking for Liling*, 256–70, which focusses on the trial and execution of the author's brother, Rafael R. Roces Jr., in August 1944. For the trials in November, see Willoughby, *Guerrilla Resistance Movement*, 588–619. Lim's name, rendered as "Vicente Rimu, Filipino, [age] 56," is found on p. 612. The other individuals with whom he was captured are listed after him in the "Record of Trial on 24 November." That Sakakida witnessed Lim's execution was told to me by Roberto Lim, but see also the account in his autobiography (*Pushing the Envelope*, 131). Rillo had been told that Lim had been killed at North Cemetery; Sakakida told Roberto Lim that the execution took place at adjacent La Loma Cemetery. For Escoda's death, supposedly as a result of "infectious disease," see Hartendorp, *Japanese Occupation of the Philippines*, 2:595, and Escoda, *Warsaw of Asia*, 92–93. One of Escoda's children, however, is quoted by Joan Orendain (daughter of the journalist whom Galang met on Mindoro) as saying, "My father was transferred to Bilibid where he was beheaded in November 1944." See Orendain, "Children of War," 111, in Constantino, *Under Japanese Rule*.

Epilogue

1. "Commonwealth Government, Increasing strength of Collaborationist element in," 4 July 1945, RG 110, MMA.
2. GO 20, HPA, 17 Mar. 1945, superseded by the more stringently worded GO 135, HPA, 18 Aug. 1945 (copies in box 1550, RG 407, Philippine Archives, NA). For a discussion of these orders and their (non)implementation, see Worcester, "Philippine Army, Dissension in," 17 May 1945; "Philippine Army Officers, Questions concerning loyalty of," 22 June 1945; "G.O. #20," 24 July 1945; "G.O. 20, Court martial of Maj. Sobrepena under," 6 Aug. 1945; and "General Orders No. 135," 10 Sept. 1945, RG 110, MMA. See also the discussion in Berlin, *Before Gringo*, 31–36.
3. Moran, Baclig, Garcia, and Segundo IDPFs; Martelino to Monihan, 11 Feb. 1946, Ganley Papers.
4. "Report of Proceedings of Board of Officers re case of Salvador Reyes," 12 Feb. 1946, and "Cases of Loyalty Board no. 2," 6 May 1946, box 1550, RG 407, Philippine Archives, NA. On the cotton growers' association, see Ikehata and Jose, *Philippines under Japan*, 176–95. Laurel had appointed Garcia executive officer of the national rice warehouse or granary (Bigasang Bayan, referred to as "Biba"). The army concluded that Garcia remained loyal despite having worked for "Japanese sponsored agencies" during the war. He was nonetheless forced to retire. See Garcia personnel file, NPRC.

5. *An Act to Authorize the Appointment of Officers on the Active List of the Philippine Scouts in the Regular Army, and for Other Things*, Public Law 96, *U.S. Statutes at Large* 63 (1949), pt. 1:169. The act also accommodated two remaining non-Filipino officers of the Philippine Scouts.
6. Kalaw, "My Activities Under the Japanese Regime"; Teodoro Kalaw Jr., affidavit, 10 Nov. 1947, "General Lim's Guerrillas" file, box 273, RG 407, Philippine Archives, NA; Abaya, *Betrayal in the Philippines*, 151–52; Romulo to Osmeña, 28 Aug. 1945, and Romulo to S. P. Lopez, 18 Sept. 1945, Romulo Papers.
7. Rogers, *Bitter Years*, 292–93; Eisenhower to MacArthur, 8 Nov. 1946, box 74, Pre-Presidential Papers, Principal File, EPL.
8. Worcester to CO, 7th Fleet Intelligence Center, 22 June 1945, RG 110, MMA; "Collaboration and Collaborators—Philippine Version," 15 May 1945, box 42, Hayden Papers. No author's name is attached, but the text of this article is nearly identical to that found in Abaya, *Betrayal in the Philippines*, 151.

Bibliography

Archival Sources

United States National Archives, Washington, D.C., and College Park, Md.

RG 24	Records of the Bureau of Naval Personnel
RG 65	Records of the Federal Bureau of Investigation
RG 77	Records of the Office of the Chief of Engineers
RG 94	Records of the Adjutant General's Office, 1780s–1917
RG 153	Records of the Office of the Judge Advocate General
	Homma, Masaharu. *Before the Military Commission Convened by the Commanding General, United States Army Forces, Western Pacific, United States of America v. Masaharu Homma.* 1945. Microfilm.
RG 165	Records of the War Department Special and General Staffs
RG 319	Records of the Office of the Chief of Military History
RG 331	Records of Allied Operational and Occupation Headquarters, World War II
RG 350	Records of the Bureau of Insular Affairs
RG 395	Records of U.S. Army Overseas Operations Commands, 1898–1942
RG 407	Records of the Adjutant General's Office, 1917–
	Philippine Archives Collection
RG 496	Records of GHQ SWPA and U.S. Army Forces, Pacific

MacArthur Memorial Archives and Library, Norfolk, Va.

RG 1	Records of the U.S. Military Advisor to the Philippine Commonwealth, 1935–41
RG 2	Records of Headquarters, U.S. Army Forces Far East (USAFFE), 1941–42
RG 3	Records of Headquarters, Southwest Pacific Area (SWPA), 1942–45
RG 15	Materials Donated by the General Public
RG 16	Papers of Maj. Gen. Courtney Whitney
RG 18	Papers of the Chief of Staff, U.S. Army, 1934–35
RG 23B	Selected Papers of Maj. Gen. Charles A. Willoughby
RG 32	Oral History Collection
RG 53	Papers of Wendell W. Fertig
RG 58	Papers of Charles Parsons
RG 110	Papers of Frederick Worcester
RG 135	Papers of Michael and Elizabeth Norman

Manuscript Collections *(by subject name)*

Almond, Edward M., Papers. USAMHI
Baldwin, Hanson, Papers. George C. Marshall Foundation Library, Lexington, Va.
Bandholtz, Harry H., Papers. BHL
Batson, Matthew, Papers. USAMHI

Belote, William and James, Papers. USAMHI
Callahan, James W., Papers. USAMHI
Casey, Hugh, Papers. Corps of Engineers Office of History, Alexandria, Va.
Davis, Thomas J., Papers. EPL
Edmonds, Walter, Papers. Air Force History Research Agency, Maxwell AFB, Montgomery, Ala.
Forbes, W. Cameron, Papers. Houghton Library, Harvard University, Cambridge, Mass.
Fortier, Malcolm, Papers. Private collection
Ganley, Eugene, Papers. USAMHI
Gonzales, Bienvenido, Papers. UPDA
Grunert, George, Papers. USAMHI
Hagood, Johnson, Papers. The South Carolina Historical Society, Charleston
Hall, Roderick, Collection. Filipinas Heritage Library, Manila
Harrison, L. Scott, Collection. MMA
Hayden, Joseph, Papers. BHL
Howard, Roy W., Papers. LOC
Inglesby, John, Collection. The South Carolina Historical Society, Charleston
Ivins, Charles F., Papers. USAMHI
James, D. Clayton, Papers. Special Collections, Mitchell Memorial Library, Mississippi State University, Starkville
Johnson, Harold K., Papers. USAMHI
King, Edward P., Papers. USAMHI
Laurel, Jose P., Papers. Jose P. Laurel Memorial Foundation, Manila
Lee, William L., Papers. EPL
Lilly, Edmund J., Papers. USAMHI
Lilly, Edmund J. POW Papers. Combined Arms Research Library, Ft. Leavenworth, Kans.
Lim, Vicente P. Original Letters, USNA Library
Malay, Armando J., Papers. UPDA
Mallonée, Richard, Papers. USAMHI
McCann, Kevin, Papers. EPL
Montgomery, William H., Papers. USAMHI
Morton, Louis, Collection. USAMHI
Murphy, Frank, Papers. BHL
O'Laughlin, John, Papers. LOC
Onorato, Michael, Collection. Hatcher Graduate Library, University of Michigan, Ann Arbor
Parker, John H., Papers. USMA Archives
People's Court Papers. UPDA
Pershing, John J., Papers. LOC
Pierce, Clinton, Papers. USAMHI
Quezon, Manuel Luis, Papers (1). PNL
Quezon, Manuel Luis, Papers (2). BHL microfilm ed.
Romero, Rufo, Papers. Private collection
Santos, Paulino. "Diary of General Paulino Santos." Hoover Institution Archives, Stanford University, Stanford, Calif.
Segundo, Fidel, Diary. http://philippinediaryproject.com

Stimson, Henry, Papers. Manuscripts and Archives, Yale University Library, New Haven, Conn.
Swanton, Donovan, Papers. USMA Archives
Taft, William Howard, Papers. LOC
Toland, John, Papers. LOC
Valdes, Basilio, Diary. http://philippinediaryproject.com
Wainwright, Jonathan, Papers. USAMHI
Wood, Leonard, Papers. LOC
Woodring, Harry, Papers. Kansas Collection, University of Kansas Library, Lawrence

Government Reports and Documents

Annual Report of the Bureau [later, Director] of Civil Service to the Governor-General of the Philippine Islands. 1913, 1914.
Annual Report of the Chief of Staff of the Philippine Army, for the Fiscal Year from January 1 to December 31, 1936. Manila: Commonwealth of the Philippines, Philippine Army, 1937.
Annual Report of the Governor-General of the Philippine Islands. Various years.
Annual Report *of the President of Philippines to the President and the Congress of the United States.* 1936–40.
Annual Report of the War Department. Various years.
Army Register. Various years.
Bureau of Insular Affairs. *A Pronouncing Gazetteer and Geographical Dictionary of the Philippine Islands.* Washington, D.C.: War Department, Bureau of Insular Affairs, 1902.
Census of the Philippine Islands, 1903. 4 vols. Washington, D.C.: United States Bureau of the Census, 1905.
Census of the Philippines, 1939. Vol. 2. Manila: Commission of the Census, 1940.
Congressional Record. Various years.
Decorations, United States Army, 1862–1926. Washington, D.C.: War Department, Office of the Adjutant General, 1927.
Foreign Relations of the United States, Diplomatic Papers, 1942. Vol. 1, *General, The British Commonwealth, The Far East.* Washington, D.C.: Historical Office, Department of State, 1960.
Headquarters, Philippine Constabulary. *Official Constabulary Register.* Manila: Bureau of Printing, 1915–35.
International Military Tribunal for the Far East. *The Tokyo War Crimes Trial.* Edited by R. J. Pritchard and S. M. Zaide. Vol. 6. New York: Garland, 1981.
Journal of the Philippine Commission. Vols. 8, 9. Manila: Bureau of Printing, 1915–16.
[MacArthur, Douglas.] *Report on National Defense in the Philippines.* Manila: Commonwealth of the Philippines, Office of the Military Adviser, 1936.
Meidling, George A. *Engineers of the Southwest Pacific, 1941–1945: Reports of Operations [of the] United States Army Forces in the Far East, Southwest Pacific Area Army Forces, Pacific.* Vol. 2, *Organizations, Troops, and Training.* Washington, D.C.: Government Printing Office, 1947.
Messages of the President [of the Philippines]. Manila: Bureau of Printing, 1937–41.
[Munson, Edward.] *Psychology of the Filipino* [and] *Conversation with Major-General Leonard Wood, Governor-General of the Philippine Islands.* Manila: Headquarters Philippine Department, 1925.

Order of Battle of the United States Land Forces in the World War. Vol. 3, pt. 2. 1949. Reprint, Washington, D.C.: Center of Military History, United States Army, 1988.

Philippine Legislature. *Laws of the Fourth Philippine Legislature.* 2 vols. Washington, D.C.: Government Printing Office, 1918.

———. *Public Laws Enacted by the Philippine Legislature.* Vol. 30. Manila: Bureau of Printing, 1935.

Philippine National Assembly. *Diario de sesiones de la period inaugural de sesiones.* Vol. 1. Manila: Bureau of Printing, 1940.

Philippine Operations Record, Phase I, Nov. 1941–July 1942. [Tokyo?]: U.S. Army Far East Command, 1946. Also known as "Japanese Monograph no. 1."

Report of the Philippine Commission to the Secretary of War. 1909, 1912, 1915.

Reports of General MacArthur. 2 vols. 1966. Reprint, Washington, D.C.: Center of Military History, United States Army, 1994.

Roster and Directory [of] United States Troops serving in the Philippine Department. Manila: Headquarters, Philippine Department. 1917–19.

Taft, William Howard. *Special Report of Wm. H. Taft, Secretary of War, to the President on the Philippines.* Manila: Bureau of Printing, 1908.

United States. *Japan and Its Occupied Territories during World War II.* Washington, D.C.: University Publications of America, 1977. Microfilm, reel 10.

U.S. Army. *Civil Affairs Handbook: The Philippines.* U.S. Army Service Forces, 1945.

U.S. Congress. House of Representatives. *Hearings before the House Committee on Military Affairs on Army Appropriations Bill for Fiscal Year 1908–09.* 60th Cong., 1st Sess., 1908.

U.S. Congress. House of Representatives. *Hearings before the House Committee on Military Affairs on the Military Academy Appropriation Bill for the Fiscal Year Ending June 30, 1913,* 62nd Cong., 2nd Sess., 1912.

U.S. Congress. Senate. *War Department Appropriation Bill for 1938; Hearings before the Subcommittee of the Committee on Appropriations.* 75th Cong., 1st Sess., 1937.

Newspapers and Journals

Army and Navy Journal
Army and Navy Journal of the Philippines
Cablenews-American
Citizen Army
Commoner (Bacolod)
Iloilo Enterprise-Press
Khaki and Red
Manila Daily Bulletin
Manila Times
Manila Tribune
New York Times
New York Tribune
Philippine Collegian
Philippine Magazine
Philippines Free Press
Philippines Herald
Washington Post

Published Books and Articles

Abaya, Hernando. *Betrayal in the Philippines.* New York: A. A. Wyn, 1946.

Abraham, Abie. *Oh God Where Are You?* New York: Vantage Press, 1997.

Agoncillo, Teodoro A. *The Burden of Proof.* Quezon City: University of the Philippines Press, 1984.

———. *The Fateful Years: Japan's Adventure in the Philippines, 1941–1945.* 2 vols. 1965. Reprint, Quezon City: University of the Philippines Press, 2001.

Alexander, Irvin. *Surviving Bataan and Beyond.* Edited by D. J. Caraccilo. Mechanicsburg, Pa.: Stackpole, 1999.

Ambrose, Stephen E. *Eisenhower: Soldier, General of the Army, President-Elect, 1890–1952.* New York: Simon and Schuster, 1983.

Ancheta, C. A., ed. *Triumph in the Philippines.* Manila: National Book Store, 1977.

———, ed. *The Wainwright Papers.* 4 vols. Quezon City: New Day, 1980–82.

Ashton, Paul. *Bataan Diary.* N.p.: privately published, 1984.

Atienza, Rigoberto J. *A Time for War: 105 Days in Bataan.* Manila: privately published, 1985.

Ayres, Leonard P. *The War with Germany: A Statistical Summary.* 2nd ed. Washington, D.C.: Government Printing Office, 1919.

Baclagon, Uldarico S. *Filipinos in the Allied Intelligence Bureau.* Makati City, Phil.: privately published, 1989.

———. *Last 130 Days of the USAFFE.* Manila: privately published, 1982.

———. *The Philippine Resistance Movement against Japan.* Manila: Veterans Federation of the Philippines, 1965.

———. *They Served with Honor: Filipino War Heroes of World War II.* Quezon City: DM Press, 1968.

Baja, Emanuel A. *Philippine Police System and Its Problems.* Manila: Pobre Press, 1933.

———. *Philippine Police System and Its Problems.* Book 2. Manila: Philippine Education Co., 1939.

Baldwin, Hanson. *Great Mistakes of the War.* New York: Harper and Brothers, 1950.

Bankwitz, Philip. *Maxime Weygand and Civil-Military Relations in Modern France.* Cambridge, Mass.: Harvard University Press, 1967.

Bartsch, William. *Doomed at the Start.* College Station: Texas A&M University Press, 1992.

Bataan and Corregidor: Battleground of the Brave. Manila: National Media Production Center, 1977.

Beck, John Jacob. *MacArthur and Wainwright: Sacrifice of the Philippines.* Albuquerque: University of New Mexico Press, 1974.

Beebe, Lewis. *Prisoner of the Rising Sun.* College Station: Texas A&M University Press, 2006.

Berlin, Donald L. *Before Gringo: History of the Philippine Military, 1830 to 1972.* Manila: Anvil, 2008.

Bernstein, David. *The Philippine Story.* New York: Farrar, Straus, 1947.

Berthoff, R. T. "Taft and MacArthur, 1900–1901: A Study in Civil-Military Relations." *World Politics* 5, no. 2 (1953): 196–213.

Blair, Emma, and James Robertson, eds. *The Philippine Islands, 1493–1898.* Vol. 49. Cleveland, Ohio: Arthur H. Clark, 1907.

Bland, Larry I., ed. *The Papers of George Catlett Marshall.* Vols. 1, 3. Baltimore: Johns Hopkins University Press, 1981–91.

Blesse, F. A. "The Filipino Fighting Man: An Appraisal of the Men Charged with Defending the Philippine Commonwealth." *Philippines* 1, no. 8 (1941): 6–7.

Boyce, William D. *United States Colonies and Dependencies.* Chicago: Rand McNally, 1914.

Boyt, Eugene P. *Bataan: A Survivor's Story.* Norman: University of Oklahoma Press, 2004.

Braisted, William R. *The United States Navy in the Pacific, 1897–1909.* Austin: University of Texas Press, 1958.

Brougher, W. E. *South to Bataan, North to Mukden: The Prison Diary of Brigadier General W. E. Brougher.* Edited by D. Clayton James. Athens: University of Georgia Press, 1971.

Buenafe, Manuel E., ed. *The Voice of the Veteran.* Manila: Philippine Educational Promotion, 1971.

———. *Wartime Philippines.* Manila: Manila Education Foundation, 1950.

Buencamino, Felipe. *Memoirs and Diaries of Felipe Buencamino III.* Makati City, Phil.: CopyCat, 2003.

Buencamino, Victor. *Memoirs of Victor Buencamino.* Mandaluyong, Phil.: Jorge B. Vargas Filipiniana Foundation, 1977.

Bunker, Paul D., and Keith A. Barlow. *Bunker's War: The World War II Diary of Col. Paul D. Bunker.* Novato, Calif.: Presidio Press, 1996.

Cannon, M. Hamlin. *Leyte: The Return to the Philippines.* Washington, D.C.: Office of the Chief of Military History, Department of the Army, 1954.

Cariño, Ranulfo. *A Brief History of the 21st Division, Philippine Army.* Quezon City: Office of the Chief of Military History, Armed Forces of the Philippines, 1971.

Casillan, Marcelo G., Sr. *My Life and Times.* Dagupan City, Phil.: privately published, 1999.

Catalan, Primitivo M. *A Brief History of the 81st Division, Philippine Army.* Quezon City: Office of the Chief of Military History, Armed Forces of the Philippines, 1973.

Catalan, Primitivo M., and Eduardo A. Calderon. *A Brief History of the 51st Division, Philippine Army.* Quezon City: Office of the Chief of Military History, Armed Forces of the Philippines, 1974.

Cave, Dorothy. *Beyond Courage: One Regiment against Japan.* Las Cruces, N.M.: Yucca Tree Press, 1992.

Challener, Richard. *The French Theory of the Nation in Arms.* New York: Russell & Russell, 1965.

Chester, Alvin P. *A Sailor's Odyssey.* Miami: Odysseus Books, 1991.

Chunn, C. E., ed. *Of Rice and Men.* Los Angeles: Veterans Publishing, 1946.

Chynoweth, Bradford. *Bellamy Park.* Hicksville, N.Y.: Exposition Press, 1975.

Clark, Frank S. *The Chronicle of Aunt Lena.* Charlotte, N.C.: privately published, 1962.

Clements, Hendrick A. *The Presidency of Woodrow Wilson.* Lawrence: University Press of Kansas, 1992.

Coates, Austin. *Rizal: Philippine Nationalist and Martyr.* 1968. Reprint, Manila: Oxford University Press, 1982.

Coffman, Edward M. "The Philippine Scouts, 1899–1942: A Historical Vignette." *ACTA*, no. 3 (1978): 68–79.

———. *The Regulars: The American Army, 1898–1917.* Cambridge, Mass.: Harvard University Press, 2004.

Coffman, Edward M., and Peter F. Herrly. "The American Regular Army Officer Corps between the World Wars: A Collective Biography." *Armed Forces and Society* 4, no. 1 (1977): 59–73.

Coleman, John S. *Bataan and Beyond.* College Station: Texas A&M University Press, 1978.

Collins, J. Lawton. *Lightning Joe: An Autobiography.* Baton Rouge: Louisiana State University Press, 1979.

Condit, Kenneth W., and Edwin T. Turnbladh. *Hold High the Torch: A History of the 4th Marines.* Washington, D.C.: Headquarters U.S. Marine Corps, Historical Branch, G-3 Division, 1960.

Condon-Rall, Mary Ellen, and Albert E. Cowdrey. *Medical Service in the War against Japan.* Washington, D.C.: Center of Military History, United States Army, 1998.

Constantino, Renato, ed. *Under Japanese Rule: Memories and Reflections.* Quezon City: Foundation for Nationalist Studies, 1994.

Cooling, Benjamin Franklin. "Dwight D. Eisenhower at the Army War College, 1927–1928." *Parameters* 5, no. 1 (1975): 26–36.

Cooper, John Milton, Jr. *Woodrow Wilson: A Biography.* New York: Alfred A. Knopf, 2009.

Coox, Alvin D. *The Unfought War: Japan, 1941–1942.* San Diego, Calif.: San Diego State University Press, 1992.

Cornejo, Miguel R., comp. *Cornejo's Commonwealth Directory of the Philippines.* Manila: privately published, 1939.

Daroy, E. Vallado. *Nobody Gathers Seashells and Gun Shells Anymore.* Quezon City: New Day, 1981.

Dauncey, Mrs. Campbell. *The Philippines: An Account of Their People, Progress, and Condition.* Boston: J. B. Millet, 1910.

Davis, Benjamin O., Jr. *An Autobiography.* Washington, D.C.: Smithsonian Institution Press, 1991.

De Guzman, Jovito Varias, ed. *Women of Distinction: Biographical Essays on Outstanding Filipino Women of the Past and the Present.* N.p.: Bukang Liwayway, 1967.

De Vera, Ruel S. *The Zero Hour: The Personal War of Basilio J. Valdes.* Makati City, Phil.: Bookmark, 2001.

De Veyra, Manuel E. *Doctor in Bataan, 1941–1942.* Quezon City: New Day, 1991.

Dizon, Lino L. *East of Pinatubo.* Tarlac: Tarlac State University, 1998.

Dod, Karl C. *The Corps of Engineers: The War against Japan.* Washington, D.C.: Center of Military History, United States Army, 1987.

Doeppers, Daniel F. *Feeding Manila in Peace and War, 1850–1945.* Madison: University of Wisconsin Press, 2016.

Donovan, William. *P.O.W. in the Pacific.* Wilmington, Del.: Scholarly Resources, 1998.

Drea, Edward J. *In the Service of the Emperor.* Lincoln: University of Nebraska Press, 1998.

Dyess, William E. *The Dyess Story.* Edited by Charles Leavelle. New York: G. P. Putnam's Sons, 1944.

Eisenhower, Dwight David. *At Ease: Stories I Tell to Friends.* Garden City, N.Y.: Doubleday, 1967.

———. *Crusade in Europe.* Garden City, N.Y.: Doubleday, 1948.

———. *Eisenhower: The Prewar Diaries and Selected Papers, 1905–1941.* Edited by Daniel D. Holt and James W. Leyerzapf. Baltimore: Johns Hopkins University Press, 1998.

———. *The Papers of Dwight David Eisenhower.* Edited by Alfred D. Chandler Jr., Stephen E. Ambrose, Louis Galambos, Daun van Ee, Joseph P. Hobbs, Elizabeth S. Hughes, and others. 21 vols. Baltimore: Johns Hopkins University Press, 1970–2001.

Eisenhower, Susan. *Mrs. Ike: Memories and Reflections on the Life of Mamie Eisenhower.* New York: Farrar, Straus, and Giroux, 1996.

Elarth, Harold Hanne, ed. *The Story of the Philippine Constabulary.* Los Angeles: Philippine Constabulary Officers Association, 1949.

Elliott, Charles B. *The Philippines to the End of the Commission Government.* Indianapolis: Bobbs-Merrill, 1917.

———. *The Philippines to the End of the Military Regime.* Indianapolis: Bobbs-Merrill, 1916.

Enosawa, G. H. *Manuel L. Quezon: From Nipa House to Malacañan.* 1940. Reprint, Manila: Manuel L. Morato, [c. 1993].

Escoda, Jose M. *Warsaw of Asia.* Quezon City: Giraffe Books, 2000.

Falk, Stanley L. *Bataan: The March of Death.* New York: Curtis Books, 1962.

Faust, Karl Irving. *Campaigning in the Philippines.* 1899. Reprint, New York: Arno Press and The New York Times, 1970.

Fields, John W. *Kangaroo Squadron: Memoirs of a Pacific Bomber Pilot.* N.p.: privately published, 1982.

Fine, Sidney. *Frank Murphy: The New Deal Years.* Chicago: University of Chicago Press, 1979.

Fletcher, Marvin E. *America's First Black General: Benjamin O. Davis, Sr., 1880–1970.* Lawrence: University Press of Kansas, 1989.

Forbes, W. Cameron. *The Philippine Islands.* 2 vols. New York: Houghton Mifflin, 1928.

Foreman, John. *The Philippine Islands.* 3rd ed. 1906. Reprint, Manila: Cacho Hermanos, 1985.

Forman, Sidney. *West Point: A History of the United States Military Academy.* New York: Columbia University Press, 1950.

Fortier, Malcolm. *Life of a P.O.W. under the Japanese.* Spokane, Wash.: C. W. Hill, 1946.

Friend, Theodore. *Between Two Empires.* New Haven, Conn.: Yale University Press, 1965.

Galang, Ricardo C. *Hammer and Anvil.* Quezon City: Phoenix, 1989.

———. *Secret Mission to the Philippines.* Manila: University Publishing, 1948.

Galang, Z. M. *Leaders of the Philippines.* Manila: National Publishing, 1932.

Ganoe, William A. *The History of the United States Army.* New York: D. Appleton and Co., 1924.

General and Flag Officers of the Philippines. Quezon City: Registry Committee, Association of General and Flag Officers, 1977.

Ghormley, Ralph M., comp. *Military Order of the Carabao Centennial History.* N.p.: Military Order of the Carabao, 2000.

Gilbert, Paul T. *The Great White Tribe in Filipinia.* Cincinnati, Ohio: Jennings and Pye, 1903.

Gleeck, Lewis E., Jr. *The American Half-Century, 1898–1946.* Manila: Historical Conservation Society, 1984.

———. *Laguna in American Times.* Manila: Historical Conservation Society, 1981.

———. *The Manila Americans.* Manila: Carmelo and Bauermann, 1977.

Gloria, Claro. *All the Way from Bataan to O'Donnell.* Quezon City: privately published, 1978.

Go, Puan Seng. *The Hour Had Come.* Grand Rapids, Mich.: Douma Publications, 1958.

Golay, Frank H. *Face of Empire: United States–Philippine Relations, 1898–1946.* Madison: Center for Southeast Asian Studies, University of Wisconsin, 1998.

Gopinath, Aruna. *Manuel L. Quezon: The Tutelary Democrat.* Quezon City: New Day, 1987.

Guerrero, Jaime L. *Waiting for the Enemy.* Quezon City: Central Book Supply, 2010.

Gumban, Edgarto T. *Bataan Company Commander.* N.p.: privately published, n.d.

Gunther, John. *Inside Asia.* Rev. ed. New York: Harper and Brothers, 1942.

Gwekoh, Sol H. *Manuel L. Quezon: His Life and Career.* Manila: University Publishing, 1948.

Halsema, James J. *E. J. Halsema: Colonial Engineer.* Quezon City: New Day, 1991.

Hamm, Margherita Arlina. *Manila and the Philippines.* London: F. Tennyson Neely, 1898.

Hancock, H. Irving. *Life at West Point.* New York: G. P. Putnam's Sons, 1902.

Harrison, Francis Burton. *The Cornerstone of Philippine Independence.* New York: The Century Co., 1922.

———. *Origins of the Philippine Republic: Extracts from the Diaries and Records of Francis Burton Harrison.* Edited by Michael P. Onorato. Ithaca, N.Y.: Cornell University Department of Asian Studies, 1974.

Hartendorp, A. V. H. *History of Trade and Industry of the Philippines.* Manila: American Chamber of Commerce, 1961.

———. *The Japanese Occupation of the Philippines.* 2 vols. Manila: Bookmark, 1967.

Hayden, Joseph R. *The Philippines: A Study in National Development.* New York: Macmillan, 1942.

Hayes, Thomas. *Bilibid Diary: The Secret Notebooks of Commander Thomas Hayes.* Edited by A. B. Feuer. New York: Archon Books, 1987.

Heisinger, Duane. *Father Found: Life and Death as a Prisoner of the Japanese in World War II.* Longwood, Fla.: Xulon Press, 2003.

Hill, Alva J. "The Philippine Army during the World War." *Philippine Forum* 2, no. 1 (1936): 52–61.

History of the Philippine Army, 1897–1945. Manila: Army Historical Division, Philippine Army, 1982.

Hoge, William M. *Engineer Memoirs.* Washington, D.C.: United States Army Corps of Engineers, Office of History, 1993.

Hough, Frank, Verle Ludwig, and Henry Shaw. *Pearl Harbor to Guadalcanal.* Washington, D.C.: Headquarters U.S. Marine Corps, 1958.

Hunt, Frazier. *MacArthur and the War against Japan.* New York: Charles Scribner's Sons, 1944.

———. *The Untold Story of Douglas MacArthur.* New York: The Devin-Adair Company, 1954.

Hurley, Vic. *Jungle Patrol.* New York: E. P. Dutton, 1938.

Ikehata, Setsuho, and Ricardo T. Jose, eds. *The Philippines under Japan.* Quezon City: Ateneo de Manila University Press, 1999.

Ind, Allison. *Allied Intelligence Bureau.* New York: David McKay, 1958.

[Infante, Mariano, comp.] *Golden Anniversary, 1941–1991.* [Manila:] 41st Division Foundation, 1991.

Ingham, Travis. *Rendezvous by Submarine.* Garden City, N.Y.: Doubleday, Doran, 1945.

Jackson, Calvin. *Diary of Col. Calvin G. Jackson, M.D.* Ada: Ohio Northern University Press, 1992.

Jacobsen, Gene S. *We Refused to Die.* Salt Lake City: University of Utah Press, 2004.

Jalandoni, Venicio. *A Silent Sacrifice.* N.p.: privately published, 1998.

James, D. Clayton. *The Years of MacArthur.* 3 vols. Boston: Houghton Mifflin, 1970–1985.

Jamias, Cristino. *The University of the Philippines: The First Half Century.* Quezon City: University of the Philippines Press, 1962.

Japanese Military Administration. *The Official Journal of the Japanese Military Administration.* Vol. 3. Manila, 1942; reprint, War Department, n.d.

Jolly, John P. *History [of the] New Mexico National Guard, 1606–1963.* [Santa Fe:] New Mexico National Guard, Adjutant General's Department, 1963.

Jose, Ricardo T., ed. *The Book on the Japanese Occupation: World War II and the Japanese Occupation.* Quezon City: University of the Philippines Press, 2006.

———. *Captive Arms: The Constabulary under the Japanese, 1942–1944.* Quezon City: College of Social Sciences and Philosophy, University of the Philippines, 1997.

———. *The Philippine Army.* Quezon City: Ateneo de Manila University Press, 1992.

———. "The Philippine National Guard in World War I." *Philippine Studies* 36 (1988): 275–99.

———. "Remembering World War II in the Philippines: Memorials, Commemorations and Movies." In *Globalization, Localization, and Japanese Studies in the Asia-Pacific Region: International Symposium,* 115–34. Kyoto: International Research Center for Japanese Studies, 2010.

Jubal, Exequiel D., and Soloman A. Asturias. *A Brief History of the 41st Division, Philippine Army.* Quezon City: Office of the Chief of Military History, Armed Forces of the Philippines, 1974.

Kalaw, Maximo. *The Case for the Filipinos.* New York: The Century Co., 1916.

———. *The Fighting Filipinos.* Manila: privately published, 1966.

———. *Self-Government in the Philippines.* New York: The Century Co., 1919.

Karig, Walter, and Welbourn Kelley. *Battle Report: Pearl Harbor to Coral Sea.* New York: Farrar & Rinehart, 1944.

Knox, Donald. *Death March: The Survivors of Bataan.* New York: Harcourt Brace Jovanovich, 1981.

Kramer, Robert S. *One Out of Eleven.* Atlanta: privately published, 1992.

Kumai, Toshimi. *The Blood and Mud in the Philippines: Anti-Guerrilla Warfare on Panay Island.* Iloilo, Phil.: Malones Printing, 2009.

Kushner, Ervan F. *Bogged Down in Bora Bora: A History of the 198th Coast Artillery Regiment (Antiaircraft) on Bora Bora Island, 1942–1943.* Paterson, N.J.: E. F. Kushner Books, 1984.

Labrador, Juan. *A Diary of the Japanese Occupation.* Manila: Santo Tomas University Press, 1989.

Lapham, Robert, and Bernard Norling. *Lapham's Raiders: Guerrillas in the Philippines, 1942–1945*. Lexington: University Press of Kentucky, 1996.
Larkin, John A. *Sugar and the Origins of Modern Philippine Society.* Berkeley: University of California Press, 1993.
Larson, Clarence. *A Long March Home.* Fergus Falls, Minn.: privately published, 1998.
Laurel, Jose P. *War Memoirs of Dr. Jose P. Laurel.* Manila: Jose P. Laurel Memorial Foundation, 1962.
Lee, Clark. *They Call It Pacific.* New York: Viking Press, 1943.
Lee, Henry G. *Nothing but Praise.* Culver City, Calif.: Murray & Gee, 1948.
LeRoy, James A. *The Americans in the Philippines.* 2 vols. 1914. Reprint, New York: AMS Press, 1970.
Lewis, Graydon, ed. *Intercept Station C: From Olongapo through the Evacuation of Corregidor.* Denver, Colo.: Naval Cryptologic Veterans Association, 1983.
Lichauco, Marcial P. *"Dear Mother Putnam": A Diary of the War in the Philippines.* Manila: privately published, 1949.
———. *Roxas: The Story of a Great Filipino and of the Political Era in Which He Lived.* Manila: Kiko Printing, 1952.
Lim, Roberto H. *Pushing the Envelope.* Pasay City, Phil.: Mapua House, 2010.
Lim, Vicente. *To Inspire and to Lead: The Letters of Gen. Vicente Lim, 1938–1942.* With an introduction by Edilberto C. de Jesus. Manila: privately published, 1980.
Linn, Brian. *Guardians of Empire.* Chapel Hill: University of North Carolina Press, 1997.
———. "Guerrilla Fighter: Frederick Funston in the Philippines." *Kansas History* 10, no. 1 (1987): 2–16.
———. *The Philippine War, 1899–1902.* Lawrence: University Press of Kansas, 2000.
MacArthur, Douglas. *Reminiscences.* New York: McGraw-Hill, 1964.
Malcolm, George. *The Commonwealth of the Philippines.* New York: D. Appleton-Century Co., 1939.
Mallillin-Jamboy, Evelyn. *Resistance Movement in Lanao.* Iligan City, Phil.: MSU-Iligan Institute of Technology, 1985.
Mallonée, Richard C. *Battle for Bataan: An Eyewitness Account.* Novato, Calif.: Presidio, 1980.
Manchester, William. *American Caesar.* New York: Dell Publishing, 1978.
Manikan, Gamaliel. *Guerilla Warfare on Panay Island in the Philippines.* Manila: Sixth Military District Veterans Foundation, 1977.
Marquez, Adalia. *Blood on the Rising Sun: A Factual Story of the Japanese Invasion of the Philippines.* New York: DeTanko, 1957.
Mason, John T., Jr., ed. *The Pacific War Remembered: An Oral History Collection.* Annapolis, Md.: Naval Institute Press, 2003.
Matson, Eva Jane. *It Tolled for New Mexico: New Mexicans Captured by the Japanese, 1941–1945*. Las Cruces, N.M.: Yucca Tree Press, 1994.
May, Mary Cathrin. *The Steadfast Line: The Story of the 27th Bombardment Group (Light) in World War II.* 4th printing. Tallahassee, Fla.: privately published, 2006.
McCoy, Alfred W. *Closer than Brothers.* Manila: Anvil, 1999.
———. *Policing America's Empire.* Madison: University of Wisconsin Press, 2009.
McCoy, Alfred W., and Ed. C. de Jesus, eds. *Philippine Social History: Global Trade and Local Transformations.* Quezon City: Ateneo de Manila University Press, 1982.

McElhenny, William S., et al. *Armor on Luzon: A Research Report*. Ft. Knox, Ky., The Armor School, 1950.

Meixsel, Richard B. "American Exceptionalism in Colonial Forces? The Philippine Scout Mutiny of 1924." In *Colonial Armies in Southeast Asia*, ed. Karl Hack and Tobias Rettig, 171–94. London: Routledge, 2006.

———. *Clark Field and the U.S. Army Air Corps in the Philippines, 1919–1942*. Quezon City: New Day, 2002.

———. "Major General George Grunert, WPO-3, and the Philippine Army, 1940–1941." *Journal of Military History* 59, no. 2 (1995): 303–24.

———. "Manuel L. Quezon, Douglas MacArthur, and the Significance of the Military Mission to the Philippine Commonwealth." *Pacific Historical Review* 70, no. 2 (2001): 255–92.

———. *Philippine-American Military History, 1902–1942: An Annotated Bibliography*. Jefferson, N.C.: McFarland, 2003.

Miller, E. B. *Bataan Uncensored*. 1949. Reprint, Little Falls, Minn.: Military Historical Society of Minnesota, 1991.

Miller, Edward S. *War Plan Orange*. Annapolis, Md.: Naval Institute Press, 1991.

Miller, Francis Trevelyan. *General Douglas MacArthur: Fighter for Freedom*. Chicago: John C. Winston, 1942.

Miller, J. Michael. *From Shanghai to Corregidor: Marines in the Defense of the Philippines*. Washington, D.C.: History and Museums Division, Headquarters U.S. Marine Corps, 1997.

Millett, Allan R., and Peter Maslowski. *For the Common Defense: A Military History of the United States of America*. Rev. ed. New York: The Free Press, 1994.

Mojica, Proculo L. *Terry's Hunters*. Manila: privately published, 1965.

Molina, Antonio M. *Dusk and Dawn in the Philippines: Memoirs of a Living Witness of World War II*. Quezon City: New Day, 1996.

Morison, Samuel Eliot. *History of United States Naval Operations in World War II*. Vol. 3, *The Rising Sun in the Pacific, 1931–April 1942*. Boston: Little, Brown, 1948.

Morton, Louis. "The Decision to Withdraw to Bataan." In *Command Decisions*, edited by Kent Roberts Greenfield, 151–72. Washington, D.C.: Center of Military History, United States Army, 2000.

———. *The Fall of the Philippines*. Washington, D.C.: Office of the Chief of Military History, 1953.

———. "The Philippine Army, 1935–1939: Eisenhower's Memorandum to Quezon." *Military Affairs* 12 (1948): 103–7.

———. *Strategy and Command: The First Two Years*. Washington, D.C.: Office of the Chief of Military History, 1962.

———. "War Plan Orange: Evolution of a Strategy," *World Politics* 11, no. 2 (1959): 221–50.

Munda, Amado A. *The Last Days of General Santos*. Cotabato, Phil.: privately published, n.d.

Murray, Williamson, and Allan R. Millett, eds. *Military Innovation in the Interwar Period*. Cambridge: Cambridge University Press, 1996.

Navarro, Edmundo G. *Beds of Nails*. 3rd printing. Manila: privately published, 1988.

Nelson, Linnea A., and Elma S. Herradura. *Scientia et Fides: The Story of Central Philippine University*. Iloilo: Central Philippine University, 1981.

Nier, T. J., and A. R. Menke, comps. *The Gleim Medal Letters, 1971–1997.* 2nd ed. San Ramon, Calif.: Orders and Medals Society of America, 2001.
Oatman, Earl R. *Only the Beginning.* Riverside, Calif.: privately published, 1991.
Ochosa, Orlino A. *The Tinio Brigade: Anti-American Resistance in the Ilocos Provinces, 1899–1901.* Quezon City: New Day, 1989.
Olson, John. *Anywhere-Anytime.* N.p.: privately published, 1991.
———. *O'Donnell: Andersonville of the Pacific.* N.p.: privately published, 1985.
Ongpauco, Fidel L. *They Refused to Die.* Gatineau, Quebec: Levesque Publications, 1982.
Ongpin, Guido R. *The Story of the Philippine Packing Corporation, 1926–1966.* [Manila?]: [Philippine Packing Corporation?], 1966.
Onorato, Michael. *A Brief Review of American Interest in Philippine Development and Other Essays.* Rev. ed. Manila: MCS Enterprises, 1972.
O'Reilly, Edward S. *Roving and Fighting: Adventures under Four Flags.* New York: The Century Co., 1918.
Paredes, Ruby R., ed. *Philippine Colonial Democracy.* Quezon City: Ateneo de Manila University Press, 1989.
Peña, Ambrosio P. *Bataan's Own.* Manila: 2nd Regular Division Association, 1967.
———. *The Story of the 1st Regular Division.* Quezon City: Military History Branch, Armed Forces of the Philippines, 1953.
Pestaño, Rolando S. *A Brief History of the 31st Division, Philippine Army.* Quezon City: Office of the Chief of Military History, Armed Forces of the Philippines, 1976.
Petillo, Carol Morris. *Douglas MacArthur: The Philippine Years.* Bloomington: Indiana University Press, 1981.
Philippine Commission of Independence. *Beautiful Philippines: A Handbook of General Information.* Manila: Bureau of Printing, 1923.
Philippine Normal School, Manila, Philippine Islands, Catalogue for 1917–18. Manila, 1919.
The Philippine Scouts. Fort Sam Houston, Tex.: Philippine Scouts Heritage Society, 1996.
Phillips, Claire, and Myron B. Goldsmith. *Manila Espionage.* Portland, Ore.: Binfords & Mort, 1947.
Pobre, Cesar P. *History of the Armed Forces of the Filipino People.* Quezon City: New Day, 2000.
Pogue, Forrest. *George C. Marshall: Education of a General.* New York: The Viking Press, 1963.
Poncio, John Henry, and Marlin Young. *Girocho.* Baton Rouge: Louisiana State University Press, 2003.
Porter, Catherine. *Crisis in the Philippines.* New York: Alfred A. Knopf, 1942.
Potts, Adam. "1914 in the Philippines." In *The Ten Year Book*, 31–32. West Point, N.Y.: U.S. Military Academy, Class of 1914, 1926.
Pringle, Henry F. *The Life and Times of William Howard Taft.* Vol. 1. New York: Farrar & Rinehart, 1939.
Quezon, Manuel L. *The Good Fight.* New York: D. Appleton-Century Co., 1946.
———. *Filipino People* 2, no. 10 (1914): 23.
Quinn, Michael A. *Love Letters to Mike.* 2nd ed. Steilacoom, Wash.: Circle Q Press, 2004.
Quirino, Carlos. *Chick Parsons.* Quezon City: New Day, 1984.

———. *Filipinos at War.* Quezon City: Vera-Reyes, 1981.
———. *Quezon: Paladin of Philippine Freedom.* Manila: Filipiniana Book Guild, 1971.
Ramsey, Edwin Price, and Stephen J. Rivele. *Lieutenant Ramsey's War.* New York: Knightsbridge, 1990.
Register of Graduates and Former Cadets of the United States Military Academy. West Point, N.Y.: Association of Graduates, 1990.
Ridgway, Matthew B. *Soldier: The Memoirs of Matthew B. Ridgway.* As told to Harold H. Martin. New York: Harper and Brothers, 1956.
Rio, Eliseo D. *Rays of a Setting Sun.* Manila: De La Salle University Press, 1999.
Robinson, Wirt, ed. *General Cullum's Biographical Register of the Officers and Graduates of the United States Military Academy*, vol. 6B, *Supplement, 1910–1920.* Saginaw, Mich.: Seeman and Peters, 1920.
Roces, Alfredo. *Looking for Liling.* Manila: Anvil, 2000.
Rogers, Paul P. *The Bitter Years: MacArthur and Sutherland.* Westport, Conn.: Praeger, 1991.
Romulo, Carlos P. *I Saw the Fall of the Philippines.* Garden City, N.Y.: Doubleday, Doran, 1943.
Root, Elihu. *The Military and Colonial Policy of the United States.* Cambridge, Mass.: Harvard University Press, 1916.
Rosen, Melvin H. *History of the Philippine Scouts Field Artillery.* Falls Church, Va.: privately published, 1995.
Rosenfeld, Harvey. *Richmond Pearson Hobson: Naval Hero of Magnolia Grove.* Las Cruces, N.M.: Yucca Tree Press, 2000.
Rosinger, Lawrence K. "The Philippines—Problems of Independence." *Foreign Policy Reports* 24, no. 8 (1948): 82–95.
Rostker, Bernard. *I Want You! The Evolution of the All-Volunteer Force.* Santa Monica, Calif.: RAND, 2006.
Roth, Dennis Morrow. *The Friar Estates of the Philippines.* Albuquerque: University of New Mexico Press, 1977.
Roxas, Manuel. "Brief Summary of the Activities of Manuel Roxas during the Japanese Occupation." In *Documents on the Japanese Occupation of the Philippines*, edited by Mauro Garcia, 238–58. Manila: Philippine Historical Association, 1965.
Rutledge, Tilman J. *My Japanese POW Diary Story.* New York: Vantage Press, 1997.
Salamanca, Bonifacio S. *The Filipino Reaction to American Rule.* 1968. Reprint, Quezon City: New Day, 1984.
Savary, Gladys. *Outside the Walls.* New York: Vantage Press, 1954.
Sayre, Francis Bowes. *Glad Adventure.* New York: Macmillan, 1957.
Schaffer, Ronald. "General Stanley D. Embick: Military Dissenter." *Military Affairs* 37, no. 3 (1973): 89–95.
Schultz, Duane. *Hero of Bataan: The Story of General Jonathan M. Wainwright.* New York: St. Martin's Press, 1981.
Selleck, Clyde. *The War Diary of Gen. Clyde Selleck.* Manila: Historical Conservation Society, 1985.
Sevilla, Victor J. *Bataan Odyssey.* Manila: Salesiana Publishers, 1988.
Sexton, William. *Soldiers in the Sun.* Harrisburg, Pa.: The Military Service Publishing Co., 1939.
Sinco, Vicente G. *The Government of the Commonwealth of the Philippines.* Manila: Community Publishers, 1938.

Smith, Jean Edward. *Lucius D. Clay: An American Life.* New York: Henry Holt, 1990.
Smith, Robert Ross. *Triumph in the Philippines.* Washington, D.C.: Office of the Chief of Military History, 1963.
Sonnichsen, Albert. *Ten Months a Captive among Filipinos.* New York: Charles Scribner's Sons, 1901.
Sorley, Lewis. *Honorable Warrior: General Harold K. Johnson and the Ethics of Command.* Lawrence: University Press of Kansas, 1998.
Stanley, Peter W. *A Nation in the Making: The Philippines and the United States, 1899–1921.* Cambridge, Mass.: Harvard University Press, 1974.
Steinberg, David Joel. *Philippine Collaboration in World War II.* Manila: Solidaridad Publishing House, 1967.
Sturtevant, David R. *Popular Uprisings in the Philippines, 1840–1940.* Ithaca, N.Y.: Cornell University Press, 1976.
Summerall, Charles. *The Way of Duty, Honor, Country: The Memoir of General Charles Pelot Summerall.* Edited by Timothy K. Nenninger. Lexington: University Press of Kentucky, 2010.
Swinson, Arthur. *Four Samurai.* London: Hutchinson, 1968.
Tagarao, Silvestre L. *All This Was Bataan.* Quezon City: New Day, 1991.
Taruc, Luis. *Born of the People.* New York: International Publishers, 1953.
Taylor, John R. M. *The Philippine Insurrection against the United States: A Compilation of Documents with Notes and Introduction.* 5 vols. Pasay City, Phil.: Eugenio Lopez Foundation, 1971.
Thomas, Ed. *As I Remember: The Death March of Bataan.* Sonoita, Ariz.: privately published, 1990.
Thorpe, Elliott R. *East Wind, Rain: The Intimate Account of an Intelligence Officer in the Pacific, 1939–1949.* Boston: Gambit, 1969.
Toland, John. *But Not in Shame.* New York: Random House, 1961.
———. *The Rising Sun.* New York: Random House, 1970.
Topham, Anne. *A Distant Thunder: Intimate Recollections of the Kaiser's Court.* Pound Ridge, N.Y.: New Chapter Press, 1992.
Twichell, Heath, Jr. *Allen: The Biography of an Army Officer.* New Brunswick, N.J.: Rutgers University Press, 1974.
Underbrink, Robert L. *Destination Corregidor.* Annapolis, Md.: United States Naval Institute, 1971.
U.S. Military Academy. *The Howitzer, 1914.* West Point, N.Y., 1914.
Vance, John R. *Doomed Garrison—the Philippines (a POW Story).* Ashland, Ore.: Cascade House, 1974.
Verzosa, Vicente L. *What Price Valor.* Manila: privately published, 1962.
"Vicente Lim." *Assembly* 7, no. 4 (1949): 12–13.
Villamor, Jesus. *They Never Surrendered.* As told to Gerald S. Snyder. Quezon City: Vera-Reyes, 1982.
Villarin, Mariano. *We Remember Bataan and Corregidor.* Baltimore: Gateway Press, 1990.
Watson, Mark Skinner. *Chief of Staff: Prewar Plans and Preparations.* Washington, D.C.: Historical Division, Department of the Army, 1950.
White, W. L. *They Were Expendable.* New York: Harcourt, Brace & World, 1942.
Whitehead, Arthur. *Odyssey of a Philippine Scout.* Tucson, Ariz.: privately published, 1989.

Whitman, John W. *Bataan: Our Last Ditch.* New York: Hippocrene Books, 1990.
Whitney, Courtney. *MacArthur, His Rendezvous with History.* New York: Alfred A. Knopf, 1956.
Wickberg, Edgar. *The Chinese in Philippine Life, 1850–1898.* New Haven, Conn.: Yale University Press, 1965.
Williams, D. R. *The United States and the Philippines.* Garden City, N.Y.: Doubleday, 1926.
Willis, Henry Park. *Our Philippine Problem.* New York: Henry Holt, 1905.
Willoughby, Charles A. *The Guerrilla Resistance Movement in the Philippines, 1941–1945.* New York: Vantage Press, 1972.
Willoughby, Charles A., and John Chamberlain. *MacArthur: 1941–1951.* New York: McGraw-Hill, 1954.
Wise, William. *Secret Mission to the Philippines.* New York: E. P. Dutton, 1968.
Wissolik, Richard David, and Katie Killen, eds. *They Say There Was a War.* Latrobe, Pa.: Saint Vincent College Center for Northern Appalachian Studies, 2005.
Worcester, Dean. *The Philippine Islands and Their People.* New York: Macmillan, 1898.
Young, Donald J. The *Battle of Bataan.* Jefferson, N.C.: McFarland, 1992.
Young, Kenneth Ray. *The General's General: The Life and Times of Arthur MacArthur.* Boulder, Colo.: Westview Press, 1994.

Unpublished Manuscripts

Franklin, Charles, comp. "History of the Philippine Scouts, 1899–1934." Washington, D.C.: Historical Section, Army War College, 1934.
Magtoto, Amado B. "Rock of Bataan." N.p.: n.d.
Manzano, Narciso L. "Memoirs of Col. Narciso L. Manzano, USA, Ret." N.p., ca. 1983.
Rich, Albert T. "Fort San Pedro 22." Iloilo, Phil.: U.S. Army, Division of the Philippines, Department of the Visayas, 1903.
Santos, Paulino. "Speeches: Formal, Informal, and Extemporaneous, Delivered by Major General Paulino Santos, Chief of Staff, Philippine Army." Manila: Publication Division, Adjutant General Service, 1938.
Steinberg, David Joel. "Interviews of Prominent Filipinos." Manila, 1969.

Dissertations and Theses

Anselmi, V. A. "Colonel Robert Besson: Japanese Prisoner of War, 1941–1945." Master's thesis, Northwestern State University of Louisiana, 1985.
Carpenter, Suzanne G. "Toward the Development of Philippine National Security Capability, 1920–1940." PhD diss., New York University, 1976.
Maniago, Jo Ann Barker. "The First Peace Corps: The Work of the American Teachers in the Philippines, 1900–1910." PhD diss., Boston University, 1971.
Masi, Anthony. "MacArthur's Defense of the Philippines in the Perspective of the United States Press." Master's thesis, University of Maryland, 1968.
Meixsel, Richard. "An Army for Independence?: The American Roots of the Philippine Army." PhD diss., Ohio State University, 1993.
———. "United States Army Policy in the Philippine Islands, 1902–1922." Master's thesis, University of Georgia, 1988.

Nye, Roger H. "The United States Military Academy in an Era of Educational Reform, 1900–1925." Phd diss., Columbia University, 1968.

Rimando, Juanito R. "Brigadier General Vicente Lim and the 41st Division in Bataan." Master's thesis, University of the Philippines, 1978.

Woolard, James. "The Philippine Scouts: The Development of America's Colonial Army." Phd diss., Ohio State University, 1975.

Index